D0206059

DISCARDED

DISCARDED

Date Due

BRODART, INC.	Cat. No. 23 233	Printed in U.S.A.

DES PLAINES, ILLINOIS   60016

OAKTON COMMUNITY COLLEGE LIBRARY
DK274.   1980   C001
THE   INI   WORLD   5

DISCARDED

DISCARDED

The Soviet Union in World Politics

DISCARDED

About the Book and Editor

The Soviet Union in World Politics
edited by Kurt London

Despite assertions that the goal of Soviet foreign policy is no longer world revolution — a view enhanced by the détente of the '70s — Soviet history suggests that the USSR has always followed the imperatives of both communism and nationalism. This collection of essays looks at the results of these dual motivations. Examining the impact of Soviet policies and actions on key nations and regions throughout the world and highlighting their significance as agents for change in the international arena, the authors present an overview of world politics today, as well as an in-depth study of Soviet international behavior.

Kurt London is professor emeritus at George Washington University's Institute for Sino-Soviet Studies, of which he was founder and first director. He was also adjunct professor at the Naval Post-Graduate School at Monterey.

The Soviet Union in World Politics

edited by
Kurt London

11080

OAKTON COMMUNITY COLLEGE
DES PLAINES CAMPUS
1600 EAST GOLF ROAD
DES PLAINES, IL 60016

Westview Press / Boulder, Colorado
Croom Helm / London, England

All rights reserved. No part of this publication may be reproduced or transmitted in any form or by any means, electronic or mechanical, including photocopy, recording, or any information storage and retrieval system, without permission in writing from the publisher.

Copyright © 1980 by Westview Press, Inc.

Published in 1980 in the United States of America by
    Westview Press, Inc.
    5500 Central Avenue
    Boulder, Colorado 80301
    Frederick A. Praeger, Publisher

Published in 1980 in Great Britain by
    Croom Helm Ltd.
    2-10 St John's Road
    London SW11

Library of Congress Catalog Card No. 79-19503
ISBN (U.S.): 0-89158-263-0
ISBN (U.K.): 0-7099-0415-0

Printed and bound in the United States of America

OAKTON COMMUNITY COLLEGE
DES PLAINES CAMPUS
1600 EAST GOLF ROAD
DES PLAINES, IL 60016

Contents

Part 3
The Role of Soviet Armed Forces

Part 4
An Overview of Soviet Foreign Policies

Preface

After the brief period of uneasy East-West collaboration during World War II, the international equilibrium — such as it was — deteriorated into Stalin's cold war. As the superpower status of the USSR solidified, the impact of its foreign policy compelled other states, directly or indirectly, to formulate their policies with a wary eye toward possible Soviet reprisals. This situation effected immense changes in the political map of the world that almost certainly would not have occurred without the Soviet threat.

Some observers have asserted that the Soviets no longer seek their traditional goal of world conquest through revolution. Since the early 1970s and the advent of détente, such views have been expressed quite forcefully (and hopefully) in the West. Indeed, the Soviets seemed to show unusual cooperation after President Nixon's visit to Moscow. But world history since 1918 demonstrates that Soviet foreign policy cannot be accepted at face value.

The West, particularly the United States, was so infatuated with the idea of détente that it did not seem to notice that the Kremlin was denigrating the concept by emphasizing the Leninist theory of "peaceful coexistence." In communist thought this meant that a communist nation should strive for a modus vivendi with nations of different social systems while continuing the ideological and political struggle. In contrast to the West, the Soviets denied that détente was indivisible. This strategy, still not fully appreciated in the United States, was eminently successful. It created the appearance that the Soviets no longer sought world revolution. As a result, many observers believed that the USSR need no longer be regarded as a revolutionary power but rather as a traditional nation-state.

The Kremlin often reiterated, in strong language, that détente would not rule out Soviet military intervention wherever "wars of national liberation" occurred. The Kremlin also asserted that East-West détente did not imply an "artificial restriction of objective processes of historical development." Western sovietologists are familiar with the significance of such "objective processes"; unfortunately, statesmen and diplomats rarely are. Western hopes for an improvement of East-West relations are ill-founded and only highlight the need for a worldwide survey of the results of Soviet foreign policy. (For an excellent in-depth analysis of détente and peaceful coexistence, see *Research Notes on U.S.-Soviet Affairs,* no. 1, July 1978, edited by Mose L. Harvey and Foy D. Kohler of the Center for Advanced International Studies, in association with the University of Miami, Coral Gables.)

This anthology presents the results of an investigation of the effect of Soviet foreign policy on the international relations and policies of other nations. It is a revised and expanded version of an earlier analytical work on the Soviet position in the world. The outstanding contributions to this work were provided by experts who not only understand the nature and rationale of Soviet foreign policy but who are also familiar with the political, social, economic, and geographic conditions of individual areas of the world.

It is a privilege to express my thanks to the Earhart Foundation in Ann Arbor, Michigan, for a grant that supported this research. I also thank the many experts who encouraged me to pursue the project.

Kurt London

The Contributors

William J. Barnds, formerly a senior research fellow at the Council on Foreign Relations, is now a professional staff member with the United States Senate Committee on Foreign Relations. He is the author of *India, Pakistan and the Great Powers,* and other works.

Galia Golan is director of the Soviet–East European Research Centre of the Hebrew University of Jerusalem and senior lecturer in political science and Russian studies. She is the author of *Yom Kippur and After: The Soviet Union and Middle East Crisis; The Czechoslovak Reform Movement: Communism in Crisis 1962-1968;* and *Reform Rule in Czechoslovakia: The Dubcek Era 1968-69.*

Bernard K. Gordon, who first visited Southeast Asia in 1956, is professor of political science at the University of New Hampshire. He is the author of *Toward Disengagement in Asia: A Strategy for American Foreign Policy; The Dimensions of Conflict in Southeast Asia;* and other books. He was guest professor at the Center for Southeast Asian Studies at Kyoto University, Japan.

Leon Goure is professor of international studies and director of Soviet studies at the Center for Advanced International Studies, University of Miami, Coral Gables. His publications include: *The Siege of Leningrad; Soviet Military Strategy* (coeditor); *Military Indoctrination of Soviet Youth; Science and Technology as an Instrument of Soviet Policy; Convergence of Communism and Capitalism: The Soviet View;* and *Soviet Strategy in the Seventies: From Cold War to Peaceful Coexistence.*

William F. Gutteridge, M.A. (Oxon.), is professor of international studies and director of complementary studies at the University of Aston in Birmingham. He is the author of four books: *Armed Forces in New States* (1962); *Military Institutions and Power in the New States* (1965); *The Military in African Politics* (1969); and *Military Regimes in Africa* (1976).

Harold C. Hinton is professor of political science and international affairs at the Institute for Sino-Soviet Studies, The George Washington University. His works include: *Communist China in World Politics; The Bear at the Gate: Chinese Policymaking Under Soviet Pressure;* and *An Introduction to Chinese Politics.*

Kurt London is professor emeritus of George Washington University and the founder and first director of its Institute for Sino-Soviet Studies. Among his books are: *The Seven Soviet Arts; Backgrounds of Conflict: Ideas and Forms of World Politics; How Foreign Policy Is Made; The Permanent Crisis; The Making of Foreign Policy—East and West; Unity and Contradiction: Major Aspects of Sino-Soviet Relations* (ed.); *New Nations in a Divided World* (ed.); *Eastern Europe in Transition* (ed.); and *The Soviet Union: A Half Century of Communism* (ed.).

Charles Burton Marshall served as a staff consultant to the Committee on Foreign Affairs of the House of Representatives, a member of the Policy Planning Staff of the Department of State, and as professor of international politics at the School of Advanced International Studies of The Johns Hopkins University. Since retirement from teaching, he has been active as a consultant on foreign policy and national defense. His books include: *The Limits of Foreign Policy; The Cold War: A Concise History; The Exercise of Sovereignty;* and *Crisis over Rhodesia: A Skeptical View.*

Robert L. Pfaltzgraff, Jr. is professor of international politics at the Fletcher School of Law and Diplomacy, Tufts University. Concurrently, he is president of the Institute for Foreign Policy Analysis, Cambridge, Massachusetts, and president of the United States Strategic Institute, Washington, D.C. His publications include: *Contending Theories of International Relations; The Study of International Relations; Soviet Theater Strategy: Implications for NATO; The Atlantic Community in Crisis; Arms Transfers to the Third World; The Cruise Missile: Bargaining Chip or Defense Bargain?; The Other Arms Race: New Technologies and Non-Nuclear Conflict;* and *The Superpowers in a Multinuclear World.*

Morris Rothenberg, a former director of the State Department's Office of Research on the Soviet Union and Eastern Europe, is currently a vice president of the Advanced International Studies Institute and adjunct professor at the University of Miami, Florida. His publications include *Whither China: The View from the Kremlin* (with Leon Goure) and *Soviet Penetration of Latin America.*

Alvin Z. Rubinstein is professor of political science at the University of

Pennsylvania. He is author of a number of books on Soviet and Communist affairs, including *Red Star on the Nile: The Soviet-Egyptian Influence Relationship Since the June War; Yugoslavia and the Nonaligned World;* and *The Soviets in International Organizations.*

Leonard Schapiro is professor emeritus of political science with special reference to Russian studies, London School of Economics and Political Science, University of London. Professor Schapiro holds an LL.B. and is a barrister-at-law, a Fellow of the British Academy and of University College of London, and an honorary foreign member of the American Academy of Arts and Sciences. His major publications are: *The Origin of the Communist Autocracy; The Communist Party of the Soviet Union; The Government and Politics of the Soviet Union; Rationalism and Nationalism in Russian Nineteenth Century Political Thought; Totalitarianism;* and *Turgenev: His Life and Times.*

Hugh Seton-Watson is professor of history at the school of Slavonic Studies, University of London. His numerous publications include: *Eastern Europe Between the Wars; The East European Revolution; The Decline of Imperial Russia; Pattern of Communist Revolution; Neither War Nor Peace; Nationalism and Communism; The Russian Empire 1801–1917;* and *Nations and States.*

Adam B. Ulam is professor of government and a former director of the Russian Research Center, Harvard University. Among his books are: *Titoism and the Cominform; The Unfinished Revolution; Lenin and the Bolsheviks; Expansion and Coexistence: History of Soviet Foreign Policy, 1917–1967; Stalin and His Era;* and *Ideologies and Illusions.*

Part 1

**The Nature of
Soviet Foreign Policy:
A Conceptual Appraisal**

1

Totalitarianism in Foreign Policy

Leonard Schapiro

The term "totalitarian" has had a very checkered career. It has been used polemically and with great lack of precision and applied to political and historical situations as well as political systems. There are those who argue that the term is at worst misleading and at best outmoded and that it confuses rather than clarifies political analysis. I have tried elsewhere to meet some of the main arguments that have been advanced in recent years against the retention of the label "totalitarian" for any of our contemporary societies; I have argued that with proper limits and precautions the term still has a valid place in the language of politics.[1]

In regard to the Soviet Union a strong case certainly can be made for the view that, because of the many changes that have taken place in its political system since Stalin's death, it is misleading to use the same term for the USSR in, say, 1939 or 1952 and the USSR today. A strong case but not an entirely convincing one: Although the Stalin-scale terror is gone and, above all, the form of completely personal rule that Stalin developed by the end of the years of the Great Terror, nevertheless there remain many salient and distinctive features that still clearly differentiate the Soviet Union (and its satellites and imitators) from other societies, even the most authoritarian.

This argument, which will be elaborated below, is more particularly apt when the question of foreign policy is at issue. For one of the most significant recent changes in the Soviet political system is the fact that the leader, with a form of personal rule that cut across all legal and constitutional boundaries, seems to have been replaced by a collective oligarchy in which the leading figure, Leonid Brezhnev, cannot ignore his colleagues, whatever the degree of preponderant influence he has in fact acquired over the years. This is, of course, a most important general change. Yet it is much less evident where foreign policy is concerned.

It has become clear over the past few years that Brezhnev has been assuming a dominant role in the design and conduct of Soviet foreign policy and has completely eclipsed his most important partner in government, Alexei Kosygin, the chairman of the Council of Ministers, in whose province foreign policy strictly falls. Brezhnev is the architect of the new Soviet policy in relation to both Europe and the United States. Whatever opposition he may have encountered, it has been Brezhnev who has conducted the discussions and paid the relevant foreign visits. In April 1973, he clearly received an endorsement of his policy from the Plenum of the Central Committee of the Communist Party of the Soviet Union (CPSU), and the quite unprecedented variety of prominent speakers was obviously designed to show that any past opposition to Brezhnev's foreign policy was now at an end. The introduction of the ministers of foreign affairs and the defense as full members of the Politburo at this Plenum (again, virtually unprecedented), may also have strengthened Brezhnev's control over foreign policy and related defense policy. For these two ministers were thereby brought under the direct control of the Politburo and above all its chairman, Brezhnev; previously they had been only indirectly controlled by the Politburo's policy as interpreted to them by the chairman and the Presidium of the Council of Ministers.

It may well be that there has been quite an extensive and significant erosion of totalitarianism in the Soviet Union in the past twenty years. But if the argument outlined above is correct, it would follow that the erosion is likely to have had less effect in the sphere of foreign policy than in the area of domestic policy. Speculation over dissent on foreign policy inside the Politburo is a favorite pastime of journalists — in their accounts both Khrushchev's and now Brezhnev's careers so often hung in the balance depending on their success in placating the "hawks" or satisfying the gentler "doves." But there has been relatively little evidence to support these extravagant speculations. No doubt foreign policy failures have been used by potential rivals in the Politburo to weaken an opponent or even to topple one, in the case of Khrushchev. But the most important issues at stake are invariably domestic; on foreign policy there usually seems in retrospect to have been a surprising degree of unanimity.

It is true that Soviet policy toward the Vietnam War changed sharply after the fall of Khrushchev. But there were other reasons for this — the military situation for one. Policy toward China, after a short lull, remained the same — allowing for differences of style. It was not for these reasons that Khrushchev fell but for his internal policies, which made him powerful enemies.

Many of the rumors of alleged dissent on policy in the Soviet Union are plainly put out to deceive a credulous Western public. Shelest was the real hardliner on Czechoslovakia, while the others wavered; Shelest was the real opponent of "détente" with the United States: these were recent inspired rumors. The intended moral for the West was that those remaining in the Politburo since April 1973 are authentic peace-loving "doves" who deeply regret the invasion of Czechoslovakia and are genuinely anxious for real "détente." Such is the advantage of a foreign policy in which police, press, and diplomacy all act as one disciplined machine.

Space does not permit an extensive analysis of totalitarianism, to which an enormous literature has been devoted. But the least that must be undertaken is a search for what appear to be the dominant features of the system under discussion in order to examine how far and in what way these features apply to the conduct of foreign policy. The dominant features are derived from a study of the three societies to all of which the term "totalitarianism" was applied in the English language both between the wars (despite assertions to the contrary in the literature) and after World War II — Mussolini's Italy, National Socialist Germany, and the Soviet Union under Stalin.

These features are three in number. The first is "totality": the concentration at one central point of all ultimately effective power over the whole life of the country and over all individuals. The central point is of course the leader — even if in practice the leader delegates his power or is forced to share it for a greater or lesser time. This power can be put into effect in spite of and in disregard of any existing established checks or barriers — such as the law, private morality, or parties, groups, or institutions with discrete and clearly defined functions. In this process ideology plays a vital part, in particular the position of exclusive monopoly the ideology enjoys (thus distinguishing totalitarian ideology from anything comparable in pluralist societies).

It should be particularly noted that the characteristic nature of this kind of total power is very different from "state" power, however extensive. "State" implies some kind of legal order, some system of established, discrete institutions. On the contrary (and this was particularly evident in National Socialist Germany), total power is equally hostile to the established state power and to society as a whole, and it imposes its will on and control over both in equal degree. This aspect of total power — which becomes particularly relevant when considering control of foreign policy, and which has been much neglected in the literature of totalitarianism — cannot be further discussed here and the interested reader must be referred to other works.[2]

The second main feature of totalitarianism is a corollary of the first. It is the lack of independence of any institution, and the lack of strict differentiation of functions between institutions. Take, for example, the institution of law. In countries governed by law, the law is intended to act as an independent yardstick for determining the limits of power of different elements in the machine of government as well as the extent of individual rights. In its codes and its constitution the Soviet Union claims to be governed by law. In practice there has never been a period in Russian history, let alone Soviet Russian history, when the actual source of power—the emperor, the executive, the CPSU, or whatever—could not ignore, circumvent, influence, or at least neutralize the legal frame work or the courts.

All governments no doubt flout or try to flout the law in greater or lesser degree at one time or another. But most governments know when they are doing so and there tends to be a public outcry when they are found out. This was to some extent true in Russia during the period of the reforms, between 1864 and 1917. It is not true of Soviet Russia, where the authorities, from Lenin to Brezhnev, have held the profound conviction (whatever they may have found it convenient to say) that laws are a facade and do not apply to those at the top. The members of the "democratic movement" in the Soviet Union today have occasionally reported that their endeavors to insist on their legal rights when they come up against the KGB are met with the rejoinder that the law "does not apply" to them. This boast is not strictly true even in practice in the Soviet Union today, but it is illustrative of a deeply ingrained attitude of mind that characterizes the totalitarian society and its officials.

The third characteristic feature of the totalitarian society is its purpose: world Communist power or Aryan domination over inferior races, coupled with a mission to transform man or mankind. The totalitarian rulers, unlike the rulers of a police state, are not content merely to stay in power and suppress their enemies and critics. They have to persuade themselves that they have a historic mission to perform, a mission that gives them some special rights over their fellow men. This conviction imbues them with the sense of self-righteousness and determined hypocrisy that so strongly characterizes today's Communist rulers in their dealings with the outside world.

These three aspects of tolitarian rule are of the greatest relevance when one examines the peculiar characteristics of totalitarian foreign policy, especially the last of the three characteristics—the sense of a determined purpose. Of Hitler's determined purpose there is no need to say much, except to record the obvious fact that if the statesmen of the United States and Europe (including Stalin) had paid a little more serious attention to the avowed, explicit, and often repeated "ultimate purpose" of National Socialism the history of the past fifty years might have been very different.

The avowed purpose of Soviet Russia has been less crudely formulated and has changed in the course of the past six decades with respect to both timetable and emphasis. But it has not changed in its essential feature, which is and always has been a world in which what is usually described as "socialism," and which in practice means state capitalism administered by a Communist party oligarchy, prevails.

This comparatively simple picture, admirably suited to the monistic nature of a totalitarian regime, has been obscured by a number of factors. Among these are the apparent, frequent tactical retreats from the general purpose; certain flexibilities of policy that are quite inconsistent with the existence of a Soviet blueprint for the imposition of world socialism; and the fact that in many respects the Soviet Union behaves in the same way as other aggressive, chauvinistic, expansionist world powers. These facts have led some people to draw the inference that communism is no longer a relevant factor and that the current approach is simply old-fashioned, imperialistic Russian foreign policy with traditional aims. It is suggested that each of these implied or explicit denials of an ultimate purpose in Soviet policy is fallacious.

One can distinguish three main phases of Soviet foreign policy since 1917, separated by two major tactical retreats or, at any rate, changes of position. The first phase, until the end of 1920 or the beginning of 1921, was characterized by a determined if somewhat unrealistic belief that revolution was imminent in the main industrial countries. Naturally enough this euphoria could not lead to any serious doctrine of foreign policy; it was only after the realization that the capitalist world was going to survive for quite a while that a policy was evolved for long-term coexistence with it.

Broadly speaking this new policy rested on several premises. First, that trade and diplomatic relations with the capitalist powers could be advantageous to Soviet Russia. Second, that the nature of the political systems of the major capitalist powers made them particularly vulnerable to political subversion and propaganda from the Soviet side. Lenin's *Infantile Disease of Leftism in Communism* remains a monument to the Soviet view of policy in conditions of coexistence.

Indeed Lenin never tired of emphasizing that the capitalists' greed for profit would blind them to the fact that in building up revolutionary Russia they would be bolstering their avowed enemy. A private memorandum by Lenin, never officially published but beyond question authentic, puts the Soviet calculation in terms that cannot be improved on. After emphasizing that the "deaf-mute" capitalists will only too readily believe Soviet assertions that their government organs are quite independent of both party and Comintern, he adds that the capitalists

> will open their doors wide to us, and through these doors will speedily enter the emissaries of the Cominterm and of our party, investigation organs in the guise of diplomatic, cultural and trade representatives. . . . They will open up

credits for us, which will serve us for the purpose of supporting Communist
parties in their countries. They will supply us with the materials and
technology which we lack and will restore our military industry, which we
need for our future victorious attacks on our suppliers.[3]

Lenin certainly believed that in the last resort the capitalists would stand
and fight and that the socialist countries, with the support of the colonial
peoples, would be victorious. So far as the last part is concerned — the role
of the colonial peoples in helping on the final victory of world socialism —
this has remained a cardinal principle of Soviet policy. In the past few
years, the active military and political support of what in Soviet eyes are
wars of liberation — such as the overthrow of colonial regimes in Angola and
Mozambique and the extension of the African insurrection to the whole of
Southern Africa, and bolstering the cause of the Palestinian Arabs — has
become an all-important part of the pursuit of the ultimate aim of weakening the "capitalist" powers and forwarding world socialism. However, much
less has been heard in Soviet ideological statements in recent years of the inevitability of war between the "socialist" and the "imperialist" camps. In the
time of Khrushchev this change of dogma derived avowedly from the belief
that modern weapons are of such destructive power that their use would
destroy both sides, and that war has therefore become unthinkable. Since
the fall of Khrushchev, and the progressive growth of Soviet military might
— and, one must add, what must look to the Soviet leaders as the decline of
the Western will to resist the advance of communism — the argument based
on destructive power is no longer used. In fact in recent years Soviet
military doctrine has repeatedly emphasized that nuclear weapons have not
altered the basic position, and that a nuclear war must be prepared for and,
if it should come, be won. That the possibility that a nuclear war may be
fought in the end is present in Soviet thinking is further underlined by the
development since 1972 of an elaborate civil defense program in the Soviet
Union, and by technological aspects of Soviet general defense policy.[4]

The use of an overwhelming military presence and the maximum espionage and subversion presence are part of what has always been described in
Soviet terminology as "ideological struggle," which is repeatedly asserted as
the necessary concomitant of "peaceful coexistence." As Brezhnev said on
27 June 1972:

While pressing for the assertion of the principle of peaceful coexistence, we
realize that successes in this important matter in no way signify the possibility
of weakening the ideological struggle. On the contrary, we should be
prepared for an intensification of this struggle and for it to assume an increasingly more acute form of struggle between the two social systems.[5]

In essence this view is the logical implementation of Lenin's policy of combining trade and correct diplomatic relations on the one hand with subversion and political warfare on the other.

The difference between the third and second stages, as outlined above, should not be exaggerated, for two reasons. In the first place, Soviet policy has never been militaristic in the sense of taking risks in order to pursue its aims by force. The Soviet Union's military moves since World War II have either been miscalculations (as in the invasion of Korea, when it was misled by Dean Acheson's assertion that South Korea was not within the American "defense perimeter") or made in the certainty that they would not be opposed by force (as in Hungary in 1956 and Czechoslovakia in 1968). Conversely, on the rare occasions when the West has stood firm in the face of Soviet aggression, Soviet response has bordered on panic surrender—as over Cuba in 1962.

The fact is that military might for the Soviet Union is seen primarily as a political weapon, a means of furthering political aims by military blackmail or intimidation. The overwhelming strength the Soviet Union has built up against the forces of NATO is such a political force; its full potential is designed to unfold as the political and military influence of the United States in Europe declines (this is the Soviet Union hope and intent). The Soviet navy, which has been greatly developed in recent years, is intended not as a combat force so much as a force that can rapidly support a political uprising favorable to the Soviet Union before anyone else can get there.

This intimate link between the armed forces and foreign policy was characteristic of Lenin's outlook from the start, since Lenin, who greatly admired Clausewitz, drew no firm distinction between war and politics, and whose specific contribution to twentieth century foreign policy is its militarization. For Lenin as for Clausewitz, war and politics were alternative means to the same end—victory—to be selected as circumstances dictated. Moreover the rules of warfare applied fully to politics, in particular the concentration of overwhelming strength at the decisive point and the mobilization of political forces in support of the military advance.[6]

The fact that Soviet military theorists stress in their writings that a nuclear war cannot be excluded as a real possibility, that if it does occur it must be successfully defended and—in occasional writings—that the best defense may in some circumstances be a preemptive strike, raises an important question: what influence does the military have on policy decisions? The answer to this question brings into relief a central aspect of Soviet totalitarianism in its relation to foreign policy, namely the integration of the military machine into the civilian, and the complete subordination of the military to control of the Communist party. This does not mean that the military have no voice in decision making, let alone that they do not influence policy. But it is the case that in the last resort it is the party which decides; and that the kind of conflicts which in some other countries have resulted in duality of policy do not arise in the Soviet Union. It can therefore be assumed that if the military are allowed to debate the question of nuclear war, they do so with the full approval of the party. It also means that any decision involving the risk of nuclear war will always be a party decision.[7]

The fact that Lenin himself believed there would be an ultimate military clash loses much of its relevance. The use of military force as a political weapon was indeed part of his outlook. However the use of military force as an integral part of foreign policy, which involves the maintenance of enormous forces in what are supposed to be times of peace, presents great problems of expenditure and morale that would be quite insuperable for a power that did not pursue a "total" policy and did not exercise as nearly as possible total control over its population and resources.

Thus these different phases of Soviet foreign policy are quite consistent with, indeed are only consistent with, a continuing ultimate purpose of "world socialism." But some are inclined to doubt this ultimate purpose, arguing that Soviet foreign policy over the years shows such a variety of tactical moves and changes of line that it is quite impossible to infer the existence of any plans for world revolution. The argument is indisputable; the inference is false.

There has never, it is true, been any evidence that the Soviet Union has at any time acted according to some master plan in its progress toward "world socialism." On the contrary, the evidence is conclusive that the Soviet Union pursues its course with full regard for the strengths and weaknesses of its antagonists as it encounters them—retreating before the former, exploiting the latter. "World socialism" is in no sense a blueprint, but it is essentially a compass. The course is set; although the needle may and must veer frequently from the course, it always returns to it as soon as circumstances permit. There have been some failures, such as Cuba—but even here the Soviet Union succeeded in extracting virtual recognition of Communist Cuba by the United States in exchange for abandoning a rash gamble that the Soviet Union had no available means of supporting at the time (1962).

Also, one frequently encounters the argument that Soviet policy aims are no more than Russia's traditional foreign policy aims, which Russia under any government would pursue if it had the necessary armed might. This argument is true in part; certain aspects of Soviet policy are traditional to Russia and have been embarked on by the Soviet Union as and when its military power—or what it could make the United States believe was its military power—grew strong enough. Such aims include the search for a warm water outlet for Soviet ships, for control of the Baltic Sea, and for the creation of a land barrier to the West on Soviet European frontiers.

However, it would be erroneous to ignore the additional dimension created by over fifty years of reiterated ideology — the self-declared righteousness, the denigration of opponents, the drive, the purpose, the sacrifice — in short, all the aspects of foreign policy that all countries display in time of war. The point is that the Soviet Union always behaves as if at war and believes this, if only because in many senses it is true.

Also, the militarization of the population is something no democratic state could hope to achieve in times when there were no actual or imminent hostilities. Nor indeed could any dictatorship achieve this militarization without total control over its population and resources. It is for this reason, if for no other, that the often reiterated Soviet fears of aggression from the Western powers carry little conviction. It is also worth noting that, in contrast to the intensified "ideological struggle" that is so often emphasized as the other aspect of "peaceful coexistence," the period of "peaceful coexistence" between Stalin and Hitler after the pact of August 1939 was characterized by total silence on the Soviet side of the subject of the National Socialist regime. In the case of Hitler there evidently was a real fear on the Soviet side that abuse might provoke an attack; in the case of Western powers today there evidently is not.

The character of total militarization in Soviet foreign policy is thus in turn dependent on the totalitarian nature of Soviet power internally. This must now be examined in more detail in the light of the short analysis of totalitarian rule with which this chapter began. The question of the dominant purpose has been dealt with. But the dominant purpose, and the militarized policy it serves, can only be pursued by a government that is in full control of all power; that need fear neither obstruction nor impediment from any private or public concern, institution, or vested right; and that has the means at its disposal to overcome any obstruction or impediment with relative ease. (Hitler left his "Aryan" capitalists relatively unmolested but had no difficulty in bringing them to heel when he thought it necessary, and the evidence suggests that had he been victorious an even more extensive policy of control over capital would have been embarked upon.)

Moreover such a militarized policy can only be pursued by a government that can concentrate control at one focal point to a much greater extent than can a prime minister or president who must take account not only of parliament or congress but of a vigorous free press and an opportunity for public criticism that is even less restricted in the United States than in a country like Great Britain where an official secrets act is in force.

While the single leader who has tended to emerge in the formulation of Soviet policy is relatively immune from criticism, this immunity no doubt does not extend to the secret councils of the Politburo or on occasion even the Central Committee. But this private and secret criticism does not discredit the policy of the leader, except for the rare occasions when he happens to be ousted. Moreover, as has been suggested, the use of inspired rumors and no doubt other less publicly evident instruments of deception can be used to bolster a leader who may in fact be facing severe criticism. In fact, as Brezhnev has shown over the years, skillful political manipulation of the top offices in the CPSU can, on some occasions, successfully overcome internal doubt and opposition.

The result is that in the conduct of his foreign policy a Soviet leader can convincingly display determination and ability to put a novel policy into effect — something the leader of a democratic system could not hope to do without genuine support behind him. Elections in Western democracies are regular and certain and their results usually unpredictable. The "palace revolutions" of the Soviet Union are rare enough (only one in the past twenty-seven years) for everyone to pretend that they cannot happen.

The fact that in his conduct of foreign policy the totalitarian leader can ignore or control public opinion and discount the possibility of public criticism gives him two further advantages over his democratic opposite number. The first is that a policy completely inconsistent with what has been asserted before can be pursued without either difficulty or visible loss of face. There is no evidence that a Soviet leader has been inconvenienced or has had his authority shaken by such complete reversals of policy as the Stalin-Hitler pact; or has faced serious internal difficulties over a policy of alliance with countries like Egypt that suppress their Communists; or, more recently, that Brezhnev, after years of abusing U.S. policy in Vietnam, ever hesitated about entertaining President Nixon immediately after the mining of Haiphong harbor and the outcry that followed it. Or, at all events, if Brezhnev did face opposition on this issue and in general on the policy of so-called "détente" with the United States — as was rumored in connection with Shelest's removal from the Politburo in April 1973, although the official charge against him was Ukrainian nationalism — he had little difficulty in overcoming it. A leader of a democratic society could easily have fallen from office on such an issue.

But the totalitarian leader enjoys a second advantage as the result of his control over public opinion and sources of information, an advantage the Soviet Union has always made great use of. No Soviet leader, from Lenin to Brezhnev, has failed to attach supreme importance to the battle for the minds of his opponents. It is toward this end that the whole machinery of state propaganda is directed, aimed at the populations of the countries of the non-Communist world, designed when necessary to drive a wedge between the population and its government, to neutralize or cast doubt on information about Soviet life or policy unfavorable to the Soviet Union, and the like.

This is all familiar enough—although whether the full effectiveness of this propaganda over the past fifty years is always realized in the West is another matter. But the totalitarian leader, because of his control over information inside his own country, derives a special benefit in his conduct of foreign policy and plays a very significant role in the propaganda process. The benefit is twofold. First, he can bolster the alleged success of his policy in a non-Communist country by citing the views of pro-Communist groups of no importance or influence in their own countries. In so doing he can rely on the ignorance of his own countrymen, remaining confident that they will be unable to assess the true worth of the information presented to them. But the leader can also, through his control over internal expression of opinion, create an impression of internal solidarity and support that may be quite false but which adds to his authority when dealing with the outside world.

In recent years the Soviet Union has failed to keep some dissident voices from being heard outside the Soviet Union. Although these voices have been raised mostly on internal issues of civil rights, including the right to emigrate, on occasion they have certainly extended to foreign policy issues, such as the invasion of Czechoslovakia. This voice of dissent has been a serious breach in the totalitarian armor. All evidence at present points to the fact that the Soviet authorities regard the repair of this breach by more severe repression as a high-priority task. It is easy to see why, from their point of view, this should seem the proper approach; whether they will succeed is another question. What is certain is that it is not in the interests of any power that does not wish to see the influence of the Communist bloc advanced to help the Soviet authorities to silence dissent in their own midst. (This position is discussed below in connection with "Eurocommunism.")

The Soviet leader thus derives great advantages from his controlled propaganda machine and his control over internal news and opinion, even if today the latter cannot always be maintained at the high degree of perfection he would wish. But the most curious aspect of the interrelation between the leader's foreign policy and his propaganda machine is the way his policy in practice helps to consolidate and expand a position that starts off as no more than propaganda—if only by wearing down the patience of his opponents.

This is illustrated by a Soviet diplomatic technique that has been skillfully adapted to the policy of an expanding power. Underlying it is the proposition the Soviet Union treats in all negotiations as unassailable, unchallengeable, and indeed outside the limits of discussion: All "socialist" advances are progressive, historically determined, and therefore irreversible. By contrast, any attempt to overthrow or weaken a "socialist" regime is counterrevolutionary and reactionary and the Soviet Union is justified in helping to restore "socialism" where it can. The importance of this doctrine, which was fundamental to Leninism, becomes readily apparent when—by sheer persistence, double-speak, and exhaustion—it is successfully foisted on powers that do not adhere to it.

This may be illustrated by the position of East Berlin. The status of Berlin as a whole was regulated by agreement among the four Allies after World War II, and plainly no one power had the right to alter that status. Yet this is precisely what the Soviet Union did after 1958 when it recognized East Germany and encouraged the transfer of control over East Berlin to the newly recognized state, which the other Allies did not recognize. Thereafter the Soviet Union not only refused to discuss the status of East Berlin but proceeded by various forms of harassment, both directly and indirectly through its satellite East Germany, to create a West Berlin problem (although the status of West Berlin was still regulated by the four-power agreement). In 1971, when Brezhnev formulated his foreign policy, recognition of East Germany was one of its central features. He has now achieved this recognition—in return for concessions on West Berlin. These concessions, even if as substantial as claimed by the German Federal Republic, do not include any concessions on East Berlin, which was not a question on the agenda.

Thus, over a period of some twenty years, a combination of propaganda, some intimidation, and skillful foreign policy leadership has enabled the Soviet Union to consolidate a "socialist gain."[8] This is far from the only example that could be cited on the unity of leadership and propaganda. It is difficult to imagine the success of this technique in the absence of unified, total control over the formulation and conduct of foreign policy.

When necessary the totalitarian leader can also, to a greater degree than his democratic opposite number, ignore the advice of his military leaders— though it must be emphasized that this is only a matter of degree. A prime minister or president can, and at times does, ignore his military advisers. But he runs the risk of resignations, public criticism, party splits, and government changes—all the not easily predictable consequences of the working of the democratic machine. Khrushchev ignored his military advisers over the Cuban adventure in 1962. It was a relative though not complete failure, and it apparently threw Khrushchev into a panic; at least this seems the only reasonable explanation of the fact that his signal to President Kennedy of 26 October has never been published by the United States. No doubt the Cuban incident was one of the reasons Khrushchev was persuaded to abandon much of his defense policy, which was characterized by overreliance on nuclear weapons. Nevertheless it is worth reflecting that, with a less resolute and skillful reaction than that of President Kennedy, the gigantic bluff over Cuba might have succeeded; it might have yielded greater dividends for the Soviet Union than it did.

Such then are some of the advantages a totalitarian leader can enjoy in the conduct of foreign policy given his immunity from public control and his insulation from public opinion and debate. The Soviet leader in particular derives additional strength from the ideological assertions and certainties that have been nurtured by over fifty years of political warfare.

It is now time to look at some of the advantages deriving from the nature of the rule exercised by the leader of a totalitarian society and his ruling elite. It is of interest in this context to note that it is in the overall *political* leader that this totality of control over foreign policy is concentrated—a fact underlined by the normal absence from the Politburo, the policy-making apex of the Soviet government system, of both the minister of foreign affairs and the minister of defense. The elevation of these two ministers to the Politburo in April 1973 does not seem to have altered this situation.

However, the fact remains that since Stalin's death—and of course during Stalin's period of virtual one-man rule—Soviet foreign policy has been largely formulated by the man who as chairman of the Politburo necessarily wields more power over all aspects of the country's life and resources than any other individual—in other words, the first or general secretary of the CPSU.

Khrushchev, it is true, combined the offices of first secretary of the party and chairman of the Council of Ministers after 1958 (semiformally after 1955) and Brezhnev does not. But Brezhnev succeeded, certainly by the end of the sixties if not before, in asserting a degree of control over foreign policy that effectively eclipsed the chairman of the Council of Ministers. After allowance has been made for the elements of collective consultation, interest pressures, economic demands, and other similar factors that operate on all governments, it is not far wrong to regard Soviet foreign policy as more of a one-man show than could be possible in any parliamentary or presidential system.

High on the list of Soviet advantages in the conduct of foreign policy is government control over foreign trade and the absence of private, uncontrolled capitalist enterprise. Negatively this means that economic pressures for trade will not be allowed to work to the detriment of overall policy. Thus, on the non-Communist side, a policy of economic isolation of the USSR—assuming that such a policy is in the interest of the non-Communist world, which is at any rate an arguable case—would inevitably be defeated by commercial pressures on the governments concerned. Or again, in developing trade with the Soviet Union and China, technological skills or long-term credits might well be so vital to the USSR or China that valuable political concessions could be exacted in return.

There would be nothing reprehensible about demanding such concessions. Communists are realists and are prepared to pay a price for something they want badly enough. But in conditions of private enterprise
where the state has no monopoly of foreign trade, it is difficult if not impossible for a government to restrict or direct the foreign commercial dealings of the private enterprises so as to correlate them with the government's
political objectives. There is, of course, no difficulty about such correlation
on the Soviet or Chinese side.

As with trade, so with many other aspects of national life. In theory the
totalitarian leader can bring into one coordinated plan his education policy,
his economic policy, his diplomacy, his international lawyers, and his intelligence officers, to name only a few. Judging by results, for example, in
Africa, for some time, but no longer to anything like the same extent, one
might be tempted to say that better advice might have been obtained from
old-fashioned, independent academic study than from some of the non-
sense that emanated from the Communist-controlled institutes.

But there are many cases where the drafting of students to their subjects
and their jobs may well be usefully correlated with a change in foreign
policy, or where the faculties and institutes of international law can be
relied on not to produce inconvenient academic criticism of government
policy but on the contrary to produce political arguments suitably dressed
up as scholarship.

Similarly it is no doubt a convenience to have the required number of
linguists available when embarking on foreign policy operations in an area
that has hitherto been left unexplored. The coordination of intelligence
with foreign policy is not peculiar to totalitarian systems. Naturally enough
the bunglings and failures, or just misfortunes, of intelligence operators will
on occasion cause acute embarrassment to the Soviet authorities; even the
Soviet propaganda machine at times finds such errors difficult to deal with.
But at all events the Soviet leader is spared the harassment of his own press,
parliament, politicians, and public opinion.

He probably enjoys yet another advantage in this respect. There is no
doubt that in planning intelligence operations to fit in with their foreign
policy both Khrushchev and Brezhnev have been careful to avoid too much
risk that the former might have the effect of wrecking the latter. But they
have been able to take a fairly high degree of risk. This is the result of long
experience and of disposing of a much larger and more widely spread intelligence service than their adversaries.

It is also not unrelated to the fact that for half a century, ever since the
last years of Lenin and the early years of the Comintern, Soviet Russia has
been sedulously striving—with some limited success—to persuade the

Western world that it is all right for Communist Russia to preach co-existence and practice subversion at one and the same time, while anyone who points to this inconsistency may be attacked for "cold warmongering" or the equivalent.

We have so far been concerned with the advantages a totalitarian leader enjoys in the conduct of his foreign policy vis-à-vis his democratic adversary. It is now time to look at some of the limitations, disadvantages, and weaknesses of totalitarian foreign policy and to strike some general balance.

One of the main factors limiting the totalitarian leader's freedom of action in his foreign relations is his constant preoccupation with maintaining himself and his associates in power. For the outside world he needs to create, by manipulating public opinion, the appearance of a legitimacy he cannot risk exposing to freely held elections. But at home he must calculate the extent to which he can compel and the extent to which he must conciliate; on this calculation far-reaching decisions of foreign relations will necessarily depend.

Thus, since the death of Stalin, decisions to purchase grain abroad in order to counteract bad harvests and farming inefficiency have been related to the fact that the growing demand for higher food consumption is no longer regarded as something that can be regulated by repressive measures as it was under Stalin. This kind of consideration applies to other matters of internal government as well. Stalin did not hesitate over the degree of terror he was prepared to use or the number of victims he was ready to immolate. But Stalin's was virtually a one-man government; neither of his successors has been able to achieve this extent of power, and it is unlikely for the foreseeable future that the top leaders of the USSR will permit any one of their number to acquire such power.

And so the Soviet leader, be he Khrushchev or Brezhnev, finds himself still, to a significant extent, limited by having to take some account of outside opinion in pursuing his policy internally. He must balance the degree of odium he acquires against his skill in deceiving the outside world and the degree of risk (hitherto very small indeed) that his treatment of intellectuals or national minorities will seriously affect trade or cultural contacts or anything else the Soviet Union is seeking to obtain from the non-Communist world.

However it should be noted that when the Soviet Union is really convinced of the need to act — if, for example, it feels that the security of its own rule is at risk — it will act with complete disregard for the effect on outside opinion. The invasions of Hungary and Czechoslovakia in 1956 and 1968 illustrate this principle very well. In each case the Soviet leaders must have been well aware of the severe shock their actions were bound to cause to even their most loyal supporters overseas. In both cases the fear that the Soviet bloc would break up, or that the disintegration of Communist rule in a satellite would spread to the Soviet Union itself, was sufficient to overcome any reluctance there may have been to act.

However, with this important qualification, outside opinion, potential loss of left-wing good will, reluctance to tarnish the Communist image, and the like are all factors that can exercise some restraint on a Soviet leader's actions. One would have thought that the Western powers would make much more use than they usually do of this reality in order to force concessions in their own favor upon the Soviet Union. But this they very seldom seem to do, and for two reasons.

One is the mistaken belief that attempts to interfere in Soviet internal matters will give the Soviet Union a right to interfere in the internal affairs of others — mistaken because the Soviet Union has for sixty years claimed and exercised what it considers its right, in the interests of promoting socialism or as self-appointed champion of human liberties, to interfere constantly in the affairs of other countries. And the Soviet Union will certainly continue to do so however those other countries act toward it.

The second and main reason why Western countries so often fail to exploit any hold they may have over the Soviet Union is that, in dealings with countries where free enterprise prevails, the Soviet authorities can and do deal with individuals and individual firms that operate mainly with their own interests in mind; the actions of these individuals simply are not coordinated or to any considerable degree controlled by the governments concerned.

The one limitation that has not hitherto proved much of a restraining influence on Soviet leaders is fear of internal public criticism. This is not only to be explained by the degree to which a Soviet government controls the expression of opinion; it is also partly due to the tradition of indifference to foreign policy, or at least the ingrained feeling that has always prevailed in Soviet Russia — that foreign policy is something completely outside public control.

Moreover the propaganda machine builds up the successes of foreign policy and plays down the failures; it succeeds very effectively in conveying a picture of one great unrelieved Soviet success story in the pages of the internal party press. And success is very popular with the Soviet public, as with any other. It is little concerned to probe such questions as the rights and wrongs of what appear to the average Soviet citizen as troublesome and ungrateful Czechs — for it was a small minority indeed inside the Soviet Union that viewed the 1968 invasion with anything but satisfaction.

Such then are the main limitations on the totalitarian conduct of foreign policy. It also has certain disadvantages. The Soviet system may be better adapted than others at training sufficient numbers of linguists, for example, to serve its foreign policy needs. But it can break down very badly when it comes to the pursuit of the true facts. Ideology, lack of high standards of scholarship, lack of general free access to non-Soviet sources, restrictions on travel — these and many other factors have often operated to produce an inadequate academic and historical basis for foreign policy, especially in new and unfamiliar areas.

Africa is a case in point. Although Soviet study of Africa has been improving, it was for years bedeviled by dogmatic preconceived assumptions based more on theory than on the realities of African life. The natural results were the repeated occasions in the past ten or fifteen years when Soviet policy in a particular part of Africa (Guinea, Ghana) ended in failure.

Again, although the extent to which the Arab-Israeli war of 1967 was actively encouraged by the Soviet Union is open to conjecture, there can be no doubt that the Soviet Union attached undue weight to the preponderance of weapons and equipment supplied to Egypt and failed to attach sufficient weight to the incapacity of the Egyptians to use them. Had it been otherwise the Soviet Union would surely have attempted, both earlier and more vigorously, to dissuade the Egyptians from provoking the Israeli attack.[9]

It is probably true, however, that although the present Soviet leaders are liable to miscalculate in this or similar manner because of the inadequacy of their objective study of the facts, they are unlikely to make mistakes on the magnitude of Stalin's mistakes — his blind confidence in the security of his bargain with Hitler, for example, in defiance of all the evidence. Stalin's foreign policy was one man's creation in which no one else played any part; for all the power and influence Brezhnev has accumulated in the sphere of foreign policy, there is no parallel between his position and Stalin's.

But mistakes will continue to be made, although certainly in the past decade the indications are that the research on which successful foreign policy must be based is improving in the Soviet Union. It is not easy, for lack of evidence, to estimate the value of the research side of the Soviet intelligence service. Its espionage and subversion sides are in many respects outstanding. No doubt the research necessary to service espionage and subversion must be excellent. But this kind of research is different from what historians and political scientists in Western universities mean by research — an all-around, objective examination, not necessarily limited by or geared to any particular, practical political purpose.

It is unlikely that the Soviet leaders can get this kind of research from their intelligence service. If the facts were better known, it might well turn out that one of the disadvantages of Soviet foreign policy is overreliance on the intelligence service for the kind of analysis that ought to be but usually is not provided by truly independent Soviet universities, scholars, and institutes.

Overreliance on the intelligence service may be a handicap to the Soviet Union in other respects. For example, it is extremely difficult to see what advantages the Soviet Union has derived from repeated unsuccessful attempts to subvert certain foreign governments and install governments favorable to itself—in Yugoslavia, for example, in Albania, and probably in China. The real successes of Soviet control in obtaining a stranglehold over a foreign government through its intelligence service have invariably followed either military conquest, as in the case of the KGB's control over Czechoslovakia, or an economic stranglehold, like the one that gave the KGB control in Cuba.

Although space does not permit full discussion of the question, a sketch of totalitarian foreign policy as exemplified by the Soviet Union would be incomplete without some reference to the three main respects in which Soviet control over a wide area has been diminished since Stalin's death: the loosening of the Communist bloc, the relative independence of the nonbloc Communist parties, and the break with China. Each of these factors has reduced the monolithic strength of the Soviet Union as the leader of a world movement; each has certainly reduced the total nature of Soviet power, whatever strains and discontents may have been seething underneath. Yet these strains should not be exaggerated unduly.

The members of the Communist bloc, or some of them, may be striving for some degree of political and economic independence from the tutelary power of the Soviet Union. Romania, Hungary, and Poland, at any rate, are casting lustful glances at the European Economic Community. Romania has tried at every opportunity to demonstrate that its foreign policy is not always a carbon copy of the Soviet Union's. Yet, despite these small shoots of independence, the Soviet Union can continue to rely on a very solid bloc of powers whose destinies, in the last resort, must depend on the strongest Communist state and whose regimes would not last one hour if communism should ever collapse in the USSR.

The bloc may no longer be monolithic, even in appearance. But its value to the total foreign policy of the USSR remains immeasurably greater than any other system of client powers or alliances between unequals in the world today. For one thing, and this is no mean advantage, the Soviet Union can fully utilize as part of its general intelligence service network—an important adjunct to its foreign policy—the intelligence services of the various bloc countries.

Insofar as independence of action is concerned, of course, the Communist parties in the noncommunist countries are greatly changed from the days of the Comintern when they were obedient tools of Soviet foreign policy. Since Stalin's death they have successfully persuaded the Soviet Union—or forced it to accept as inevitable—that their political progress in their own countries is directly related to the degree to which they can persuade their fellow countrymen that they are no longer merely the tools of a foreign power. And so discordant and critical voices have been heard in the various Communist parties on the subject of Soviet policy toward Czechoslovakia in 1968, on policy toward Israel, on Soviet anti-Semitism, on Soviet treatment of intellectuals, even on the European Economic Community.

Indeed, the emergence of a degree of independence in the tactics pursued by the Communist parties of certain countries — including Italy, France, Spain and Great Britain — is a significant break in the totalitarian armor. However, the breach must not be exaggerated so far as foreign policy is concerned. But one aspect of this phenomenon (which has been nicknamed "Eurocommunism") is particularly damaging and disturbing to the Soviet Union, as is evident from Soviet reactions to it. This is the increasingly open and strident criticism by these parties of the abuse of human rights inside the Soviet Union. This development has become particularly important in the past few years since the Helsinki Final Act was signed, among others, by the Soviet Union in 1975 and revised at Belgrade in 1977. The fact that this Act obliges states to respect civil rights (in a way that the Soviet Union has never done and plainly did not intend to do when it signed the Act) has emboldened courageous dissenters to urge fulfillment of its obligations by the Soviet authorities. This, in turn, has led to increasingly savage repressions inside the Soviet Union, and the repressions have outraged public opinion in most Western countries, and notably in the USA. In the USA, in particular, this repressive Soviet policy, in flagrant violation of the Helsinki Act, has put in jeopardy the policy of so-called "détente" inaugurated in 1972. In other Western countries, regard for the opinion of the voters whom they hope to attract has forced some Communist parties to voice protests against Soviet conduct. From the Soviet point of view, this has two undesirable consequences, even if the Soviet leaders may be regarded as fairly indifferent to outside opinion. First, it endangers what the Soviet Union regards as the main fruits of détente: Western trade, especially in technological methods and equipment, and credits; and what they see as the growing respectability of Communist parties. Up to date, neither the West nor the Soviet Union has drawn the right inference from this situation — the West, that it should withhold trade and credits until the Helsinki Act is complied with; and the Soviet Union, that it may in the end lose more by the repressive policy which it pursues toward internal critics than it gains in what it regards as internal security.

However, even if the Soviet Union may have lost subservient agents, has it not gained, in the pursuit of its general foreign policy aims, perhaps a more convincing chorus of advocates in the Western world? For again, in the main essentials the Communist parties continue to support Soviet foreign policy aims. And can it be doubted that the electoral victory of a Communist party in Italy, say, or in France would be of inestimable value to the Soviet Union in its general aim of weakening the North Atlantic Alliance, even if Italian or French Communists continued to berate the Soviet authorities for such matters as ill-treating Solzhenitsyn?

The breach with China is in a different category and raises issues that far exceed the modest aims of this chapter.[10] There is no doubt that considerable damage has been done to the strength and unity of world communism by the emergence of a second center of authority, in open conflict with the first, on the interpretation of the sacred canon and on the conduct and development of revolution.

Because of this schism both Khrushchev and Brezhnev repeatedly tried to procure the condemnation as heretics by the Communist parties of the world of the Chinese Communist party. All these efforts failed and have now apparently been abandoned. Their failure was indeed a measure of the degree of independence Communist parties have acquired in their relation to the Soviet Union, no doubt in part as the result of the emergence of Communist China. The existence of a hostile Communist China gravely impairs one aspect of the Soviet Union's "total" conduct of its foreign policy. The limitation on Soviet action imposed by the existence of China extends mainly to Asia. This factor may have the effect, indeed may already have had the effect, of reducing Soviet interest and diplomatic activity in Asia and intensifying Soviet interest in what have always been the areas to which the Soviet Union devotes its primary attention—Europe and the United States.

Such then are the advantages and disadvantages, the strengths and weaknesses, of the totalitarian system of foreign policy, as exemplified by the Soviet Union. There can be no doubt that in many respects its purpose, its unity, its immunity from internal criticism and pressure, its freedom from the vagaries of private enterprise, its comparative freedom in fixing priorities in disregard of internal political factors, all give the totalitarian leader considerable advantages over his democratic opponent. Even if there are important limitations on the "total" nature of his conduct of policy, the advantages would seem heavily to outweigh the disadvantages.

Experience, however, seems to suggest that there may be two respects in which totalitarian foreign policy can prove particularly vulnerable. First, it is essentially rigid—in terms of its ideology, its view of the world, its purpose, and the nature and extent of its knowledge and understanding of foreign countries. It is slow to adapt to a changing world, reluctant to abandon a dogma, inhibited by traditional categories of political judgment. All these limitations could prove serious handicaps if the Soviet Union should be faced in the future with diplomatic opponents who understand Soviet methods and purposes and who are not too ready to be deluded by phrases and bluffed by a well-worn technique for dealing with the "deaf-mute" capitalists whom Lenin so vividly sketched over fifty years ago.

Second, Soviet diplomatic success has always depended much more on skill in exploiting the weaknesses of opponents than on the strength of the Soviet case. Time and again, when faced with determined opposition to its ploys, the Soviet Union has been forced to retreat. If, as seems to be the case, the Soviet Union is entering a policy phase in which it recognizes that it will long be dependent on economic and technological support from the Western world, the United States and Western Europe will have only themselves to blame if they fail to exact a full political price for such support.

At the time of this writing (January 1980) the Soviet invasion of Afghanistan, and the possible threat that it may pose to Iran and Pakistan, have led to a reappraisal by the United States and the other NATO powers of the extent, if any, to which their relatively liberal policy of trade with the USSR should continue.

Notes

1. Leonard Schapiro, *Totalitarianism* (New York: Praeger, 1972).

2. Hans Buchheim, *Totalitarian Rule: Its Nature and Characteristics,* trans. Ruth Hein, annotations Kurt P. Tauber and Ruth Hein (Middletown, Conn.: Wesleyan University Press, 1968).

3. This document, which was first published in 1961, was discovered in 1924 by the painter Annenkov, who was charged with examining Lenin's papers shortly after his death in order to prepare a selection of drawings, paintings, and photographs of Lenin. Annenkov knew Lenin's handwriting and took a copy of the letter. The style, the place where the document was found, and the character of Annenkov all leave no doubt that the document is authentic. Whether it was ever sent to whomever it was intended for, presumably Chicherin, is another matter. The full text will be found in *Novy Zhurnal,* no. 65 (New York, 1961), pp. 146–147.

4. For a discussion of these questions and an examination of the evidence, see *The Strategic Intentions of the Soviet Union,* report of a Study Group of the Institute for the Study of Conflict, London, March 1978.

5. *Pravda,* 28 June 1972.

6. For a recent discussion of this theme, see Richard Pipes, "Principles of Soviet Foreign Policy," *Survey* 19, no. 2 [87] (Oxford, Spring 1973), pp. 41–61.

7. For a full discussion of this subject and for the evidence, see the report referred to in note 4.

8. I am indebted to Professor Pipes for this example.

9. Whether or not the Soviets goaded the Egyptians into attacking Israel in Oc-

tober 1973 is also a matter of conjecture. Since Brezhnev seems eager to maintain the East-West "détente," there is some doubt that he actively supported a new war at a crucial state of U.S.-USSR economic negotiations. It appears that the Politburo is divided on the détente issue, and the possibility of underhanded manipulations by "hawkish" members cannot be entirely ruled out. In any event, the internal pressures in Egypt and Syria apparently had reached a boiling point that the Soviets could not control.

10. Some discussion of the subject by Harold C. Hinton will be found in Chapter 7.

2

The Soviet Union and the Rules of the International Game

Adam B. Ulam

The Russian Revolution opened a new era in modern history. This is one of those rare platitudes that needs to be repeated rather than eschewed. Consider the European state system, which for the years 1648 to 1918 was virtually synonymous with the world system. During that period the ideological-religious character of the given state was at most of secondary importance insofar as its role in world politics was concerned. There were only occasional and short-lived exceptions to this rule.

The First French Republic between 1793–1794 and 1800 constituted a challenge to every other major state system in Europe, and ideological proselytizing was an important element in its drive for expansion. But beginning with the Napoleonic phase these ideological pretensions of the French state became, if not completely eradicated, then subdued by other elements. The expansionist thrust of the First Empire came to reflect no specific ideology but French nationalism and even more than that, Napoleon's personal and dynastic ambitions. His bid for European domination was no longer coupled with an ideological challenge to every other form of government. Eventually the French armies were defeated by the same principle and emotion that had led to their dazzling successes: nationalism.

Between 1815 and 1914 no state declared itself the carrier of a universal ideology or sought the overthrow of other forms of government. To be sure, Nicholas I's Russia was a self-proclaimed defender of the principle of legitimacy or, as we might call it anachronistically, of counterrevolution. But this stance, like the Holy Alliance of Nicholas' predecessor, was designed for the preservation of the status quo rather than the propagation of a specific ideology, and in any case both attempts at "freezing," so to speak, the political system of Europe of 1815 soon met with failure.

In brief, any citizen, not to mention any statesman of nineteenth-century Europe, would have had difficulty accepting the thought that there could be a state that would demand and enjoy all the international appurtenances of "normal" statehood and membership in the community of nations at the same time that its professed aim and ideology was to subvert all other existing forms of government. Nothing resembling such a situation had existed since the religious wars of the sixteenth and early seventeenth centuries. Even the First French Republic did not explicitly seek destruction of nonrepublican forms of government in countries with which it was not at war. Paris was not the center of an international movement with adherents in Vienna or Petersburg plotting the overthrow of their governments. "Friends in peace, enemies in war" was the ruling maxim of international relations in the era that came to an end on 7 November 1917.

It is rather startling to reflect that the people who carried out the Bolshevik Revolution had, only three years before, shared in this concept of international relations. The vision of an eventually socialist world enshrined in the Second International did not include the notion that the first state to become socialist would have any international obligations on that account.

One can search in vain in the Russian radical literature prior to 1914 for any hint of the foreign policy of a socialist Russia. To be sure, the prospect of such a Russia appeared quite distant. It would have been fantastic to think of backward Russia as the standard-bearer of militant Marxism. If such a vision ever passed before the eyes of Lenin, or for that matter Mártov, they must have thought only of revolutionary Russia as an example to the rest of Europe rather than of Russia as the center and directing force of a disciplined international movement.

With the outbreak of the European war Lenin repudiated the social-democratic tradition of the Second International and made his celebrated appeal for a return to the earlier militant essence of Marxism. Implicit in this appeal were two assumptions: (1) the European state system as it had existed since 1815 had broken down; (2) the moving force in international relations was to be class struggle, which would at once replace and absorb the national question as the main element of world politics. The new role of the Soviet state was to arise from the fact that the first assumption turned out to be amply justified, the second one only partially so.

In the first flush of their enthusiasm after taking power, the Bolsheviks believed that a completely new revolutionary era had dawned over Europe. If their country of the "half savage, stupid and heavy people of the Russian villages and countryside," to quote Gorky,[1] had become the stage of the first Victorian socialist revolution, if Russia's relatively small and backward working class had seized power, could one doubt that before too long the workers of Berlin, Paris, and London would follow suit?

All the cautions of the old social democracy, the schemes of stages of historical development carefully worked out by Karl Marx suddenly became obsolete. With World War I capitalism had committed suicide. In Lenin, as in most other Bolsheviks, the revolutionary triumphed over the historical determinist. So it was foolish to worry about foreign policy in the old sense of the word, or about other appurtenances and trappings of traditional statehood.

Trotsky, the commissar of foreign relations, a man normally of the most practical cast of mind, explained to a petitioner for a job that there was hardly anything worthwhile to do in his department: "I myself took this job so I would have more time for the Party work. All there is to do is to publish the secret treaties, then I will close the shop."[2] There was a messianic feeling that the irresistible wave of revolution would surge through a Europe weary of the economic system and civilization that had brought the frightful bloodbath.

This feeling received its first check at Brest Litovsk. It is the ratification of the humiliating and disastrous treaty that marks the true beginning of the Soviet state. Before then communism can be described as enthusiasm that seized power. By March 1918 this revolutionary enthusiasm became embodied in a state that, apart from its self-professed mission to carry out the world revolution, had to perform traditional tasks of statehood: to collect taxes, to build roads, to engage in diplomatic negotiations. After their victory the Soviets addressed European workers over the heads of their governments. But at Brest their emissaries affixed their signatures to the treaty along with those of His Majesty the German Emperor, His Apostolic Majesty the Emperor of Austria, and the King of Hungary. This was the first and the most fundamental lesson in political realism that the rulers of the infant state absorbed.

Revolutionary enthusiasm lingered on and did not receive its definite check until the days in September 1920 when the defeated Red Army reeled back from Warsaw. It was only then that the vision of the world kingdom of socialism gave way to weary resignation to the purgatory of capitalist encirclement. Russia, Lenin acknowledged, would have to exist within a system of states and coexist with capitalism.

The very nature of this coexistence was from the beginning to have a profound influence on the character of the Soviet state and in the longer run, even before the USSR became a world power, on that of other states.

The uniqueness of the Soviet regime proceeded not only from its Communist ideology but also from what might be called its existentialist nature. We may today observe how the character of certain states — Israel is the example that comes most readily to mind — is shaped not only by their political structure but also by the challenge to their very existence from the hostile forces surrounding them. The external threat is not an occasional one and it does not touch on a territorial dispute or rivalry over spheres of influence or trade; it is directed at the very essence and existence of the political organism. In some ways this threat can become an element of strength for the regime; the mentality of the state of siege endows the given society with cohesion.

The Soviet regime has developed the exploitation of external danger to the level of an art. This is not to argue that at times the danger was not real or felt as such. Still, capitalist encirclement has been much more than an occasional propaganda weapon in the armory of Soviet communism. It has been a continuous theme in Soviet internal and external politics, an invaluable means for whoever holds power in the USSR to suppress opposition and dissent.

There was perhaps some superficial logic in the argument around 1921–1922 that the weak and isolated Soviet state could not afford the luxury of free political debate and that not only other Marxist parties but any organized attempt at dissent within the Communist party had to be suppressed. The erstwhile capitalists and landowners were just waiting for internal divisions and chaos to attempt, with foreign help, to fasten their yoke on the people of Russia.

But even today, with Russia a world superpower, with the last of pre-1917 capitalists moldering in the grave, a similar argument is being used to justify the ban on dissent in the arts, to prohibit publication of certain novels, to jail or expel those who claim liberties spelled out in the Soviet constitution. The enemy is always there awaiting a chance, unreconciled to the existence of the first state to enshrine socialism as its ruling ideology.

There is no question that it was a masterly exploitation of this motif that enabled Stalin to erect his edifice of tyranny. At crucial points in his struggle for absolute power he invoked the foreign danger to cow his opponents and silence the scruples of his own partisans. It is difficult to see how the party rank and file would have acquiesced in the destruction of Lenin's companions led by Trotsky except for Stalin's ability to persuade the party between 1924 and 1928 that his rivals were "objectively" working for the enemy. And one decade later he was able to destroy them physically by "proving" that they were in fact agents of Berlin and Tokyo.

Many of those who recoiled from his schemes of social engineering — which brought about famine, death, and the destitution of millions — had their hands stayed by the dictator's argument that the sufferings of mass collectivization were necessary if Communist Russia was to survive. The existence of foreign danger and the permanence of international crisis has thus become a fixed principle of the Soviet philosophy of government and in fact might be described as a principal working tenet of current Communist ideology.

We might now indulge in a brief epistemological disquisition. How is this tenet of Communist faith actually regarded by its high priests? In their own innermost thoughts do they perceive foreign dangers to be as concrete and constant as their oratory has led many to believe?

Even in their public pronouncements Soviet leaders have given us a hint of their basic ambivalence on this point. Speaking at one of the most danger-fraught times for the Soviet state, Lenin could still give this amazingly sober and optimistic appraisal: "We are in a situation in which the raging waves of imperialist reaction which appear at any moment to overwhelm the small island of the Socialist Soviet Republic, time and time again break against each other."[3]

Uncompromising hostility to the Soviet system is a basic tendency of world capitalism. But so are rivalry and inner conflicts characteristic of capitalist-imperialist systems. The first tendency requires that the Soviet Union never let its guard down, never assume that permanent peace is achievable as long as capitalism remains. The second bestows on the Soviet Union an attribute no social system or regime possessed in the past: indestructibility. The very forces of history preclude the possibility of Communist Russia being attacked by a superior combination of powers. This, then, had been the counterpoint of the Soviet philosophy of international relations. We say "had" for, as we shall see, nuclear weapons and the rise of another but potentially hostile Communist power has called for a reexamination of those basic tenets and challenged the whole ideological basis of the Soviet state.

For most of its existence the USSR, that is, its rulers, defined its role in international relations quite differently from that of any state in the past. Due to its ideological character Soviet Russia had different obligations and faced different dangers than a "normal" state. Therefore the USSR claimed, and what is rather amazing, achieved a special status in international relations.

It was to be treated as a regular member of the community of nations, yet unlike other states its rulers never made a secret of the fact that they sought and hoped for an overthrow of other forms of government. To be sure, Soviet diplomacy worked strenuously to maintain the fiction that there is a definite distinction and separation between the Soviet leaders in their capacity as governors of their state and as guides of international communism. But already in the beginning, and against the advice of his more timid diplomats, Lenin refused to lend any plausibility to this fiction by having government figures keep away from the Comintern. "There can be no question of me and Trotsky leaving the Executive Committee," he wrote Foreign Commissar Chicherin.[4]

Soviet leaders pleading for diplomatic recognition and foreign credits thus continued as members of the body that issued inflammatory revolutionary appeals, drew scurrilous characterizations of bourgeois politicians in France and Britain, and in general interfered in the most flagrant manner in the internal politics of countries with which the Soviet Union sought normal diplomatic and trade relations.

The very fact that neither Lenin nor his successors sought to conceal their roles as spiritual and political directors of a world revolutionary movement illuminates the fact that as politicians the Communists discounted the alleged danger that as ideologists they incessantly invoked. Had they been really convinced of the imminence of a capitalist attack from abroad, it is reasonable to assume that they would have chosen to be more hypocritical, to try to disguise more effectively their role as international revolutionaries. But as Lenin wrote in the same letter to his foreign commissar, for Soviet dignitaries to resign from their Comintern posts would only create the impression of weakness. And a principle the Soviet regime has observed to this very day, and one that has served it well, is that to create the impression of weakness among foreigners is much more dangerous than to maintain the posture of ideological hostility.

By 1933 the Soviet Union obtained what it had sought so persistently and unflinchingly since 1919: special status in the community of nations in terms of a virtual acknowledgment by other major states that the USSR had the right to all the usual appurtenances of statehood and diplomatic and commercial intercourse even though its professed philosophy was one of hostility to every other form of government and despite the fact that an international movement centered in and directed from Moscow had as its professed aim the spread of communism to all corners of the world.

Major powers that have recognized the Soviet regime as the legal government of Russia, concluding with the United States in 1933, have often demanded and sometimes exacted that Soviet Russia formally renounce its interference in their internal affairs. But except in the case of the United States it is difficult to believe that such assurances were sought seriously rather than as a gesture. Certainly by 1933 it was almost humorous to expect the Soviet government, as Maxim M. Litvinov pledged in a formal note to the U.S. Department of State,

> to refrain, and to restrain all persons in Government service and all organizations of the Government or under its direct or indirect control . . . from any act overt or covert, liable in any way to injure the tranquility, prosperity, order or security of any part of the United States. . . . Not to permit the for-

mation or residence on its territory of any organization or group . . . which has as its aim the overthrow or the preparation for the overthrow . . . of the political or social order of the whole or any part of the United States.[5]

That such pledges were sought could in itself be taken as proof that the old diplomatic order had disintegrated beyond any hope of reconstruction.

But by the time the Soviet Union took its place as a full member of the world community of states its status as such was still more paradoxical, and by the pre-1914 standards more scandalous, than had been the case in the twenties.

Until roughly 1925–1926 it could still be claimed with some superficial validity that the Soviet Communists were members of a world movement in which their country played the leading but not absolutely dominant role. But by 1933 it was clear that the rulers of Russia were not mere participants in a world revolutionary movement and it could not be claimed that, although enjoying a special status among their fellow revolutionists, they were not the absolute masters. With Stalin at the helm, foreign Communists were now obedient servants of the Soviet Union, foreign Communist parties an extension of Soviet power. After 1928–1929 a decision made in the Kremlin was as binding on the Communist party organizations in Paris and Prague as it was in Kiev or Minsk.

With the Sixth Congress of the Comintern, the tactics as well as personnel policies of foreign Communist parties passed under the direct control of Moscow. Official recognition of the USSR thus amounted to a virtual acknowledgment by the major powers that they could have normal diplomatic relations with a state that claimed and received from a number of their own citizens loyalty superior to that they acknowledged to their own government.

Ironically, it fell to the country that has traditionally been most jealous of the principle that the loyalty of its citizens should be rendered exclusively to their own government to recognize most vividly the universalistic pretensions of the Soviet state. On his visit to Moscow in 1935 following the signing of the Franco-Soviet pact, the French foreign minister, Pierre Laval, sought and received Stalin's approval of an internal policy of the French government, a formal declaration that was thought necessary to make the French Communists support their country's defense effort: "Comrade Stalin expressed complete understanding and approval of the national defense policy pursued by France with the object of maintaining its armed forces at a level consistent with its security requirements."[6]

Thus a right-wing French government pleaded with the leader of the world Communist movement to sanction its internal policies and thereby make them acceptable to a number of its own citizens!

Even when the growing fascist threat made the Soviet Union anxious for allies abroad, its government refused to play down its role as the directing force of the world Communist movement. The farce that Foreign Commissar Litvinov chose to enact before the American ambassador in 1935 speaks for itself: William C. Bullitt expostulated with Litvinov that the approaching Seventh Congress of the Comintern would, in view of the participation of American Communists, constitute a violation of the Roosevelt-Litvinov agreement of 1933.

> Litvinov said: "What, is there to be one?" I answered, "yes, on the twentieth of this month." Litvinov replied with a broad grin, "You know more about the Third International than I do. The other day when I was talking with Stalin I said I had heard there was to be a meeting of the Third International on the tenth of this month. Stalin replied, 'Is there?' He knew about it no more than I do."[7]

The Laval and Bullitt incidents do not require a comment, but we might pause to enquire the reasons that made the Western powers accept such an unprecedented state of affairs. They are to be sought first of all in the destruction of the European state system wrought by World War I. The cornerstone of this system was the principle of state sovereignty.

The Treaty of Versailles failed to restore the old system. In fact, by imposing severe restrictions upon the sovereignty of the defeated powers, notably Germany, Versailles helped establish the notion that state sovereignty was *not* the basic foundation of the international order. The Western powers' intervention in the Russian civil war, sporadic and ineffective though it was, further weakened legally, and even more psychologically, the case for holding the Soviet Union accountable to normal rules of international intercourse. If capitalist powers had tried to overthrow the infant Soviet state, could one by any logic deny this state the right to have special friends and partisans abroad?

More basically, after 1918 the democratic ethos became a powerful force in international relations. This sounds and is paradoxical, for this date marks the opening of the intense challenge to democratic and liberal institutions throughout the world. But it is precisely in the name of democratic principle that the forces inimical to democracy were to score their greatest gains: The doctrine of national sovereignty became unavailing in the face of the democratic one. Public opinion in democratic countries found it difficult to resist the argument that the feelings of the majority of the Germans in Austria and Sudetenland possessed a higher validity than the legal rights of the Austrian and Czech states. And it was equally difficult for the French or British governments to suppress political organizations or opinions in their own countries merely because they reflected the wishes and served the interests of a foreign power.

By the same logic the Soviet Union could not be blamed for the fact that a number of British or American citizens shared the ideology and political premises of its rulers. In fact, acquiescence in the Soviet Union's unusual role in international relations preceded the toleration of local Communist parties by the democracies.

Persecution and chicanery against those parties by many democratic governments could be traced to the parties' ostentatious hostility to democratic institutions, especially in the twenties and early thirties, rather than to their link with the USSR. Weimar Germany found no incompatability between its virtual alliance with the USSR and political and legal measures directed against the German Communists. And Fascist Italy, which relatively early established diplomatic ties with Moscow, was not inhibited by this fact from suppressing the Communist party and imprisoning its leaders.

The challenge the Soviet Union represented to the world order was thus unique in its nature. The response, or rather the lack of response, of other powers to this challenge contributed to the final demise of the world order in the thirties. For it was then that the ideological principle finally prevailed over state sovereignty as the strongest element in international relations.

The initial and very considerable successes of Hitler could be traced to his masterly exploitation of the changed rules of the game that were signaled by the Versailles Treaty but brought into full prominence by the existence of the new type of state, the USSR. Anticommunism was more than Hitler's propaganda stock in trade; it was a technique that enabled weak and isolated Germany to obtain allies and, most important, time for rearmament.

It is often alleged that Hitler "got away" with his trampling over Germany's treaty obligations and his aggressive posturings from 1933 through 1938 because of fears of communism in the West. This is true enough. But a large part of his success must be traced to the breakdown of the general principle of international obligation and the norms of international comity, which had occurred before and largely because of the USSR. It would have been an international scandal and quite possibly *causus belli* for the Tsar of All Russias to publicly express Russian territorial claim to Eastern Galicia on the ground that the majority of its inhabitants were Little Russians (as the Ukrainians were called in tsarist Russia).

But Hitler's public claims to foreign territories, whether rationalized on the grounds that the German race needed *Lebensraum* or that the territories in question were inhabited by Germans, did not automatically brand him as the enemy of *the* European order in the eyes of the other powers, as Louis

XIV and Napoleon had been branded for advancing similar expansionist claims. Hitler's *claims* were no more shocking than those advanced by the Soviet Union by virtue of its role as the Fatherland of Socialism; in fact, to some conservative circles in the West, even to people who had little sympathy for fascism as such, Hitlerism appeared a welcome counterforce to communism.

A world order, even a rudimentary one such as prevailed prior to 1914, must be based on the assumption that some legal norms such as national sovereignty are superior to considerations of nationalism and ideology (the distinction itself is awkward, integral nationalism and racism as in Hitler's creed being a species of ideology). However ridiculous or immoral the "little wars" of the nineteenth century may appear to us, they were limited and of brief duration because none of the contestants sought the overthrow of its enemies in the name of a "higher" principle.

What kept the Crimean War "small," for example, was not its limited scope — it involved, after all, three of Europe's five major powers of the time — but the limited objectives of the contestants. One can readily envisage that had this war taken place some fifty years later it would have turned into a total war, not so much because of changes in the nature of warfare but because it could not have failed to assume an ideological character. The French and British would have proclaimed it a war against tsarist autocracy; the Russians would have invoked — as a matter of fact, they tried intermittently and ineffectually throughout the century — the principle of natural self-determination, to be applied, to be sure, not to their own but to the Turkish empire. World War I already bore a quasi-ideological character ("Prussian militarism," the espousal by the Central Powers of a variant of national self-determination as evidenced in their abortive moves on the Polish question, the Wilsonian rhetoric).

Paradoxically, the legalistic and conservative order established by the Congress of Vienna enabled liberal and eventually democratic institutions to take root in a number of countries. The result of World War I, fought in the name of lofty principles, was to make the world very unsafe indeed for democracy.

The Soviet Union adapted very skillfully to the drastically changed nature of international relations. After 1933 its position appeared to be the acme of paradox. Here was a state that proclaimed itself opposed to every other existing form of government and yet claimed to be a firm supporter of the international order threatened by fascism. Lenin had branded the League of Nations a "league of imperialist brigands," yet in 1934 the USSR entered the League.

Hitler's dramatic successes in the 1930s should not make one overlook the fact that he failed in his first and most basic diplomatic objective: to isolate the USSR and to be acknowledged as a defender of the European order against communism. His anti-Communist posturings gained adherents among some groups and politicians in the West and contributed, although not nearly as much as is commonly believed, to French and British toleration of his early treaty violations and aggressions.

But the British and French governments did not turn to Hitler to help save them from international communism. Once their hopes of appeasing Hitler were exposed as illusory, they went to Stalin to help save them from war and, if that was impossible, to help them in a war against resurgent Germany.

The official myth sedulously propagated by Soviet propaganda and still believed by many in the West — that the USSR patiently tried to collaborate with the democracies and only when repulsed by them turned regretfully to a treaty with Germany — cannot obscure the brilliant achievement of Soviet diplomacy. Alone among the great powers in 1939, the Soviet Union achieved its aim: to gain territorial aggrandizement while remaining at peace.

The Franco-British hopes of drawing Russia into an alliance and thus preserving peace turned to ashes; so did Hitler's dream that the French and British, dazzled by the Soviet-German pact, would let him have his will with Poland. To be sure, Stalin's brilliant gambit was, within two years, to bring him close to an irretrievable disaster — but then, who in 1939, including the German general staff, could have realized the full extent of the French army's weakness?

But it was not merely Stalin's diplomatic skill (and unscrupulousness) that enabled him to first pose as a defender of democracy and then, in the name of the interests of the Fatherland of Socialism, to forge an alliance with Hitler. There was an ample warrant in the ideology for both courses of action. It was Hitler who compromised what little ideological content there was in his hideous doctrine by signing with Stalin.

Stalin could revert to the traditional Communist tenet in international relations: differences between capitalist states were those of degree rather than of substance. A major and prolonged war between the main capitalist powers would create a favorable climate for the spread of revolution. Thus, quite apart from personal and nationalist reasons, Stalin could claim that the course he took in 1939 was in full accordance with the Communist doctrine. It was not his fault that some people in Britain and France thought that around 1934–1935 the character of the Soviet state had changed drastically, that the Popular Front period represented more than just a phase in the foreign policy of his country, and that he would obligingly pull

British and French chestnuts out of the fire, risking in the process the destruction of his own regime, if not indeed of the whole Communist experiment.

The Grand Alliance of the USSR with the United States and Britain demonstrated once again the incongruous character of the Soviet state and its position in the community of nations. The Western allies could not accept the simple fact that the USSR became their partner in the war because and only because Russia had been attacked by Hitler. If for the Germans the Japanese became "honorary Aryans," then for the British and Americans, and especially the latter, for the duration of the war Stalin became an "honorary democrat."

Pretense notoriously leads to self-deception. Even if the most humane type of Communist rather than Stalin had disposed of Russia's policies during the war, he still could not have fulfilled the hopes that Western public opinion and official American (if not British) circles had entertained about the Soviet Union's postwar behavior in international relations. Unfounded illusions during the war, an unfounded disillusionment following it — here in a nutshell is the main source of America's unhappy experience with the USSR and the world.

The tragedy (for such it is) is compounded by the fact that, while the basic ideological incompatibility between the two superpowers could not have been wished away, some of its disastrous consequences could have been avoided by greater realism on the part of the West. Stalin could not have been transformed into a Jeffersonian democrat recognizing the sanctity of popular elections. But he did entertain the possibility of the Soviet Union becoming an imperial power in the traditional sense of the word. In the very beginning of the Grand Alliance he formulated his proposals in a rather crass way. The Anglo-Soviet treaty of alliance was to be supplemented by a secret protocol that would provide for the Soviet Union to retain its 1941 frontiers (i.e., its territorial gains from the period of Soviet-Nazi collaboration) in return for the British right to bases in France, the Low Countries, Norway, and Denmark. But apart from the crudity of such proposals they testify to Stalin's readiness to consider the postwar world in terms of spheres of influence.[8]

Any and all such attempts broke down because of American refusals even to consider the sinful idea of spheres of influence. Russia was, in Washington's view, to be integrated into the world system with peace guaranteed through the United Nations. The result was predictable: The Soviet Union got *its* sphere of influence but the Western Allies did not get theirs. Eastern Europe was firmly in the Soviet grip by 1946, while much of American policy during the next two decades would consist of devising stratagems and policies to protect Western Europe from the Soviet and/or Communist danger.

Furthermore there is much to suggest that hard, businesslike bargaining could have enabled Poland, Czechoslovakia, and other nations to preserve their internal autonomy while remaining within the Soviet sphere, that is, to have the status of today's Finland rather than to undergo the brutal process of Communist *Gleichschaltung*. Not only the United States but also the alleged objects of its solicitude were thus destined to pay a high price for American virtue and repugnance for power politics.

It is not here suggested that with a different attitude by the West the Soviet Union would have washed its hands of the international Communist movement at the end of the war. But there is a great deal of evidence to support the contention that for a considerable period of time the USSR might have deemphasized the use of foreign Communists as an auxiliary arm of foreign policy.

The Comintern was dissolved in 1943. The great Communist parties of the West—the Italian and French—were, and with more than just a hint from Moscow, pursuing moderate policies within the context of parliamentary government. The Sino-Soviet treaty of August 1945 showed that the USSR expected Chiang's regime to remain the main political force on the Chinese mainland for a long time. All such maneuvers suggest that Stalin was leaving himself an option of observing certain rules of the international game, *provided that those rules were spelled out clearly by his Western partners*. But they were not.

Washington, which after 1945 charted the direction of Western policies, no longer sought to bargain with the Soviet Union. The United States had expected the USSR to behave in a manner consonant with the United Nations Charter; since the USSR did not, the American policymakers concluded that the usual tools of diplomacy were unavailing when dealing with this mysterious power.

Absurd expectations succeeded grotesque apprehensions. If the Soviet Union violated its wartime pledges and the UN Charter, this meant it might at any point launch its armies in a drive to the English Channel. In April 1946 the ambassador of the country that had a monopoly on the atom bomb and at the time produced half of the world's industrial output asked the leader of a state whose economy still lay shattered by a war in which it lost more than twenty million men, "What does Russia want and how far is Russia going to go?" And Stalin not very reassuringly answered, "We are not going much farther."[9]

American naivete could not be reassuring to Stalin—quite the opposite. If the United States at the height of its power failed to realize its strength and bargaining assets, this meant that the Soviet Union should cash in on its opportunities before the Americans woke up and tried to mount a basic challenge to the new Soviet position both in Europe and elsewhere.

It was therefore easy for Stalin to see the Marshall Plan not merely as the means to put Western Europe on its feet but as a sinister scheme to use the rearmed West as America's cat's-paw to reverse Russia's postwar expansion and deny it the fruits of victory. If so, East European countries had to be more firmly bound to the USSR, their governments and societies shaped by the Communist mold.

There was likewise no reason for Moscow to press the Chinese Communists to moderate their ambitions and content themselves with just Manchuria. A Communist China, or even a China torn by civil war, was bound to distract American attention and resources from Europe. This is yet another and more startling paradox: It was the weakness of America's *original* reaction to the Soviet usurpations that fed Stalin's fears and apprehensions for the future and set the stage for the cold war. The West's confused and contradictory policies led the Soviets to fear an *eventual* war; Russia's ominous and self-imposed isolation moves, such as the Berlin blockade and the 1948 Communist coup in Czechoslovakia, made the West fear *imminent* Soviet aggression. Here then was a tragedy of errors, or rather of mutual misperceptions, that largely shaped the postwar world.

The Cominform born in 1947 was a ponderous Soviet response to what was perceived as the long-range American threat. The Communist Information Bureau of nine parties might well have been called the "Anti–Marshall Plan Bureau." Its second function was to exercise control over the Communist parties that now ruled as the Kremlin's deputies in their own countries.

The whole effort was transparently clumsy. The Soviet Union did not need the Cominform to keep the French or Bulgarian Communists in line. But it was obviously hoped that this would be a more decorous way of synchronizing the policies of foreign Communists and making sure that they would combat the nefarious designs in the West. Once it failed in its first test, when the Yugoslav Communists refused to submit their dispute with Moscow to the "imported" arbitration of the Cominform, the latter obviously became a fifth wheel, and its dissolution in 1956 was hardly noticed.

Stalin's obsession with the Marshall Plan and its alleged military implications and his personal pique at a Balkan upstart whom he suspected, also falsely, of harboring ambitions to become completely independent from the USSR were to have fateful and irreversible historical consequences. The period of the Berlin blockade, which began in the early summer of 1948 and ended in May 1949, coincided with the time when the Chinese Communists scored their greatest and decisive successes in the civil war. With a confrontation with the United States, with real war not inconceivable (even though Stalin did not believe the risk was great), the USSR obviously was not going to put a brake on the Chinese Communists' progress and their welcome diversion of Washington's attention from its European schemes.

This was not the time to negotiate with the Americans about what had obviously been the original Soviet aim in China—a Communist state but confined to northeast China and Manchuria (which would have given the Soviet Union a Chinese satellite rather than a rival Communist power). And after the Berlin confrontation ended in the summer of 1949 even Stalin could not have stopped Mao's forces, in view of their dazzling victories and the complete collapse of Chiang's regime.

The rise of Communist China transformed many of the basic perspectives of Soviet foreign policy. Between 1933 and 1950 the Soviet Union was accepted as a normal member of the community of nations; at the same time the Soviet state claimed and received the loyalty of a worldwide movement on account of its ideological character. The Soviet Union had been the sole "exporter" of revolution, the sole arbiter of tactics of Communist movements everywhere. After World War II, the USSR became one of two superpowers and yet, like the weak and backward Russia of the twenties, it still basked in the protective feeling and affection of millions of supporters and sympathizers throughout the world.

Now this enviable situation was gone forever. No longer would the USSR be able to enjoy complete freedom of maneuvering, confident that no matter how drastic or unexpected its policies—say, the Nazi-Soviet pact—they would be met with a chorus of approval from every Communist party in the world.

How did Stalin propose to deal with the new problem? We have only scraps of information about his dealings with the Chinese leadership, but they throw some fascinating light on Sino-Soviet relations during that phase. It is clear that Stalin counted first of all on his unmatched prestige to secure at least outward deference and obedience from Peking. But even the megalomaniac despot realized that China could not be treated in the way he dealt with Bulgaria. The Sino-Soviet treaty of 1950 envisaged the Chinese repossessing Port Arthur and the Manchurian Railway. Stalin now hastened to offer Soviet military help for Mao's consolidation of his power over the mainland. We are indebted to a recent Soviet source for an interesting piece of information: "Soviet aviation units took part in the concluding phase of the [civil] war, having been sent there in accordance with the Sino-Soviet Treaty of February 14, 1950."[10]

But it is clear that Stalin did not confine himself to soothing Mao's pride and providing him with belated help. The Manchurian part of the Chinese Communist empire at first enjoyed an autonomous position, being ruled by people with special ties to Moscow, headed by Kao Kang. It was only following Stalin's death that Mao moved, in December 1953, "to remove or to push aside those leaders of the Party, who were known as partisans of increased proletarian influence in the Party and of friendships with the Soviet Union."[11] In 1955 Kao Kang died in jail.

The story of the Korean War suggests strongly that it was exploited by the USSR, if not indeed instigated for the purpose of preserving Soviet leverage over Peking. After China's involvement, Soviet air units moved into Manchuria, ostensibly to protect China from American air raids.[12] But it is at least reasonable to conjecture that this was the means of establishing Soviet presence in that rich province should Chiang's forces with American support descend on other parts of China and rekindle the civil war.

Stalin's death was bound to put an end to such games, at least for some time to come. His successors were conscious of how the awe and imperturbability the late despot had exuded masked various internal and external weaknesses of the Soviet Union. They could not and would not conduct foreign policy in the same way. Above all they realized that their position might be weakened, perhaps fatally, by any realization, whether in the West or even in their own country, of the precarious nature of Sino-Soviet relations.

It is revealing to note that the announcement of Malenkov's assumption of leadership was accompanied by a picture showing him with Stalin and Mao, as if in addition to the late dictator's blessing he also had the approval of the head of the nation that for the next seven years would be officially referred to as the Great People's Republic of China.[13] For both internal and external reasons the Kremlin needed the "unshakable friendship of the Soviet and Chinese people," and it had to pay a price.

For some twenty years the relationship between the Soviet Union and foreign Communists had been fairly one-sided: To the USSR accrued most of the advantages of this relationship, to foreign comrades most of the dangers and costs. Now the Soviet leaders hastened to appease Peking. Economic and technological help was extended to China on a much more generous scale than originally planned in Stalin's time. The special position of the USSR in Manchuria and Sinkiang was liquidated with no resistance by Moscow.

In 1954 Khrushchev headed a delegation to China and it fell to him to negotiate the final state of the liquidation of the Soviet presence on Chinese soil: Port Arthur and the East Chinese Railway were turned over to Peking; the joint companies (Stalin's favorite method of exploiting fellow Communist states) were liquidated, their total assets going over to the Chinese. For Mao this was evidently only a beginning: Mongolia should be returned to Chinese suzerainty, he told his visitors!

Developments in the international field during the next five years left the Kremlin no option but to continue what was in fact a policy of appeasement of Peking. The years 1956–1957 were a time when the leadership of the CPSU was shaken by serious internal dissensions. It was imperative for the Kremlin to receive public support from China, and that support did not come free. In October 1957 the Soviets took a step that would have been unimaginable in Stalin's time: They promised to help China develop its nuclear technology and, as the Chinese were later to reveal, the agreement included the promise that the USSR would deliver to its ally a sample atom bomb.[14]

Both sides were under no illusion as to the nature and reasons for their collaboration. Peking was aware that time was growing short for its exploitation of the Soviet predicament. A détente with the United States would enable the Kremlin to face a public rupture with China with greater equanimity. Understandably Mao had every reason to press the Soviet Union toward a more militant posture vis-à-vis America, to constrain Moscow to support anti-Western revolutionary movements all over the world. The Soviets chafed under these constraints. As a semi-official source says,

> In August–September 1958 in an attempt to intensify the "Big Leap" through the means of creating a center of tension close to China, Mao and his partisans embarked, without any consultation with the USSR . . . upon provocative artillery shelling of islands in the Taiwan Straits. . . . As it became known later, the Maoists had counted on the possibility of starting there a "local war with the U.S. and of involving eventually the USSR in it."[15]

History thus caught up with the USSR. What had been the source of additional strength, of a privileged position with respect to other states, now also became a burden, a source of entanglements and dangers. Communist China's declaration of independence vis-à-vis the Soviet Union was to affect much more than just Sino-Soviet relations; it was bound to change the Soviet position within the whole Communist movement. No longer would the USSR enjoy a completely free hand in foreign affairs, able to perform the most breathtaking maneuvers and shifts in its policies, confident that no matter how much they might hurt the interests of foreign Communists the latter would obediently follow Moscow's wishes.

Some foreign parties, notably Albania's, went completely over to Peking's camp. Others, such as North Vietnam's, saw the conflict between the Communist giants as an opportunity for maneuvering between the two and asserting a degree of independence of both. The Sino-Soviet break, which became public knowledge in 1960, meant that any conflict between the interests of a given Communist party and that of the USSR could no longer be resolved by Moscow automatically and without fear of unfavorable repercussions. Peking became a fervent advocate of what might be called the underprivileged members of the Communist family: of those parties whose revolutionary strivings were either ignored or restrained by Russia out of concern to avoid a dangerous confrontation with the United States.

Much as they saw through the Chinese game, and in fact by the early 1960s came to believe that Mao wanted nothing less than to force them into a war with America, the Soviet leaders were still vulnerable to such pressures. The loyalty of foreign Communists could no longer be taken for granted; it had to be fought for in competition with China.

Thus the Soviet regime was forced to offer repeated proofs of its "internationalism" and its solicitude for anti-Western revolutionary movements throughout the world, even though by doing so it was frustrating or at least delaying thoroughgoing détente with the United States and definitive settlement of the German problem, which have been cardinal objectives of Soviet policy since the middle fifties.

An outside observer, when first confronted with the evidence of the Sino-Soviet split, might well have concluded that its logical outcome would have to be a basic change in the Soviet Union's foreign outlook and policy. The USSR would become explicitly what it already was in fact: a status quo power. The umbilical cord linking the Soviet state to the international Communist movement, if not severed, would become attenuated. It obviously made no sense to export revolution if—and here China offered a constant and irrefutable proof—each new state entering the "camp of socialism" brought with it new headaches for the USSR: entanglements, expense, danger.

Even within its special preserve—Eastern Europe—the USSR had to tolerate a semi-independent posture by Romania. Other and loyal East European Communist regimes still had to be watched carefully—in 1968 Brezhnev might well have borrowed the American policy-makers' domino simile about Southeast Asia to justify the Kremlin's intervention in Czechoslovakia. A few more months of the Czechoslovak liberalization and the Warsaw and East German regimes would have had to follow suit or collapse in the face of popular pressure.

The maintenance of Communist regimes in Eastern Europe could no longer be assumed to bring economic profits to their protector. The pattern of Soviet exploitation that prevailed in Stalin's time could not be maintained following his death. And in the sixties the satellite empire was to become an occasional economic burden. Following the 1968 invasion Soviet economic help was extended to Czechoslovakia to keep the country's economy from crumbling. And in the winter of 1970–1971, to prevent Gomulka's fall from endangering the Warsaw Communist regime, food shipments had to be rushed to Poland.

As against the costs and dangers of ideological imperialism, the Kremlin leadership could ruefully contemplate the case of Finland. This small country, since 1945 as firmly within the Soviet sphere as any of the Communist satellites, had been allowed for a variety of reasons to preserve its internal autonomy and democratic institutions. Hence Finland's internal crises and dilemmas were of no concern to Moscow, no drain on Soviet resources. The Finnish government did not have to be watched anxiously for any signs of a flirtation with Peking; the freedom of the press in Helsinki was unlikely to lead to untoward impressions and strivings on the part of Warsaw, Sofia, or Kiev.

But neither the Sino-Soviet conflict nor the recent troubles in Eastern Europe appear to have persuaded the Kremlin to drastically alter the pattern of its relations with the world Communist movement or to abstain from ideological imperialism. In fact, as we have seen, the dispute with China has, at least until very recently, sharpened the ideological thrust of Soviet foreign policy.

During the Khrushchev era the Soviet Union sought to outbid Peking in the appeal to revolutionary movements, especially in the Third World. Moscow has decided not only to try to remain the directing center of world communism but also to become the chief sponsor of non-Communist revolutionary movements and regimes, as evidenced by the support given to practically every organized force combating the waning Western influence in the Third World. In fact fissures within the Communist bloc have apparently served to strengthen the Soviet's determination to stake a claim to yet another area of ideological influence and appeal in world politics.

Amid the official guests at the recent congresses of the Communist party of the Soviet Union there have been delegations not only from fraternal parties all over the world but also from the ruling parties of Algeria, Mali, and Tanzania. To be sure, their presence could only partly offset the absence of representatives of the largest Communist-ruled nation in the world, but the mere fact of admitting non-Communists to what had traditionally been a closed family gathering has a significance that goes beyond the symbolic.

The Soviet Union now proclaims itself to be the fatherland not only of socialism but of anti-imperialism. For a traditionalist thinking in terms of pre-1914 international law and diplomacy, this would have been an even more shocking and ominous development than the Soviet link with other Communist parties. The latter might be rationalized in terms of a worldwide ideological fraternity, masked by the polite fiction that when Suslov and Ponomarev talk with their British, French, or Argentinian comrades they do so as fellow Communists rather than members of the highest ruling body of the USSR. But this new intimate link between the Soviet Union and a variety of movements and regimes whose only common denominator is hostility to the West has an eloquence of its own.

How can one explain the persistence of this anti-Western syndrome and activity even at times, as at present, when the Soviet Union's "other" official policy seeks, and to a degree has achieved, a far-reaching détente with the United States and other Western powers?

There are several explanations, and we might state them very briefly: (1) the very momentum, so to speak, of the Soviet Union's ideological past; (2) competition with China; and (3) most basically, the very character of the Soviet regime is predicated upon its international role. Every denial of internal freedom, each restriction on the Soviet citizen's liberties, is ultimately rationalized by the image of a world divided into two hostile camps in which the forces of light — communism — are forever struggling with those of darkness — capitalism and imperialism — in a struggle that never abates even when relations between the Soviet and Western *governments* are friendliest.

Furthermore, and equally important, the Soviet regime feels that by now it has gained a prescriptive right to have what are in fact two foreign policies. It reacts strongly when the West shows the slightest sign of imitating the Soviet practice of having a bifurcated foreign policy: an ideological as well as a state one. (One may recall Khrushchev's probably not feigned indignation because the United States "celebrated" the Captive Nations Week.)

We shall presently consider how far the Soviet example has influenced the American approach to foreign policy. But right here we should just note that we have grown so used to Soviet unorthodox practices that they hardly arouse any surprise, not to mention diplomatic protests. It is no longer news when a secretary of the Central Committee and an American Communist leader sit down to a "cordial exchange of views." What would be the reaction in the USSR . . . and America . . . if a presidential assistant were to hold a similar publicly announced exchange with the head of an anti-Soviet Ukrainian or Russian emigré organization?[16] Witness the Soviet's agitation over President Carter's receiving *in his personal capacity,* a single Russian dissident.

The foregoing discussion illuminates two melancholy facts. One, a platitude: The emergence of the Soviet state and then its achievement of superpower status have, perhaps irretrievably, changed the nature of international relations and corroded the rudimentary international order that existed prior to 1914. The mainstays of that order were national sovereignty and the principle of noninterference by foreign powers in the affairs of sovereign states. To be sure, these had often been honored in breach, but still they were recognized as desirable aspirations and the necessary prerequisites of any real world order that would banish war.

The Soviet Union was the first state in modern history *explicitly* to reject national sovereignty as the basis of political legitimacy. In view of its ideological premises the Soviet state had and has to consider every non-Communist government as one de facto rather than de jure. That by itself would not have led to a heightening anarchy of international relations. It has been, after all, a tenet of the American popular philosophy of international relations that nondemocratic governments are both immoral and, in the long run, doomed by the forces of history. But in addition the Soviet Union has assumed and exercised the leadership of a worldwide movement whose stated, even though long-run, aim has been to replace every other form of government by the dictatorship of the proletariat.

Another and an almost inevitable result of the Soviets changing the rules of the international game had to be a transformation in the character of the Western powers' foreign policy, principally, of course, in that of the United States.

Once committed to an active world role, the United States — and here we mean not only the government but American public opinion — found it impossible to get a handle on the Soviet phenomenon. The United States could and did deal in a forthright manner with palpable aggression. But following the war this country became an occasional partner as well as the almost constant competitor not only of another state but also of a worldwide system.

Who was, then, the United States dealing with — the guardians of Russia's national interest or the high priests of an international ideological movement? In fighting to curb Soviet expansion, was America dealing with an imperial power, a worldwide conspiracy, or the forces of history? Could the Soviet threat — communism — be contained by enhancing the virtuousness of American policies and exacting similarly virtuous policies from its allies, or was the United States to be "realistic" — to descend into the grubby game of worldwide subversion?

Could the Russians be scared off their evil designs by a crushing superiority of power on the other side, or were they, on the contrary, to be dissuaded from their real fears by continuous examples of American high-mindedness and solicitude for freedom and democracy throughout the world? At one time or another American foreign policy during the last thirty years has reflected each of these variants.

Almost inevitably, therefore, the ideological component of American policy was enhanced by the competition with the Soviet Union and by what America's rulers and public opinion conceived to be the exigencies of the cold war. Without suggesting that this was altogether undesirable, it is clear that this aspect of the American response to what was conceived as the Soviet-Communist challenge was to have disruptive consequences both for international politics and for the inner workings of the American democracy.

In announcing the doctrine that bears his name, President Truman proclaimed the basic conflict to be between two ways of life: the Communist one, spreading "the evil soil of poverty and strife," and the democratic one, "based upon the will of the majority . . . free elections . . . guarantees of individual liberty . . . freedom of speech."[17]

This rhetoric, necessary as it may have been to convince the American taxpayers to assume additional and unaccustomed burdens, still appeared to suggest that the United States was engaged in an ideological crusade rather than a sober endeavor to restore a degree of stability to international relations. America's power was enlisted once more in a drive to make the world safe for democracy, rather than safe from war, and for the right of individual states to be free from direct or indirect aggression.

Many of the contested areas—Iran, Turkey, certainly Kuomintang China—could not be described as free in the sense the term is employed in the lexicon of American politics. The time would come when public opinion would demand evidence of irreproachable democratic virtues from each of the allies and protégés of the United States, and when it was found wanting many Americans would conclude that this country had no business protecting those countries' independence.

Thus the ideological veneer of the policy of containment was destined to contribute to the paradoxical situation of recent years when, to many critics at home and abroad, the United States stands revealed not as defender of international security and order but as an enemy of social and political change throughout the world. Yet what most critics and moralists overlook is the lesson of one of the most justifiable and rewarding acts of post–World War II U.S. foreign policy: the decision to extend American help to a regime that by no stretch of the imagination could be characterized as democratic and in no sense could be described as opposed to social and economic change, Tito's Yugoslavia.

Here was a government that, although utterly lacking in democratic or capitalist virtues, showed its determination to preserve, or rather to retrieve, its national independence as well as the capacity to do so barring an invasion by an overwhelming force. American aid to Communist Yugoslavia could be seen as an act of sheer power politics. Yet in extending a helping hand to a Communist dictatorship, the United States stumbled into an acknowledgment of what must be the basic principle of international morality: the right of any state, no matter what its ideological complexion, to be free from foreign domination. Livelihood must come before virtue, proclaimed an ancient philosopher. And international security must come before democracy or social progress as the foundation of a viable international order.

The Soviet state, or rather the privileged position this state has assumed in its foreign relations, has thus deflected even its rivals from perceiving what must be the guiding principle of an effective endeavor for peace. The ideological virus that has infected the world body politic could not be conjured away by contrivances like the United Nations.

When the United States, in exasperation over this predicament, sought a formula for an ideological counteroffensive against what was perceived as the Soviet drive for world domination, this served only to deepen the crisis the world had reentered immediately following the war. *Both* superpowers have rationalized their ideological imperialism in terms of higher principles that allegedly transcend national sovereignty. What made matters worse from the Western point of view was, of course, the fact that America's was bound to be ineffective. Unlike the Soviet Union, the United States has not disposed of the loyalty of a disciplined world movement that would unquestioningly follow its commands.

Furthermore, a democratic society is badly equipped to sustain a prolonged ideological crusade. It is expected—by its own people, by its allies—to adhere rigorously to its professed ideals in international relations and not to dilute them in the slightest through realpolitik or national interests. The Soviet state has not, at least until recently, suffered from similar disadvantages. The Monroe Doctrine has in effect collapsed; the Brezhnev Doctrine (which should really be called the Stalin Doctrine) has been doing quite well, at least insofar as Eastern Europe is concerned.

But we are not concerned here primarily with U.S.-Soviet relations. Our inquiry relates to the problem of how the Soviet Union has affected the general character of international relations and politics. We have seen that until 1914 there existed what might be called a rudimentary international order. It was far from providing for the equality of its member states, still less for a peaceful resolution of international disputes. Yet in theory this system expressed certain basic aspirations and stipulated the necessary conditions for a world order, the cardinal of them being national (or to be more precise, state) sovereignty.

The rise of the Soviet state and the international Communist movement inevitably posed a basic challenge to the effort to reconstitute this international order after the catastrophe of the world war. Soviet membership, first in the League of Nations and then in the United Nations, could not in itself counteract the disruptive effect of the Soviet Union on normal (again in its pre-1914 sense) functioning of international politics. Whatever obligations the USSR assumed by virtue of its membership in the world organizations and whatever one thinks of the Soviet record in abiding by them, it is clear the Russian leaders never even pretended that in assuming such obligations they were abdicating their role as the guides of a worldwide supranational movement whose legitimacy derived from an ideology (as interpreted by themselves) and not from any international covenant.

The challenge to the Russian leadership of the Communist movement, the virtual certainty that the monolithic unity of this movement can never again be restored, has not thus far resulted in what might be called the secularization of the Soviet state. In fact, while Soviet policies toward acknowledged ideological rivals have become more conciliatory, over the last twenty years Soviet ideological pretensions have grown more all-embracing. Moscow has emerged as a sponsor of a revolutionary ecumenism but one that, unlike Rome's, does not imply a liberalization of the practices of the true church itself.[18]

Influence and power outside their own country are seen by the Soviet leaders as a necessary condition for the preservation of their regime in its full autocratic rigor. Stalin could easily afford the collapse of the Greek Communist rebellion or Tito's defection. But the Cuban fiasco contributed to Khrushchev's fall, and his successors felt that Czechoslovak liberalization posed a serious threat to their own methods of governing the Soviet people. They are convinced that they must lead and score successes abroad lest their leadership be threatened at home.

Accordingly they maintain, even though they may suspect that it is not so, that the slogans and goals of world communism are as relevant and important to the security of the Soviet state today as they were in the twenties and thirties. They go on proclaiming the inherent contradictions within the capitalist world while turning a blind eye to those within the socialist camp. In many ways Soviet foreign policies (and, incidentally, domestic ones as well) are currently in a state of what by analogy with the Fourth French Republic might be called "immobilisme," and it would be foolhardy to soon expect a Soviet DeGaulle who would liquidate Soviet ideological imperialism the way the French statesman shed his country's colonial burden.

Détente has not changed or even strongly affected the characteristics of Soviet foreign policies. In fact, the period since its inception, the last eight years, has vividly demonstrated how enduring are these characteristics. The series of international agreements, culminating with the accords signed between the USA and the USSR during President Nixon's visit to Moscow in 1972, was hailed by many in the West as ushering in a new era in international relations, with the Soviet Union cooperating toward the goal of world stability.

Yet even on their face, those agreements promised but a continuation of troubled coexistence. They registered the two superpowers' determination to avoid a nuclear war, and to regulate (certainly not insofar as the USSR was concerned, to arrest) the armaments race. As Moscow has viewed it, détente must not be allowed to limit its freedom of action or to impair the ability to play the international politics game according to its own rules. A friendlier *tone* in its relations with the West was indicated, i.e., by Russia's current economic troubles, and hence the need for Western credits and technology. But the USSR did not propose to purchase Western goodwill by altering its traditional policies. Where the West saw a promise of stability and of terminating the condition of "neither peace nor war" that has plagued the world since 1945, the Soviet leaders discerned new ways and opportunities of expanding their country's power and influence.

The differences in the Soviet and Western views of détente and in the general philosophy of international relations come out vividly in the juxtaposition of two texts. One is an excerpt from the declarations signed by Brezhnev and Nixon, purporting to define the principles upon which the intercourse between the two superpowers was to be based: "Both sides recognize that efforts to obtain unilateral advantage at the expense of the other, directly or indirectly, are inconsistent with these objectives. The prerequisites for maintaining and strengthening peaceful relations between the USSR and the USA are the recognition of the security interests of the parties, based on the principle of equality and the renunciation of the use or threat of force."

As against that declaration, reminiscent in its tone and unrealism of the Litvinov note of 1933, we may counterpose a statement by a North Vietnamese official, explaining why his government felt confident that it could with impunity violate the Paris accords of 1973 and proceed in 1975 to conquer South Vietnam: "The internal contradictions within the U.S. administration and among U.S. political parties had intensified. The Watergate scandal had seriously affected the entire United States . . . [It] faced economic recession, mounting inflation, serious unemployment and an oil crisis."[19] It is safe to say that similar conclusions must have been reached by the Soviet Politburo when it decided "to obtain unilateral advantage" by authorizing the recent intervention in Afghanistan, and the Cubans' descent on Angola and intervention in other parts of Africa. The whole notion of an international order based upon agreements and independent of the correlation of forces at the given moment is probably not only unacceptable but genuinely incomprehensible to the Soviet leadership. Obviously, in view of America's and Western Europe's new vulnerabilities and social and economic travails, détente in 1980 cannot put the USSR under the same obligations, require the same restraint, that it did in 1972. And were he felt impelled to speak frankly, Brezhnev would probably echo another indiscreet admission by a foreign Communist, this time a Filipino at the Twenty-Fifth Party Congress: "The confrontation of socialism with imperialism in Indochina has demonstrated that with the help of the Soviet Union, one can achieve national liberation without threatening either world peace or détente."

Is it possible even to envisage the Soviet Union at some future point recognizing that its interests might best be served by an international system "based on the principle of equality and renunciation of the use or threat of force"? To answer we must conclude with another platitude which needs to be repeated: It is the disarray and weakness of the West, spiritual rather than military or economic in its essence, which has led to the present melancholy state of international affairs, and enabled the USSR to act as the catalyst of the forces destructive of the old world order. And as long as that condition of the West persists, communism, though incapable of erecting an alternative world order, will continue to challenge and encroach on what remains of the old. It is a recognition of these ineluctable facts that must precede any future attempt to piece together a world community.

Notes

1. Maxim Gorky, *O Ruskom Krestyansive* (Berlin, 1922), p. 22.

2. S. Pestkovsky, "The October Days in Petrograd," in the *Proletarskaya Revolutsya,* no. 10 (October 1922), p. 99.

3. From a speech on 14 May 1918, in Jane Degras, ed., *Soviet Documents on Foreign Policy,* vol. 1: *1917–1924* (London: Oxford University Press, 1953), p. 78.

4. *Leninskiy Sbornik* [Collected notes and papers by Lenin], vol. 36 (Moscow: State Publishing House, 1959), p. 338.

5. Jane Degras, ed., *Soviet Documents on Foreign Policy,* vol. 3: *1933–1941* (London: Oxford University Press, 1953), p. 36.

6. Ibid., p. 132.

7. *Papers Relating to the Foreign Relations of the United States: Russia 1933–39* (Washington, D.C.: Government Printing Office, 1941), pp. 221–22.

8. See Adam B. Ulam, *Expansion and Coexistence: History of Soviet Foreign Policy, 1917–1967* (New York: Praeger, 1968), pp. 331–32.

9. Walter Bedell Smith, *My Three Years in Moscow* (New York: Lippincott, 1950), p. 50.

10. V. I. Glunin, A. M. Grigorev, K. V. Kukuskin, and N. N. Nikiforov, *Noveyshaya Istoria Kitaya* (Moscow, 1972), p. 246.

11. Ibid., p. 266.

12. Ibid., p. 259.

13. The picture in *Pravda* of 10 March 1953 was a composograph of a photograph taken at the signing of the Sino-Soviet alliance on 14 February 1950, when in addition to the three gentlemen in question, a score of other officials were gathered for the occasion.

14. Ulam, *Expanse and Coexistence,* p. 599.

15. Glunin et al., *Noveyshaya Istoria Kitaya,* p. 319.

16. We may console ourselves with the reflection that in the past Communist China was willing to tolerate a somewhat similarly abnormal pattern of relations between Washington and Peking. We had de facto diplomatic relations with the People's Republic at the same time that we had a de jure link with and were pledged to defend another Chinese regime viewed by Peking as a rebel one. To be sure, the Chinese Communists viewed this as but a temporary accommodation and realistically as an efficacious way of eroding U.S. protection of Taiwan.

17. Harry Truman, *Memoirs,* vol. 2: *Years of Trial and Hope* (New York: Double-day, 1958), p. 106.

18. Perhaps emblematic of the whole current state of relations is the issue of a dialogue between Catholicism and Marxism as advocated by certain circles within the Church. The Communists are quite willing to carry out such a dialogue, *provided it takes place in the West.* At home they insist on a monologue.

19. *New York Times,* 26 April 1976.

Part 2

**Regional Case Studies
of Soviet Foreign Policies**

3

Eastern Europe

Hugh Seton-Watson

The object of this chapter is not to provide a chronological survey of the relations between the Soviet Union and Eastern Europe but to consider the impact of Soviet policies on that region (the broad region lying between the areas of compact German, Italian, and Russian population—including, for present purposes, the Belorussians and the Ukrainians under the term "Russian")[1] at decisive moments since 1917, and to ask the following questions: What was specific to the Soviet impact? In what respects did that impact differ from the impact of previous great powers, such as the Ottoman empire, the Hapsburg monarchy, or the tsarist empire?

In Stalinian and post-Stalinian mythology, the October Revolution was, for the peoples of Eastern Europe as for other peoples living farther away from the borders of Russia, the decisive event making possible the self-determination of oppressed nations and marking a new phase in the struggle of the working class against capitalism. For example, the establishment in 1918 of an independent state of Czechs and Slovaks was the result not of the activities of that enemy of the workers, Thomas Masaryk, or of the victory of his masters, the Western imperialist powers, or of the armed struggle of Czech and Slovak volunteers in various Allied armies, or even mainly of the Czech and Slovak peoples in the homeland. It was, instead, the Bolshevik Revolution in Russia that brought liberty to Czechs and Slovaks; it was Lenin and Stalin who by their wisdom and heroism created Czechoslovakia.

The truth is less glorious and far more complicated. It is true that the events of 1917 in Russia made a profound impression all over Eastern Europe. However it was the February Revolution that first aroused the hopes of the German and Magyar workers and of the subject nations of the Hapsburg monarchy. The May 30 declaration of the South Slav and Czech deputies to the reassembled Reichsrat in Vienna preceded Lenin's armed insurrection by five months but was certainly inspired by the revolutionary situation in Russia. The revolutionary mood among workers, intellectuals, and peasants in Central Europe grew as the situation in Russia developed, up to and after the October Revolution.

But the main change brought by the October Revolution was the collapse of Russian military power, which affected different nations of Eastern Europe in different ways. From February 1917 onward the non-Russian peoples of the Russian empire had increased their political demands. As the victorious German and Austrian armies marched eastward, escape from Russian domination became a serious prospect for these peoples but it also brought the prospect of German domination in place of Russian. Poles viewed this change with very mixed feelings; Ukrainians, Belorussians, and Lithuanians (and perhaps also Latvians and Estonians) on balance welcomed it. In the Danubian and Balkan countries, however, there was much less joy.

It is true that the Bolshevik slogans of self-determination and the demagogic performances of Trotsky and his colleagues at Brest Litovsk aroused hopes for the non-Magyars and non-Germans of the Hapsburg monarchy, but it did not take very long to see that revolutionary rhetoric was no match for German military power. For Serbs and Romanians, both in the two kingdoms and in Austria-Hungary, Brest Litovsk was a disaster, and this was hardly less true for Czechs, Slovaks, Croats, and Slovenes. Further south the victory of Lenin seemed to guarantee to the Bulgarian small-power imperialists their ill-gotten gains at the expense of Serbs and Greeks.

Fortunately for these disappointed nations, the Western Allies defeated Germany and they obtained the independence or national unity for which they had fought. They also obtained a good deal more, abusing their moment of victory (through association with the victors) to place large numbers of Hungarians, Germans, Macedonians, and Ukrainians under their rule. For this, historians are entitled to blame them and their Western patrons. But historians simply make themselves ridiculous when they deny that these nations had legitimate national aspirations; that many Western statesmen felt genuine sympathy for these aspirations; and that a victory of German imperialism, furthered by Bolshevik surrender, would have destroyed them.

It was after the collapse of Germany in 1918 that a second aspect of the Bolshevik victory in Russia—less obvious at first than the immediate aspect of Russian military collapse—became evident. This was the ambition of the Bolsheviks to promote revolution in Europe. Revolutionary rhetoric from Moscow and panic fears among Western politicians and capitalists created hysterical passions for or against Soviet Russia that bore very little relation to realities in Central and Eastern Europe.

Far from wishing to follow the Russian example, the German workers' councils (at first sight the equivalent of Russian soviets) were voted out of existence by their own freely elected delegates in December 1918, in favor of a "bourgeois parliamentary" constituent assembly. The Berlin insurrection and the Munich "soviet republic" of early 1919 were mere flashes in the pan. The Soviet Republic lasted longer in Hungary, where it was supported by the hope of nationalist army officers that Russia would save Hungary's old frontiers. In the end, though, the Romanian army sufficed to suppress it. In Romania and Poland triumphant nationalism and the hope of land reform — realized in the former but frustrated in the latter — combined with ancient distrust of all things Russian to keep Bolshevik influence minimal.

Pilsudski's defeat of the invading Red Army in 1920 put an end to hopes of Red revolution in Eastern and Central Europe. The only substantial Communist party that was left was the Bulgarian. It in turn quarreled with its potential ally, the Peasant party, and in 1923 — having failed to help Stamboliisky's government in its hour of danger — the Communists made a hopeless rebellion of their own, which was bloodily suppressed. In all these events the advice of the Russian revolutionary experts entrenched in the newly founded Comintern was rather less than helpful.

Nevertheless the possessing classes in Eastern Europe did not lose their fear of communism or their identification of this deadly threat with the vast resources of mysterious, malevolent Russia. Hungarian and Polish landowners, Romanian and Balkan rising capitalists and their West European associates, quailed from time to time at the floods of bloodcurdling rhetoric proceeding from Moscow. Their fears enabled governments to restrict such liberties as had been gained by earlier political struggles and to resist such plans for social progress as were put forward by democratic politicians, on the grounds that these would give openings to Bolshevik subversion. Political opponents were denounced as Communists or unconscious tools of Communists.

It was not only the rich who were frightened by the Communist bogey; as enemies of peasant property and persecutors of religion, the Soviet rulers appeared to menace whole peoples. Forced collectivization of agriculture and the horrors of the First Five-Year Plan, vividly if not always accurately reported in the world press, strengthened the argument. Czechoslovakia was the only country in which the upper and middle classes were not much impressed by the Bolshevik bogey. This was not so much thanks to any innate superior political wisdom of the Czechs as because the Czechs — who had never had much direct contact with Russians — preserved a sentimental pan-Slavism, firmly founded on ignorance and wishful thinking.

If obsession with an illusory revolutionary danger was one consequence of the October Revolution in Eastern Europe, another was a gap in the

European power system, which particularly affected the peoples of the Danube Valley and the Balkans. Russia had in effect withdrawn from Europe. Entrenched behind the Kremlin walls, preoccupied with the task of turning Russian society upside down, the Soviet leaders paused from time to time to chant a few hymns of hate addressed to the capitalist world.

Meanwhile, with Russia absent and Germany prostrate, the French could feel they were — or at least ought to be — the masters of Europe; the Italians could play little games of being a new Austria-Hungary; and the British could turn their backs and wash their hands of it all, interrupting this ploy occasionally with a snort of protest at some event they had scorned to anticipate and become powerless to remedy.

The East European governments aped their protectors. The Little Entente rulers basked in the rather weak and filtered sunshine of French culture; the Hungarians and Bulgarians eagerly attached themselves to Il Duce and did their best to adopt his morality; and Pilsudski brooded in angry isolation (both before and after making himself dictator) on the future of Poland as a great power.

All this came to an end fairly soon after Adolf Hitler was called to power by President Hindenburg. The Soviet rulers were at first happy to see in power a fanatical nationalist under whom their obsessive nightmare, a reconciliation between Germany and its vanquishers — which must by definition be intended as preparation for an onslaught by the whole capitalist world on the homeland of the toilers — seemed most unlikely to be realized. But when Hitler made an agreement with Poland in January 1934, thus apparently replacing the Prussian tradition of alliance with Russia against Poles by the Austrian tradition of encouraging Poles against Russia, the Soviets thought again. By the end of 1934 the Soviet Union was in the League of Nations; in the following year the Franco-Soviet and Soviet-Czechoslovak pacts were signed. Russia was back in the European power system.

During this period even conservatives in Britain and France were increasingly alarmed and repelled by the spectacle of the Third Reich, and it began to look as if something like the pre-1914 Triple Entente might reemerge to hem in Germany. At this time Mussolini also was very far from enthusing over his northern admirer. Hitler's attempt to annex Austria, his former homeland, by the *putsch* of 25 July 1934 — which cost Chancellor Dollfuss his life but did not capture power in Vienna — caused Mussolini to strike one of his most impressive pseudo-Colleoni attitudes — with jutting jaw, fiery rhetoric, and Italian divisions mobilized on the Brenner.

These trends were reversed partly by the Ethiopian war, which cut off Italy from the West and made the Duce listen to the Führer's blandishments, but still more by the war in Spain.

From 1934 to 1937 the idea had been growing up in the West that the Soviet Union was now a "respectable" power. The days of that frightening revolutionary fanatic Lenin were now long past. Stalin was another sort of man; he was restoring badges of rank in the Red Army and the people he had shot were revolutionaries.

There was no keener advocate of the *Salonsfähigkeit* of Stalin than Central Europe's veteran incurable optimist, President Eduard Beneš of Czechoslovakia, who believed that he had placed Stalin in his debt by forwarding to him "evidence" of the "treason" of Tukhachevsky and other Soviet marshals. But this rosier view of the Soviet Union quickly faded.

In the war in Spain, ideological passion, which had been apparently languishing in Russia, burst into bright flame. Spanish anarchists and various leftists were accused of burning churches, raping nuns, and murdering priests. The atrocities were doubtless exaggerated, but some of them did take place. The fact that the Spanish Communists, now implacable champions of bourgeois morality and parliamentary democracy, were in no way to blame for the atrocities did not prevent their identification, in European conservative minds, with all the old horrors of bolshevism. The international "image"—this useful word was not current in those times—of the Soviet Union suffered. This development was in no way Stalin's fault, but Fascist propagandists all over Europe made the best of the situation. The Spanish war was represented as a new version of religious war. European civilization was being defended against Red bestiality, or democracy was being defended against Fascist terror, depending on your point of view.

In such a climate of opinion the prospects for cooperation between the Western capitalist powers and the Soviet Union rapidly receded. In the West, many democrats who were far from Communists rallied to the Spanish Republican cause and many others of a more conservative frame of mind who were far from Nazis showed a preference for Franco. But Stalin no longer seemed a likeable fellow, nor did the Soviet Union seem *bündnisfähig*.

While all eyes were on Spain, Hitler went ahead with the political penetration of Eastern Europe. Western governments lost their will to oppose his designs. One important point in this process can rightly be regarded as Stalin's fault: the mass purge from 1936 to 1939. Information in the West was not then very good, but it was known that something like half the officers above the rank of major had been removed. Military attachés and Defense Ministry officials did not need to have pro-Fascist sympathies to have their doubts about the value of an ally with an army that had had treatment of this sort. The colonels and generals who advised their governments were perhaps inclined to be oversensitive to the fate of other colonels and generals. But the fact remains that, whether it was a matter of professional bias or common sense, the purges had an impact in the Munich surrender, which in turn determined the fate of Eastern Europe.

The revival of ideological passion had also been affecting the East Europeans for some time. Here the Spanish war played its part, but more important were the effects of the economic depression on these mainly agricultural economies. Poverty, discontent, and political extremism all grew together. It was the Fascists who were the most successful. Especially in Romania and Hungary, they were able to produce a mixture of nationalist and social radicalism that proved attractive not only to students, unemployed members of the intellectual professions, and persons seeking an opening in business but also to peasants and workers. The enemy against whom the various discontents were directed was "the Jew," the sinister author of both capitalism and communism, of both liberal and Marxist false doctrine.

In neither country did the Fascist movements achieve power by their own efforts, but in both they had a powerful influence on public opinion as well as rulers, pressing the latter to ape the style of Hitler and Mussolini, to go along with their foreign policies, and to think in terms of war against Soviet Russia.

By contrast, discontent in Yugoslavia, Bulgaria, and Greece, especially among the educated members of the younger generation, inclined to antifascism and at least a certain benevolence toward the Soviet Union and communism. In all three countries Communists formed fairly small but very active minorities, enjoying wide public sympathy.

Poland, of all the East European countries, was the least affected by genuine political extremism. Pilsudski's successors in power aped Fascist slogans but did not reflect public opinion, which consisted mainly of peasant democracy and democratic socialism. Most Poles distrusted communism because it was associated with Russia. There was widespread anti-Semitism in Poland—which had three million Jewish citizens—but Hitler's men failed to mobilize this feeling on behalf of the Third Reich; fascism and National Socialism were distrusted for their association with Germany.

Repulsed by his French ally at the time of the Munich surrender, Stalin took a new look at his foreign policy and ended up with the Molotov-Ribbentrop pact, or Fifth Partition of Poland, of August 1939. The British and French governments had little right to moral indignation, considering how they had behaved a year earlier.

More serious is the argument that Stalin misjudged the military realities of 1939 and paid heavily for this in 1941. Thanks to Russian neutrality the Germans were able to do to France in 1940 what they had not been able to do, thanks to the Imperial Russian Army, in 1914. Having handed over the whole European continent for Hitler to conquer, the Russians had no second front to help them when Hitler turned east. They feared, not without reason, that if they had made an alliance with the West in 1939 their Western allies would have stood by while Hitler attacked Russia. But even if this had happened the Russians would have been better off than they turned out to be in 1941. For in 1939 public pressure in the West for action on the western front would have produced results before Hitler's armies had reached Moscow. The Western armies were in existence in 1939; in 1941 they had ceased to exist and no public clamor could create them until some years had passed and millions of Russian soldiers had perished.

Be that as it may, the impact of the Molotov-Ribbentrop pact on Eastern Europe was quite unambiguous. The homeland of the toilers of the world, openly adopting the methods of Empress Catherine II, grabbed a third of Poland without firing more than a shot or two, and a chunk of Finland after surprisingly hard fighting. Nine months later the three Baltic republics, eastern Moldavia (or Bessarabia), and northwestern Moldavia (or northern Bukovina) were similarly "liberated."

Having conquered Western Europe from the North Cape to the Pyrenees, Hitler paused to consult his Soviet ally before finishing off what remained of neutral independence in the Balkans. When Molotov came to Berlin in November 1940, he was offered a sphere of influence in the Persian Gulf area. Molotov had no moral objections to accepting this offer; what he did not like about it was that it was not enough. He also asked for a dominant position in Bulgaria and a strategic base in the Straits of the Black Sea. This was too much for Hitler, who decided to put into operation his long-prepared plans for the invasion of Russia.

War with Russia would of course have come in any case one day, for Hitler's hatred was unchanging. But this should not blind us to the fact that the war with Russia which began in 1941 was sparked by Stalin's greed for power in the Balkans and at the Straits.

Looking back at the impact of the Soviet Union on Eastern Europe during the first quarter-century of the Soviet regime, the main impression is of the yawning gap in Europe—the absence of Russia. The gap was imperfectly concealed by a smokescreen from which emerged occasional displays of revolutionary pyrotechnics—fiery monsters that burst upward and dissolved in midair without a trace.

In the mid-1930s the output of rhetoric diminished as the Soviet government sought to enter into diplomatic combinations with other governments. Its first efforts were marked by ignorance, dogmatism, and greed; however these were not unusual features of great power diplomacy at the time and the two great West European democracies can hardly boast a nobler record. At the same time it is worth repeating that, although the Soviet effort was not notably worse than that of Chamberlain or Daladier, it also was not notably better. And Stalin did do one thing that they did not: He destroyed half his officer corps and a large part of his administrative and industrial leadership.

The Soviet regime was saved from the disastrous situation of 1941 by the bravery of the Russian people in arms and the skill of the Russian officers, many of whom had been only recently recalled to arms from the prisons, torture chambers, and concentration camps to which Stalin's special security tribunals had sent them in 1937 and 1938. The comparison of 1941–1944 with 1812, which was the theme of Soviet propaganda at home and abroad, was about as well justified as any simple historical comparison can be. The combination of blind obedience and willing self-sacrifice displayed by the serfs of Alexander I had its parallel in the similar attitudes of the *kolkhozniki* and underpaid unskilled factory workers conscripted into Stalin's armies.

It is also fair to point out Stalin's own great merit as a leader, which was strikingly similar to that of Alexander I — although both men have been ill treated hitherto by historians and commentators, who have paid more attention to such glamorous figures as Kutuzov and Zhukov. It was the tsar alone who decided in 1812, against the preferences of most of his advisers including even Kutuzov, to ignore any offer of peace from Napoleon. It was the tsar who also decided, against still more strongly held opinions among his advisers, that it was not enough to drive Napoleon out of Russia and that the Russian army must pursue him into Europe and destroy his power completely. It was Stalin who made the same decisions in regard to Hitler.

It is here that the resemblance ends. In 1814 the Russian armies entered Paris. They had been welcomed in Germany and France along the way, and they had shown discipline and good behavior that astonished the population. Even in Poland they had been kept fairly well under control. In 1945 the Russian soldiers got only as far as Berlin and Vienna, but they left an impression of unrestrained savagery in the memories of the civil population — in countries allied with Hitler but also in countries he had conquered.

Intellectuals living beyond the English Channel or the Atlantic Ocean could calmly explain this behavior by the atrocities committed by Hitler's hordes in Russia and by the fact that many Russian soldiers had had no leave, and no contact with women, for three years. At the receiving end it was hard to be so calm. A bitter Hungarian pun spoke of the three catastrophes in Hungarian history: the Tatar devastation, the Turkish devastation, and the Russian liberation (*tátár dulás, török dulás, felszabadulás*).

This experience must have its place in any brief survey of the "Soviet impact" on Eastern Europe.

When the deluge was over, Europe was a different place. The effect of the Bolshevik Revolution had been, as we have seen, to create a yawning gap in the system of European great powers. The effect of Hitler's aggression against Russia and his defeat by the Red Army was to destroy that system altogether. In 1945 only one of the European continental great powers was left — Soviet Russia. On the western periphery its military power was matched by that of the United States, still flanked by Britain, which had not yet embarked on the process of economic exhaustion and political abdication that were to gather speed in the 1950s. The dividing line through the middle of Europe was set up where the Western and Soviet armies met and, with some modifications, has been maintained since then.[2]

In Eastern Europe the territorial settlement was dictated by the Soviet Union. In the Danubian and Balkan lands, essentially the frontiers of 1919–1920 — the "Versailles Diktat" Lenin and his colleagues had so bitterly denounced — were restored. Some small changes were agreed upon with the other allies, and in fact these changes were in the direction of greater justice from the point of view of Wilsonian national self-determination: Southern Dobrudja was left in the possession of Bulgaria (having been ceded in 1940 by Romania at the orders of Hitler and Mussolini with the approval of Stalin); Yugoslavia acquired from Italy the so-called Venezia Giulia, with a Slovene or Croatian majority population; and Greece received from Italy the islands of the Dodecanese.

If Wilsonian principles were observed in the south, in the north the state interests of Soviet Russian imperialism prevailed. The three Baltic republics were annexed once more, Finland gave up more territory, and Romania lost not only northern Bukovina (with a Ukranian majority population) but also the whole of Bessarabia, in which Romanians formed a clear majority. In June 1945 the restored government of Czechoslovakia formally ceded its former eastern province, Ruthenia, which Soviet authorities had in a practical sense taken over some monthes earlier.

Most important of all, the Polish state was shifted massively westward. The eastern third of prewar Poland was annexed by the Soviet Union, and in return the Poles were allowed to annex formerly German territory up to the Oder and western Neisse rivers. Finally, the Soviet Union annexed a chunk of East Prussia, demonstrating that it was now master by changing the historic name of Königsberg to Kaliningrad.

It might be argued that in his combination of high-sounding principles and territorial greed Stalin was again unconsciously imitating Alexander I. But there can be no doubt that on the economic side Stalin outdistanced his predecessor. Heavy reparations were exacted from the defeated states. In Germany Stalin was able to take wealth only from the region his troops occupied, although his men did put into practice Lloyd George's earlier — but then unfulfilled — injunction to squeeze the orange until the pips pop out. In Romania and Hungary the wealth extracted was far larger than official figures suggested at first sight, due to manipulation of nominal prices and massive requisitions by the Soviet Army. In both these countries also, "joint companies" were set up in inportant branches of the economy; under such arrangements the Soviet government, as owner of expropriated former German properties — including former British, French, and American capital previously expropriated by the Germans — was nominally "associated" with the Romanian or Hungarian government but in practice controlled the whole enterprise.

In formerly Allied countries, victims and not satellites of Hitler, the situation was no much better. The Czechoslovak government was obliged to give the Soviet government control over its uranium, now particularly valuable in the post-atomic age; the Polish government had to sell to the Soviet Union, at an uneconomic price, so large a proportion of its coal output that it was unable to take advantage of the postwar demand for coal in world markets.

All these developments show the determination of the Soviet leaders to grab as much as they could, in old-fashioned imperial style. Their justification was simply that they had suffered more than anyone else, that they had brought liberation, and that they must be compensated by both the aggressors and the victims — for the victims owed them their liberty. The reasoning was not very different from that of Raymond Poincaré in the 1920s.

But there was another dimension to the Soviet victory. The Soviet Union was supposed to stand for socialism — for the promise of a new and better society for all, an end to the exploitation of man by man, advance into the sunlit future of communism. In Eastern Europe it was not only the Communists who were inspired by such visions and therefore had hopes of Soviet victory.

Capitalism in Eastern Europe did not seem to have achieved much. It had led to economic depression and this had brought the Fascists to power. Hitler's rule had brought first pitiless oppression and then the devastation of war. The Western democracies stood for the capitalism that had failed and then handed Eastern Europe over to Hitler. It was true that the British had paid their debts since 1940 and that American power had decided the issue on the world scale. But it was the Russians who had borne the main burden of the struggle and they had a different vision for the future — one that had not yet been tried out and found wanting in Eastern Europe.

Terrible periods of destruction always create utopian longings: People feel that after such horrors there can be no simple return to the old past, that there must be a brighter future, a new deal, a new commonwealth. Such was the mood in World War I, in the Russian Revolution, in 1812, in the great catastrophes of human history far back into the past.

In 1945, of course, Eastern Europe still had embittered champions of the old order, men who had lost power and wealth and feared for their lives, who hoped for yet another war—this time between the victors—from which they might gain. But they were not very many and they kept rather quiet. Among the intellectual professions, especially among the educated youth, the workers, and to a large extent also the peasants, Soviet victory was viewed with hope. Even the horrors of the passage of the Soviet Army did not destroy that hope; when war was over, many people hoped, the wise men who thought in terms of world socialism would assert their will.

It is essential to remember that this feeling was widespread. For the essential truth is that it was soon made clear that the Soviet leaders had one answer to all problems. They had a monopoly of Marxist-Leninist "scientific" wisdom. Their institutions, their policies, their methods of coercion and persuasion must be applied everywhere. Soviet ideological enthusiasm, which was as important a part of the picture as Soviet material and territorial imperialism, led to the same result. And inevitably the principal victims of the process that now set in were not so much the defeated reactionaries as the revolutionaries or reformers who had their own visions of how their nations should achieve liberty and social justice. The victims were peasant leaders, democratic socialists, and those Communists who wished to use humane methods and who respected their own national traditions.

The historical facts can hardly be disputed by any one who examines them rationally. But the facts can be variously interpreted.

It is increasingly argued that the tragic fate of the East Europeans was brought upon them as much by Western as by Soviet policy. The bitter mood of Stalin is attributed to the hostility toward him of the Western leaders, especially after the death of Roosevelt. Already in 1942 the refusal to start a second front caused Stalin to suspect the Allies' motives. The Allies gave material help but it was small in relation to Russia's needs. When the war ended the Russian people were on the verge of starvation, their cities and industries devastated, while the American economy was booming and the American people had the highest overall standard of living known to history.

As the war ended more and more diatribes against communism were heard from prominent public figures in the West. Western capitalists, Stalin was bound to believe, were ganging up to exploit the resources of the world and to force Soviet Russia into submission. Postwar aid to suffering Russia was cut off. Stalin probably assumed that the atom bomb was dropped on Hiroshima not so much to force Japan into surrender as to intimidate Russia. President Truman decided to use the new atomic threat to promote new tough policies. The wartime agreements on spheres of influence in Europe were to be scrapped, to the disadvantage of the Soviet Union. Faced by such hostility, what could Stalin do but entrench himself in the areas he held, insist on unreserved obedience, and treat all East Europeans who showed any Western sympathies as enemy agents?

There is some truth in these arguments. The fact that Stalin was profoundly suspicious of Western motives was well known at the time. Indeed one may say that the Western press in 1944 and 1945 was obsessed with the need to allay suspicion, to explain everything patiently to the Russians, and to do nothing that might conceivably arouse further suspicion.

It is true that Stalin resented the delay in creating a second front, but it is also true that there were powerful military arguments in favor of the timing adopted and that in any case Russia was only in such desperate need of a second front in 1941, 1942, and 1943 because Stalin had refused the Western powers a second front in 1939 and 1940.

It is also true that public figures in the West from time to time made hostile statements about the Soviet Union, but it is also true that these were far outnumbered by the friendly statements by still more prominent persons and that the British and American press and radio poured forth unending paeans of praise for the Soviet ally. That there should be hostility is not surprising in view of the unswerving hostility of official Soviet attitudes to Western governments since 1917; what is surprising is how little hostility there was.

As for the atom bomb, the fact that it strengthened the Western position in relation to the Soviet ally and led to a tougher attitude on the part of President Truman was easily apparent to any newspaper reader in 1945: it hardly needs to be established by the painstaking researches of revisionist Western historians, admirable though these may be.

As for the division of spheres of influence, this is a more complex matter. The truth is that the future of Eastern Europe was a subject of conflict between the Western governments and the Soviet Union throughout the wartime alliance; insofar as the origins of the cold war are found in Eastern Europe, they must be traced much further back than 1945.

The most difficult single problem was Poland. British Prime Minister Winston Churchill, bound by alliance to Poland and eager to cooperate closely with the Soviet Union, made great efforts to bring about a reconcilation between the two; in this he was supported by the Polish premier, General Sikorski. But there were three main difficulties.

The first concerned Poland's eastern border. The main obstacle to Polish-Russian agreement ever since the end of the eighteenth century, this border was more responsible than any other single factor for the breakdown of the 1815 settlement, the revolts of 1831 and 1863, and the Polish-Soviet war of 1920. The frontier proposed by Stalin in 1943 corresponded approximately to the easternmost boundary of the area of compact Polish population. Beyond this line there were indeed substantial Polish minorities — and it was true that Polish culture had been prevalent for many centuries and its traces were still to be found — but the majority of the population was of Belorussian, Ukrainian, or Lithuanian nationality. Whether this was a good reason for incorporating these non-Polish nations in the Soviet Union was of course by no means certain, but there was a good case for arguing that they should not be incorporated into Poland.

But the Polish leaders could hardly be expected to see matters in this way. They passionately felt they could not surrender Polish territory until a sovereign Polish parliament had considered the issue. Their insistence on this legal argument was reinforced by their moral abhorrence of the means by which Stalin had come into possession of eastern Poland: by a robber's bargain with Hitler. Nothing would shake them. Churchill tried hard in 1943 and 1944, insisting that acceptance of Soviet territorial claims offered the only hope — an increasingly slender hope — of assuring the sovereign independence of a smaller Polish state, and perhaps even of saving the ancient Polish city of Lwow.

The second difficulty was the mutual ideological hostility of the Polish and Soviet leaders. The prewar Polish regime had been socially reactionary and politically repressive, its leaders inclined to ape the style of the Fascists. But these elements were not predominant in the large Polish emigration after 1939. In the underground state in Poland, which was in regular contact with the exiled government and recognized its authority, the most important political groups were the democratic peasant movement and the Socialists (PPS). These democratic forces were perfectly willing and even eager to cooperate with the Soviet Union, but only on the basis of equality with the right to decide their own political future and their own tactics in resisting the Germans. But it became increasingly obvious that the Soviet leaders' aim was to impose Communist leadership and Soviet domination on them.

The third difficulty concerned the Polish army to be formed on Soviet soil from the Polish soldiers taken prisoner by the Red Army in 1939. The Polish government had detailed information on these prisoners and repeatedly asked the Soviet government for information about them. Gradually an army was assembled but several thousand Polish officers, whose names were known, did not reappear. Friction grew between the Polish army and the Soviet authorities, for which the Poles were no doubt partly to blame, and in July 1942 the force was allowed to leave Russia through Iran to fight against Hitler on other fronts. Nearly a year later, in April 1943, the German government announced that it had found a mass grave of more than 2,000 Polish officers in the Katyn forest in western Russia. The propaganda motives of the Germans were of course obvious, but the evidence showed that the officers had been massacred by Soviet executioners and further research in later years confirmed this view.[3] It may be presumed, although it has not been proved, that the rest of the missing officers suffered a similar fate elsewhere.

No government in wartime can be expected to show indifference to the fate of thousands of its officers. The Polish leaders, despite frantic efforts by their British allies to deter them, formally asked the International Red Cross to investigate the matter. The Soviet government made this the excuse to break off relations with the Polish government. From this time on Soviet propaganda denounced the exiled leaders as Nazi accomplices and made no secret of Soviet intentions of creating a Polish army and a Polish government of their own, firmly controlled by obedient Communists.

When Soviet troops entered formerly Polish territory, the Polish resistance units that contacted them were treated not as allies but as enemies. When Warsaw rose against the Germans in August 1944, the Soviet Army stood idly by. There may have been compelling military reasons for its inaction, although these were not stressed at the time. It is also arguable that the Polish resistance command was foolish to start the revolt, for political reasons, without previously ascertaining the Soviet attitude.[4] Nevertheless the Soviet attitude—noisy demand for action by the Poles until August 1944, then inaction combined with denunciation of Polish adventurers who allegedly wasted Polish lives in vain—had a shattering impression on Poles and, despite the efforts of the Western press to play it down, on Allied opinion. But this was not the end of the story. In March 1945 the surviving leaders of the Polish resistance were invited to meet the Soviet military authorities so they might be sent to Moscow to take part in the Allied-sponsored negotiations for the formation of a new Polish government. They accepted the invitation—and were arrested, tried in Moscow for crimes against the Red Army, and sentenced to long terms of imprisonment.[5]

These developments irremediably poisoned the relations not only of the Polish exiles with all the Allies but also of the Western governments with the Soviet Union. From at least 1942 onward the Polish problem was a major source of disagreement. In retrospect it cannot be doubted that the Soviet Union's constant purpose, ruthlessly pursued, was to subject Poland to its will and to force the Western powers to accept terms that not only clashed with their interests but also dishonored them as statesmen. Stalin was completely successful in this endeavor, which had been completed before the atom bomb was made available (the successive stages need not concern us here).

The question of the agreed spheres of influence in southeast Europe is also more complicated than it seems. The divisions proposed by Churchill were intended only for the duration of the war. More important, the concept of predominance was understood quite differently by the two sides. The Western leaders were perfectly willing to have the Soviet Union be the dominant power throughout Eastern Europe (except Greece) in the sense that the foreign policy of all these countries should in future be subordinated to Soviet foreign policy. This is in fact what became established practice in regard to one country only, namely Finland. What the Western governments had not intended was that exact copies of the Soviet political and economic power apparatus should be imposed by force on all these countries, or that any individual citizen who expressed political sympathy for Western institutions or policies, or even maintained personal friendships with Westerners, should be considered guilty of treason. When it became clear that this was to be Soviet practice, first the Western representatives on the spot, then the Western governments, and finally Western press and public opinion became loudly indignant.

It is true that Stalin stood by while British troops suppressed by force the Greek Communist resistance movement in December 1944. Yet the cases are not exactly parallel. The Greek Communists made war on the Greek government recognized by the British (and by the Americans and Russians), and that government asked for British armed aid. But there was never any question of armed insurrection by peasant democrats or socialists against the Soviet-sponsored governments of Romania, Bulgaria, and Hungary. This is a real difference, and one need not approve of the anti-Communist Greek government of George Papandreou in order to recognize it.

It is also true that in Romania and Hungary there were supporters of the old regime who did their best to intrigue with the British and American missions, and there may have been individual members of those missions who were foolish enough to listen to such talk — although listening is not the same as acting or advising one's government to act. The truth is that the Soviet leaders had marked down for destruction the non-Communist democratic parties and ruthlessly carried out their purpose.

To return to the original question of the difference between the impact of the Soviet Union and that of previous great powers, the specific quality of Soviet domination in essence is very simple. Stalin was not content to dominate the external relations of the East European states; he insisted on imposing his own totalitarian model on each and every one of them.

The chronological stages of this process have often been described and need not be repeated here. But a few words are needed on three aspects of the process—political, economic, and cultural.

The political structure, familiar to all students of communism, was imposed ready-made. It is worth noting, however, that this was not the classical model of Lenin's day but the more developed model of Stalin's prime. The essence of Lenin's model was that the Communist party should dominate and infiltrate all other hierarchies of power—armed forces, police, ministerial bureaucracy, industrial management, and the various "public" (*obshchestvennie*) organizations. Stalin modified this substantially. When he was at the height of his power, it can hardly be said that the Communist party dominated all the other apparatuses. Stalin paid lip service to the primacy of the party but in fact the party was reduced to one of several apparatuses manipulated by the autocrat, of which security police, army, and industrial management were equally important.

It was this Stalinist model that was imposed in Eastern Europe. It required that in each country there should be a pocket-sized Stalin, with direct access to the Boss. Such were Rákosi in Hungary, Gottwald in Czechoslovakia, Dimitrov and then Chervenkov in Bulgaria, and to a rather lesser extent Bierut in Poland and Gheorghiu-Dej in Romania. Of course it is not possible to be quite sure about the extent of these men's power. Stalin no doubt checked up on them from time to time by independent channels, and in any case a colonial autocrat is a different breed than a metropolitan autocrat. Yet the general pattern was unmistakable.

Imitation of the Soviet apparatus of economic power began at the end of the 1940s: nationalization of industry, use of trade unions to recruit an unskilled labor force, draconian labor discipline, Stakhanovism, "socialist competition," state farms, collective farms, and machine-tractor stations. Practical implementation was not always so close to Soviet practice as the similarity of slogans and directives from above would suggest. Policies were carried out much less brutally than in the Russia of the 1930s—which does not mean that there was not much injustice and resentment. Pressure on all classes of the population was most intense in 1951 and 1952, and this was certainly connected with the Soviet Union's military needs during the Korean War. After Stalin's death, pressure was relaxed and collectivization of agriculture was slowed down. After October 1956 collectivization was abolished altogether in Poland but resumed and carried to its conclusion in the other countries. In the late 1960s there was much talk of economic reform and diversification of policies. In Czechoslovakia the experiments were brought to a halt after the crisis of 1968, but they persisted in Hungary and to a lesser extent in Bulgaria.

Throughout Eastern Europe from the late 1940s regular ceremonial kowtows had to be made before the superior culture of the Soviet Union. This soon proved to mean a good deal more than expressions of admiration for "scientific socialism" as expounded and practiced by the glorious party of Lenin and Stalin: It also included the duty of paying homage to the culture of the great Russian people.[6] This involved a good deal of rewriting of national history to accord with Russian national prejudices and a good deal of denial of national cultures. The method was perhaps most striking in the case of Romania.

The Romanian national revival, from the eighteenth century onward, had been based on the myth (part truth, part fiction) of the Latin origin of the Romanian people and on the very real help received from France and to some extent Italy. Romanian schools and cultural life were dominated by French influence, while the neighboring peoples of Slavic speech were known only to Slavonic specialists. In the 1950s a systematic effort was made to reverse this whole tradition. Cultural links with France and Italy were severed; Russian was given first place as a foreign language in Romanian schools; national history was rewritten to show that the Romanians' best friend had always been the great Russian people; and there was some attempt to make greater use of the Slavic words in the rich vocabulary of the Romanian language in preference to the Latin words, and even to suggest that the Romanians were a Slavic people and their language a Slavic language. All this was entirely counterproductive. Romanian children obstinately refused to learn Russian and continued to learn French, from their parents or their parents' friends, and the old Latin mythology grew stronger than ever. The attempt at Russification embittered Romanians both inside and outside the Communist party.

"Nationalism" became the enemy after the excommunication of Yugoslavia in 1948. This event was caused not so much by any real opposition to Soviet foreign policy from Tito's government as by Stalin's invincible distrust for a group of men who had fought their way to power by their own efforts and could not be handled as simple agents. Once the breach had come, and the Yugoslav Communists had defied Stalin's will and gotten away with it, Stalin was resolved to root out the nationalist heresy in all other parties. The purges were carried out in the style of Moscow in 1936–1939, but the number of victims was much smaller. Soon Zionist sympathies, or even Jewish origin, were added to "nationalism" as objective criteria for arrest.

The impact of the purges varied considerably. It was greatest — with about half the membership of the central committees removed — in Czechoslovakia and Hungary, both of which had once had strong social democratic and bourgeois liberal parties. In Poland, of which the same was true, the purge was much less drastic; the reason may be that, in a party that had already been dissolved once by the Comintern (in 1938) and suffered from its identification with the national enemy, the built-in opposition to further mass purges was strong enough to compel moderation on Stalin's part.

Stalin's death was followed by a period of relaxation. The result, as so often when repressive regimes behave more mildly, was an increase of discontent. First came the riots in Plzeň and the East German rising in the summer of 1953, then the riots in Poznan in June 1956, followed by the Polish leadership crisis and the Hungarian Revolution of the following autumn. There followed a period of repression in Hungary, of whittling away of newly won liberties in Poland, and of anxious tightening of control in the other countries.

In the 1960s, as the conflict between Russia and China became common knowledge, the East European Communist leaders found that they had some room to maneuver in relation to Moscow and used this to increase their effective sovereignty and — in most cases — to make life more pleasant for their subjects. On the Adriatic coast the conflict between Moscow and Peking enabled the Albanian leader Enver Hoxha — who disliked the "liberalizing" trends in neighboring Yugoslavia and had nationalist motives for hatred of Serbs — to move into the Chinese camp.

In the late 1960s came the ferment in Czechoslovakia, reaching its climax in Alexander Dubček's attempt to achieve "communism with a human face" and ending with Soviet military occupation. On this occasion Wladyslaw Gomulka had the distinction of presiding over the only occasion when Polish troops had marched shoulder to shoulder with Prussians and Russians into a neighboring country. But this triumph did not save him from the wrath of the Polish shipbuilding workers who took over the harbor cities of Gdansk and Szczecin at the end of 1970. The peoples of Eastern Europe were still in a cage, but it was more spacious and comfortable and the bars were wrapped around with thick layers of felt.

The state of ferment continued in the second half of the 1970s. It was stimulated by the proceedings of the Helsinki Conference of 1975, which turned out to be something of a boomerang for its Soviet initiators. The discussions on "basket three," and the formal acceptance by the Soviet government and its East European clients of a commitment to respect human rights offered new opportunities to dissenters in most of these countries. The Belgrade Conference of 1977–1978 ended in stalemate, and the Soviet rulers brazenly inflicted savage punishments on Soviet subjects who had monitored their nonimplementation of Helsinki. Brezhnev and his team did not hesitate to proclaim their perjury before the eyes of the whole world — they calculated, perhaps correctly, that indifference, defeatism, guilt-complexes, and commercial interests in the West, together with anti-Western nationalism and antiwhite racism in the excolonial or semicolonial world would quickly distract attention from Soviet misdeeds.

However, the tensions in Eastern Europe remained clearly visible. In Poland a new attempt to raise food prices in June 1976 set off a series of workers' riots similar to those of January 1971; the brutal treatment of workers by the police led to new political activity by the intellectuals, already infuriated by the abject submission of Poland to the Soviet Union enshrined in the projected new constitution; and the powerful Catholic Church gave its blessing to both types of resistance. For the next two years the unity between the main social classes, as well as between Christians and unbelievers, in opposition to the regime, kept Poland in a potentially explosive condition. To some extent two sets of social organizations existed side by side, including unofficial trade unions and unofficial universities. Fear of disaster, which might spread beyond Poland's frontiers, imposed self-restraint alike on the Polish opposition, the Polish Communists and the Soviet government, which was an encouraging sign. Neverthless at the outset of 1980 the latent explosive quality of Polish public life had not diminished.

In Czechoslovakia the Charter 77 Movement, essentially a mass petition for the implementation of the Helsinki obligations, attracted support mainly from intellectuals but also from workers. The Prague government did not relax its dictatorship, but it treated the protesters somewhat more mildly than in the past. In East Germany the most striking event of these years was the revolt of the Communist apparatchik Rudolf Bahro, who published in West Germany a book ruthlessly analyzing the GDR's system of tyranny and exploitation, but insisted on remaining at home to face persecution. The posture of this Communist heretic recalled inevitably that of Martin Luther: "Hier steh' ich fest, ich kann nicht anders." Unlike his predecessor, he had no Electoral Prince to protect him, and received a heavy prison sentence.

In the Balkan sector there were many uncertainties in the late 1970s. In Romania there was conflicting evidence as to the extent of President Ceauşescu's resistance or submission to Soviet domination. In Yugoslavia, as President Tito advanced in age, future political trends were subject for speculation at home and abroad. In Albania, too, though Enver Hoxha was not quite 70 (while Tito was 81), a succession problem seemed likely to arise before very long. Albania's foreign orientation was also in process of change, since Enver Hoxha, who appeared to have had a preference in Chinese politics for the Gang of Four, was rejected by the government of Hua Kuo-feng and Teng Hsaio-p'eng.

What then is the balance of the Soviet impact on Eastern Europe after fifty years, and especially after the last twenty-five?

The difficulty of answering this question, formidable in any case, is much increased by the smokescreen of moralizing rhetoric in which the subject has long been enveloped. The main fault here lies without doubt with the Soviet spokesmen. For decades it was an unshaken dogma that all policies bearing the mark of Stalin's unique genius must be little if at all short of perfection. Since his death the quality of infallibility has been transferred to the collective leadership of the CPSU.

The events of 25 October 1917 established once and for all, in Soviet eyes, the monopoly of Marxist wisdom in the minds of Lenin and his close collaborators and their ability to represent the interests of the workers of the world. Since then, by a process that can only be compared with the apostolic succession in the Catholic Church, this wisdom has been transmitted to later generations.

There have been some regrettable "mistakes" along the way. About half of those who were elected to the Central Committee proved between 1917 and 1934 to be agents of the German, British, Japanese, or other intelligence services, or at least to be enemies of the people—or else they were innocent victims of a bloodthirsty maniac who was able to hold control over the Communist party, despite its wisdom, for more than a quarter-century. But these "mistakes" are of small account: The infallible wisdom remained and remains a matter of dogma.

Possession of a monopoly of Marxist-Leninist science allegedly enables the Central Committee precisely and exhaustively to understand the past, present, and future of human society. Consequently Soviet foreign policy —including, of course, policy toward Eastern Europe—differs from the foreign policy of all other states in that it is "scientifically" based. But this is not all.

Other states pursue what their rulers claim are the state's interests, although of course they are the interests of the ruling class; the Soviet Union claims not to pursue class or state interests but to be wholly devoted to the cause of peace and human happiness. Conversely, whatever aim the Soviet government pursues at any particular moment *is* the cause of peace and human happiness. The relations of the Soviet Union with the states of the socialist camp are said to be determined by pure disinterested generosity. For example, all commercial dealings between the Soviet Union and these states are considered acts of self-sacrificing aid on the part of the Soviet Union.

A striking historical example of brotherly aid, outside the commercial field, was the action of August 1968, when the Soviet Army, assisted by units from other brotherly socialist armies, liberated the workers of Czechoslovakia from a government chosen by the ruling Communist party—a government that, according to the lies circulated by the Western press, enjoyed the support of the Czech and Slovak peoples but that in reality was betraying the cause of socialism and was despised by all truly Marxist-Leninist Czech and Slovak workers.

This is essentially what the publicity machine of the Soviet Union has been asserting for decades and is still asserting, ably seconded by the publicity machines of the other states of the socialist camp. The doctrine has not varied, although the volume and the crudity of the language have varied a good deal according to time and place.

It is almost impossible for observers who do not accept, or who are not coerced into echoing, this doctrine not to be exasperated by this hypocrisy. Westerners who are not professional academic observers of the East European scene but who are from time to time concerned with it—in particular, journalists and professional politicians—react and overreact.

In the Dulles era a moralizing counter-rhetoric grew up: "The Communists" were seen as the very incarnation of evil. As long as a real "Iron Curtain" almost completely prevented mutual contact, the myth of the utter wickedness of the Communist East persisted, increasing the confusion still further. In the 1960s when Western travelers were able to go to Communist lands and found that the people they met were normal, decent, and friendly, not only did the myth of Communist wickedness dissolve (which was entirely to be welcomed) but it began to be assumed that all previous observations on the hostility of the Soviet government and its conquest and domination of Eastern Europe also were untrue. Later still, as opposition to the Vietnam War rose in the United States, it came to be assumed not only that the anti-Communist rhetoric of the Dulles era was unjustifiable but that the United States was at least mainly, and perhaps even exclusively, responsible for all that had gone wrong in world politics since 1945.

The Western mind, and above all the Anglo-Saxon Protestant journalistic mind, still seems incapable of appreciating that political conflicts are not between absolute good and absolute evil and that one's enemies may be upright and admirable people but they remain enemies. Those in the mass media seem condemned forever to oscillate between self-righteousness and self-flagellation.

Let us then try, difficult though it may be, to escape from this climate and to see the balance of the last quarter-century.

Throughout Eastern Europe there has been massive industrial progress. This was much needed. Before 1941 the whole region except the Czech lands suffered from massive agricultural overpopulation, underemployment, and low productivity. It was clear to all serious observers at that time that there must be a vast transfer of labor from the fields to the factories. This has happened under Communist leadership, with strong support from the Soviet leaders. One may therefore argue that the impact of the Soviet Union has been constructive, insofar as it has accelerated industrialization.

Against this it may be argued that the types of industry chosen have distorted the national economies; that in one of the most advanced areas, the Czech lands, industrial management is less efficient and far more wasteful of manpower than before 1938; and that agricultural output has been little improved. Whether East European economic development would have been more successful without Soviet domination certainly cannot be proved or disproved. But it seems fair to give some share of credit, for what *has* been achieved, to the Communists and their Soviet patrons.

It is equally true that there has been a massive development of schools and colleges and that this too has had strong Soviet support. It is certain that the schools have been used as instruments of crude political indoctrination, but this has not prevented the emergence of first-class professional and scientific ability. The new intellectual elite has been recruited, certainly to a much greater extent than previously, although perhaps not quite to the extent that is asserted, from among children of workers and poor peasants who would have had little chance of higher education before 1945. This is one of the proudest achievements of the era of Soviet domination. But characteristically the Soviet leaders, like other imperial rulers of the past, have earned little gratitude from those they benefited. It was precisely the young generation of educated people from plebian homes who provided the driving force in the movements of 1956 in Poland and Hungary and 1968 in Czechoslovakia.

If the creation of new intellectual elites has been all too successful, indoctrination with Soviet mythology through the schools has been a failure. Tinkering with national mythologies to the advantage of Soviet or pre-Soviet Russian nationalism has only strengthened the devotion of the East European peoples to their old myths. This is particularly true of Romania, Hungary, and Poland. Denunciation of the decadent West seems only to have increased the appetite of the East Europeans for Western culture. One of the sadder and more ridiculous features of the East European scene before 1941 was the determination of all intellectually ambitious young people to rush to the fountains of wisdom in Paris or Vienna, London or Berlin, combined with complete indifference or contempt toward the languages, cultures, or history of neighboring people. This remains little changed (and perhaps slightly increased) in the Eastern Europe of the 1970s.

During the last twenty-five years there has been completed in all Eastern Europe a process familiar from the history of other European nations: the diffusion of national consciousness from the political elite downward into the whole population. Already by the 1930s, if not earlier, this process had been completed among the Czechs and the Slovenes—both economically efficient and well-educated modern nations—and to a lesser extent among the Serbs, Bulgarians, and Greeks, who were economically and culturally less advanced but had a strong equalitarian feeling and a very well developed political sense. In the rest of the region, in each state—quite apart from the existence of national minority groups—there were two separate nations: a Europeanized upper nation and a lower nation of poor and unskilled peasants. The relative percentages of population between the two nations, their attitudes toward each other, and the opportunities to rise from the lower nation to the upper nation, varied. For example, in Romania the Europeanized section was proportionately smaller, and the lower nation was probably on the whole more backward, than in Hungary; but in Hungary class hatred against the upper nation was more bitter, and the opportunity of rising from below was smaller, than in Romania.

By the 1970s this situation had changed. Economic development, urbanization, and mass education had molded Romanians, Hungarians, Poles, and Croats into single nations—although of course within each nation great differences in power, wealth, and prestige remained. The common ethos that welded them together was an amalgam of socialism and nationalism, but of the two ingredients the second was the stronger. The socialist nationalism of the Romanians of 1970, for example, owed at least as much to the Latin mythology of the nineteenth-century Romanian nationalists as to the influence of Marx or Lenin.

Since 1945 the peoples of Eastern Europe have had "socialism" imposed on them and have come to accept it as a fact of life; for those under forty years of age, it is difficult to imagine that society could be other than "socialist." Since 1945 the peoples of Eastern Europe also have become modern European nations, and this transformation has taken place under the leadership of Communist governments. Of these two major developments, the second is the more important.

It must also be said that in Yugoslavia, after a period in which it looked as if reconciliation between the Yugoslav peoples, and especially between Serbs and Croats, was making progress, there was a revival of bitter nationalism in the 1970s. This was caused not by external influences but by the very process of the formation of modern nations (especially among the Croats) discussed above.

Between the wars bitter nationalist conflicts existed within several and between all of the East European states. It was widely believed that Communists, having a supranational ideology, might be able to bring new solutions to these conflicts. Even opponents of Soviet domination entertained such hopes. They were disappointed. Soviet domination did, it is true, "freeze" certain conflicts of this sort. There is still bitter latent hostility between Romania and Hungary about Transylvania, but this question has been successfully kept out of international politics since 1945. On the other hand the conflict between Yugoslavia and Bulgaria about Macedonia has been manipulated by the Soviet government since 1945 in quite old-fashioned imperialist style. The conflict between Yugoslavia and Albania, and between Serbs and Albanians inside Yugoslavia, escaped Soviet control in the 1960s since both Yugoslavia and Albania became quite independent of the Soviet Union.

The greatest Soviet success in the manipulation of nationalism was the exploitation of the "German danger," especially in Poland. In the period of Gomulka's rule in particular, Germany served the regime as an all-purpose scapegoat. As Gomulka's rule became more and more distasteful to one section after another of the population, all that he could do was to maximize anti-German propaganda, arguing that only his government and its Soviet patrons could protect Poland from German revenge. All the while, Poles were becoming less anti-German as the years went by, while in the Federal Republic Konrad Adenauer's rigid stance was gradually replaced by a much more flexible and conciliatory attitude in Bonn.

However, when the formal reconciliation between Poland and the Federal Republic came, it was only in small part due to a change of heart among politicians or people in either country; the main reason was that the Soviet government had decided a reconciliation was to its immediate economic advantage and that coming to terms with Bonn would benefit overall Soviet international diplomacy. Having made up their minds on this new course, the Soviet leaders simply ordered the Polish Communists to toe the line.

In general it is probably true that national antagonisms between East European nations are now milder than in the 1930s, but this should not be exaggerated. Insofar as this is true, it can be explained more easily by the passage of time than by any scientific Marxist-Leninist wisdom learned from Moscow. It can also be explained in large part by the fact that in all the East European states of the socialist camp frustrated national resentment is directed above all against a single object—the Soviet Union.

There are well-informed people in the West who maintain, whether with indignation or satisfaction, that a balance of power has been established in Europe, maintained not by European great powers, as in the past, but by two extra-European superpowers: Western Europe is the American sphere of influence, Eastern Europe the Soviet. There is some obvious truth in this, but reality is not quite so simple.

The essence of spheres of influence, in the classical sense, was that the dominating power controlled the foreign policy of the lesser states in its sphere and intervened in their affairs if it believed that its vital interests were directly and seriously threatened; otherwise it left them to their own devices. This may be said to be the case in the relationship between the

West European states and the United States today (although it is very much open to argument), but in the relationship beween the East European states and the Soviet Union it applies to one case only: Finland. Elsewhere the Soviet rulers have not been content to control the foreign policy of the lesser states and impose their will in matters of major strategic security. Instead the Soviets have insisted on imposing copies of their own political institutions, have insisted that they alone shall decide what modifications of these institutions are legitimate, and have tried to remold the national cultures and rewrite national history in accordance with the cultural and historical dogmas of Soviet Russian imperialism.

The case of Czechoslovakia is perhaps the most revealing. President Beneš was willing unreservedly to adapt his foreign policy to Soviet requirements. Stalin, however, still found it necessary to destroy Czechoslovak democracy, to impose Communist party dictatorship of the Soviet type, and to follow this up by a purge of the party carried out by the Stalinian methods of falsification and torture. The modern history of Czech and Slovak independence was then rewritten to suit Soviet legend. The only episode in the eighty-seven years' life of the president-liberator, Thomas Masaryk, that mattered to the Soviet cultural dictators was that for some months in 1918 he had been involved in conflict with Lenin's regime (although he himself had done his utmost to avoid armed conflict between the Czech legions and the Bolsheviks and had strongly advised the Western allied governments against armed intervention in the Russian civil war). For this sinful episode Masaryk was posthumously punished by being made a historical un-person, and his long career in the service of his nation became an un-career.

In the mid-1960s, under the comparatively "liberal" regime of Antonín Novotny, this veto was gradually withdrawn and Czech historians could once again write the truth (albeit with an understandable Marxist slant) about their national history. Then came the crisis of 1968: Czechoslovakia was "liberated" by the Soviet Army; history was refalsified, or liberated from bourgeois (or human-faced Communist) objectivism; and historians were dismissed on a mass scale — with the lucky ones allowed to take jobs as tramway conductors, the unlucky ones reduced to unemployment.

The truth is that since 1945 there has not been, and there is unlikely to be in the near future, a division of spheres of interest in Europe. What there has been is an extension of the Soviet Russian empire to the Elbe, the Bohemian forest, and the Drava. Within the empire, domination in the classical sense has not been enough. Domination has been supplemented by national humiliation. The degree of humiliation has varied: For some years it has virtually disappeared in Romania, and it is rather mild in Hungary. But the principle has been maintained. The result has been to maintain

Central and Eastern Europe as one of the most politically explosive regions in the world. Americans and Englishmen may be indifferent to their own history: nobody has tried to deprive them of it. In Central and Eastern Europe it is not only professors of history who care about their nation's past or national mythology; workers and peasants too feel passionately about it, as has been shown again and again in the last century and a half. To a Western intellectual imbued with conventional liberal wisdom, this may seem deplorable; it is nonetheless true.

In summary, the essential and peculiar impact of the Soviet Union on Eastern Europe, the one aspect that distinguishes it from the impact of the many despotisms, native and foreign, that preceded it, is just this: the insistence on national humiliation.

Though it is arguable that both Russia and Europe would have fared better ever since 1945 if Stalin had been statesman enough to give to his other western neighbors the status he gave to Finland, there was a powerful reason why, thirty years later, Brezhnev and his colleagues did not dare to risk a reversal of Stalin's policies. If they had been willing to allow the Poles, Czechs, and others their own indigenous cultures, without distortion of their history and literature in the interest either of Bolshevik dogma or of Great Russian imperial self-esteem, then inevitably the Ukrainians and Georgians and Tatars and countless others would ask for the same. This in turn would lead, the Moscow Communists were convinced, to separatism, and the existence of the Soviet empire would be endangered.

The East European nations must therefore be subjected to cultural interference and national humiliation in order that the non-Russian half of the Soviet population might be kept under Russian rule—at a time when almost all West European empires had been decolonized, and the few remnants were the object of a massive worldwide Moscow-orchestrated hate campaign under cover of which Soviet military and naval power were being extended all over the world. There is thus a direct connection between the imperial multinational nature of the Soviet Union, the submerged simmering hostility of a hundred million subject Europeans to their Soviet Russian overlords, and the escalation of hatred against the West throughout the Muslim lands and Africa.

The implications of this connection deserve a few words more. The price which the Soviet rulers know that they have to pay for their policies is the continuing explosive state of Eastern Europe. Yet this state of affairs cannot be attributed by them to any defects in Soviet policy, which is by definition scientifically "correct." It can be explained only by the poisonous influence of the "capitalist world" that is the neighbor of all but one East European state.[7] Yet the Western capitalist governments that spread their poison to the east have been showing themselves increasingly weak-willed, guilt-ridden, and gullible in their dealings with the Soviet Union and with the new states of the Third World; and though they may retain a technological lead over the Soviet economy, and certainly produce for their citizens far more of the sophisticated and agreeable luxuries of modern life than Soviet citizens can enjoy, yet their military strength, and that of their American patrons, has been steadily declining in relation to that of the "socialist camp." What can the rising generation of Soviet bureaucrats and officers, too young to remember the war of 1941–1945, make of these contradictions and paradoxes? What, they may well ask, is Soviet military power for, if not for use? How much longer will their cautious but aging seniors be able to calm their zeal?

Notes

1. This definition of the region excludes Germany, including that portion which has become a part of the Soviet Empire in the form of the German Democratic Republic, aptly described as neither German nor democratic nor a republic. The omission is deliberate, for it is not possible to discuss the GDR systematically except in connection with the German problem since 1945 as a whole. Nevertheless there will at times be references to the GDR in the following pages, and a good deal of what has been said of the other countries is applicable with little modification to the GDR too.

2. Western forces were withdrawn from parts of central Germany and western Czechoslovakia that they had entered in the course of military operations, in order to comply with the boundaries for occupation zones previously agreed to by Churchill, Roosevelt, and Stalin. In the region of Trieste some territory was later ceded to Yugoslavia. Yugoslavia itself from 1948 onward ceased to be part of the Soviet bloc while remaining outside the Western bloc as well.

3. See J. K. Zawodny, *Death in the Forest* (Bloomington: Indiana University Press, 1962).

4. For a well-informed discussion of this question, see Jan Ciechanowski, *Powstanie warszawskie* (London, 1971).

5. It is interesting that the distinguished revisionist historian Gar Alperovitz, in his *Atomic Diplomacy* (New York: Simon and Schuster, 1965) emphasizes the rigidity of the Western governments in the Polish question in the period of preparation for the San Francisco conference on the United Nations (where Poland was without representation owing to Allied inability to agree on a united Polish government) without once mentioning the arrests of the resistance leaders, whose fate was the object of frantic if ineffective Allied diplomatic activity at the time.

6. We must note the difference between Great Russian (*velikorusskii*), which is a linguistic category, and "great Russian" (*velikii russkii*), which introduces an element

of moral admiration. It was the second term, with frequent use of the ritual adjective "great," that became mandatory in the reign of Stalin and did not disappear under his successors.

7. East Germany, Czechoslovakia, Hungary, and Bulgaria have "capitalist" neighbors on land, Poland across a narrow sea. Only Romania has no "capitalist" neighbor, though Yugoslavia is, by Soviet standards, regrettably infected by the consumer-society values of Western capitalism. Possibly it is the enclosed position of Romania that causes the Soviet leaders to permit in that country a degree of cultural renationalization greater than elsewhere.

4

Western Europe

Alvin Z. Rubinstein

The expansion of Soviet military power into the center of Europe has been the most significant and enduring consequence of the Second World War. It gave rise to the cold war and constitutes a permanent threat to the nations of Western Europe. Far exceeding the wildest dreams of the most imperialistic tsars, Soviet rulers, by virtue of their growing military strength and the continued sway they hold over an Eastern Europe whose control they deem essential to their national security, have had a profound effect upon the policies of the Western countries. Their expansionism has given rise to the incompatible conceptions of security sustaining the East-West conflict, which, however, has changed greatly since 1945, in response to changing perceptions and power balances.

The Soviet leadership has grown more sophisticated and does not view Western Europe as a political unit, hence Moscow's increasingly differentiated policy. Despite its sustained military buildup and forward deployment of conventional forces far beyond what might be presumed necessary to control Eastern Europe or deter an attack by NATO, Moscow does not seem bent on all-out war. Certainly, the Western perceptions of threat in the 1960s and 1970s has been far less than in the 1940s and 1950s, notwithstanding the quantum growth of Soviet power, including nuclear parity with the United States. Moscow pursues a variety of policies designed to ensure Soviet hegemony in Eastern Europe and a measure of influence in Western Europe. At a minimum, it seeks the preservation of its imperial system; at maximum, political predominance on the European continent. Congenial neutralization rather than communization impels Moscow's policy toward Western Europe. The elements of continuity and change in Soviet policy emerge clearly from an examination of the key issues that have absorbed Soviet attention since 1945.

I

In the early postwar years, Soviet policy toward Western Europe was determined by Stalin's priorities in Eastern Europe. Whatever may have been his interest in encouraging a full withdrawal of American power from Europe, in dominating all of Germany, and in promoting the prospects of Western European Communist parties, Stalin sought first and foremost to rebuild the devastated Soviet economy and consolidate Soviet rule in Eastern Europe. To do this, he was willing to sacrifice or at least subordinate his other, longer term, aims in Europe. Though a cunning statesman, he pressed Sovietization and Stalinization in the areas controlled by the Red Army with such harshness and impatience that he aroused deep-rooted fears in a sorely weakened and vulnerable Western Europe that reacted with a collective defense that he had hoped to prevent.

Moscow initially favored an exploitative and "Carthaginian solution" to the German problem: extensive reparations; the cession of the Oder-Neisse territories to Poland as compensation for the Soviet absorption of eastern Poland; the expulsion of twelve million Germans from Eastern Europe; and the establishment of a Moscow-controlled Communist party in power in East Germany. However, by mid-1946, Moscow adopted a more conciliatory position, seeking to obtain a voice in the management of the Ruhr and to disrupt the Western decision to treat Germany's economy as part of the overall effort to advance Western Europe's economic recovery. It also eased its pressure on Turkey for territorial and military concessions after the Truman Doctrine was proclaimed in March 1947 and cautioned the French and Italian Communists against an attempt to seize power.

Stalin saw in the American proposal to aid Europe's economic recovery, formalized in June 1947, a challenge to Soviet rule in Eastern Europe, and he came out strongly against the Marshall Plan, even though a minimal Soviet participation might have killed the enterprise in the U.S. Congress and prolonged Western Europe's internal weaknesses. The satellitization of Soviet-occupied areas took precedence over normalization of relations with the West. The Stalinization of Eastern Europe, and with it the crystallization of the cold war, received Moscow's imprimatur in September 1947, at the founding conference of the Cominform. Moscow used the Cominform to tighten its control over Eastern Europe and serve notice on the West that its influence would no longer be tolerated in the area. What had been introduced as a temporary arrangement among victors became institutionalized as the division of Europe between adversaries.

In 1948 the full impact of Stalin's isolationist and absolutist course became evident: no deviation from total subservience to Moscow was tolerated. In February, the Communists engineered a coup in Prague; in June, West Berlin was blockaded and Yugoslavia excommunicated from the Cominform. The events in Prague and West Berlin gave impetus to Western rearmament and the subsequent grand reconciliation between Western-occupied parts of Germany and the rest of Western Europe. The Yugoslav affair triggered massive purges and ever more repressive measures in Eastern Europe and opened an irreparable schism in the international Communist movement; after Stalin's death, Titoism became the midwife to national communism in Eastern Europe and forced Stalin's successors to grope for ways of reconciling substantial measures of autonomy with the preservation of essential Soviet strategic interests.

The Berlin blockade was Stalin's most explicit challenge to the Western position in Germany. Several considerations may have prompted the move. First, if the Western powers could be forced out of Berlin and the entire city brought under Soviet control, Moscow would have greatly enhanced its prospects for controlling Germany; certainly, it would have weakened the West's position in their zones of occupation. Second, the Soviet Union sought to discourage the establishment of West Germany as an independent country within the Western camp. Third, an Allied retreat in Berlin would have strengthened the Communists in the politically vulnerable countries of Western Europe and placed those regimes under considerable pressure, thereby deflecting their attention away from what was happening in Eastern Europe and from a reconciliation with the Germans. Fourth, it would have given an irresistible aspect to Soviet expansionism. Finally, once the blockade took on the form of a protracted crisis and show of wills, Stalin may have used it to test U.S. determination. A year later, the U.S. willingness to bear the cost of the airlift convinced Stalin to end the crisis. Stalin failed not only to drive the Western powers out of Berlin, but also to prevent the establishment of the Federal Republic of Germany (FRG) on 23 May 1949. And, though he retaliated in kind by setting up the German Democratic Republic (GDR) six months later, he set in motion a Western reaction that was to have far-reaching implications for East-West relations and the future of Europe.

The Berlin crisis, the continued presence of sizeable Soviet forces in the middle of Europe, and the Sovietization of Eastern Europe, reinforced Western perceptions of threat and weakness and of an insatiably expansionist Soviet Union that could be checked only by a countervailing buildup of military strength. To this end the North Atlantic Treaty Organization (NATO) was created on 4 April 1949. Intended as a defense against a possible Soviet attack, NATO sealed the division of Europe into rival military blocs. In the early years, its military credibility depended on the nuclear supremacy of the United States. It also proved to be the politically feasible way of integrating the West Germans into the West.

Moscow bitterly criticized NATO and drew on European fears of a militaristic and revanchist Germany to forestall West German rearmament. It orchestrated Communist-organized "peace groups," playing on Western antiwar sentiment and exploiting intra-NATO disagreements on how to deal with the German question and the Soviet Union. But with Moscow's success in detonating a nuclear bomb in 1949, the triumph of communism in China, and the Korean War, the West placed a premium on developing an adequate defense.

In retrospect, we can discern Stalin's innate conservatism in foreign policy. His goals were national rather than international, Russian not Communist. He regarded Eastern Europe as a necessary buffer for Soviet security. He did not seek to overrun Western Europe by force. Rather he sought to keep the West divided and weak in order to proceed with the consolidation of the new Soviet order in Eastern Europe. In this he failed because so insistent was he upon imposing the Communist form of rule on his East European satrapies and maintaining the Red Army in the center of Europe in order to ensure their loyalty that he was unable to mitigate the appearance of threat to the West. He failed, too, to prevent the rearmament of the FRG and its membership in NATO. Indeed, Western Europe was never more united than when Stalin's Soviet Union seemed to be most threatening.

II

Stalin's death in March 1953 ushered in an era of Soviet foreign policy notable for its flexible approach to Western Europe. A mixture of blandishment, pressure, need, and growing military power (especially since the mid-1960s), Soviet policy has shown remarkable persistence and continuity, and a tenacious pursuit of priorities.

Stalin's postwar objectives had been relatively clearcut: to establish effective control over Eastern Europe; to prevent a revival of German power; to obstruct Western Europe's recovery; to promote the withdrawal of U.S. power from Europe; and finally, to keep NATO weak and forestall West German membership in the Western coalition. His successors have faced more subtle challenges and difficult problems. In Eastern Europe, they seek to preserve yet decentralize their imperial system: Soviet needs, bloc pressures, and changes in the European environment and the international Communist movement have required constant recalibration of the limits of autonomy for members of the Soviet bloc; autonomy is doled out to satisfy pent-up nationalist desires without jeopardizing the stability and cohesiveness of Moscow's security community. They have sought international recognition for the GDR and acceptance of the permanent division of the country. Their policy toward Western Europe poses several dilemmas. How far can they reduce tensions and thereby encourage a reduction in the American military presence in Europe without opening themselves to increased demands for autonomy from their client states? How far can they press their quest for military superiority without triggering a Western reaction? Are Soviet goals better served by West European integration, with the diminished American influence that is implied therein, or by a Western Europe of weak nation-states indifferently coalesced in a NATO dominated by the United States? Can the political status quo be maintained in a period when Moscow seeks expanding economic cooperation? How can the incompatibilities in the simultaneous courtship of the Federal Republic and France be minimized? As always in Soviet foreign policy there are multiple objectives, and as these are continually shifting in importance, success depends as much on opportunity as on astute management.

For a combination of domestic and intrabloc reasons, the post-Stalin Soviet leadership was in need of a détente. In June 1953 riots by East Berlin workers sent shock waves through the Soviet bloc. Moscow decided to grant the satellites chunks of autonomy and discard the excesses of Stalinist tyranny. In the spring of 1955, Soviet leaders dropped their previous insistence that an Austrian peace settlement be linked to a solution of the German problem. The Austrian State Treaty was signed with surprising speed on 15 May 1955. It committed Austria to permanent neutrality, in return for which the Soviet Union and the Western powers ended their occupation and established Austria as an independent state. The treaty was significant because, together with Moscow's relinquishment of the Porkkala base in Finland, it marked the first disengagement of Soviet military power from a forward position in Europe. By these concessions Moscow hoped to prevent the Federal Republic's rearmament and military integration into NATO. Indeed, it went so far as to suggest that NATO and the Warsaw Pact—the Soviet counterpart of NATO established the day before the Austrian treaty was signed—be fused into an overall European security system. It is questionable whether Soviet leaders expected the West to entertain such a proposal seriously. But they did nurture an image of Soviet "reasonableness" and set in motion a series of diplomatic exchanges aiming at a normalization of Soviet–West European relationships.

During the past generation, the Soviet theme in Europe has been "peaceful coexistence." Notwithstanding the Soviet interventions in Hungary in 1956 and Czechoslovakia in 1968, Moscow has "liberalized" its rule in Eastern Europe and sought to improve relations with Western

Europe. While seeking to maintain strategic control in its part of Europe, it has devoted much energy and attention to its relations with Western Europe. Soviet policy was clustered around a number of distinct but inter-related issues involving the two Germanies, France, NATO, European security, and economic cooperation. In the course of examining these issues, other aspects of Soviet policy and aims will become evident.

III

Soviet policy toward Western Europe gives pride of place to the problem of Germany. For more than a century, Moscow has alternated between fascination with and fear of German discipline, drive, and productivity. Since 1945 there has been really nothing to indicate that Moscow ever seriously contemplated the reunification of Germany: Stalin's note of 10 March 1952 did hold out this prospect in return for permament neutraliza-tion and virtual disarmament, but it was very likely more a ploy to kill the European Defense Community and West Germany's integration into NATO than a serious proposal for fundamentally restructuring the Euro-pean political alignments that made possible Moscow's position in middle Europe. Moreover, a unified and Communist Germany could only be a Soviet planner's nightmare, a threat to the Soviet imperium in Eastern Europe and, ultimately, to the security of the Soviet Union itself. Perhaps on no issue is the irrelevance of Marxist-Leninist ideology to the behavior of the Soviet state more manifest.

From 1955 on, the Soviet Union cultivated Western acceptance of the territorial status quo in Europe, recognition of the division of Germany and the legitimacy of the GDR, a weakening of ties between West Berlin and the FRG, and a minimal level of rearmament by the Federal Republic. Khrushchev decided to revive the Berlin problem as a pretext for pressur-ing the West on these issues. On 27 November 1958, he provoked a crisis, insisting that West Berlin be set up as a "free city," guaranteed by the four former occupying powers and the two existing German states, and that the Western powers withdraw from the city. Khrushchev's pseudo-ultimatum was extended for almost three years, as the Soviet government avoided any precipitous action: there was petty harrassment of traffic from the Federal Republic to West Berlin, but no repeat of 1948, as the West held firm. Frustrated and in need of some visible sign of achievement to still his critics in the Kremlin and help East German party boss Walter Ulbricht, whose regime was hemorrhaging from the flight of refugees, most of whom were skilled workers essential to economic development, he agreed to a politi-cally humiliating move. On 13 August 1961, without warning, the Berlin wall was put up, physically sealing off the two sectors of the city. A monument to Communist weakness, it helped Ulbricht and permitted Khrushchev to save face. The "crisis" petered out, especially after the upturn in Soviet-American relations that followed the Cuban missile crisis of October 1962, and it ended on 12 June 1964, when the Soviet Union and the GDR signed a twenty-year Treaty of Friendship, Mutual Assistance, and Cooperation. The treaty was reassurance for Ulbricht, who had feared a Soviet deal with Bonn at his expense. But more important, by ending the Berlin crisis, Moscow was able to proceed on a new tack toward Western Europe.

Within hours after Ulbricht had signed the treaty and left Moscow, Khrushchev held a talk with the ambassador from the Federal Republic to discuss a new Soviet policy and a proposed visit to Bonn. Aware of the advantages of improved bilateral relationships with key Western countries, Khrushchev aimed for greater influence on FRG politics, particularly for arms limitation and abnegation, rather than for any overall settlement. He believed that a major Soviet initiative could aggravate intra-NATO tensions and prevent the FRG from acquiring control of or developing nuclear weapons; and he hoped to use the spectre of another Rapallo to extract concessions from the FRG's allies. His son-in-law, Alexei Adzhubei, visited Bonn in July, and the following month Khrushchev announced his intention of travelling to the FRG. However, two months later he was deposed by his closest associates, some speculate because of his German policy, but more likely the proximate causes were related to domestic issues.

By 1966 Khrushchev's successors adopted his line and explored ways of improving Soviet-FRG relations: they dropped the "demand" for a German peace treaty, kept Berlin quiet, stressed the need for a "European security treaty," without offering details, and permitted the repatriation of many Soviet citizens of German origin — a decision that had been made by Khrushchev. At the Twenty-third Congress of the CPSU in March–April 1966, Foreign Minister Andrei Gromyko declared that the "normalization and improvement of relations with the Federal Republic of Germany" depended, in effect, on the Bonn government's renouncing nuclear weapons and accepting the existing frontiers of all states in Europe; and he called for a European security conference. The matter dragged on inconclusively until after the Soviet occupation of Czechoslovakia in August 1968, when polemics in the Soviet media against the Federal Republic dropped sharply, and Moscow hinted at a desire to continue the talks. The discussions were given new impetus in March 1969, when the Soviet ambassador in Bonn made a point of briefing the government about the Chinese "aggression" on the Ussuri River: faced with tension in the East, Moscow coveted normalization in the West. A few days later, the Political Consultative Committee of the Warsaw Pact, meeting in Budapest, repeated the oft-made

Soviet proposal for "the holding of a general European conference on questions of security and cooperation in Europe." Soviet overtures received a welcome reception in Bonn with the coming to power of the Social Democratic Party (SPD) in October 1969.

SPD Chancellor Willy Brandt's *Ostpolitik* meshed with Brezhnev's *Westpolitik.* Convinced that reunification was unlikely in the foreseeable future, and desirous of easing the situation of West Berliners, reducing the hostility between the FRG and GDR, and opening the way for better relations with Eastern Europe, Brandt abandoned Bonn's previously revisionist line and expressed a willingness to recognize the territorial and political status quo in Europe. On 28 November 1969, the Federal Republic signed the non-proliferation treaty, renouncing any right to acquire, develop, or use nuclear weapons; on 7 December 1969, at Brandt's initiative, talks opened in Moscow on renouncing the use or threat of force between the two countries; and on 1 February 1970, a major economic agreement was reached under which the FRG agreed to provide 1.2 million tons of large diameter pipes on favorable terms, financed by a consortium of German banks, in return for which the Soviet Union was to deliver natural gas over a twenty-year period starting in 1973. Key Soviet military, political, and economic objectives were within reach.

The capstone of the Soviet diplomatic strategy was the signing, on 12 August 1970, of the treaty in Moscow between USSR and the FRG under which they agreed to settle their disputes by peaceful means. The treaty further stipulated that the two parties: "undertake to respect without restriction the territorial integrity of all States in Europe within their present frontiers; declare that they have no territorial claims against anybody nor will assert such claims in the future; regard today and shall in future regard the frontiers of all States in Europe as inviolable such as they are on the date of signature of the present Treaty, including the Oder-Neisse line which forms the western frontier of the People's Republic of Poland and the frontier between the Federal Republic of Germany and the German Democratic Republic." For Moscow, the treaty meant that the Federal Republic accepted the division of Germany, the reality of the GDR, and the renunciation of nuclear weapons; it was the augury — and essential precursor — of what Moscow was to achieve at Helsinki five years later, namely, Western recognition of Soviet hegemony in Central and Eastern Europe; and it accelerated the acquisition of advanced technology and extensive credits from the FRG — an objective that was increasingly important for Moscow.

Brandt's only condition for satisfying Soviet desires was an acceptable arrangement for West Berlin. After very difficult negotiations lasting from March 1970 to August 1971, the four powers — the Soviet Union, the United States, France, and Britain — signed an agreement that went a long way toward improving the condition of the West Berliners: unimpeded civilian transit traffic to West Berlin (which is situated 110 miles inside of the GDR) from the Federal Republic by road, rail, and waterways was assured; West Berlin could maintain its special relationship with, but not be part of, the FRG; and West Berliners were to be granted easier access to visit family in the GDR. The 1970 treaty was ratified by the German parliament in May 1972, but by a very narrow majority, because Brandt's opponents felt that he had given away too much for too little.

That Moscow was keen on Brandt's *Ostpolitik* was evident: in May 1971, it forced the aged and antiaccommodationist Walter Ulbricht to resign from the party secretaryship (he died on 1 August 1973) and replaced him with the more compliant Erich Honecker, who was prepared to subordinate the GDR's long-term aims and make concessions to FRG demands on West Berlin; by implication, it eschewed the use of the city's vulnerability as a lever against the Federal Republic. Moscow has downgraded the GDR's political goals in its quest for greater influence over the FRG and in order better to exploit intra-NATO conflicts.

Economic cooperation with the Federal Republic is also important to the Soviet Union (and for the GDR, which received more than three billion dollars from Bonn during the 1971–1978 period for the upkeep of transit routes and other projects linked with West Berlin). By 1978 the FRG had become its leading non-Communist trading partner and source of high technology imports. Soviet imports include a vast iron and steel complex, turbines for the natural gas pipeline to Eastern Europe and the FRG, electronic equipment for petrochemical plants, trucks, and heavy machinery. Most of this has been financed by long-term German credits, estimated at upwards of ten billion dollars. During Brezhnev's visits to the Federal Republic in 1973 and 1978, economic relations loomed large, as did Soviet attempts to curtail the arms buildup and persuade the Germans to agree to a mutual renunciation of the neutron bomb. Clearly, détente with the Federal Republic is a crucial component of the overall Soviet strategy of promoting "mutually advantageous" economic and political ties with the rest of Western Europe.

IV

After assuming power, the Brezhnev-Kosygin leadership continued Khrushchev's "opening to the West," with its attention to France. The Soviet media had long castigated French colonialism in Southeast Asia and North Africa, and when Charles de Gaulle returned to power in 1958, Moscow attacked him for seeking to establish a military dictatorship and for refusing to grant independence to Algeria. But this soon changed as Khrushchev saw opportunities to exploit French differences with Bonn, London, and Washington: he did not permit the Soviet interest in penetrating the Third World to interfere with his European policy. Nor was the relationship without its difficulties.

Perhaps nowhere is the complexity and often indeterminate character of Soviet policy toward Western Europe more apparent than in Moscow's attempt simultaneously to court the Federal Republic and France. When it tries to attract the one, it often dismays the other. With the FRG, the USSR suggests the ultimate of a Rapallo-type relationship, leaving vague the issues of unification and the military power that such a German state would require to pursue an independent policy, all of which are anethema to Paris. With France, Moscow stresses the Franco-Russian alliance in two world wars and the dangers of "German militarism."

De Gaulle's grant of independence to Algeria was welcomed in Moscow, but it was his dissatisfaction with NATO, his rejection of the U.S. proposal for a multilateral nuclear force, his opposition to West European economic and political integration, his quest for a reduced American role in Europe, his acceptance of the Oder-Neisse boundary, and his readiness to improve relations with Moscow unilaterally that accounted for the Kremlin's interest in the French connection. It saw France as the "Achilles heel" of NATO and found congenial the Gaullist preference for a Europe of cooperating but nationalistic and independent sovereignties, which conflicted starkly with the "Atlanticist" formulations so favored by American and British officials. As one Soviet writer noted, "A powerful France holds no menace for the Soviet Union or its interests. On the contrary, the more France asserts her greatpower independence, the easier it will be for us to work in common for solution of the pressing problems of Europe and the world." De Gaulle's distinctive blend of unsentimental realism and striking purposiveness (for example, his veto of the British application for membership in the Common Market in January 1963) intrigued Moscow so much that it was not deterred from pressing for closer bilateral relations by his *force de frappe,* his refusal to sign the nuclear test ban treaty or discuss arms control, his tenacious opposition to Soviet pressure during the Berlin and Cuban crises, and his cultivation of a special relationship with Bonn.

President de Gaulle's visit to the Soviet Union in June 1966 came during the halcyon stage of the Soviet courtship, scarcely three months after he had informed NATO of his intention to withdraw France's participation in the integrated military commands and had indicated the desirability of a shift of venue for NATO's headquarters (from Paris to Brussels). Soviet leaders sought to encourage de Gaulle's weakening of NATO and urged more intimate Franco-Soviet ties: the Moscow Declaration of 30 June 1966 announced the plan of the two governments "to continue regular consultations." Moscow tried to strengthen the relationship, but after the Soviet invasion of Czechoslovakia, which coincided with the twilight of de Gaulle's political career, a certain disenchantment and constraint developed in Paris. High level visits have been continued by succeeding French presidents Georges Pompidou and Valery Giscard D'Estaing, and Soviet leaders have regularly returned them, but the mood has not been the same.

By the early 1970s, France edged back toward military cooperation with NATO and noticeably muffled the acid exchanges with its allies that were so characteristic a feature of the de Gaulle era. Moscow is under no illusions that France can disengage itself from the Atlantic alliance and play a completely independent role in Europe, but it finds promise enough in the neo-Gaullist propensities that shape the outlook of French leaders and the tenor of the French domestic politics to seek agreement with France on the convergent strands of the two countries' foreign policy. Thus Moscow, like Paris, supports the preservation of the territorial status quo in Europe, a non-nuclear FRG, a diminished role for the United States in Europe, a NATO of modest size, and expanded East-West economic cooperation. Both retain a vestigial uneasiness over the danger of a resurgent German nationalism and militarism. Overall, France is useful to the Soviet Union in the ongoing process of détente, which is favored by each country. Its demands are few and its contributions are important to the advancement of Soviet aims. For example, in the economic and technological realm, France has led the way to the Soviet market. In October 1964, it extended the USSR a seven-year credit for 356 million dollars, which was used to finance chemical plants and equipment, making France the first member of the European Economic Community (EEC) to break with the community's previous five-year limit on credits to the Soviet Union. A ten-year Franco-Soviet trade agreement was concluded in October 1971 during the first of Brezhnev's visits to France; and during Brezhnev's visit in December 1974, a far-reaching accord was reached under which the USSR will deliver natural gas over a twenty-year period and France will provide several important industrial plants, including a massive complex for the production of aluminum. By the late 1970s, France had become the USSR's second most important Western trading partner—a distant second to the Federal Republic.

The Soviet state-to-state relationship with France has taken precedence over encouragement to the French Communist party at electoral time. There is little evidence to suggest that Moscow is prepared to jeopardize the former to benefit the latter. Rather, it seems determined to have friendly relations with France serve as a model of what Moscow seeks to establish with other West European countries. The Soviet strategy is peaceful co-existence, with the term détente added because of its popularity with

Western leaders. Whatever the term, the theme is Soviet reasonableness and accommodation; what is not said, but is crucial to the reality that Moscow seeks to fashion, is the role that military power plays in advancing political goals. The Soviet military buildup along NATO's central front has been well reported, because a Soviet strike across the North German plain would threaten the nerve centers of the alliance, but what is less known is the awesome power and diplomatic pressure that Moscow directs along the northern tier of Western Europe.

V

Short on population but long on strategically prime real estate, Scandinavia comprises about one-third of non-Communist Western Europe. Its political-military role is of crucial importance to the Soviet Union: on the Baltic side, it controls the approaches to Leningrad and the Baltic SSRs; on the Atlantic side, Norway is situated astride the approaches to the Kola Peninsula, where the Soviet network of military installations is considered by Western intelligence analysts to be the most heavily concentrated system of air, naval, and missile bases in the world. The Kola Peninsula was chosen for this military buildup because it offers the shortest trajectory route from the Soviet Union over the top of the world to targets in the United States, and safeguards the sea and air lanes to key military and industrial sites in the Soviet north.

The Soviet Union desires the neutralization of the Nordic area, i.e., Finland, Sweden, Norway, and Denmark. Finland's neutrality and policy of deferring to Soviet wishes on most foreign policy issues was introduced in 1944 by former Prime Minister J. K. Paasikivi, and has been the centerpiece of Finnish statecraft ever since. For 800 years a dukedom of Sweden, Finland acquired independence only after World War I, having been part of the Russian empire for more than a century. After 1945, having sided with Germany, it was forced to cede eastern Karelia, including the ice-free port of Petsamo (Pechenga), to the USSR. Under the 1948 Soviet-Finnish Treaty of Friendship, Cooperation, and Mutual Assistance, the Finns agreed to consult with the Soviet government should Moscow feel threatened by Germany or any country that is allied with it, that is, any member of NATO. These consultations severely limit, but do not eliminate, Finland's possible initiatives in foreign affairs. For most of the post-1955 period, Moscow has pursued a moderate policy toward Finland, a reward for its accommodation in foreign affairs.

Sweden followed a policy of neutrality in the two world wars, but it is well armed and would presumably resist any invasion. It has never seriously considered joining NATO and argues for keeping the Nordic area nuclear-free, which sits well with Moscow and reassures it on the security of its Baltic flank.

Moscow's awareness of Norway's strategic importance was an outgrowth of World War II, when German submarines operated out of occupied Norway to interdict American Lend-Lease shipments to Murmansk. After the war, a slice of territory taken from Finland made the Soviet Union Norway's neighbor in the far north along 110 miles of bleak, frozen wasteland that Norwegians say is land the strategist remembered but God forgot. To the east of Norway's northernmost district of Finnmark, the Soviet Union has three ice-free ports of Petsamo, Severomorsk (a new naval base), and Murmansk, located 15, 60, and 100 miles from the Norwegian frontier, respectively. Their security is a prime Soviet concern.

Norway is a staunch member of NATO, but it has no desire to fuel Soviet apprehensions or precipitate a crisis through any misperception of its behavior. To allay Soviet anxieties, Norway (and Denmark) announced in 1961 that no nuclear weapons would be introduced on its territory; nor would it house NATO bases or permit NATO exercises near the Soviet border. It has also kept force levels in Finnmark at a low threshold and been slow to develop radar facilities and military bases there so as not to cause the Soviets undue alarm over their defensive and missile capabilities. Moscow would prefer that the Nordic countries officially agree to the establishment of a nuclear-free zone in the area, but neither Norway or Sweden is prepared to foreclose the possible option of acquiring nuclear weapons should this ever be deemed necessary.

While suspicious of Norway's membership in NATO and the silent war of electronic eavesdropping and intelligence surveillance that continually goes on, Moscow has thus far accepted Norway's self-imposed limitations as evidence of a desire not to threaten Soviet security, and seems likely to continue to do so as long as no power other than Norway controls the approaches to the Kola Peninsula. But since all Soviet ships and submarines must pass through the Norwegian Sea en route to the Atlantic Ocean, it cannot be happy at the monitoring of Soviet naval deployments. Control of Finnmark would, of course, seal this gap in Soviet military secrecy.

Soviet policy towards Norway is overwhelmingly strategic, but economic considerations are starting to impinge in ways that foreshadow future tensions. These center on the Svalbard-Spitzbergen archipelago that commands the approaches to the Kola Peninsula. In 1920 Norwegian sovereignty there was internationally recognized, but the archipelago was demilitarized and the 40 signatories to the treaty—including the Soviet Union—were granted most-favored-nation treatment, allowing them the same rights as Norwegians for fishing, mining, and other commercial ventures. In addition to Norway, only the Soviet Union has heretofore been active, maintaining a coal mining concession: the approximately 2,000 Soviet miners do not produce as much as the 1,000 Norwegians. The discovery of oil has greatly enhanced the area's importance, some estimates holding that 40 percent of the world's reserves of oil may exist in the Arctic region. Moreover, the Barents Sea is a rich fishing area. Negotiations between Norway and the Soviet Union for delineating national jurisdictions over the seabed and the seas surrounding the Svalbard-Spitzbergen archipelago are underway. The prospect of international oil companies drilling in their backyard makes the Soviets very nervous, and Moscow may decide to press for an exclusive Soviet-Norwegian sovereignty in the area. Soviet long-term intentions toward Norway should emerge from the lengthy legal discussions now underway. It is against this background that the growing Soviet military boldness in the area needs to be evaluated: "Naval and air exercises move westward into the Norwegian Sea. The number of reconnaissance flights over Finnmark and adjacent districts increases. Unidentified submarines are detected in the fjords."[1] By exposing Norway's military weakness and vulnerability, Moscow serves notice of its opposition to any Norwegian-NATO buildup that might alter the Soviet preponderance of military superiority in this strategic sector; and it may expect to obtain additional concessions in the bargaining over the boundaries of the continental shelf.

VI

A major hurdle for Moscow's promotion of détente and normalization of relations in Europe has been its ambivalence toward West European integration and unity. Ideologically hostile, in accordance with the canons of Marxist-Leninist scripture, Moscow holds that the drastic and desperate measures of "monopoly capital" to stave off the inevitable collapse of capitalism may bring a temporary reprieve, but that they lead to increased international tensions and a further deterioration in the condition of the working class. At the operational level, "the Europe of Trusts," as the edifice of supranational institutions is called, politically limits the Soviet Union's freedom of diplomatic maneuver, ability to play one capitalist country against another in order to extract maximum commercial benefit, and economic penetration of that part of the Third World that has been able to fashion a special relationship with the EEC. Though preferring bilateral diplomacy, Moscow could not indefinitely ignore the EEC, which came into being with the Treaty of Rome in March 1957.

The subject of considerable discussion in Moscow, the EEC was acknowledged to have brought about an accelerated rate of economic growth and unexpected stability to member countries. Khrushchev publicly denounced it in May 1962, but this capitalist creation forced him to offer proposals for strengthening the economic structure of COMECON: paradoxically, for his "socialist commonwealth" to compete and deal with its capitalist counterpart, the nations of Eastern Europe were allowed greater measures of autonomy, thus further complicating Soviet hegemonial ambitions. When de Gaulle vetoed Britain's application for membership in the EEC in January 1963, Moscow was elated, seeing this as vindication of Leninist expectations. However, propaganda aside, it could not ignore the Common Market's vitality. The Soviet policy of détente in Europe, the eagerness for expanded economic relations with Western Europe, the pressure from West European Communist parties who sensed the general support that the EEC enjoyed in their respective countries, the interest of the East Europeans in more economic, technical, and cultural "windows to the West," and the desire for a *status quo cordiale* with Western Europe to offset the widening rift with Peking all wrought a change in Soviet perceptions and attitudes.

In March 1972, in a speech marking the subtle evolution in Soviet policy from unrelenting hostility to incipient accommodation, Brezhnev implicitly recognized the EEC:

> The USSR is far from ignoring the actual situation in Western Europe, including the existence of such an economic group of capitalist countries as the "Common Market." We attentively follow its evolution and its activities. Our relations with its members, naturally, will depend on the extent to which they, on their part, recognize the realities existing in the socialist part of Europe, in particular the interests of COMECON countries. We are for equality in economic relations and against discrimination.[2]

The process of working out a satisfactory agreement between the EEC and COMECON has been difficult. Romania, Hungary, and Poland took the lead in trying to adjust to the community's requirements, but they were limited by Soviet restraints, which may be eased by improved East-West relations. After an unproductive eighteen-month period, the EEC accepted an invitation in September 1974 from the secretary-general of COMECON to send a delegation to Moscow. The talks in early 1975 yielded little except for the first official contacts. In 1977, when the EEC imposed a 200-mile limit on North Sea fishing, Moscow sent an official Soviet delegation to Brussels; for the first time it opened actual negotiations for mutual concessions, thereby according de facto recognition of the EEC. Whatever may be Moscow's readiness to negotiate, it will proceed warily, hypersensitive to the effects on Soviet–East European and West European–East European relationships. Politics is still in command in the Kremlin, economic advantages to the contrary notwithstanding.

VII

The central political objective permeating almost all Soviet diplomatic moves since 1945 was Western recognition of the post–World War II territorial and political status quo in Europe. To this end, and to forestall the European Defense Community and West German rearmament, Moscow started to lobby for a European Security Conference as early as 1954 and bruited it often in the 1960s, but the Western powers were cool to the idea. By 1970, the mood changed in the West; interest in an accommodation with the Soviet Union and improved East-West relations was strong. The USSR was now acknowledged to be a superpower in every military sense of the term: it enjoyed essential equivalence with the United States in nuclear weapons and delivery systems and a numerically commanding advantage in conventional forces. Moreover, though the Soviet Union remained solidly entrenched in Eastern Europe, it was allowing increasing measures of autonomy and its own social-political system had relaxed since the Stalin period. Washington's interest was evident in the unseemly haste with which it had swept the Soviet invasion of Czechoslovakia and the "Brezhnev Doctrine" under the rug and urged Strategic Arms Limitation Talks (SALT), no doubt also hoping that Moscow's interest in a limitation on strategic weapons would have a salutary effect on U.S. efforts to reach an agreement with Hanoi for an end to the American involvement in Vietnam. With the 1970 Soviet-FRG treaty, the 1971 Quadripartite Agreement on Berlin, and the Soviet acceptance of American and Canadian participation, Western opposition weakened to a Conference on Security and Cooperation in Europe (CSCE). Moscow overcame what was perhaps the last hurdle when Brezhnev, in May 1971, challenged the West to judge the Soviet Union's peaceful intention by "tasting" the wine of negotiations, offering to meet NATO's demand for parallel but interrelated talks on the reduction of forces in Central Europe.

Deliberations on CSCE started in Helsinki on 22 November 1972. When the Final Act was signed by the heads of state of 35 countries on 1 August 1975, the Soviet Union realized a 30-year ambition. Though officially only a political statement of intent and not a treaty or a legally binding document, the Final Act in effect ratified the existing frontiers in Europe. It was a political settlement of World War II and recognized Soviet hegemony over the Communist half of Europe. Still, the Soviet triumph was not unmixed. The Helsinki Conference may have given the East Europeans ammunition to use against Moscow in their quest for greater autonomy and expanded contacts with the West, but more time must elapse before the validity of this proposition can be assessed. The Final Act expressed those general principles that are the staples of international summitry: sovereign equality of states, inviolability of frontiers, territorial integrity of states, nonintervention in the internal affairs of other countries, the renunciation of force or the threat of force to change existing frontiers, and so on. It now remains to be seen to what degree these principles will be implemented.

Basket 1—as the set of principles on security, confidence-building measures (CBMs), and disarmament is called—was of most interest to Moscow. By noting that "The participating states regard as inviolable all one another's frontiers as well as the frontiers of all states in Europe, and therefore they will refrain now and in the future from assaulting these frontiers," it filled Soviet needs. The Western Powers contented themselves with CBMs such as the prior notification of major military maneuvers, the notification of smaller military exercises, and the exchange of observers at maneuvers. While voluntary in nature, the CBMs were working through late 1978 and held out some prospect for a future easing of military tensions. Basket 2 deals with economic and technological cooperation, issues also of interest to Moscow. However, it is Basket 3, which was included at the dogged insistence of the West Europeans and which constitutes a potpourri of political principles on the freer flow of people, ideas, and information, that contains the fly in the CSCE ointment Moscow so readily bought. The importance given by the Carter administration to human rights has, willy-nilly, marred the process of Soviet-American détente and turned the CSCE follow-up meeting at Belgrade (October 1977 to March 1978), which was supposed to review the progress and problems of CSCE since Helsinki, into a mini-confrontation. Moscow sees the lapsing of SALT I in October 1977, the brouhaha over Soviet intervention in Africa, and the checkered course of Soviet-American economic relations as political and military consequences of the ideological motivation behind President Carter's concern with human rights.

Of far greater potential importance for Soviet policy than CSCE are the MFR talks that began officially in Vienna on 30 October 1973 (preparatory meetings were held from 31 January to 28 June 1973). Originally termed Mutual and Balanced Force Reduction (MBFR), the official title is the Conference on Mutual Reduction of Forces and Armaments and Associated Measures in Central Europe, commonly referred to as MFR. MFR was the price Moscow paid for CSCE. Its outcome will determine the military component of détente in Europe. Ironically, just as Moscow's harvest from Helsinki may prove less than it originally anticipated, so, too, NATO may find MFR more a problem for the Atlantic alliance than for the Soviet Union.

MFR reveals the multiple and adaptive nature of Soviet policy. Though not at all enthusiastic in the beginning, Moscow tries to use MFR to stabilize its present favorable military advantage in Europe. One way is to weaken NATO, not merely militarily but politically as well. Moscow considers NATO an aggressive military bloc dominated by the United States, but it appreciates the existing differences in national positions and seeks to exploit them, playing off one member or faction against another. NATO's failure to resolve essential policy questions on strategy, interoperability and standardization of weapons, and new weapons, such as the neutron (enhanced radiation) bomb and cruise missiles, is grist for the Soviet mill. These conflicts may encrust still further the Soviet belief in the divisive propensities inherent in relations among capitalist countries and lead Moscow to wait for the right time and circumstance to capitalize on these disagreements. Thus are ideological predilections and perceptions reinforced by political phenomena.

Perpetuation of a favorable military balance depends on checking the growth of the Bundeswehr. Through arms reduction and limitation, Moscow hopes to place ceilings on the military forces of the Federal Republic. An opening wedge in this drive may be seen in the Warsaw Pact proposal, submitted on 8 June 1978, which agreed for the first time that both sides should have an equal number of troops in Central Europe and that no country would be permitted to increase its forces above present levels.

Among the other issues that Moscow has raised are the limitation on NATO forward-based systems (FBS), a treaty on the renunciation of the first use of nuclear weapons, and a limit on the size of military maneuvers. Disengagement as a way of encouraging a withdrawal of U.S. forces has cropped up repeatedly. For example, in the late 1950s Moscow proposed a demilitarized zone of 400 kilometers on either side of the Elbe. Several variants have been suggested, including one for the establishment of a nuclear-free zone that would include Poland, Czechoslovakia, and the two Germanies. Finally, the Soviet Union uses MFR as a forum to convince the West Europeans of the harm that the deployment of the neutron bomb would do to the negotiations aiming at a reduction of forces in Central Europe.

Soviet political strategy in Europe rests on a strong military base. Despite anticipated major economic difficulties in the 1980s, the Soviet Union shows no disposition to stabilize, much less reduce, military expenditures or the modernization of its strategic and conventional forces. The buildup of strategic forces pushed by Khrushchev and accelerated by Brezhnev in the mid-1960s gives no sign of tapering off. No longer do Western experts talk of NATO's military superiority. The discussion now centers on the nature and extent of Moscow's military superiority, nuclear weapons aside.

The characteristics of Soviet military policy in Europe are important to any consideration of the range of Moscow's probable and possible political objectives. Briefly, these characteristics are high conventional force levels and their strong forward deployment; a commitment in Soviet doctrine "to wage and to win a campaign" with *all* weapons available, i.e., including nuclear arms; an impressive buildup of mobile battlefield cover for moving combat forces (the emphasis is on SAM-8s and SAM-9s); a substantial numerical advantage in tanks, motor-rifle divisions, and artillery over NATO forces; improved and highly effective logistical support; and the buildup of what Richard Burt has called "Eurostrategic weapons," i.e., nuclear-capable strike aircraft and medium and intermediate range mobile missiles, that include the most advanced and MIRVed SS-20, which was deployed in late 1977 and has a 3,000 mile range and so is not considered a strategic weapon or covered by SALT.[3] Soviet forces maintain a high level of combat readiness and they are consistently modernized and given deeper penetration capability. The Soviet Union is deploying a new generation of tactical or "theater" nuclear surface-to-surface missiles: the SS-21, which replaces the very short range "FROG"; the SS-22, with a 500 mile range, which replaces the "SCUD" that had a 180 mile range; and, most threatening of all the Eurostrategic weapons, the mobile SS-20s, which can hit targets anywhere in Western Europe from movable platforms in the Soviet Union.

VIII

That a major Soviet military buildup is underway in Central Europe is undisputed: Soviet forces are being equipped and trained to fight a blitzkrieg war. Nonetheless, NATO officials do not believe Moscow intends an all-out aggression against Western Europe. Several explanations may help illumine the Kremlin's *military*. First, massive military power is perceived as the best defense, not only against any NATO attack or attempt to intervene in Eastern Europe, but also against attempted national Communist defections or uprisings. Second, the Soviet leadership, like its czarist predecessor, values redundancy. As the saying goes, "Russians feel more comfortable with three armies too many than three divisions too few." Overinsurance is axiomatic in Soviet military doctrine. Third, if war erupts, Moscow wants an overwhelming retaliatory capability. In recent years, it seems to have shifted from the expectation that the next European war would be nuclear and predicates a war-winning strategy on the forward deployment of massive conventional forces that are expected to neutralize the nuclear option. Some British analysts contend that Soviet troops are being trained to live off the land, carry sufficient ammunition with them during rapid forward thrusts, and achieve a decisive victory before NATO could react. The ability to strike suddenly, with minimal reinforcement, is expected to provide the clout to deter or to demolish, as need requires.

Fourth, by forward deployment, the Soviet Union seeks a critical edge over NATO and the eventual acquiescence to Soviet military superiority in Central Europe. Expecting that in the short run NATO may react by intensifying its military buildup and by modernizing (and this is a matter of concern to Moscow), the Soviets think that the West has a short memory and will in time accept the forward Soviet deployment as the norm for a tolerable balance of power in Europe. Finally, since the mid-1970s, Soviet commentators have called attention to the downturn in détente and NATO's growing modernization program, most recently the decision of the NATO Defense Council in December 1979 to deploy a new generation of theater missiles capable of hitting targets in the Soviet Union from bases in Western Europe. The Soviets fear the trend in NATO is toward increased defense budgets and weapons modernization, hence their own sustained programs.

Politically, the Soviet Union prefers an orderly and stable environment in Western Europe; it does not like changes that might complicate the realization of its specific objectives: a non-nuclear German Federal Republic and a modest U.S. presence, both of which are keys to keeping NATO minimally potent; a Western Europe of nation-states at a low level of integration; a worsening of West European–U.S., and especially FRG–U.S. relations; assured access to West European technology and markets; and better leverage over West European Communist parties whose ideological assertiveness and prospects for sharing power are beginning to complicate Soviet hegemony in Eastern Europe and leadership of the world Communist movement. Moscow aspires to become security manager of Europe and assumes that this can best be attained in an atmosphere of détente and through expanded bilateral relations with the existing capitalist governments.

Soviet diplomacy is active and resourceful. On 6 October 1979, during a speech in East Berlin, Brezhnev unexpectedly announced the unilateral withdrawal of up to 20,000 Soviet troops in the coming year, 1,000 tanks, and other equipment from East Germany. He also offered to reduce the number of medium-range "theater" missiles based in the European part of the USSR, if no new missiles were added to NATO's arsenal. Moscow's aim is to forestall the deployment of 572 new medium range missiles that are intended to counter Soviet missiles targeted against Western Europe. Brezhnev also made propaganda capital out of a military liability, since the tanks to be withdrawn from the GDR are obsolete. He hopes intra-NATO dissension will eventually surface and defeat the campaign for the deployment of new missiles in much the same way it affected the NATO decision not to deploy the neutron bomb.

If Moscow does indeed have a long-term political strategy for an ideal relationship with the countries of Western Europe, it would be that commonly referred to as "Finlandization."[4] With due apologies to the Finns, this term is used to signify a process whereby the Soviet Union influences the domestic and foreign policy behavior of non-Communist countries in a way that leads them to follow policies congenial to or approved by the Soviet Union. It is a policy of special constraints where Soviet interests and preferences are involved, in which governments are overly careful, beforehand, in dealing with the Soviet Union and in acting on issues of special interest to Moscow.

True, reality is more complex than the theories or conceptual formulations that seek to explain it. While the behavior of Austria and Finland does suggest a preoccupation with the wishes of Moscow, the NATO countries are far from manifesting the telltale signs of Finlandized states. If the Finlandization of the West should come to pass, it would be a consequence not just of Soviet strength but also of Western weakness — debilitating domestic politics, intra-alliance bickering, a contraction of power under the guise of advancing détente, and a lack of commitment to professed ideals and institutions. Naturally Moscow will try to exploit the disarray in the West and induce a lowering of its guard. True, too, for the moment, at least, the Kremlin seems committed to the same general policy in the 1980s that has brought it such handsome benefits in the 1970s. But although it is heir to constraints, dilemmas, and problems that frustrate and divert its diplomacy from desired paths, Moscow seems, looking back at its behavior in recent decades, to have always been attentive to longer range schemes for the attainment of key objectives and the ordering and management of European affairs. Soviet pragmatism should not obscure Moscow's outlook and ambitions.

Notes

Part of the research for this essay was done in the course of investigating the strategic and political implications for NATO of Soviet policy in the Mediterranean area, work on which was begun during the summer of 1977 with a NATO Research

Fellowship. The views are the author's own and are not to be construed as in any way representing official NATO policy. The author, however, expresses his appreciation to NATO for its assistance.

1. *New York Times,* 20 June 1977.

2. *Pravda,* 21 March 1972.

3. John Erickson, "The European Military Balance," *Proceedings of the Academy of Political Science,* vol. 33, no. 1 (1978), pp. 111–13, 121.

4. For an examination of the applicability and nonapplicability of this concept, see George Ginsburgs and Alvin Z. Rubinstein, eds., *Soviet Policy Toward Western Europe* (New York: Praeger Publishers, 1978).

5

The Middle East

Galia Golan

Soviet Interests in the Region

The Middle East has traditionally and historically held great interest for the powers in the Kremlin, whether they be tsarist or communist. Access to warm waters from the Black Sea as well as geographic proximity to the country's southern borders were long factors influencing Russian interests and policies in the area; such factors have not in fact altered much over the years. Nonetheless, these traditional interests have formed only one component of Soviet motivation and policies in the area as interests of other types have appeared or became functional throughout the Soviet period. While these traditional interests contained an element of strategic factors, the latter became in time the dominant Soviet interest in the area, particularly in the era of Soviet-American nuclear competition. With this shift came an expansion of Soviet interests beyond the border countries of Turkey and Iran — which nonetheless remained important — to the Mediterranean Sea and countries further south.

Whereas the Soviets had earlier demonstrated a limited strategic interest in the region motivated by the desire to drive the West, particularly the United States, from the area, the increased importance of the strategic factor with regard to the Middle East, and with it the increased importance of the area itself in Soviet foreign policy, was traceable to two interconnected phenomena of the late 1950s and early 1960s. In this period a certain change was discernible in Soviet strategic thinking — a change that had been brewing for some years but that probably received a decisive push as a result of the Cuban missile crisis. Soviet strategic thinking under Khrushchev had been based upon and focused around nuclear power. While this may have been an improvement over Stalin's technological shortsightedness,[1] Khrushchev's strategic approach tended to neglect other considerations, such as the conventional forces on the sea and in the air; it also proved to be an insupportable drain on the Soviet economy. The Soviet missile venture in Cuba was itself an attempt to overcome just these problems, but its failure glaringly demonstrated the gaps in Khrushchev's nuclear strategy. For the crisis revealed Moscow's basic military weakness vis-à-vis the United States when it became necessary to find a non-nuclear answer to a nuclear crisis situation. More generally it demonstrated Moscow's weakness at a global level, in contrast to the already apparent American capability to intervene or act in any number of far-flung theaters of action. While playing a contributory role to Khrushchev's fall from power a few years later, the Cuban crisis opened the way for strategic development which had in fact already been started in a limited fashion, specifically the development of the Soviet fleet, and its forward deployment in the world's seas in an effort to gain flexibility and increased military options for the Kremlin.

The intensive expansion of Soviet naval power, which became apparent in the 1960s, was due also, however, to a development that preceded — and probably contributed to — the Cuban missile venture: the appearance of the American Polaris nuclear submarine, a seaborne nuclear-weapon launcher to which the Soviets had virtually no answer. It was to meet this challenge, as well, that the Soviets shifted to forward deployment of their fleet, relying heavily on the development of antisubmarine warfare, despite all the difficulties involved in the latter. Thus, the more general expansion of the Soviet fleet in the pursuit of global flexibility in military-strategic competition primarily with the United States and its allies, combined with the more specific response to the deployment of the Polaris in the Mediterranean Sea, occasioned the opening of the Soviet Mediterranean squadron and, with it, an upgrading of the Middle East in Soviet strategic considerations.[2] The direct connection with the Polaris was evident not only from the timing of the opening of the squadron but also from later developments, for as the Americans placed a modified Polaris and then the Poseidon in the Indian Ocean, thereby targeting Soviet industrial centers from seaborne launchers still further away, Soviet ships began to appear in that arena as well. And, indeed, for all that the Mediterranean squadron was targeted against the American Sixth Fleet and southern Europe, the overall thrust of Soviet strategy as it developed in the 1960s appeared, already, to be south-southeastward, in the direction of the Indian Ocean.[3]

The expansion of the Soviet fleet brought with it other Soviet undertakings, for inasmuch as the Soviets had not developed aircraft carriers (the decision to do so apparently came in the 1960s, the first two such carriers entering service only in the 1970s), Moscow sought not only shore facilities for its fleet but air bases as well for the aircraft necessary for the protection and functioning of the fleet.[4] It was this requirement that transformed the Soviet interest in the Middle East states, specifically Egypt, into a primarily strategic-military one as Moscow sought these support facilities for its Mediterranean squadron. Egypt was the focal point of this venture, mainly because of the relative suitability of its ports and airfields but also because of its geopolitical position in that part of the world and the relative stability of its regime. Thus, prior to the Six-Day War the Soviets sought port facilities in Egypt and by the late 1960s had undertaken the development not only of these facilities but of some six air bases as well.[5] With the expulsion of Soviet military advisers from Egypt in 1972 and the subsequent deterioration of Soviet-Egyptian relations, Moscow sought a strategic alternative in Syria and, later, in Libya, concentrating on naval and air facilities. Given the broader scope of Soviet strategic interests, however, Soviet efforts were not limited to the needs of the Mediterranean squadron and the area of what are known as the Arab confrontation states (in the Arab-Israeli conflict). The same interests at play in this area applied further southward as well. Indeed, with the development of the Poseidon and, particularly, the Americans' Trident missile, a sea-launched missile with a range of 6,000 miles, the Indian Ocean—and its peripheral states—assumed an increasingly important position in Soviet thinking.[6] Moreover, locations further west even in the Mediterranean became feasible targets for Soviet military interests once Moscow succeeded in improving its own means of supporting its fleet and larger numbers of long-range aircraft. Thus, the indecision and instability of the Soviet military presence in the area of the confrontation states, including Syria as well as Egypt, could be compensated for by facilities in states to the west such as Libya and Algeria. Internal differences of opinion in the Soviet Union, specifically within the military, may also have been at play, the relative strategic importance versus the risks of Soviet military involvement in the area possibly evoking controversy. In any case, by the mid-1970s the Soviets' strategic interest in the confrontation states, while still operative, was diminished somewhat, the interest particularly in the Indian Ocean area as the coming confrontation point between Soviet and American strategic forces (and a stepping-off point for crisis intervention in Asia) appearing to have surpassed it at least slightly.

It was the strategic interest above all, however, that dictated the massive Soviet move into and investment in the Middle East–confrontation states area in the 1960s, and it was to serve this interest that the Soviets sought to stabilize, expand and strengthen their political position in the area. Inasmuch as the major strategic interest had appeared only in the 1960s, the basis for political influence had already been laid in the previous period, i.e., the 1950s, when Moscow's interest in the area had been primarily political. At that time Moscow had sought to bolster the neutralist, anti-imperialist tendencies of the Middle Eastern states with the objective of combating and eliminating American influence, both in the region and globally, as well as in international forums such as the United Nations.[7] Once the strategic interest shifted from what might be called a defensive-passive one to an offensive-active search for a Soviet military presence, the political objective became an auxiliary factor. Penetration of the local regimes, expanded influence and where possible friendship treaties were pursued so as to protect and further Soviet military interests. As a result, the 1970s saw, virtually for the first time, not only the Soviet quest for military bases beyond its direct sphere of influence but also the bid for treaties with Egypt, Syria, Iraq, Somalia, India, and other countries where political alliance was desired for the acquisition and maintenance of military facilities. This effort was not successful with Syria, for example, and the treaty with Egypt came, basically, too late (May 1971) to reverse the already apparent deterioration in Soviet-Egyptian political relations which it was, nonetheless, meant to check.

It might be argued, and indeed there apparently were those within the Soviet leadership who did so, that the only political link sufficiently strong to serve Soviet interests on any stable basis could not be created with bourgeois nationalist or even so-called progressive regimes but rather — and only — with Communist governments. Even further, it may have been argued that the ideological interest in the advent of such regimes should take precedence over strategic interests, military objectives playing only a subsidiary role to achieve and protect the ideologically oriented effort. Aside from the *realpolitik* considerations regarding the feasibility and likelihood of achieving this ideological goal, as well as the risk its pursuit might engender to Soviet state (strategic) interests in the region or elsewhere, the answer to this dilemma could be found in ideological formulations themselves. Lenin had once formulated a framework for action in nonindustrialized countries whereby, because of the absence of a genuine or large proletariat, progress towards socialism was to be pursued first by cooperation with bourgeois nationalist elements' struggle against outside imperialist powers and for what was called a national-democratic revolution. The latter, by introducing the bourgeois democratic freedoms, would provide a more conducive atmosphere for Communist action (possibly even a place for them in a coalition), which could then lead to the second stage, socialist revolution. According to this doctrine, local Communists were to join forces with the bourgeois nationalists for the first stage and lead them, from within, onto the next stage. Stalin's rather dogmatic application of this policy in China in the 1920s was a total failure, leading to the virtual destruction of the Chinese Communist party and the general (though not total) abandonment of this theory for some time. Following World War II, for example, certain exceptions notwithstanding, Soviet policy had no room for such compromises; the world was seen as divided into two hostile camps — the capitalist versus the Communist — and the task of Communists was to lead a struggle for socialist revolution even in the underdeveloped world. In the early 1950s, particularly after Stalin's death, this more aggressive approach was moderated by the recognition both of the inherent danger of such a confrontation policy in the nuclear era and also of the possibilities existing within the underdeveloped countries emerging from colonialism and rapidly becoming a "Third World." In support of these countries' tendency to neutralism — a policy which served Moscow's efforts to eliminate Western influence and military presence in the Third World, there was a return to Lenin's approach. Communists were again told to postpone their revolutionary struggle, to be satisfied (as the Soviets were) with an anti-imperialist struggle in alliance with local nationalist, even bourgeois nationalist, forces. There were occasional exceptions to this dictum; in certain cases in which Moscow was under pressure for a more revolutionary position because of a Chinese presence (e.g., the Sudan in the early 1970s) or the chances for success were overwhelming, the risk of Western (U.S.) intervention minimal (such as the PDRY), the orders were different. But on the whole, in the Middle East as elsewhere in the Third World, Moscow's policy meant support of the local government often even to the detriment of the local Communists (e.g., in Egypt where the party was told in 1965 to dissolve itself, its members individually to join Nasser's ruling party; in Syria, where the Communists split over Moscow's orders to accept what was clearly to be a junior position in a purely formal coalition with the ruling Ba'th party).[8] In addition to the Leninist ideological framework, other ideological justifications were preferred, such as the concept of "progressive regimes," "Arab socialism," and the like. What was, in effect, at play, however, was the subordination of ideological interests to the strategic one. This did not mean total neglect of the former; indeed, since the Brest-Litovsk Treaty Russian foreign policy has proceeded on the dual paths of party-ideological-revolutionary activity on the one hand and state-strategic-political activity on the other. Where the two have clashed, or threatened to clash, however, at least in the post-Stalin period, preference has been given to the second path, the major considerations regarding the value of risk-taking along the first path being the objective chances for success and the possibility of outside, particularly American, response.

If the primary Soviet interest in the Middle East is strategic, the political interest instrumental, in service of the strategic interest, and the ideological interest a long-term less operative one, the Soviets' economic interest in the region is open to some speculation. The economic importance of the area for the West, i.e., the growing dependence upon Middle Eastern oil need not predicate a similiar Soviet interest or dependency. The Soviet Union it-

self is one of the world's most important oil producers, while a cardinal rule
of Soviet foreign trade policy has been strictly to avoid dependence upon
outside resources. These two factors, combined, have accounted for the fact
that Moscow imports extremely little Middle Eastern oil and, certain
Western estimates notwithstanding, apparently has no plans to do so in any
significant manner. Rather, for all the expense and difficulty involved, Soviet energy plans are posited upon development of Soviet sources in Siberia
with or without outside (American, Japanese) technological assistance.[9]

Middle Eastern oil and natural gas supplies have been of marginal
economic value to the Soviet Union insofar as they have become part of
package deals that enable the Soviets to acquire these resources on a barter
basis (from Iraq, Syria, and Iran, for example), while selling these same resources themselves on the world market for hard currency. More important, however, has been the indirect Soviet interest in Middle Eastern oil
supplies for Eastern Europe in order to ease, somewhat, the burden upon
the Soviet Union to meet Eastern European demands. Thus East European
importation of Middle Eastern oil could free certain quantities of Soviet oil
for sale on the hard-currency market or for the Soviets' own domestic
uses.[10] Yet, for all that the Soviet Union has encouraged the East Europeans to increase their purchases in the Middle East, no significant shift in
supplies has occurred—in part because the same policy of avoidance of
dependence upon non-Communist suppliers holds for Moscow's satellites
as well as for Moscow, in part because the Soviet Union itself derives some
economic benefit from its oil sales to Eastern Europe at new higher prices.
At most one might speculate that the Soviets do have an interest, nonetheless, in Middle East oil for its East European allies, but the application of
this interest has yet to take on the proportions that would either explain the
massive Soviet investment in the region in the 1960s or take precedence
over the other, specifically the strategic, Soviet interest in the Middle East.

Oil need not constitute a primarily economic interest, however. The
ability to control or influence the flow of Middle Eastern oil upon which
Western Europe, Japan, and even to some extent the Americans are dependent would certainly augment Soviet power in the context of East-West
competition. From this point of view Moscow has indeed sought first of all
to limit Western control or influence over the oil-producers, and, secondly,
to improve its own relations and position with these states. Thus, Soviet
propaganda has concentrated on the nationalization of the Middle East oil
companies, and Soviet activities—diplomatic and trade—have increased,
particularly in the Persian Gulf area. Some progress was made at least in
Soviet-Kuwaiti relations, for example, but Moscow's success with the major
oil powers, Iran and Saudi Arabia, has been virtually negligible, especially
in view of the animosity of the latter and the fear of the former vis-à-vis the

Soviet Union, and the complexities of the inner Gulf as well as inter-Arab relationships themselves. Moreover, given the importance the Americans attach to the unimpaired flow of Middle Eastern oil to world markets and the Soviets' own involvement in these markets, it is not certain that the Soviet leaders are particularly anxious to tamper with the flow of these supplies or risk East-West confrontation over the oil lanes. One might conclude, therefore, that although the Soviet Union does have an interest in Middle Eastern oil, for a variety of reasons, this interest is neither as clear-cut nor as important over the long-run as other, particularly the strategic, interests.

Moscow may have economic interests in the Middle East other than those connected with oil. Although no figures are available, the Soviet Union has become an arms merchant in the area, demanding dollar payments for equipment formerly provided on a generous credit basis to a number of its clients in the area. Such payments were demanded from Egypt as early as 1973 and, although Moscow accorded Syria a long moratorium on the former's military debt, Saudi Arabia reportedly provided cash for partial payment of post-1973 supplies.[11] Similarly, the Soviet air-defense offer to Jordan in 1976 called for hard-currency payments, although the accompanying Soviet demand for the stationing of military personnel in Jordan caused the deal to fall through.[12] Inasmuch as it is difficult to identify cash transfers, or their size, for the purchase of Soviet arms, it is impossible to determine if they are of sufficient economic importance to constitute a motivating factor in Soviet Middle East policy. From one point of view such payments do fall under the general category of the trend, since the mid-1960s, towards more balanced, less one-sided (and unprofitable) Soviet trade relations with Third World countries. Whereas once Soviet military supplies to the Middle East constituted something of an economic burden,[13] cash payments may have changed the situation. Soviet proposals for limitations of the Middle East arms race, however, would suggest that the Soviets do not consider the change significantly lucrative — in any case not sufficiently lucrative to warrant toleration of the growing American role in arms supplies and, also, the risk of nuclearization of the military components of the region.

Judging, therefore, from an economic point of view, the Middle East would appear to be marginal in Soviet thinking, even with regard to oil supplies for Eastern Europe. At the same time, Soviet trade policies reveal a slight shift of Soviet interests south-southeastwards, for the favorable trade and credit terms once offered the confrontation states have given way to demands for a return on the Soviet investment, while the share of the richer oil states, able to pay their way, in overall Soviet trade and oil relations has increased.[14] The promise of greater cooperation with a post-Shah

Iran could in fact convert at least this part of the Middle East into a major economic interest for the Soviet Union, provided that post-Shah Iran alters its emerging policy of hostility toward the Soviet Union.

Factors Affecting Achievement of Soviet Interests in the Region

The pursuit of the various, and changing, Soviet interests was facilitated by a number of factors that contributed to certain successes. The very entrance of the Soviet Union into the Middle East scene in the mid-1950s was made possible by the collapse of imperialist rule in the area, the retreat of the British, and the rise of a Third World neutralist philosophy. Given the limited nature of Soviet interests at this time, the situation was in fact quite conducive to Soviet success. The Soviet Union itself was not perceived by the Arab world as an imperialist power; rather the image of champion of the anti-imperialist struggle had taken hold. Inasmuch as the Soviets' ideological interests were also muted, and the local regimes' claims to progressiveness were accepted by the Kremlin, and inasmuch as Soviet political demands were limited mainly to the neutralists' anti-Western position in international forums and the like without any accompanying demand either for identification with the Soviet Union or a physical (i.e., military) presence, the Soviets could maintain this image. Moreover, the Soviet economic model was attractive to these emerging nations, with its emphasis upon strong central control, state planning, and rapid industrialization. While Moscow had to be careful not to tread on the toes of the landed-interests, as distinct from the vast peasant population, on the question of agrarian reform, the Soviet approach was not doctrinaire at this time. Soviet economic assistance was more than generous, conceived of as an instrument to further Soviet political interests with almost no regard for cost-benefit considerations, return on investment, or even practicality. The purpose was to impress, both the recipient country and the world, by means of large, ostentatious projects.

The West was much less generous from an economic point of view, as demonstrated by the American-Western failure to provide the necessary assistance to Egypt in its Aswan Dam project. Thus, to a certain degree, Western default aided the Soviet penetration effort of the 1950s. This was not entirely a matter of a lack of Western interest; the British Suez venture and the American efforts for a Baghdad Pact demonstrated some interest. But such willingness, and, in the case of Britain, capabilities, were limited, leaving the door open for Soviet generosity. Even later, as the British withdrew from areas further south and east, it could be argued that the Soviets were merely filling a vacuum or were at least assisted by this retreat.

An important contributing factor to the Soviet move into the area was, of course, the conflict situation in the region. Indeed, it was probably the Soviet willingness to support and assist the Arabs in their struggle with Israel which, more than any other factor, enabled Moscow to gain many of its political-strategic objectives. Beginning with the Soviet-backed Czechoslovak arms deal with Egypt in 1955 and Soviet political support in response to the Suez crisis, through the Six-Day War, Soviet resupplies, and direct military assistance in the War of Attrition, an Arab dependency upon Soviet military and political support appeared to have been created. There was a direct correlation between the accommodation of Soviet strategic interests, in the form of naval and air facilities, and Soviet willingness to equip, train, and otherwise assist the Arab military position. Tension in the area, at least Arab-Israeli tensions, appeared to serve Soviet penetration efforts, highlighting, as it did, not only the Arabs' need for Soviet assistance but the polarization of the superpowers' position and America's commitment to the enemy side, Israel. The positive contribution of the conflict situation to Soviet interests was so great that it was even arguable that Moscow actively sought continuation of the conflict, possibly even its aggravation (in the form of the Six-Day War, for example), so as to ensure Moscow's own continued presence in the area.[15]

Yet neither the conflict situation nor many of the other above factors were quite so clear-cut or static; indeed in time, or from certain aspects, they militated, together with other factors, against the Soviets' achievement of their interests. For example, the advantage the Soviets enjoyed because of their identification with the anticolonialist rather than colonialist world was gradually corroded. As their penetration of Middle East, particularly Egyptian, military-security and even political realms increased, with the Soviets attempting to influence events through persons sympathetic or beholden to them, the Arabs gradually began to perceive them as another imperialist power. This image was fortified by the actual Soviet bid for bases, the behavior of Soviet advisors and personnel in the host country, and a Soviet tendency to treat the Arab leaders in an imperial manner, often disregarding their requests or even humiliating them. And, therefore, if in the past Islam worked against Soviet ambitions to improve its position by ideological efforts (or efforts to promote the Communists), even the "progressive" regimes balked at infringement upon their independence. In the case of Egypt, this led to the actual expulsion of the Soviets and abrogation of the mutual friendship treaty; with Syria, this meant refusal to enter such a treaty, and policies contrary to Moscow's preferences with regard to such things as the local Communist party or the Lebanese civil war; in the case of Iraq, it meant refusal to grant the Soviet Union extraterritorial rights for naval facilities or political concessions on the international scene.[16] This Arab independence, even to the point of defying Soviet attempts at arms blackmail, increased significantly with the rising importance of the petro-dollar, and the accompanying rise both in the importance and influence of the oil-rich states, particularly Saudi Arabia.

A factor that further complicated Soviet efforts in the region was the Arab world itself, with its shifting alliances, rivalries, and conflicts. While Soviet friendship with Iraq, for example, produced difficulties for improved Soviet relations with Iran, Iraqi-Syrian animosity much more severely complicated Soviet policies in the area. Similarly, the Syrian-Egyptian and the Egyptian-Sudanese-Libyan relationships, with all their changing component factors, often confronted Moscow with serious policy dilemmas. The Egyptian-Syrian union in 1958, the Egyptian backing for Nimeiry in the days of the abortive leftist coup against the latter in 1971, the Syrian invasion of Lebanon in 1976 are just a few examples. Particularly detrimental to Soviet interests in the region was the rising influence of Saudi Arabia, whose anti-Soviet position carried with it the potential for influencing not only Egypt, for example, but even the loyalties of Syria and the PLO. Nor does the periodic cohesion of the more radical states — such as Libya and Iraq, or Libya, Iraq, and elements of the PLO — necessarily counter this problem, for the radicals' "Rejectionist" position regarding the Arab-Israeli conflict and other issues does not always or entirely suit Moscow's own policies.

Indeed, disagreement between the Soviet Union and its Arab client-states on various issues of substance was another serious limiting factor on Moscow's achievement of its interests. It was not only the Soviets' imperial attitude towards Egypt that led Sadat to expel the Soviet military advisers in 1972, but also — and mainly — Moscow's growing détente with the United States and, in particular, its opposition to another Arab military offensive against Israel (opposition that expressed itself in denial of certain Egyptian arms requests). Similarly, there have been serious Soviet differences with the more radical Arab states and the PLO regarding the issue of a "political" versus a "military" solution to the Arab-Israeli conflict, specifically the matter of the Geneva peace conference and Security Council resolution 242 which carries with it recognition, and the idea of security, for Israel.[17] And, as already mentioned, serious substantive differences arose between Moscow and Damascus over the Lebanese problem. Many of these problems arise, however, because of still another factor which is very much at play with regard to the Middle East, i.e., the global factor or the superpower relationship.

While it was the superpower relationship with its competition, strategic–balance of power and defensive considerations that accounted for the major Soviet investment in the area in the 1960s, it was this same relationship, competition, etc. that limited Moscow's moves and policies in the region. As is the case in almost all Soviet foreign policy decisions, the estimated American response was and is the ultimate consideration in Soviet Middle East calculations. Although Soviet leaders and literature often spoke of applying détente to the Middle East, mainly as a means of limiting the risks of superpower competition there and, following the Yom Kippur War, as a means of at least sharing in the developments involving the area, there is little evidence of any Soviet (or American) linkage of the détente issue with that of the Middle East. The contentions of Sadat, Qaddafi, and others notwithstanding,[18] Soviet behavior particularly during the Yom Kippur War, but also before and after it, strongly suggested that the Kremlin was willing to undertake certain risks to détente which, it calculated, could be handled and in time overcome. Much more limiting, however, was the risk of superpower confrontation; this was to be avoided at all costs, even though such a dictate created serious problems for Soviet-Arab relations. From this point of view Soviet risk taking was great in the late 1960s, when Soviet involvement was at its height, but even at this time Moscow sought to restrain the Arabs, both by control of types of armaments supplied and by persuasion, so as to avoid all-out Arab-Israeli war and the concomitant danger of Soviet-American confrontation.[19] It was on this issue, in essence, that Sadat parted with the Soviets, Soviet caution persisting even when Moscow decided to renew arms supplies to Egypt in early 1973 in view of Sadat's determination to act with or without the Soviet Union. It was this caution that prompted the Soviets once again to risk disfavor in the eyes of the Arabs by pressing the latter to agree to a cease-fire almost immediately after the opening of hostilities in October 1973 and continuing these pressures until a Soviet-American cease-fire was more or less imposed, based on resolution 242 and calling for negotiations—both of which had, at least until then, been unacceptable conditions for such parties as Iraq, Syria, and the PLO. The Soviets did send massive material assistance to the Arab war effort, but this represented compensatory action designed (unsuccessfully, as it turned out) not only to preserve Moscow's prestige in the region but also to prevent an Arab defeat of the dimensions which might precipitate a call for Soviet military intervention.[20] Given the continued volatility of the Arab-Israeli conflict even after the war, and the growing American involvement in the region, this major limiting factor remained operative.

Thus, the very conflict situation that had facilitated Soviet entry into the area tended in time to become extremely dangerous, even counterproductive. If the conflict could have been strictly controlled it might have retained its value for Soviet purposes; but given the highly volatile nature of the conflict itself, declining Soviet influence over its Arab clients (notwithstanding arms blackmail attempts), particularly with the rise of Arab independence in connection with the petro-dollar, as well as the increased American involvement, the Arab-Israel conflict began to lose much of its usefulness. In part the Soviets themselves were responsible for this, for their reluctance to fulfill the role of "war-maker" greatly reduced their usefulness to the Arabs. And if they were unwilling to provide the war option, they were virtually unable to provide anything else. They could not play as potentially an effective role as the Americans in bringing about a settlement inasmuch as they, unlike the Americans, had no leverage over Israel. Nor could they significantly compete with the Americans in the peaceful area of economic assistance once the Americans decided to move into this sphere of activity. Not only Egypt but even Syria and Iraq were to become somewhat less certain Soviet allies from this point of view. These problems did not, however, outweigh the negative aspects of maintenance of the conflict situation, but, as we shall see below, they did affect Soviet behavior in the area.

Another factor that may affect Soviet policy in the Middle East lies within the highly speculative area of Soviet domestic considerations. Possible linkage between domestic Soviet economic considerations and economic ventures abroad can be and has been demonstrated to a large degree, both in the area of the energy problem and the armaments issue.[21] Similarly one can posit a number of Soviet military and political interests upon which Soviet foreign policies are based. It is much more difficult, however, to connect these relatively objective findings with the existence of differences of opinion within the Soviet decision-making elite or with domestic disputes which have played a role one way or another in Soviet policy towards the Middle East, for example. That the massive Soviet involvement in the Middle East was generally unpopular amongst the Soviet public was evident from the manner in which Soviet media handled the subject, but public opinion as such probably had little to no effect on decision making in this area.[22] The opinions expressed by various research institutes and journals, as well as the daily press, may be of somewhat greater importance, insofar as these organs may be the domain or under the influence of a particular person or group within the ruling elite.[23] Differences, even to the point of conflicting views, can indeed be found in Soviet publications and propaganda, although it is very difficult to determine whether these constitute natural variations intended by the regime, reflecting possibly some division of labor, dictated perhaps by the expected audience, or if they are indeed expressions of genuine disputes or differences of opinion.

There would appear to be or have been some disagreement with Soviet

Middle East policy from the ideological quarter, i.e., from persons object-
ing to the preference for government-to-government, including bourgeois
governments, relations at the expense of local Communist and radical national liberation movements. Shelepin was identified with this point of
view, and while he was head of the Soviet trade union movement, the trade
union daily *Trud* appeared to express a dissenting view on the massive Soviet military involvement in Egypt, for example, while giving more attention to ideological issues connected with progressive groupings and decisions, specifically the Palestinian issue and the PLO.[24] Similarly, Podgorny
and Ponomarev tended toward more radical statements with regard to the
Middle East, including more frequent references to the Palestinians, when
compared with Brezhnev and Kosygin.[25] This may have been due to the
role of these two leaders with regard to national liberation movements and
nonruling Communist parties. By the same token, there may have been
those representing the economic sphere who demanded greater return on
the Soviet investment in the Middle East, while there may have been
military figures who expressed concern over the danger of Soviet-American
confrontation in this region, over the problem of advanced types of Soviet
weapons systems falling into Western hands because of Arab failures, or
simply over the diversion of resources to this venture as distinct from other
branches or theaters of Soviet military operations.[26] Arab sources have
spoken of serious internal Soviet opposition, for example, to the Soviet
assumption of responsibility for Egyptian air defenses in 1970.[27] On the
other hand, there may have been those within the military, for example,
who welcomed the opportunity to test new systems and techniques, or those
who sought this opportunity for expansion of the fleet and support facilities.[28] As distinct from the ideological issue, however, differences of views
on these subjects are almost impossible to prove, with the exception of an
occasional unusual remark in the military press. Those journals and even
personalities most identified with détente do appear to have been most interested in a negotiated settlement in the Middle East, while organs or persons identified with Russian nationalism or anti-Semitism (in the latter
case, Ukrainian publications, for example) appear to take a more aggressive line with regard to the Soviet presence in the region. While one
might contend that differences such as these do exist, one can only guess as
to the role they have actually played as factors determining policy decisions.
Moreover, the Soviets themselves tend to hint at if not actually propagate
the view that differences of opinion exist, probably as a tactic to influence
the other side to a particular position or at the least to justify certain Soviet
positions. The former was indeed a tactic used in conversations with PLO
leaders, as well as with Israel in rumored contacts over the years.[29]

The Soviet Position

A stock-taking of the Soviet position in the Middle East following twenty-five years of activity, and as the Brezhnev era draws to a close, reveals a sharply ascending and then descending curve that tends in the direction of overall failure. This failure is by no means complete, however. In the political-ideological sphere one could point to the Soviet treaty with Iraq, the legalization of the Syrian Communist party and its inclusion in a front with the ruling Ba'th party. One could also point to the Marxist orientation of South Yemen, improved Soviet relations with Libya, Kuwait, Jordan, and, potentially Iran, as well as significantly improved relations with Turkey, and an identification with the PLO as that movement has gained in world recognition. Yet, judging from the point of view of success or failure in achieving Soviet political-ideological interests in the area, the conclusions are less positive. In the country that was the very cornerstone of Soviet efforts in the region, Egypt, the failure has been most dramatic and almost total. Egypt abrogated the 1971 Friendship treaty in 1976, purged itself of Soviet sympathizers to a very large degree, moved against the already illegal local Communists and local leftists, as well as severely curbed all contact with the Soviet Union, frequently and violently criticizing the latter's policies on an almost regular basis while building its foreign policies on a westward orientation.

In the case of Syria, as we have seen, the Soviets have been unsuccessful in achieving sufficient political influence to curb Syrian independence or even significantly influence the policies of Damascus. The local Communists are but *very* junior partners in the political sphere, subject to periodic restrictions and suppressions. Moreover, for all that Syria replaced Egypt as Moscow's major ally amongst the confrontation states, the demonstrative independence of Damascus continuously raises the possibility (in Moscow's considerations) of a westward turn by Syria in the style of Cairo (and possibly in alliance with Cairo and Riyadh), despite the leftist more radical orientation of the Syrian regime. Soviet inroads with Iraq are much deeper, but both Iraq and Libya constitute highly problematic and erratic political partners, the latter offering no room for progress in the ideological sphere and both staunchly (and effectively) resisting Soviet controls or even influence. Moreover, Soviet policy with regard to the Eritrean problem raised serious problems for Moscow's relationship with these radical states. Even in the case of the apparently successful developments in South Yemen, the Soviet position is complicated by interests in North Yemen and a desire not to provoke Saudi Arabia, in view of nascent Soviet hopes for improved relations with Saudi Arabia. Relations with the PLO are still more problematic, for the PLO is neither sufficiently strong, stable, nor united enough on its own to be of great use to the Soviets, nor is it by any means totally dependent upon or even responsive to the Soviet Union. Only in the cases of Kuwait and Jordan has Soviet progress been relatively steady, but, in keeping with the limitations even of Soviet expectations regarding these states, this progress has not been of major significance, particularly with regard to a future shift towards a Soviet orientation on the part of either of them. The overthrow of the Shah of Iran was a most positive development for Soviet relations with Iran, provided Moscow manages to find the correct formula for reaching the new Islamic Republic (despite the local leftist opposition to the new regime's policies and oppression). Progress with Turkey, on the other hand, has been extremely significant, if still insufficient to have occasioned a major reorientation of this NATO state.

The vicissitudes of Soviet Middle East fortunes point, on balance, to a Soviet failure to achieve stable political and/or ideological positions in the Middle East from which Moscow's other interests might be successfully pursued. If, however, one were to reduce Soviet objectives from that of influence to something less ambitious, a case could be made for a certain Soviet success. For a major political Soviet achievement over the past twenty-five years has been the at least informal recognition of the Soviet Union as a factor to be considered in the Middle East. It is true that in the period of Henry Kissinger, American policy sought to ignore or undermine this development, and with regard to the Arab-Israeli conflict the Soviet role appeared to become so marginal that some could argue against any need to consider Moscow at all in this context.[30] Yet, the Carter administration would appear to have rejected this estimate, for even though the Soviet Union is greatly limited in its ability either to act or influence the actors in the region, it still plays a role by throwing its weight behind one actor or another, weight that is not entirely without at least potential importance given the achievement of some of Moscow's strategic interests in the region.

The Soviet military presence in the Mediterranean has indeed become a significant one. While still only a fraction of the size of Moscow's more vital Baltic fleet and greatly limited by demands upon the Black Sea fleet to which it belongs, the Mediterranean squadron has a more or less permanent roster of approximately sixty ships. While there are varying opinions as to the relative strength (and speed and versatility) of this contingent in comparison with the Americans' Sixth Fleet, the deployment of this squadron, complemented by some twenty to thirty additional vessels in times of crisis, can at least serve as a check on the Americans' freedom of action. The same can be said for the Soviet fleet further south, in the Red Sea–Indian Ocean area, although here the Soviet presence is much more limited, probably because of the strain upon the Black Sea fleet as a whole. Until more ships become available, this deployment further south, which

usually consists of approximately twenty vessels — not all of which are warships — will not constitute a serious force.[31]

At the same time, these strategic achievements have not been totally ac-
commodated by the necessary auxiliary and support facilities. In this sense
Soviet strategic interests have not been entirely achieved inasmuch as the
port and air facilities lost in Egypt, as well as Somalia, have not been fully
compensated for by moves elsewhere. Neither the Libyans nor even the
Syrians have been as cooperative as the Egyptians, nor have the Iraqis — or,
to date, the Ethiopians — been as forthcoming as the Somalis once were.
While Soviet requirements have undergone certain changes as a result of
technological and military development, such things as the deployment of
two Soviet aircraft carriers (rotating in all four Soviet fleets) have not
eliminated the continued strategic problem.

Moreover, the relative price the Soviet Union has to pay for political and
strategic benefits has significantly increased when compared with the actual
return received. Given the increased demands *and* risks involved in a Soviet
Middle Eastern presence, as well as the slight shift of at least future Soviet
priorities south-southeastward deep into the Indian Ocean, the Soviets
have shown signs of reluctance to make the necessary concessions — or pay
the price necessary — in order fully to regain their former position in the
region.[32] The lack of Soviet willingness to compromise with Egypt without
the latter's full renunciation of the United States, Moscow's risk of its
Syrian link during the Lebanese crisis, and its exaggerated demands regarding a Jordanian air defense system all point to this conclusion. In view
of these relatively new circumstances, particularly the evolution of the
limitations upon Soviet policy outlined in the previous section, the Soviets
would appear to have opted for what might be termed a minimal rather
than maximal policy, or the optimal obtainable within the present context.
This would entail two interrelated objectives: maintenance of a Soviet
presence at not too great a cost; and prevention of a total American
takeover of the area.

Such Soviet objectives could be served by a settlement of the Arab-Israeli
conflict, so long as the Soviet Union itself were a party to the settlement. As
we have seen, the Arab-Israeli conflict no longer plays the positive role it
once did in the achievement of Soviet interests and may even play a negative role in today's circumstances. Soviet thinking along these lines was apparent even in the pre-1973 two-power and four-power efforts for a settlement;[33] it probably became still more definite following the Yom Kippur
War as the negative aspects of the ongoing conflict became more acute. A
settlement would eliminate the risks associated with the conflict while,
possibly, reversing some of the negative trends affecting the Soviet presence
in the region. Specifically, Soviet participation in a settlement, particularly

in its guarantees, would provide international, formal recognition and legitimation of the Soviet Middle Eastern presence. Such formalities, however apparently superfluous, have traditionally been of importance to the Soviets, as evidenced by their persistent efforts to achieve a European security conference to formalize, permantly, East Europe's post–World War II borders. Moreover, such recognition would provide greater stability to the Soviet presence than the present, uncertain need to rely on the good will of host Arab regimes. Thus, surveillance flights in the region (including coverage of the Mediterranean area), port facilities, and the like would be ensured for the purposes of peace keeping rather than the result of a separate agreement with one leader or another. Navigational rights, as the Soviets themselves have suggested, might well be included, providing future assurances for these Soviet interests as well. That such assurances might also entail limitations probably would not interfere with Soviet interests inasmuch as their own presence, at least at sea, lags behind that of the Americans, limitations affecting also the Americans being therefore welcome. Similarly, Moscow itself has proposed limitations on the arms race following a settlement, presumably because of America's growing role in this sphere, as well as the danger of nuclearization of the region.

A settlement without Soviet participation, i.e., a "pax Americana," would not serve Soviet interests even if it did mean reduction or elimination of certain negative aspects of the situation. Yet Soviet participation itself is not an easy matter and Moscow's quest for a role in the negotiating process has involved it in a number of contradictions. The very Soviet interest in a negotiated settlement evoked the ire of the "Rejectionist" Arabs from the outset. But even amongst the more moderate elements, it was encumbent upon Moscow to champion at least close to the Arabs' maximum demands so as to offer the Arabs something beyond the more limited agreements the Americans proposed. Increasing support of the more radical Arab demands became necessary not only to distinguish Moscow from Washington but also in order to prove to the United States (and Israel) the absolute necessity of bringing the Soviet Union into the settlement process as the controller of the war option. (In time this became also a tactic to isolate and pressure pro-American elements such as Egypt.) Yet this identification with the more radical demands often prompted Soviet support for, or at least tolerance of, positions contrary to its own interests or policy. This was the case, for example, after the Israeli-Egyptian Interim Agreement of 1975 when Moscow endorsed the Syrian initiative to bring the Palestinian issue before the Security Council in hopes of obtaining a replacement for (correction to) resolution 242. The Soviets themselves preferred the Geneva conference over the UN as the forum for such discussions, and it did not believe it possible, or expedient, to tamper with resolution 242 at this time.

More serious perhaps was Moscow's alignment with the Rejection Front in response to Sadat's 1977 peace initiative and the 1979 Egyptian-Israeli Peace Treaty, primarily because of Syria's opposition to Egypt's move and, of course, the exclusion of Moscow itself. The Soviets had little choice but to support the extremist view that opposed all negotiations, resolution 242, even the Geneva conference. In all such cases the Soviet line itself did not undergo a change; rather support for the radicals formed merely one component of a dualistic Soviet position, the other being the consistent advocation of a settlement, through multilateral negotiations, to result in recognition of Israel within secure borders (specified as those of prewar 1967) as well as a Palestinian state. Maintenance of the Soviet position despite and even in argument with its more radical clients (such as the PLO) strongly suggested that Moscow was indeed committed to these positions as the most realistic and feasible ones possible. Nonetheless, here too, a certain tactic was involved, for the Soviets had to convince Israel and the U.S. that they were reasonable partners for negotiations and, therefore, a positive, rather than negative, obstructionist factor for resumption of the Geneva conference. Part of this tactic was a certain carrot and stick approach to Israel, declarations of Soviet willingness to provide guarantees and recognize Israel's 1949–1967 borders often appearing when Soviet participation in negotiations seemed imminent or likely, a borderline position such as press references to the 1947 partition plan (and its borders) when Moscow was totally excluded from the picture.[34] Yet, similar tactics were used with the PLO and the Arab states themselves, while the overall consistency of the Soviet line suggested that the basic Soviet position on a settlement, multifaceted as it was, remained relatively constant. The need to prove, at one time, Soviet usefulness and loyalty to the Arabs, the essentiality of the Soviet Union to the negotiating process, as well as Moscow's potential for positive contribution, or at least nonobstructionist behavior, posed a tactical dilemma for the Soviet Union, complicated still further by regional considerations and objectives not directly connected with the Arab-Israeli conflict.

For all that Soviet policies in the Middle East, particularly in the Arab-Israeli context, have become reactive rather than dominating and directing them, tending on balance even to failure rather than significant achievement, there is little reason to believe that the Soviet interest in the overall region of the Middle East, including the Persian Gulf and northern Indian Ocean will in fact decline in the near future. Future Soviet policies for, and position within, the Middle East will most likely be subject to most of the factors operative until now and dictated by most of the same interests. In both cases, the East-West balance of power and the East-West relationship constitute the major determinant, although shifts or reorientations within and amongst the local regimes continue to play a great role. While the overall direction of Soviet interests lies in the area of the Indian Ocean, a strengthened position in the Horn of Africa, for example, might also benefit the Soviets in their struggle for influence in the Arab-Israeli context. The latter would appear, however, to be declining in preference, while those factors that have limited Soviet influence, even at periods of peak Soviet involvement, would appear to be strengthening rather than diminishing. Changes in the Soviet leadership might well occasion a shift in Soviet tactics, support or identification with one group or another changing, possibly even precipitating, Soviet initiatives in apparently new directions. Yet the objective circumstances both of the East-West relationship and of overall Soviet interests are relatively constant, suggesting that even with the advent of a more (or less) adventuristic Soviet regime, the options and actual policies will be adjustable in only a very limited way.

Notes

1. Thomas Wolfe, "Evolution of Soviet Military Policy," in John W. Strong, ed., *The Soviet Union Under Brezhnev and Kosygin* (New York: Van Nostrand Reinhold, 1971), pp. 75–92.

2. For a discussion of the development of the Soviet fleet and the influence of the Polaris, see Michael MccGuire, "The Background to Soviet Naval Developments," *The World Today,* vol. 27, no. 3 (March 1971), pp. 93–103; Michael MccGuire, "The Evolution of Soviet Naval Policy: 1960–1974," in MccGuire, ed., *Soviet Naval Policy: Objectives and Constraints* (New York: Praeger, 1975); or John Ericson, *Soviet Military Power* (London: Royal United Services Institute, 1971), pp. 53–60; Geoffrey Jukes, *The Indian Ocean in Soviet Naval Policy,* Adelphi Paper no. 87, 1972; or Richard Ackley, "Sea-Based Strategic Forces: Mid-term Security for an Era of Nuclear Proliferation," Halifax (Dalhousie Seminar), 1974, pp. 10, 18. For Soviet references, see A. K. Koslov, "The United States in the Mediterranean: New Realities," *SSLA: Ekonomika, Politika, Ideologia,* no. 4 (April 1972), pp. 32–33; Admiral Gorshkov, "Navies in War and Peace," *Morskoi sbornik,* no. 2 (1973), p. 20, or in *Pravda,* 28 July 1974, and *Krasnaya zvezda,* 22 March 1974.

3. There is some controversy among Western observers over the authenticity of Soviet concern regarding the American strategic threat from the Indian Ocean because of the the difficulties involved in submarine detection and the variety of possibilities open to the Americans for launching positions against the USSR. See Commander Thomas A. Brooks, "Soviet Carrier Strategy," *U.S. Naval Institute Proceedings,* vol. 100, no. 4 (854: 1974), p. 103, or Bradford Dismukes, "Roles and Missions of Soviet Naval General-Purpose Forces in Wartime: Pro SSBN Operations'?" (Arlington, Va: Center for Naval Analyses, August 1974).

4. See J. C. Hurewitz, *The Persian Gulf* (New York: Foreign Policy Association, 1974), pp. 44–47; Arthur Davidson Baker III, "Soviet Major Combatants," *U.S.*

Naval Institute Proceedings, vol. 100, no. 4 (854: 1974), pp. 47–48; or Norman Polnar, "The Soviet Aircraft Carrier," *loc. cit.,* vol. 100, no. 3 (853: 1974), pp. 145–61.

5. George Dragnich, "The Soviet Union's Quest for Naval Facilities in Egypt Prior to the June War of 1967," unpublished paper, Washington, D.C., 1974, p. 19, also links this move to the 1961 Soviet loss of its submarine base in Albania.

6. See notes 2 and 3 above.

7. See Walter Laqueur, *The Struggle for the Middle East* (Washington: Macmillan, 1969), pp. 7–13, or Malcolm MacIntosh, "Soviet Policy Towards the Middle East," *Bulletin on Soviet and East European Jewish Affairs,* no. 4 (December 1969), pp. 32–33.

8. See John Cooley, "The Shifting Sands of Arab Communism," *Problems of Communism,* vol. 24, no. 2 (1975), p. 33; Robert Freedman, "The Soviet Union and the Communist Parties of the Arab World," unpublished paper, Milwaukee, Wisconsin, 1974, pp. 28–29. For Arab Communist disagreement see Kerim Mroue, "The Arab National Liberation Movement," *World Marxist Review,* vol. 16, no. 2 (1973), p. 70, and Victor Tyagunenko, "Trends, Motive Forces of the National Liberation Revolution," *loc. cit.,* vol. 16, no. 6 (1973), p. 124, which are seen by Freedman as a polemic on this issue. See also A. S. Becker and A. L. Horelick, *Soviet Policy in the Middle East* (Rand Corporation, 1970), pp. 30–35.

9. Dina Spechler and Martin Spechler, "The Soviet Union and the Oil Weapon," in Yaacov Ro'i, ed., *The Limits of Power: The Soviet Union in the Middle East* (London: Croom Helm, 1978); A. S. Becker, "Oil and the Persian Gulf in Soviet Policy in the 1970s," in M. Confino and S. Shamir, eds., *The USSR and the Middle East* (Israel Universities Press, 1973), pp. 174–85; Franklyn D. Holzman, "Soviet Trade and Aid Policies," in J. C. Hurewitz, ed., *Soviet-American Rivalry in the Middle East* (New York: Academy of Political Science, 1969), pp. 104–20; Robert Hunter, *The Soviet Dilemma in the Middle East,* Adelphi Papers nos. 59, 60 (1969).

10. Becker, "Oil and the Persian Gulf in Soviet Policy," p. 181. See also Marshall Goldman, *Détente and Dollars: Doing Business With The Soviets* (New York: Basic Books, 1975).

11. *New York Times,* 20 and 22 October 1973, 4 February 1974. INA (Iraqi News Agency), 26 April 1974; DPA, 13 April 1974 (Sadat interview); *Le Monde,* 21 December 1973, 31 March–1 April 1974, 18 April 1974; MENA, 22 September and 8 October 1974 (Sadat interviews).

12. MENA, 20 June 1977 (Jordanian military spokesman).

13. Gur Ofer, "The Economic Burden of Soviet Involvement in the Middle East," *Soviet Studies,* vol. 24, no. 3 (January 1973), pp. 329–47.

14. Gur Ofer, "Economic Aspects of Soviet Involvement in the Middle East," in Ro'i, ed., *The Limits of Power.*

15. The Soviet Union did play a role in precipitating the Six-Day War by providing reports of Israeli force concentrations on the Israeli-Syrian border. For various analyses of Soviet motivation see Yaacov Ro'i, *From Encroachment to Involvement, A Documentary Study of Soviet Policy in the Middle East,* 1945–1973 (New York: John Wiley and Sons, 1974), pp. 436–38; A. Horelick, "Soviet Policy in the Middle East," in P. Y. Hammond, *Political Dynamics in the Middle East* (New York: Elsevier, 1972), pp. 581–92. The Arabs claim, however, that the Soviets also sought to prevent them from actually going to war; Moscow probably neither expected nor

welcomed the results of the war inasmuch as Soviet prestige in the Arab world was negatively affected and the risk of superpower confrontation increased.

16. For fuller discussion of such issues, see Galia Golan, *Yom Kippur and After: The Soviet Union and the Middle East Crisis* (Cambridge: Cambridge University Press, 1977); Galia Golan, "Syria and the Soviet Union Since the Yom Kippur War," *Orbis,* vol. 21, no. 4 (winter 1976), pp. 777–802.

17. See note 16 and Galia Golan, *The Soviet Union and the PLO,* Adelphi Paper no. 131 (1977).

18. See Galia Golan, "The Arab-Israeli Conflict in Soviet-U.S. Relations: Is Détente Relevant?," in Ro'i, ed., *The Limits of Power.*

19. See Jon Glassman, *Arms for the Arabs: The Soviet Union and War in the Middle East* (Baltimore: Johns Hopkins University Press, 1975) and Golan, *Yom Kippur and After.*

20. For analysis of Soviet policy during the Yom Kippur War, see ibid.

21. Ofer, and Spechler and Spechler, both in Ro'i, ed., *The Limits of Power.*

22. See T. H. Friedgut, "The Domestic Image of Soviet Involvement in the Arab-Israeli Conflict," in Ro'i, ed., *The Limits of Power;* Golan, *Yom Kippur and After;* Dina Spechler, "Internal Influences on Soviet Foreign Policy, Elite Opinion and the Middle East," Research Paper no. 18 (Jerusalem: Soviet and East European Research Centre, 1977).

23. Oded Eran, "The Soviet Perception of Influence: The Case of the Middle East," in Ro'i, ed., *The Limits of Power;* Ilana Dimant, *Soviet Involvement in the Middle East* (Boulder, Colo.: Westview Press, 1978); Galia Golan, "Internal Pressures and Soviet Foreign Policy Decisions," unpublished paper, Jerusalem, 1973.

24. Ilana Dimant, *"Pravda* and *Trud—*Divergent Attitudes Towards the Middle East," Research Paper no. 3 (Jerusalem: Soviet and East European Research Centre, 1972).

25. Golan, *The Soviet Union and the PLO.*

26. Ilana Dimant-Kass, "The Soviet Military and Soviet Policy in the Middle East 1970–1973," *Soviet Studies,* vol. 24, no. 4 (1974), pp. 502–21; Uri Ra'anan, "The USSR and the Middle East: Some Reflections on the Soviet Decision-Making Process," *Orbis,* vol. 17, no. 3 (1973), pp. 946–77.

27. Muhammed Heikal, *The Road to Ramadan* (London: Fontana/Collins, 1976), pp. 83–86; *al-Nahar* (Beirut), 1 March 1974.

28. Dimant, "The Soviet Military."

29. See *Akhbar al-Yom,* 23 April 1977; *al-Asuba al-Arabi,* 9 May 1977 for Palestinian accounts.

30. For example, Abraham Becker, "Moscow and the Middle East Settlement: A Role for Soviet Guarantees?" *Middle East Review,* no. 8, spring/summer 1976, pp. 52–57.

31. Jukes, *The Indian Ocean in Soviet Naval Policy,* and D. O. Verall, "The Soviet Navy in the Indian Ocean," Halifax (Dalhousie Seminar), 1974, pp. 53–54. The Soviet naval presence in the Indian Ocean is drawn from the Far Eastern fleet, probably for this reason. The Suez Canal, therefore, is not as great a military interest as once thought. See above sources on this point as well.

32. An exception to this is Turkey, the importance of which has not receded.

33. See Lawrence Whetten, *The Canal War* (Cambridge, Mass.: MIT University Press, 1974), pp. 67–115, 340–61; chapters by P. M. Dadant and Ciro Zippo in Willard A. Beling, *The Middle East: Quest for an American Policy* (Albany: State University of New York Press, 1973), pp. 169–236; Martin Indyk, "Israel and Egypt in the October 1973 War: The Effects of Political and Military Dependence on Small Powers in Conflict," unpublished paper, Canberra, 1974, pp. 13–14.

34. For a more detailed analysis of this aspect of Moscow's position, see Golan, *The Soviet Union and the PLO.*

6

Africa

William F. Gutteridge

By June 1978 the magnitude of the Soviet Union's involvement in Africa left little doubt that it was the result of a deliberate strategy. The fluctuating fortunes of Russia's various interventions at different points in the African continent had up to that time left the more objective observers and scholars with reservations about her degree of commitment in the region. In a sense even after the strategy had, as it were, been revealed by a series of actions, the reservations remained, for it was not even then clear that any outside power could in the end emerge as the victor or general beneficiary of such a confused and unpredictable situation.

In spite of setbacks—almost as many failures as successes in terms of the establishment of governments responsive to Soviet influence—the USSR seems over a period of twenty years to have learned gradually how to exploit tensions and divisions in Africa to her advantage within the context of a world strategy aimed essentially at restricting the freedom of action of the West and limiting its influence. Only after the Angolan intervention in 1975–1976 did Russia finally emerge as the leading imperialist power in a new scramble for Africa.

The last scramble for Africa in the nineteenth century was, at least nominally, ended by the Treaty of Berlin in 1884, which allocated spheres of influence between competing colonial powers. Now these powers, primarily Britain, France, Belgium, and West Germany, are, except for France, reluctant to become involved again. This time, however, African states are themselves participants in the competition and by their rivalries create opportunities for external involvement.

The critical cases in Black Africa, which have given Russia, in particular, the cue, began with the civil war in Angola in 1975–1976. There two longstanding guerrilla movements, the FNLA led by Holden Roberto and UNITA led by Jonas Savimbi, had a measure of Western backing, prompted in the first case by General Mobutu from Zaire: the MPLA then invited Soviet-supported Cuban intervention which, partly as a reaction against South African assistance to UNITA in the south, attracted the recognition of most of the OAU member states when a government was established. This left the area with a potential East-West conflict with the two power groups supporting, respectively, Angola and Zaire.

Correspondingly on the east coast, in the Horn of Africa, Somalia brought the Russians in to help them to realize pan-Somali aspirations in Ethiopia and Kenya. As described later, Ethiopia's military regime in turn invited the Russians and Cubans to help them, following the withdrawal of American military aid, and by so doing placed the Soviet Union in a dilemma, the full consequences of which have yet to be seen.

Elsewhere in Africa local conflicts stimulated Russian military aid. In the former Spanish Sahara the Polisario movement brought Morocco and Algeria into more or less open confrontation, with France and the USA supporting one and the USSR the other. The rejection of Russian support by President Sadat in Egypt encouraged Colonel Qadaffy of Libya, though a profoundly anti-communist Moslem, to enter into a close military alliance with Moscow. Moscow in its turn, in an attempt to outflank Egypt, tried unsuccessfully from 1971 onwards to bring about the overthrow of General Nimeiry in Khartoum. This resulted in a reemphasis on Western links with Egypt and the Sudan.

The situation was further confused as it became apparent that not only were African countries often fostering opposition in their neighbors with outside support, but that the Marxist-Leninist states, established with communist support, were not always what they seemed. Judged by the development of Mozambique since independence from the Portuguese, governments like that of Samora Machel were likely to be more characteristically African nationalist than communist. Nevertheless, for the time being their affinity lay eastwards rather than westwards largely because the West, consisting mostly of former colonial powers, could not "win." The critical issue remained how African independence could be consolidated and the status of client state avoided. As the struggle for control over the mineral resources of Southern Africa became more acute during 1978, especially in face of the uncertainties about the future in the short term of Rhodesia and the Shaba province of Zaire and in the longer term of South Africa, so Soviet policy seemed to become more assertive. Nevertheless there were still signs of nervousness born of an awareness of their comparative lack of experience in Africa, which has seemed an especially baffling continent to Russians, particularly when dealing with leaders like Amin.

The fact is that Black Africa did not become a serious concern of Soviet foreign policy until the end of the 1950s. Earlier interest had been based upon the general revolutionary assumption that oppressed African peoples would rise against colonial authority everywhere. The emergence of active liberation movements after the Second World War did not, to begin with, attract much Soviet interest and Russia was in no position effectively to exploit the immediate postindependence difficulties of many African states. When the Soviets did attempt this in the Congo in 1960, they suffered an almost immediate rebuff with the expulsion of their embassy from Leopoldville.

Earlier, while the opportunity provided by the socialist inclinations of Kwame Nkrumah in Ghana and Sekou Touré in Guinea was cautiously welcomed, the Soviet Union clearly waited for proof that the independence of these leaders from London and Paris was real before committing itself to any substantial economic involvement.

In retrospect, the cautiousness of the Soviet approach to Nkrumah revealed a great deal about Russia's awareness of its limited experience of Africa: this was certainly still operative at the end of 1965 when UDI in Rhodesia might have been thought to have provided it with a decisive advantage as the champion of independent Black Africa.

In the case of Ghana the Soviet Union was applying the test of economic freedom, but as this in the end proved difficult to assess the Soviets thereafter switched attention to foreign policy as the prime means of determining an African nation's stance. This was in a way a reversal of Marxist interpretation and indicated what was to become a continuing emphasis on the political factor. Occasional references by Nkrumah to the different forms that colonialism and imperialism could take did not exactly reassure the Russians. Moreover, his pan-African ideals and emphasis on the liberation of Africa as a task for Africans seemed alien to communist principles.

It was not Ghanaian but Guinean independence that prompted a full Soviet commitment to Africa. Guinea's assertion of freedom from de Gaulle's France was seen as a sufficient proof of rejection of the continuing economic benefits of colonialism. Guinea's leader, Sekou Touré, in his turn felt free for his own purposes to support aspects of Soviet foreign policy, especially proposals for disarmament, and Khrushchev at last felt that he was making progress in Africa. Nevertheless the understanding displayed by the newly established African Institute of the Soviet Academy of Sciences was still slight. Its credibility was not assisted by Sekou Touré's assertion, apropos the suggested establishment of a communist party in Guinea, that communism was not the way for Africa.

While trade and aid, including allegedly snowplows, flowed to tropical Guinea, the Congo crisis in 1960 provided the Soviet Union with a more realistic African experience. In that country, even though the Soviet Union was not guiltless, Russian and African perceptions of colonialist intrigue tended to coincide. Ironically, in the light of events in 1977 and 1978 in the

Shaba province of Zaire, the Soviet Union attempted to get the United Nations to assert its right to intervene to end the attempt at secession by what was then Katanga.

It was at this point that the Soviet Union first became concerned with the Chinese challenge: the two communist powers were naturally both interested in the same African countries — those with potentially "progressive" regimes. Russian morale was bolstered by the division of the Mali Federation in August 1960, which facilitated the condemnation of the Senegalese for responding to French collusion. It was, however, Nigerian independence that forced the Soviet Union to reconsider its position vis-à-vis those countries that did not necessarily want to cut off ties with former colonial masters or seek to establish a socialist system.

It is unlikely that Russian influence played any significant part in bringing about the repudiation of the Anglo-Nigerian defense agreement in 1962, but a publicly lukewarm attitude to this act (which was described as a "paper gesture") suggests that by that time the division of Africa into the Casablanca and Monrovia groups of states was seen as ideologically and practically more important to Moscow than a particular embarrassment of a former colonial power. The hardening of the line between different categories of African states meant in one sense that the Russians now felt that they could distinguish accurately between those African leaders who were incurably bourgeois and those who were not. They were, however, reluctant to come down firmly against any particular regime and to sever ties with it. Such tactics were symptomatic of a new pragmatism on the part of the USSR without which any progress in dealing with Africa would have been almost impossible. Nevertheless there was a concentrated Soviet attack on the credentials, as free African states, of Senegal, the Ivory Coast, and Nigeria. But these countries were thought not to have made a final choice between socialism and capitalism, and there were attempts to penetrate and divide the bourgeoisie, especially in Nigeria.

Apart from the Congo, Guinea provided the Russians with their first real experience of the unpredictability of Africa. The sudden and fairly obviously justified charge that the communists were interfering in Guinea's internal affairs during 1961 caused them to switch their attention for the time being to the situation in Ghana as the most likely base for Russian influence in West Africa and led to the displacement of British advisers, especially in the armed forces. The necessity for this on the Soviet part was enhanced by the continuous Chinese suggestion that the USSR had betrayed the national liberation movements in the developing countries and did not understand African needs. Ironically the charge was that the Soviet Union was concentrating too much on economic development. There ensued a greater competition between the Soviet Union and China to finance

and support development schemes. Nevertheless, the inherent conflict between African nationalism and the interests of Soviet policy tended to be
revealed. At this point also the training of guerrillas and military support
for freedom movements in, for example, Angola, via Ghana, began to be
encouraged.

The experience of Guinea's defection caused the Soviet Union to tread
even more warily with other states and reinforced the early lesson that
trends were not necessarily permanent in whichever direction they went.

The absence of Communist parties in Africa forced the Soviet Union to
trust apparently bourgeois African leaders to lead their populations towards
socialism. In 1962 Ghana, Guinea, and Mali were regarded as "national
democratic" states: in other words, as Mikoyan put it, in a speech reported
in *Pravda* on 15 March 1962, new forms of nationalist democracy were
emerging in Africa which led not directly to socialism but to an acceptable
alternative, subsequently referred to as "noncapitalist development." The
lack of sympathy for what African leaders have continued to describe as
"African socialism" was an early sign that the aspirations of the people of the
continent were unlikely to prove directly compatible with those of the
Soviet Union. Even though Guinea was praised for its achievement of
economic independence, the ideological divisions remained. Only the isolation imposed by France on Guinea really promised a close relationship between it and the socialist countries.

In spite of their obvious preference for the apparently more progressive
regimes in West Africa, the Soviets began to assume a general patronage of
African states. But the passing of the Congo and Algerian crises made African leaders more willing to adopt a neutral stance in terms of seeking beneficial economic relationships with the West. This was true even of Guinea
and it is not hard to find traces of a rueful exasperation on the part of Soviet
diplomats at this time. Though an intensive attempt was made during 1963
and 1964 by the Russians to make Nkrumah dependent on Soviet
assistance and advice, especially for his own security, the attempt to establish an African "Cuba" was never realized. After the end of Khrushchev's
leadership, the Soviet authorities became less inclined to lavish economic
support on "progressive" states and sought more generally to encourage
amongst Africans the view that Russia was their champion and friend.
They showed almost as much reluctance as Western countries to bolster
Ghana's collapsing economy in the last days of Nkrumah, even though refugees from other African countries were being trained there to use Russian
arms in their own liberation struggles.

The occurrence of major military coups in Nigeria and Ghana early in
1966 left the Soviet Union no realistic alternative but stoic acceptance,
which had the advantage of allowing it subsequently to exploit the Nigerian

civil war situation by taking positively the side of the federal government and embarrassing Britain, in particular, by her enthusiastic willingness to supply arms. Nevertheless, the character of the coups, especially the second Nigerian event, defied ideological explanation and reinforced a trend to realism based on global self-interest that has been a feature of Soviet policy in Africa ever since. The weaknesses of even the sympathetic progressive regimes were openly proclaimed as inviting overthrow. Vladimir Kudryavtsev, who by this time had replaced I. Potekhin as the most influential Russian commentator on Africa, supported this view. This, however, did not prevent a rancorous relationship with the military regime in Ghana, which, for its part, clearly feared Soviet intervention on behalf of Nkrumah, who was then in Guinea. But, in general, a pattern of pragmatism had been established.

This pragmatism was most clearly expressed in the Soviet Union's shift from neutrality to support for General Gowon's federal government in Nigeria. This was the more remarkable because of earlier support for the Ibos as the most hopeful element in Nigerian society, seen from the Soviet point of view, and hostility to the reactionary feudalism of the North. Cynically, Kudryavtsev and other commentators now rationalized the North as heterogeneous with only an insignificant feudal stratum and as a region where in any case the whole political structure had been modified by the coups.

The first ten years of substantive Soviet contact with Africa saw a radical evolution of perceptions and goals. The optimistic assumption that countries like Guinea would rapidly become recognizable socialist states had disappeared. But the failure to establish communist regimes was compensated for by the realization that it was possible to damage or modify the influence of Western powers without necessarily realizing any local ideological gains. The revolutionary potential of African states had proved an illusion and this reinforced Soviet willingness to sacrifice the aims of socialist revolution to the immediate interests of Soviet foreign policy. The rest of the world has been slow to realize that there was no real contradiction between the two. The capricious nature of the African politics only served to underline the fact that, from the first, Russian support for socialist reform had been subordinated to the immediate objective of foreign policy, which was to confine Western influence. The 1970s have seen the Soviet Union, in spite of local setbacks, begin to develop this policy more positively, if not actually aggressively. Various events over the decade of the 1960s, beginning with the death of Lumumba and probably reaching a peak with the ousting of Nkrumah, served to demolish the conviction that the African situation naturally favored Soviet interests and the evolution of socialism. It was not just that the revolutionary potential of countries like Ghana, Guinea, and

Mali seemed progressively to dissolve but that even before that had occurred their aspirations were seen not necessarily to accord with Soviet aspirations.

In retrospect 1968 seems to have been a watershed for Soviet policy in Africa: thereafter the emphasis was not so much on cultivating ideologically promising countries but on countries that were of practical importance. In that year the prospect of radical change in Southern Africa, for example, may have seemed for the first time likely. At the same time, the Chinese challenge for the role of chief patron of the Third World and national liberation movements seemed to be waning. The changing situation in the Middle East began to make the Horn of Africa a promising area for intervention. Ironically for the West, the gradual realization on the part of the Russians that Marxist-Leninist concepts did not in any way neatly fit the African situation cleared the way for more realistic and, as it seems, effective policies.

During the 1960s Soviet support for the various African groups operating against the Portuguese in Angola and Mozambique had gradually increased, partially in response to the Chinese challenge. The Russians had also begun to show some evidence of interest in the Rhodesian situation through ZAPU (the Zimbabwe African People's Union). Their effort, however, apparently suffered a major setback following the August 1968 invasion of Czechoslovakia, which shook African faith in Moscow. In order to try to restore relationships, the Soviet front organization the World Peace Council organized a conference in Khartoum early in 1969. This amounted to a blatant attempt by the Russians to capture control of the Southern African liberation struggle by, in effect, setting up a rival to the OAU Liberation Committee. This prompted a declaration by four guerrilla movements — PAC, ZANU, COREMO, and UNITA — to the effect that the conference's real objectives were "to further Soviet cooperation with the USA for their joint domination of the world."

In retrospect, this seems to have proved a surprisingly temporary setback for the Russians in Africa. By 1971 the pattern of current Soviet strategy in Africa was in the process of being established. In March of that year, reports appeared in the press of a publication by the African Institute of the Soviet Academy of Sciences, edited by the Institute's Director, V. G. Solodovnikov, who is now Russian ambassador in Zambia. This document gave an up-to-date analysis of African political developments, with guidelines for communist activity on a long-term basis. For southern Africa, it saw no alternative to the overthrow of white supremacist governments by armed revolution. The publication described the possibility of using the "revolutionary democratic" parties in, for instance, Tanzania, Angola, and Mozambique, as instruments for the establishment of communist influence, and in line with earlier experience in West Africa suggested the desirability of working within one-party governments headed by "strong-man" nationalist leaders, because they will inevitably fade away.

This Soviet document reaffirmed concern about the subversion by China of pro-Moscow factions throughout Southern Africa. It also betrayed a sensitivity to the contemporary weaknesses of guerrilla movements, which was particularly appropriate in a year during which in general their relative failure and state of disorder did not enhance the Soviet Union's standing in African eyes.

The Somali Republic, moreover, had not at this stage become dependent on the Soviet Union in the way in which the original defense agreement between the two countries seemed to portend, and the military coup of 1969 had certainly not consolidated the political influence of the Russian military advisers there. It was, however, in the Sudan that during 1971, the USSR's policy was put to a severe test.

In Khartoum at the beginning of 1971 the momentum of Major General Gaafar el-Nimeiry's government was clearly hindered by the existence of rival communist parties in the country even though some communists held key posts in the administration of his Revolutionary Command Council. Relations with the Soviet Union and its allies remained cordial even during a purge of communist officials initiated during April that may have owed something to the influence of Colonel Qadaffy of Libya and possibly of President Sadat of Egypt. There is no doubt that Soviet support was important to Nimeiry in prosecuting the war in the southern Sudan. In July, however, came the attempted coup, apparently organized by the Sudanese Communist party, which the party quickly proved insufficiently strong to sustain. The rapid restoration of General Nimeiry to power had a catastrophic effect on Khartoum-Moscow relations, for the Sudan was a rare case in which the Soviet Union had close associations with a Marxist group at the expense of its relationship with the government as such: a well-organized party well represented in the government had betrayed Moscow into a serious error, putting at risk many communist enterprises in the Sudan.

The Sudanese Communist party was the strongest and best organized in Africa, and its leader, Abdel Khalik Mahgoub, a key figure in the international communist movement, was clearly identified with the coup against Nimeiry on 19 July and subsequently arrested and executed. It is not clear whether the Russians were aware of the preparations for the coup, but the Soviet press certainly loudly condemned the subsequent anti-communist actions of Nimeiry and on 1 August the Revolutionary Command Council recalled the Sudanese ambassador from Moscow and expelled the counselor (but not the ambassador) of the Soviet embassy in Khartoum. Though the

Russians, after a short delay, reacted with typical cynicism in covering their tracks in an attempt to restore normal relations with the Nimeiry regime, the Sudanese Communist party continued to be indicted as the originator of the July coup, and General Nimeiry moved cautiously to the right, encouraging local business in the process and, most significantly, attempting to find a way to a political rather than a military solution in the south. The Sudan provided another example, as the Congo did in 1960–1961, of the difficulty that Russian ideologists find in coming to terms with the unpredictability of Africa.

It is probably not an overemphasis to attribute to their Sudanese experience in 1971 what seemed in the following year to be a vitrual Russian withdrawal from African involvement. At the very least they were in a state of uncertainty as to how best to develop a general strategy for the increase of influence on the continent. This did not mean, however, that the Soviets altogether ceased to support liberation movements, nor did it involve eschewing propaganda arising from Britain's predicaments in Rhodesia and with President Amin in Uganda. The Chinese also were accused of trading with South Africa and Rhodesia. Only in relation to Somalia did Soviet African policy appear to be going according to plan during 1972–1973.

This relatively low-key approach continued for another year during which Russia seemed content to foster links with groups likely to prove an embarrassment to Western countries or China without risking any commitment that might have a "boomerang" effect; its choice of which guerrilla movements to support was still clearly influenced by Sino-Soviet rivalry.

On the West coast of Africa, Soviet naval vessels continued to provide a screen for the areas of the Portuguese colony that on 24 September were proclaimed by representatives of the PAIGC as "the independent republic of Guinea-Bissau." It was, however, in the Horn of Africa in the East that the principal Soviet effort was concentrated, with an obvious logic in connection with the buildup of Russsian naval forces in the Indian Ocean. The USSR confirmed its position as Somalia's largest source of aid; in spite of some criticism of delays and inefficiencies the influence achieved through the setting up of fishery and meat processing projects and also state farms was high. Though a large proportion of Somali produce had to be sold to the Soviet Union under the relevant agreements, the returns included T-54 tanks and military and civilian instructors as well as the supply of the Republic's oil requirements.

Somalia was by the beginning of 1974 completely dependent on Russia for the accommodation of students for advanced studies. There were substantial numbers of Russian advisers in the country, with the naval base at Berbera, where the Soviet Indian Ocean fleet had facilities, staffed at all levels by Russians. But among some Somalis the scale and style of the Soviet presence promoted a reaction in favor of the Chinese, whose aid seemed less obtrusive and in some ways more efficient. The signs of a growing confidence on the part of the Somali regime, provided communist and Islamic principles were reconciled, could, however, only be encouraging to the Russians.

The Soviet willingness to provide military equipment to President Amin was another evident indication of their anticipation of change in the Horn of Africa. The American withdrawal from their communication base at Kagnew near Asmara in Ethiopia and continuing Arab support for the Eritrean Liberation Front provided a context within which the Soviet Union could be seen maneuvering eventually to exploit the problems that would arise when Haile Selassie of Ethiopia and Jomo Kenyatta of Kenya, in due course, disappeared from the scene. The Ethiopian-Somali situation has perhaps not proved so simple a situation to exploit as they might have wished.

It was, however, the withdrawal of Portugal and Angolan independence that not only marked the return to Africa of great power confrontation but a significant and in some ways surprising change in Soviet policy. In Angola, Soviet support for the MPLA and U.S. aid for the FNLA were longstanding. But as has been demonstrated, the failure of any of the different manifestations of African nationalism to conform to the ideology of the Russian leaders had caused the Soviet Union to adopt an extremely cautious policy. This had been endorsed, as it were, by the realization of the ill repute that had stemmed from the invasion of Czechoslovakia. Almost to the extent of the former imperial powers, but by a more prolonged route studded with harsh experience, the Russians had come to accept that the appearance of foreign interference in the internal affairs of African states could rebound on them.

Over Angola the Russians in the last quarter of 1975 seemed suddenly to abandon the caution learned in the Sudan and elsewhere. This, compounded by their behavior in the Horn of Africa, has led to a radically different and altogether more ominous situation in Africa. The question is, at this time and likely for some time to come, whether in due course they will proceed through a series of similar rebuffs back to a cautious stance or not. For the first time, at the end of 1975, the Soviet Union, whose earlier failures in Africa had been the result of tactical errors and African unpredictability, seemed deliberately to be taking a major political risk.

The decision to recognize the MPLA government in Angola in November 1975 and to increase military support to it was particularly bold because it went against OAU policy at the time. Normally the Soviet Union had sought not to lead but to support the African organization and its members.

At this stage most of them were pursuing the policy of supporting all three liberation movements, the MPLA, FNLA, and UNITA. Some even preferred UNITA on the grounds that it owed least to external assistance and seemed to be a pawn to no one. There was at the same time the risk that the MPLA would not win the civil war, which in the very long term it may still turn out not to have done.

This unaccustomed daring shown by the USSR in an African situation can now be seen both as a calculated challenge to the West and as an indication of the importance that Russia attaches to the resources of southern Africa in a global confrontation. It is difficult to be sure whether it was a deliberate provocation to South Africa to intervene and thus prove to the African states that the Soviet Union was their champion. On the face of it, the chances of total failure, only limited success, or the long-term alienation of neighboring countries like Zambia were great.

An understanding of this evident gamble involves an appreciation not only of the African vicissitudes of Soviet policy, which have been described, but of a wider perspective. The hope of converting Africa to Marxism-Leninism was probably no greater in 1975 than it had been for some time. What was important was the Russian record in Africa and the Middle East. At that time the establishment of naval and military facilities in Somalia may have seemed, and probably was, their only recent success. President Sadat of Egypt and President Nimeiry of the Sudan had in different ways turned back Soviet influence over a period of more than five years. In the same period, the Americans in Zaire and the Chinese in Tanzania and Zambia, particularly by their discretion in building the Tanzam railway, had been relatively successful. There was even good evidence for supposing that the change in U.S. policy towards Peking had directly influenced General Mobutu's opening up relations with China. It would be wrong, even so, to see the Soviet Union's apparent volte-face over Angola as an act of desperation: from the West's point of view it would be more realistic to see it as an anticipation of the need to establish both a base and African credentials in preparation for a period in which the struggle for southern Africa was bound to escalate. On the face of it, the surprise Angolan initiative by Moscow was a successful attempt to preempt any Western decision to try to turn the tables on Russia in Africa by identifying Russia as the new imperialist power. To run the risk of a Vietnam-type enmeshment in Africa might, however, have been and might even now prove to be a high price to pay. The use of the Cubans as a willing surrogate was one obvious form of insurance against this, even though they in their turn clearly have their own reasons for wanting such a role in Africa.

The fairly rapid victory of Soviet-sponsored forces in Angola was due to American reluctance to become involved (which Dr. Kissinger perhaps belatedly discovered), on which the Russians gambled and which in its turn effectively frustrated South African participation. The Soviet Union's daring initiative produced what seemed an immediate reward. It promoted a swing away from Peking by the government of Samora Machel in Mozambique, in spite of the indebtedness of that government to Tanzania, which has always preferred China to Russia. By February 1976 a delegation of Mozambican ministers was in Moscow; the defense minister saw Marshal Grechko immediately before his death, and in May Samora Machel visited Russia at the invitation of President Podgorny. The prime objective on the Soviet part seems to have been to generate a series of commercial and related agreements in such a way as to replace the colonial trading pattern with Portugal by an alignment with Communist countries. This is clearly of a piece with statements in the Solodovnikov document of 1971: not only are the white supremacist regimes to be overthrown but Angola was the preface to their substitution by black Marxist states, if Soviet objectives are in fact to be realized. Once again, however, African realities seem so far to have precluded in Mozambique the thoroughgoing victory that the Russians may have expected. South African links remain, especially in relation to the operation of docks and railways, and there have been signs of renewed economic activity towards the West proper. This may in the end be critical not only for the immediate outcome of the Rhodesian situation, but for the political and economic orientation of a new state of Zimbabwe.

The Soviet stategy of using appropriately manipulated guerrilla forces in Africa, as in other parts of the Third World, was further demonstrated and received another setback in the Sudan in July 1976. On the night of 3 July at least 700 people died in the streets of Khartoum as the result of an attempted coup. General Nimeiry's security forces successfully resisted what was to all intents and purposes an invasion led by Brigadier Muhammed Nur Saad. He admitted that around 2000 men had been training in Libyan camps in the border area near Jebel Uweinat. These had infiltrated the Sudan to make an attack on the capital. Subsequently in a speech on 10 August General Nimeiry revealed the background to the attempt as he saw it. "We think," he said, "that behind Colonel Qadaffy there is another power, one of the powers of the world, a power which is seeking some influence on the Nile Valley." He later regarded the *Pravda* article on 30 August strongly supporting Libya in its quarrel with Egypt as a further indication of such intentions. Altogether this episode seems to confirm the Russian view of the Sudan as an important objective in achieving wider influence in East Africa and the Horn. Even the major commitment in Ethiopia can be seen in these terms, but there, as elsewhere in Africa, Soviet progress has not been wholly straightforward.

The switch during 1977 of Soviet support from Somalia to Ethiopia, following upon the ending of that country's earlier reliance on American military aid, was easily interpreted. Somalia could at that stage be represented as the challenger in the Ogaden, and Ethiopia as the defender of national boundaries. In spite of many crises in Africa since the early 1960s, determination to prevent an epidemic of secessionist movements and to resist forcible changes even of patently anomalous former imperial boundaries has been a continuous feature of OAU attitudes. In the Ethiopian case, the Soviet Union's volte-face could not only be construed as facilitating a proper defense of national sovereignty but was a means of advertising its willingness to ally with any group adopting the rhetoric of Marxist ideology. This kind of projection could eventually become important in the resolution of the problems both of Namibia and a future Zimbabwe.

In fact the pro-Ethiopian intervention by the Soviet Union was consistent with the new approach exemplified in Angola. Indeed in that country Russia only stepped up support abruptly for a faction that it had long aided, apparently in the face of the threat from the rival UNITA, which was benefitting from South African assistance. In that sense there was less political risk than in ruthlessly switching the full weight of its military support to a country formerly linked with the United States.

Already by mid-1978 the pliability from the Soviet standpoint of Mengistu's regime was in doubt. The question now seems whether military support or ideological identification is a reliable source of durable influence for any outside power in Africa. If it is not, as seems the case, then the Soviet Union must have already learned the lesson and still accepts the risk as in some ways worthwhile. An important issue is whether this portends another dramatic shift by the Russians eventually — perhaps in relation to southern Africa. Speculation on this must, however, be left to the end of this chapter.

To consider current Soviet policy in Africa in terms of immediate success or even durable influence in a particular territory is probably an error. Even if Ethiopia were to go the way of Egypt (1972), North Yemen (1975), and Somalia (1977) and expel her Soviet advisers, perhaps as a result of interference in local affairs and nationalist resentment, the validity of the long-term objective and the wider impact on Africa would not have been lost. A permanent foothold in the Horn of Africa would be attractive to the Soviet leaders, but this objective seems secondary to the urgent desire, with far-reaching implications, to become a permanent factor in African politics. By supporting Ethiopia, Russia proved to others its capability to provide massive military support at long range and may even have helped to boost the confidence of those, particularly in the Middle East, who with Soviet backing are inclined to resist the search for compromise there.

It is, in fact, this readiness to assist governments or liberation movements, more than ideological sympathy, which has given, and is likely to continue to give, Russia a predominant influence in Third World areas. The conditions for the success of this policy are, of course, tension, war, and conflict and their ending inimical to it. The establishment of peace after military victory demands not weapons but economic assistance and this the USSR is ill equipped to provide. The American unwillingness to reciprocate in military kind might be offset in terms of political advantage by a clear Western strategy involving a willingness to provide dramatic economic incentives to countries and movements that refuse to appeal for Soviet and quasi-Soviet assistance. The long-term link between economic performance and security needs stressing. The proper response to Soviet intervention in the Horn of Africa should have been a strong, clearly worded commitment to economic development, without strings other than the one mentioned, from North America and the EEC.

Soviet restraint on Ethiopia seems to have been a factor in preventing the counterattack surging into Somalia. The postwar disaffection of Mengistu's government with Russia that quickly set in was evidently related to the complexities of the Eritrean situation, where Arab repercussions are clearly at risk. The problems of achieving short-term success in Soviet terms are, however, perhaps best encapsulated in Somalia. In spite of growing hatred of the Russians spontaneously expressed on their departure at quite a low level of Somali society, President Siad Barre had worked consistently since 1961 to create classic Marxist-Leninist structures of government. Somalia, however, never approached the character of a communist state. It remained predominantly nationalist, reflecting the forces generated by the imperial partitioning of the Somali people. Nomadic life combined with the conservatism of Islam has prevented ideology penetrating Somali society much below the level of the ruling elite. A Western resident once summed up the typical Somali approach saying, "Call a Somali a fool and he will fight you. Call him a communist or a capitalist and he will kill you. They just want to do everything their way."

It begins to look as though in twenty years — after initial disclaimers of any expertise in judging Africa — the Soviet Union has begun to make sound judgments of its interests in Africa. It would be ironic if Russian realism and pragmatism displaced that of the West, which initially had the advantage of superior knowledge and experience. But the Soviet Union has a thicker skin and seems less easily put off by setbacks — setbacks of a kind that would not be easily explicable to the electorates in a democratic system like that of the United States. Russia certainly seems to have developed the capacity not to expect too much in the short term and keep its eye on ultimate goals. Its experiences with Ghana and Guinea in the early stages provided valuable lessons, the most important of which are that influence is never durable and that ideological commitment is less important than it seems. Mozambique and Angola are already beginning to confirm the characteristic realism and unpredictability of African politics. They raise the question of how far the settlement of the Rhodesian question has been bedevilled by assumptions on the part of whites and their Western friends that any government of Zimbabwe would be for long a client of the communist states unless forced into that position. This may indeed be a fundamental element in Soviet strategy — to encourage such forcing. Recent Russian gambles in Angola and Ethiopia suggest a realization on its part of how difficult it is to change the economic orientation of a state. Zimbabwean leaders will inherit an economic structure, which, both because of and in spite of sanctions, is highly centralized and integrated into the capitalist world's trading system. The encouragement to nationalists to realize where the interests of the new state will inevitably lie is the most important weapon that the West has, whatever the immediate outcome. It is ironic that the Soviet Union has realized the merits of flexibility and taking advantage of situations as they are, while the West has become more rigid (albeit handicapped by the behavior of white governments in southern Africa) in its tactics.

So far, however, this discussion of Soviet policy and tactics in Africa has not focused on their real purpose. It is not necessary to assume the intention to conquer the world, which clearly is something that the current Soviet leaders dare not contemplate. Their evident unwillingness to commit openly their own military forces (rather than the Cubans, for example) testifies to this. What they are interested in is preparing as best they can for any international eventuality. They may not be immediately seeking to establish a stranglehold on the West via communications and resources, but they would clearly like to be able to exercise critical pressures if things were not naturally running their way. It is for this reason that attention has been focused on sea and air routes round and across Africa and on mineral resources.

Long before the oil crisis of 1973 the South African government encouraged the view that the Cape Route was of fundamental importance to Western Europe and North America — the so-called free world. The problems of the Middle East and the Suez Canal and the necessity for supertankers to use the ocean route have reinforced this claim. It is estimated that 90 percent of European NATO's oil supplies and 70 percent of its strategic materials pass within a few miles of the Cape of Good Hope. The Soviet naval presence in the Indian Ocean is interpreted as a preparation for interception of this traffic. Neither the current size nor the character of the Russian forces, nor even their approach to the development of naval facilities at Aden, and originally at Hodeida and Berbera, tend to confirm this. Again the Soviet Union may be proving more realistic or sophisticated than its opponents.

Put simply, the capacity to cut off Western oil supplies would be much more easily exercised in the oil fields themselves, or in the restricted waters in and around the Persian Gulf, than over the hundreds and thousands of miles of deep water round the Cape. It is much more likely that the Russians' naval interest in the Indian Ocean is for the purposes of "showing the flag" and reinforcing the conviction that Russia is at hand and ready to play a part in African affairs when potential clients need it. The Soviets are also conscious of the danger of upsetting powers like India by bearing too heavily on what they see as their spheres of influence. In other words, the ships are at least as much symbols of a political presence as of military intention. The question of mineral raw materials, however, seems entirely another matter.

The manipulation of the mineral and other natural resources of southern Africa can play a part in either an offensive or a defensive strategy on the part of the Soviet Union in that region. To be effective, economic warfare in terms of the limitation of trade must have a direct impact on the military or economic potential of the adversary. Like other major powers, the Soviet Union is increasingly aware of the population pressures, problems of food production and supply, world attitudes to the current economic order, nuclear proliferation, and the scarcity or availability of raw materials. Relative self-sufficiency in food production, in spite of population pressures, has been one of the assets favoring continued stable governments in Rhodesia and South Africa and might remain so if a Zimbabwean regime, of whatever political complexion, could maintain its independence. These territories are better off than most countries in Africa or Southeast Asia.

This is one factor leading the Russians to attempt to influence the situation in southern Africa in their favor, for they undoubtedly perceive the resources necessary for economic growth as essential to security. Their early apparent success in Angola and Mozambique, where ideologically sympathetic (to the USSR) regimes have been established, raised the question whether African raw materials generally could be denied to the West. Angola and Mozambique also happened to have important ports providing outlets to the sea for the output especially of Rhodesia and Zambia.

The basic fact is that the Warsaw Pact countries are for the time being largely self-sufficient in raw materials, whereas the NATO powers are not. It is true, however, that the African countries concerned—and this would be even more the case with black-controlled Namibia, Zimbabwe, or Azania—need to sell their ores to survive economically. Outright denial is, therefore, not likely to be acceptable to them. Diversion and stockpiling, if the Communist powers could credibly finance it, would impose a threat to the security of the West—a threat especially acute because it might not be perceived early enough for substitutes to be developed or investigated.

Uranium, platinum, cobalt, manganese, chrome, vanadium, as well as gold are supplied from southern Africa in critical proportions to the United States, the United Kingdom, France, and the rest of Western Europe. In several cases the world's major known resources are concentrated in South Africa and the Soviet Union. As early as 1957, a Soviet expert on economic warfare, Major General A. N. Lagovisky, pointed out that modern armaments depended on a range of fairly scarce minerals, including chrome, platinum, nickel, cobalt, and titanium. Jet engines and armor-piercing projectiles in particular required special minerals in their manufacture. The major Western nations, he suggested validly, were almost entirely dependent on imported supplies.

While it seems unlikely that the Soviet Union or Cuba directly promoted the Shaba invasion that led to the prompt intervention of the French and others at Kolwezi, the situation in the former Katanga province symbolizes the potential danger. Those who forecast a decade and a half ago that the real crisis would come when and where major uranium sources and acute racial problems were seen to coincide may be proved dramatically correct. The Soviet Union is clearly not ignorant of the potential of southern Africa in this respect, even though it has no direct interest in uranium supplies from outside areas under its immediate control.

So Soviet strategy in Africa as it has evolved over the last two decades emerges now as strictly pragmatic—based on a "worst case analysis," in which Russia believes it necessary to be in a position to apply to NATO and the West generally pressures that would totally inhibit their freedom of action in other parts of the world. It is not, however, an infallible policy and the only thing that could make it so would be the development of a firm and widespread Western belief in Russian invincibility—and there is clearly a danger of this, enhanced in Africa by the determination of the white governments to label all their enemies indiscriminately as communist. The principal obstacle to the success of Soviet strategy is that which has continuously induced the setbacks which it has so far experienced. The critical factor is African nationalism or rather the desire of Africans to retain their independence. Up to a point presidents Nyerere, Kaunda, and Kenyatta as well as Hastings Banda have managed this. Not even Samora Machel nor even the Angolan leadership seem wholly compliant. As has already been suggested their need to export profitably is critical and puts a premium on maintaining links with those who want to buy, even if they may be capitalist. Though more forceful and more determined since the Angolan intervention than ever before, there are still elements of similarity in the Soviet

African experience now and in the early days of Kwame Nkrumah and Sekou Touré.

It is today not clear how far the Soviet Union will put its direct weight behind any faction in the Rhodesian affair. If the guerrilla war there is eventually replaced by a civil war between Africans, then presumably it will find it necessary to back one horse. A final attempt to establish a client Zimbabwean state obviously cannot be ruled out. But there is every sign, in spite of the apparent Angolan gamble, that the USSR intends not to get messily involved in fighting wars on behalf of unpredictable African groups. It is this which invites the speculation as to whether the USSR will for a long time ahead show its hand in the South African situation. It is not impossible to envisage circumstances in which it might suit the Russians tacitly to accept the South African status quo because they could not foresee a fairly short-term and (for their side) successful outcome. Indeed, Africans might before long be disillusioned to find that Soviet priorities and theirs do not necessarily coincide, either militarily or economically. In other words, a greater boldness and self-assurance on the part of the West in consulting their own interest in Africa could conceivably result in their eventually displacing the Soviet Union as champions of a truly independent Africa. In this, however, real fair dealing (as opposed to cynical trading) in economic matters could be decisive. The Soviet presence in Africa can now be regarded as permanent, but its utility to Africans is limited to massive military intervention where a conflict exists. The consolidation of peace is not only a matter of advice on the nature of the state security apparatus but of beginning to satisfy the mundane needs of the population.

Whether the Soviet ideological approach can contribute much to the development of an essentially African political model has yet to be demonstrated. The Westminster-Paris model, in spite of its initial appeal, has failed in this respect, and if Marxism-Leninism is to be any more successful it will need to accommodate African nationalist aspirations in a way that Moscow has so far never found easy to accept. The fact, however; remains that until real steps are taken to resolve the political problems, especially the recognition of a political status for urban Africans in South Africa, an important capacity for initiative will lie with the Soviet Union. Its propagandists will continue to exploit a situation that is only marginally of Russian creation but that continues to encourage African states to look to them for support in what they regard as the ultimate stages in the struggle for African freedom. However, priorities may be determined by the degree of Soviet involvement in other parts of the world.

7

East Asia

Harold C. Hinton

The Soviet Union's impact on the international politics of China, Japan, and Korea since World War II is a complex subject that is best approached by way of a summary of Soviet policy toward the East Asian region. If the account stresses China, that is because it has been the most important of the three countries to Soviet policy-makers, with a qualification allowed for the always threatening but never unleashed (against the Soviet Union) American military presence in Japan and Okinawa.

Soviet Interests and Policy in East Asia

It must be remembered, as it constantly is in Moscow, that the regions of the Soviet Union bordering on East Asia are thinly populated, contain Asian minorities of uncertain loyalty, and are poorly developed. Security has therefore inevitably been the major Soviet preoccupation in formulating policy toward East Asia. This is all the more true because in recent decades the region has seen the intrusion of three major military powers — Japan, the United States, and the People's Republic of China — all more or less hostile to the Soviet Union. Therefore it is not surprising that Soviet efforts to build up the industrial and military potential of the Soviet Far East date from as far back as 1929, with escalation whenever Moscow saw or thought it saw a particular reason to do so. Since the 1930s, the Soviet leadership has had an almost paranoid fear of simultaneous threats, crises, or wars in Europe and the Far East. A problem on one of these fronts has generally produced a conciliatory Soviet posture on the other.

Moscow has aspired not only to security but to influence in East Asia, although less obsessively than in Eastern and Central Europe. Since 1891, when the building of the Trans-Siberian Railway began, Moscow has sought advantageous economic relationships with East Asia as a means, among other things, to promote the economic development of its own Far

Eastern territory. The Soviet Union competed for political influence in the region with other major powers, above all the three already mentioned as perceived threats to its security.

Ideally Moscow would probably like to exclude the United States from the region and be in a position to manage China and Japan effectively. In reality it is far from this point and it actually appears to welcome a certain level of American military presence in the region as a restraint on China. The Soviet Union has sought, with varying degrees of energy, to exert a decisive revolutionary influence on the region since about 1921. This effort has had almost no success to date in Japan. Soviet policy and military intervention contributed critically in Korea, and marginally in China, to the emergence of Communist regimes after World War II, but in both cases factors to be considered below have rendered this triumph at best a doubtful blessing in Moscow's eyes.

Stalin's East Asian policy in 1945 was remarkably similar to his East and Central European policy. He wanted an occupation zone in and reparations from the defeated enemy; he failed to get them (apart from about $2 billion worth of Japanese equipment removed from Manchuria by Soviet forces) because his military reach did not extend to Japan. He wanted, and got by virtue of the Yalta and Potsdam agreements, certain territorial annexations (the Kuriles and southern Sakhalin) designed mainly to provide additional security against a possibly resurgent Japan, perhaps supported by the United States.

Stalin wanted a buffer zone and sphere of influence extending along the Soviet border from the Pacific to Kazakhstan. In the case of Manchuria, which his troops occupied for about six months after August 1945, he acquired important port and railway rights under the Yalta agreement and greatly helped to tip the balance for the Chinese Communists and against the Nationalists, but he failed in his further objective of getting the Communists to establish their main political and military bases in Manchuria under his protecting and dominating wing. Having failed in this, Stalin was not in a position to exert decisive influence on the course of the Chinese civil war south of the Great Wall or (despite temporary appearances to the contrary) on the policies of the Chinese Communist regime after it came to power in 1949.

Stalin was much more successful in Korea, since his forces occupied it down to the 38th parallel in 1945 and over the next three years turned it progressively into a Communist-controlled Soviet satellite. He also was successful with the Mongolian People's Republic, which had been a de facto Soviet satellite for two decades and which he managed to have proclaimed independent (of China) in 1945. Through covert support for local anti-Chinese resistance, he helped to prevent the Chinese Nationalists from establishing their authority over western Sinkiang and succeeded in 1950 in getting the Chinese Communists to grant him important mineral rights that turned the area into a Soviet sphere of influence for the next several years.

The Communist triumph in China presented Stalin with important potential gains as well as serious risks. It was a major asset to have China as an ally, and perhaps a satellite, rather than an adversary or a base for pressures aimed by hostile countries against the Soviet Union. On the other hand, the Communist victory was not due primarily to Stalin's intervention or influence, and the Chinese Communist movement had demonstrated much independence of mind, especially since Mao Tse-tung's rise to power about 1938. It was important to Stalin not to push Mao into duplicating Tito's performance, and through the exercise of uncharacteristic self-restraint he avoided such a catastrophe — by how wide a margin is not clear. In the course of his negotiations with Mao (December 1949–February 1950) Stalin gave the Chinese a military alliance, economic (and later military) aid, and a sphere of revolutionary influence in southern Asia; in return he got Chinese recognition of Soviet preeminence in Korea and Japan and temporary confirmation of his special position in Manchuria and Sinkiang.

Apart from the North Korean desire for unification, the main cause of the Korean War was Stalin's determination to disrupt the American plan for a peace settlement with Japan and to eliminate a potential springboard (South Korea) on the Asian mainland for the hypothetical combination of Japan and the United States, against which he had just given Mao a rather reluctant guarantee. In addition, Stalin probably wanted access to the warm water ports of South Korea to replace those in Manchuria (Dairen and Port Arthur) that he would shortly have to return to Chinese control.

When United Nations forces defeated the North Koreans and invaded their territory in October 1950, Stalin successfully urged Chinese intervention, since he was unwilling either to see North Korea eliminated as a Communist state or to intervene himself. After that he gave substantial military aid and other forms of support to the Chinese struggle against a technically superior adversary. Stalin consistently avoided direct confrontation with the United States over Korea, although at the end of his life he may have contemplated something of the sort in an effort to save the Chinese from having to sign an armistice under conditions that would prevent them from regaining control over those of their prisoners (70 percent of the total, as it turned out) who did not want to go home.

Whatever Stalin's intentions, his successors were much too preoccupied with internal matters, including jockeying for power, to risk a confrontation with the United States over Korea or anything else. Their attitude left the Chinese and North Koreans with no effective choice but to sign an armistice (27 July 1953) under whose terms they would not regain their disaffected prisoners.

So serious was the disunity within the new Soviet leadership that Chinese support for Nikita Khrushchev—which he actively courted by visiting Peking in September–October 1954 and promising the Chinese more aid and military protection than his main rival, Malenkov, was willing to extend—played some role in Khrushchev's ouster of Malenkov as premier in favor of Bulganin in February 1955. Some of Khrushchev's opponents tried without success to impress Peking by verbal formulas conceding it coleadership of the "socialist camp" with the Soviet Union.

Another concession that Khrushchev sought and secured from the Chinese, in addition to support in his struggle for leadership, was agreement to a fresh Soviet approach to the Japanese government. Tokyo's close ties with Taipei, as well as with Washington, prevented any such approach on Peking's part, but Khrushchev evidently wanted to take some initiative that might counteract the Japanese tendency toward subservience to American foreign policy, then under the influence of the formidable John Foster Dulles. Accordingly, in 1956 the Soviet Union established diplomatic relations with Japan while postponing a solution of the three main problems in Soviet-Japanese relations: a peace treaty, the territorial issue (arising from Japanese resentment at the Soviet annexations of 1945), and fishing rights.

Khrushchev was unable to see eye to eye with Peking on another issue of much greater importance to it than to him—Taiwan. Since Peking was determined to "liberate" the island from Nationalist control and alleged American "occupation," it was outraged by the conclusion of a treaty of alliance between the United States and the (Nationalist) Republic of China at the end of 1954. Peking put increased pressure on Khrushchev for military aid and political and declaratory support.

Khrushchev provided the military aid to a considerable extent but not the support, at least not in a form likely to be useful to Peking; he had no desire for a confrontation with the United States over an issue as remote and unimportant (from his point of view) as Taiwan. Next to Mao Tsetung's seniority complex, born with the death of Stalin, this was probably the earliest of the major issues in the Sino-Soviet dispute in its serious (post-Stalin) phase, and yet it was rarely mentioned in public because it had embarrassing aspects for both sides.

Khrushchev opened the Twentieth Soviet Party Congress on 14 February 1956, the anniversary of the signing of the Sino-Soviet alliance in 1950, no doubt in an effort to assure Peking of the continuing validity of that alliance despite certain innovations likely to be disturbing to the

Chinese. These were principally Khrushchev's concepts of the "noninevita-bility" of (general) war and the "parliamentary path" to power for other Communist parties (that is, the priority of political struggle over armed revolution). Both these concepts clearly reflected his fear of a thermo-nuclear war with the strategically superior United States, as did his secret speech attacking Stalin, which he must have known was bound to startle and might undermine the leaders of other Communist parties, including Mao Tse-tung.

Khrushchev's apprehensions regarding Peking's reaction turned out to be well founded, and he for his part was distressed by a wave of ideological and political innovations emanating from Mao after the spring of 1956—in large part in response to the challenge to Mao posed by the secret speech and its tendency to encourage some of Mao's colleagues to prune back his political role. Khrushchev no doubt felt some satisfaction at the fiasco that overtook Mao's Hundred Flowers Campaign (for free public discussion) in June 1957, especially since it coincided approximately with his own re-sounding triumph over the "antiparty group" led by Malenkov and Molotov. In the autumn of 1957, however, Khrushchev began to come under powerful and embarrassing pressure from Mao. Peking intoned the slogan that the "East wind [the socialist camp] has prevailed over the West wind [the imperialist camp]."

The Chinese assumption was apparently that Khrushchev—having shed his more conservative (in foreign policy) colleagues by purging the "anti-party group" and in October 1957 Marshal Zhukov, and having impressed the world and especially the United States by his first ICBM test and first Sputnik—should now be in a mood to live up to the Soviet Union's respon-sibilities as "head of the socialist camp." In Mao's eyes these consisted essen-tially of a political campaign, with overtones of military pressure but short of actual war, against the United States, with Taiwan as one of the main objectives.

In reality Khrushchev was in no mood or position for any such cam-paign. However he felt sufficiently embarrassed by Mao's pressures, and sufficiently interested in purchasing Chinese support for his idea (an-nounced at the Twentieth Congress) of a nuclear test ban, to make a massive concession to Peking in October–November 1957 in the form of a commitment to give China extensive technical aid with a nuclear warhead program and appropriate delivery systems (MRBMs). But in 1958 Khru-shchev refused a Chinese request for a direct transfer of operational nuclear weapons (probably tactical), and in June 1959 he effectively terminated the nuclear assistance program because of his growing objections to Chinese behavior, in particular Chinese resentment at his moves toward détente with the United States.

It was Khrushchev's decision, in the aftermath of the death of the re-doubtable John Foster Dulles in April 1959, to seek accommodation with the United States rather than increase his pressures on it that, more than anything else, pushed his relations with the Chinese beyond the point of no return.

There were other issues as well. Khrushchev felt the gravest ideological and political reservations about the Great Leap Forward (1958–1960), the most dramatic of Mao's innovations of that period, and about the increased Chinese militancy in foreign policy that paralleled it. The most spectacular manifestation of this militancy, and the one that distrubed Khrushchev the most, was Mao's decision to reinforce the impact of the Great Leap For-ward at home and abroad and compensate for Khrushchev's passivity (in Mao's eyes) by exerting politico-military pressures on Nationalist positions in the Taiwan Strait.

Khrushchev flew secretly to Peking at the end of July 1958 to dissuade Mao from such an adventure, but to no avail. During the ensuing crisis (late August to early October), which created at least some risk of a Sino-American war, Khrushchev made some loud declarations of support for Peking but carefully timed them so as to minimize the actual risk of Soviet involvement. He waited until November, when the Taiwan Strait crisis was safely over, before launching a short-lived period of pressures on West Berlin.

During 1959 Khrushchev clearly came to regard the Chinese as the main threat to the desired détente with the United States. When he visited Pe-king at the end of September 1959, he lectured the Chinese severely, and partly in public, for their tendency to "test by force the stability of the capitalist system," their roughness with the Indians over the Sino-Indian border dispute, their doctrinaire insistence on "armed struggle" as the primary means for revolutionizing the Third World, and the like. Understandably, he got a very cool reception.

Chinese objections to Khrushchev's dealings with the United States were probably a major reason Khrushchev used the shooting down of Francis Gary Powers' U-2 as a pretext for cancelling the Paris summit conference of May 1960. But when Peking, unappeased, continued to attack Khru-shchev's alleged passivity toward "imperialism" and revolution, he cut off all economic aid to China in the summer of 1960, at a time when the Chinese economy was already reeling under the impact of bad weather and the stresses of the Great Leap Forward. Khrushchev explained his position fully, as did the Chinese, to the astounded delegates to a major conference of Communist parties convened in Moscow in November–December 1960. He tried but failed to maneuver a majority vote against the Chinese, who successfully insisted on a rule of unanimity. The outcome was an ambiguous statement embodying much of both positions, with the result that each side subsequently claimed that its views and behavior accorded with the statement.

In 1961 Khrushchev became further infuriated by Chinese insistence on supporting Albania, with which he had developed a dispute rather similar, except in scale, to his controversy with Peking. But not all his colleagues were as anti-Chinese as he, and it was probably under pressure from them that he made some remarkably conciliatory gestures toward Peking in 1962. In the summer, in response to Chinese protests, he broke off talks with the United States on a nonproliferation agreement. He secretly urged the Indian government to avoid a border war with China, at the cost of no matter what concessions. Most important of all, he apparently hoped to use the missiles he emplaced in Cuba to exert pressure on the United States not only for a Berlin and German settlement but for the removal of American protection from Taiwan.

This plan came unstuck when Khrushchev, under a virtual American ultimatum, agreed to withdraw his missiles from Cuba. The Chinese denounced him for allegedly having agreed to "another Munich" at the expense of Castro and the Cuban people, and he transferred his support from Peking to New Delhi in connection with the Sino-Indian border war of October–November 1962. After that Sino-Soviet relations rapidly worsened. The Chinese denounced Khrushchev even more vigorously after he concluded the nuclear test ban treaty (July 1963), and they began to form "Marxist-Leninst" splinter parties, where possible, in opposition to the pro-Soviet Communist parties. Khrushchev retaliated by trying, but without success, to convene another major conference at which the Chinese would be disciplined or condemned in some way or other.

Still more serious was the emergence of a territorial dispute and the beginnings of a military confrontation between Peking and Moscow. Since 1960 small-scale crossings of the Sino-Soviet border by parties of Chinese military personnel had been occurring. Over the next two years Moscow began to strengthen its forces near the border to a limited extent. In the spring of 1962, according to a credible Chinese account,[1] Soviet consular personnel in Sinkiang incited some 60,000 dissident Kazakhs and Uighurs to flee across the border to Soviet Central Asia, and in retaliation all Soviet consulates in China were closed.

Over the next two years Peking publicly reminded the world that tsarist and Soviet Russia had taken territory (including the Mongolian People's Republic) from China and implied a desire to recover at least some of it. Technical talks in Peking during 1964 on the border issue failed to resolve the broader question of the old boundary treaties, which the Chinese regard as "unequal" and therefore in some sense invalid; in any case the talks were suspended with Khrushchev's fall. By the summer of 1964, as the detonation of Peking's first nuclear device approached, Khrushchev may actually have been contemplating some sort of military action against China. In any case, the clumsiness of his China policy almost certainly contributed to his overthrow in mid-October 1964.

His successors were anxious to improve relations with Peking, and in particular to secure Chinese cooperation in the transshipment of increased military aid to North Vietnam, which from November 1964 seemed likely to come, and after February 1965 did come, under American air attack. Accordingly, during a visit to Peking in February 1965, Kosygin proposed "united action" over Vietnam, a normalization of Sino-Soviet state relations (including an increase of trade and a resumption of Soviet economic aid), and a suspension of ideological polemics.

Mao personally vetoed all of this, except that an unpublished agreement was concluded (on 30 April) to permit transit by rail—but not by air, as Moscow also wished—of Soviet military equipment bound for North Vietnam. The Vietnamese crisis became a further source of Sino-Soviet disunity rather than a bridge across which relations with Peking could be improved as the Brezhnev-Kosygin leadership had initially hoped. Sino-Soviet relations worsened early in 1965 when Suslov insisted on reviving Khrushchev's plan for another international conference of Communist parties, an idea Mao strongly opposed.

In 1965–1966 Moscow began to perceive Peking as a serious potential military threat. It was in 1965 that Peking began to construct an ICBM testing range, an undeniable indication that it intended to become a major nuclear power. It was also in 1965 that the Japanese government launched a campaign for the recovery of civil jurisdiction over Okinawa, an outcome that seemed likely to eventually weaken the ability of the United States to contain possible Chinese expansion into non-Communist Asia.

Both of these eventualities were—and are—very unwelcome in Moscow. Accordingly the Soviet Union began a further military buildup near the Sino-Soviet border, and in the spring of 1966 it introduced significant forces into the Mongolian People's Republic, where they could play an offensive as well as a defensive role, for the first time. It is probably not a coincidence that in 1966 the Soviet Union began to show an interest in Japanese cooperation in the economic development of Siberia and the Soviet Far East, as a means (among other things) of strengthening Moscow's hold on these vast regions in the face of possible Chinese claims or pressures.

Already immersed in the preliminaries to the Cultural Revolution, Maoists in Peking did not pay much attention to these ominous developments. During 1966 Moscow watched with anger and dismay the unfolding of the Cultural Revolution, a process that involved the virtual elimination of the Communist party apparatus as a functioning, let alone leading, entity in the Chinese political system. This struck at the heart of orthodox, or at any rate Soviet-style, Leninism in China and was particularly unwelcome to Brezhnev as the head of the Soviet party apparatus. Furthermore the frenzy of anti-"revisionism" that accompanied the Cultural Revolution led to more flagrant violations of, and provocations along, the Sino-Soviet border from the Chinese side than ever before, with irritating effects on Soviet nerves.

There is some evidence that the Soviet leadership contemplated military intervention of one kind or another in the spring of 1966 and again at the end of the year but refrained because the whirlwind speed of the Cultural Revolution did not permit the emergence of any coherent anti-Maoist group that might have been willing to collaborate with the Soviet Union. Another probable restraining factor was Moscow's fear, as a result of the milder official American tone toward China and some evidence of a Sino-American understanding on mutually tolerable limits on action with respect to Vietnam, that further pressure on China might drive it irrevocably into the arms of the United States, despite the anti-"imperialist" rhetoric that accompanied the Cultural Revolution. Moscow's unhappiness was not alleviated by the Chinese People's Liberation Army's assumption of the leading role in the Cultural Revolution in 1967; Soviet propaganda began to picture China as dominated by a fiercely nationalist, anti-Leninist coalition of Maoists, bureaucrats, and military figures that was involved in some sort of collaboration with the West German "revanchists" against the Soviet Union.

The frustration that Moscow felt in its relations with China, as well as in other aspects of its foreign policy (notably the Middle East), helps to account for its decision to assert its *machismo* by invading Czechoslovakia. That action in turn alarmed Peking more than anything that Moscow had done to date and led the Chinese to coin a new term for Soviet behavior, one very objectionable to Moscow: "social imperialism."

Tension rose along the Sino-Soviet border and was reflected on the Soviet side in an increased level of patrolling along the Far Eastern frontier in February 1969. A Chinese ambush of a Soviet patrol on the frozen Ussuri River on March 2 outraged Moscow but also gave it an evidently welcome pretext for disengaging itself from a crisis then in progress over West Berlin and also an issue on which to rally the Warsaw Pact states around the Soviet political standard. Soviet forces executed a devastating retaliation at the same spot on March 15.

During the next several months, to Peking's dismay, the Soviet Union greatly increased its forces near the Sino-Soviet border, staged a number of incidents along that border, uttered various threats of nuclear and conventional attack on China, and gave Peking a virtual ultimatum to begin negotiating on the border issue by September 13 at the latest. Under this pressure, and with the good offices of Romanian, North Korean, and North Vietnamese parties at work, Peking yielded to the extent that Chou En-lai talked with Kosygin on September 11. By October 7 it had been agreed that negotiations would be held at the deputy foreign minister level, and these have been going on in Peking at intervals since 20 October 1969.

Peking has been demanding an agreement on a cease-fire and mutual troop withdrawal and (until November 1974) a new boundary treaty that would label the old ones as "unequal" without changing the actual border except in limited areas in the Far East and Central Asia, where Peking claims that the Soviet Union occupies territory not conceded under the "unequal" treaties and has rebuffed as meaningless a Soviet offer of a nonaggression pact. The Soviet Union has rejected the Chinese demands and insisted on a settlement that in effect would confirm the old treaties without branding them as "unequal," because to admit that would constitute a dangerous precedent for other sectors of the Soviet frontier. Under these conditions the talks have become basically deadlocked.

Meanwhile the Soviet military buildup in the regions near the Chinese border has continued, to a level (since mid-1973) of about fifty divisions, including about five in the Mongolian People's Republic. There appear to be three main reasons for this extraordinary performance.

First, the Soviet leadership is genuinely uncertain and apprehensive, partly for emotional and racial reasons, about future Chinese policy-making, especially as Peking's nuclear strength increases and the United States disengages militarily from Asia; Moscow wishes to deter possible Chinese adventures or expansionist tendencies in any direction by means of pressures exerted along its inland borders.

Second, Moscow probably wanted to be in a position, if possible, to influence the composition of the Chinese leadership and the direction of its policies after Mao Tse-tung's death in ways favorable to its own interests. Chinese charges that former Defense Minister Lin Piao, purged in September 1971, collaborated with the Soviet Union appear to have no foundation, however.

Third, the Chinese demon has largely replaced the West German bogey, and to some extent the American bogey, in Soviet domestic and foreign propaganda, and it is necessary to maintain the demon's credibility by showing that he is taken seriously. In the ideological and international Communist fields, Suslov in particular appears to find an anti-Chinese posture (which is no doubt sincere on his part) useful as a basis on which to seek the support of foreign Communist parties.

One of the most intriguing and elusive aspects of recent Soviet China policy involves Moscow's contacts with Taiwan. These have consisted mainly of a visit by the Soviet "journalist" Victor Louis to Taiwan in October 1968, a few visits to the Soviet Union by Chinese with Nationalist connections, and the passage of some units of the Soviet Far Eastern fleet through the Taiwan Strait on 12 May 1973, apparently without prior notification to Taipei. The main purpose on both sides is probably to put psychological pressure on Peking, an effort that appears to have had some success, rather than something more substantial.

Meanwhile Moscow has been making some progress in involving Japanese, and possibly some American, firms in development projects in the Soviet Far East and Siberia, of which the best known and probably the most important is the plan for exploitation of the Tiumen oil and gas reserves (in Western Siberia) by means of a pipeline to the Soviet Pacific port of Nakhodka. Moscow has been largely successful in separating this economic question from the difficult political issues of a peace treaty and the northern territories, as they are known in Japan (that is, the southern Kuriles and in particular the islands of Etorofu, Kunashiri, Habomai, and Shikotan, the last two of which Moscow has occasionally promised to return as part of a peace settlement).

There is no clear indication at present when, or even whether, agreement will be reached on these questions. It might be thought that Tokyo's success in improving its relations with the People's Republic of China has made Moscow somewhat more conciliatory toward Japan. To some extent this has happened, but on the other hand Peking and Moscow are each pressuring Japan by indicating that Tokyo will pay a price for any undue improvement of relations with the other.

In a series of speeches (7 June 1969; 20 March 1972; 21 December 1972) Brezhnev sketched out a rather vague proposal for a "collective security" system in Asia, by analogy with similar Soviet proposals for Europe. He defined the concept to include renunciation of force, "respect for sovereignty and the inviolability of frontiers" (a proviso obviously designed to counter Chinese and Japanese territorial claims), noninterference in other countries' internal affairs, and economic cooperation. He has denied, but not very convincingly, that the proposal is aimed at containing or competing with China and has even said that he would like Peking to be included. Soviet propaganda points to the Soviet-Indian treaty of friendship of 9 August 1971, as the main achievement to date of the "collective security" proposal. Mainly because of Peking's opposition, other Asian governments have shown only minimal interest in the Soviet proposal.

During the weeks following Mao Tse-tung's death on 9 September 1976, Moscow cautiously extended some olive branches to Peking, but they were rejected and Chinese anti-Soviet propaganda went on as before. In the spring of 1977 Moscow accordingly resumed its own propaganda war on Peking. A number of developments in the spring of 1978, including Brezhnev's visit to the Sino-Soviet border region in April, made it clear that the Soviet leadership, and its military component in particular, was vigorously refusing a Chinese demand for a drastic thinning out of the Soviet forces near the border. It even appeared that Brezhnev might be contemplating some drastic steps aimed at rendering the Chinese more manageable before his evidently failing health forced him off the stage. Moscow is clearly afraid that Peking is irreversibly hostile and is going to grow stronger as its industrial and military modernization progresses.

The Sino-Soviet Alliance in Chinese Perspective

In mid-1949 Mao Tse-tung made his famous announcement that China would "lean to one side," the Soviet side, in the cold war. This decision had probably never been in serious doubt, despite some tentative and fruitless overtures to the United States by Mao in 1945, and it had been made clear as early as 1948 in connection with the pro-Soviet Chinese Communist stand on the Stalin-Tito controversy. Some serious past differences with Stalin were more than outweighed by ideological ties, the interlinked histories of the Chinese and Soviet parties, a felt need for Soviet economic and military aid and protection, and a desire to shield Manchuria and China's Inner Asian territories from possible Soviet pressures through a good relationship with Stalin.

In December 1949 Mao went to Moscow for a two-month visit and negotiated with Stalin on a variety of important subjects. It was agreed, in effect and informally, that northeast Asia (Korea and Japan) should be an area of primarily Soviet initiative and that Mao would be free to exert what influence he could on the Communist revolutionary movements in southern Asia—of which only one, Ho Chi Minh's in Vietnam, was making any real progress. Accordingly Peking supported the Cominform's (meaning Stalin's) insistence that the Japanese Communist party stop being "lovable" and begin to struggle against the American occupation regime; Stalin in effect ordered the Indian Communist leadership to apologize to Mao for some rude remarks that some of its members had made about him, and the Soviet press conceded that the Chinese Communist revolutionary "model" had some peculiar applicability to non-Communist Asia.

Mao and Stalin evidently discussed the Korean situation in the light of the obvious American intention to conclude a peace treaty with Japan and the possible American intention (in their view) to rearm Japan. They decided that the restless Kim Il Song should be given the green light and the necessary (Soviet) military equipment to invade South Korea some time in the summer of 1950, since at least for the time being the United States was giving convincing signs of being determined not to defend South Korea if it were attacked. In this way a possible springboard for future military action on the continent of Asia by a hypothetical Japanese-American alliance would be eliminated while the opportunity was ripe.

It was against this combination that Mao persuaded the evidently some-what reluctant Stalin to give him the Sino-Soviet treaty of alliance signed on 14 February 1950. At the same time Mao confirmed for the time being the special access to the main Manchurian railways and ports that Stalin had gained under the Yalta agreement and following his intervention in the war against Japan. Mao also got a $300 million industrial credit from Stalin. In March a series of Sino-Soviet joint stock companies (actually Soviet controlled) were created in Sinkiang and Manchuria, and the Soviet Union agreed to a substantial program of industrial aid to China. Late in 1950, after Chinese intervention in the Korean War, Soviet military aid to China got under way.

The emergence of this close relationship with Moscow was accompanied in China by a massive pro-Soviet propaganda campaign that saturated vir-tually every aspect of public life. For this there appear to have been three main reasons. First, Stalin was known not to care for halfhearted col-laborators, and Mao probably wanted to ensure a continuation of Soviet aid and protection by making it abundantly clear that he was no Tito. Sec-ond, one of the Chinese Communists' drawbacks in the eyes of many Chinese was their Soviet connection and Mao probably wanted to silence these fears by demonstrating, or at least asserting, that a Soviet connection was an excellent thing because the Soviet Union was the source of virtually all wisdom. Third, the Chinese Communist leadership, including Mao, does appear to have been genuinely impressed with the achievements of the Soviet Union under Stalin and to have considered it a model worth imi-tating.

The first serious test of the new Sino-Soviet relationship occurred when the North Korean forces were driven back onto their own soil in the autumn of 1950 and United Nations forces under General MacArthur ap-proached the Manchurian border. Although the Chinese intervention in the war was probably not motivated mainly by Soviet urging, it is almost certain that Stalin wanted the Chinese to intervene so that he would not have to confront the United States himself. It is also very likely that before deciding to intervene Mao extracted a promise of substantial Soviet mili-tary aid, and Soviet protection if it should be needed. Chinese intervention in Korea in effect cancelled the earlier agreement on Soviet preeminence in northeast Asia, and it is probably not a coincidence that in late 1951, after a series of Chinese defeats in Korea, Stalin withdrew his support for the idea that the Chinese revolutionary "model" possessed a special relevance to southern Asia.

Toward the end of 1952 serious problems arose between Peking and Moscow as a result of Peking's unwillingness to yield on the prisoner issue in the face of American pressures and as a result of long and evidently inconclusive negotiations over the types and amount of Soviet aid to be extended to China's forthcoming First Five-Year Plan (1953–1957). Whatever Stalin's exact attitude on these questions may have been, it appears that he was at least more sympathetic to Peking on the first one than his successors turned out to be. In retrospect at least, Peking, and the historian as well, can look back on Stalin's last years as the golden age of the Sino-Soviet alliance.

The Sino-Soviet Dispute in Chinese Perspective

Sino-Russian and Sino-Soviet relations have long been complicated by racial antipathies and historical disputes, including Chinese memories of territorial losses since the mid-nineteenth century. For a short time after the Communist "liberation" of China, however, these problems were repressed with a considerable effort on both sides.

The death of the respected, if not necessarily loved, Stalin removed the stopper from the bottle in which Chinese anti-Soviet attitudes, actual or potential, had been contained. Mao Tse-tung considered himself senior and superior to the new Soviet leadership, whose internal quarrels and unwillingness to confront American "imperialism" he evidently despised. More and more the Chinese leadership came to feel, rightly or wrongly, that the Soviet Union was trying to use the special Sino-Soviet relationship, and the aid program in particular, to influence China's development along Soviet lines and even perhaps to make China into a glorified Soviet satellite. There may also have been a perception that the pro-Soviet propaganda campaign had failed to make much of an impression on the essentially anti-foreign Chinese people and that the Chinese Communist regime could improve its standing at home by taking a line that was more independent, if not actually anti-Soviet.

These general trends were reinforced in the mid-1950s by specific political issues, some of which have already been mentioned. Having supported Khrushchev as a more acceptable candidate than Malenkov, Peking soon came to feel deceived. It seems to have come to regard Khrushchev, correctly, as less geopolitically oriented than Stalin and disposed to give a lower priority to the interests of contiguous China than to Soviet activities in far-flung non-Communist states such as India and Egypt.

Peking regarded the Soviet Union as obligated by its status as "head of the socialist camp" to give more active aid and support in connection with the "liberation" of Taiwan, especially after the signing of the United States–Nationalist treaty of alliance at the end of 1954, than Moscow was willing to provide. The Chinese were unfavorably impressed by the fear of American thermonuclear power that permeated the Soviet Twentieth Party Congress, and Mao in particular objected to the implications and the effects that Khrushchev's attack on Stalin had on Mao's own position. Peking felt that this performance contributed to the crisis in Eastern Europe in late 1956, the Chinese reaction to which was to insist forcefully on the principle of Soviet "leadership" over the "socialist camp" and the international Communist movement. As already noted, Mao's insistence on this principle, his version of which actually combined minimal Soviet authority with maximum Soviet responsibility for promoting the interests of other Communist parties, became particularly loud after Khrushchev's political and space successes in 1957. Mao was correspondingly and increasingly disappointed when Khrushchev failed to respond with a coordinated political offensive against American "imperialism" that might have helped Peking to "liberate" Taiwan.

Meanwhile Mao had reacted to the pressures on him from certain of his colleagues, for which he must have considered Khrushchev's attack on Stalin to be at least partly responsible, with a series of supposedly creative ideological and political initiatives, of which the most important were the Hundred Flowers Campaign (1956–1957) and the Great Leap Forward (1958–1960). These initiatives clearly indicated that China was repudiating Moscow's guidance (whatever Mao might say about Soviet "leadership"), rejecting the Soviet developmental model, and even claiming to be passing the Soviet Union (ideologically and politically if not economically) on the road to "communism."

About the end of 1958 Mao began to apply the highly pejorative term "modern revisionism," which he had coined a year earlier and had first applied to Tito, to Khrushchev as well. The last straws for Mao included not only Khrushchev's performance during the Taiwan Strait crisis of 1958, which Peking was to ridicule publicly five years later, but his caution in waiting until it was over to launch his Berlin campaign. As already indicated, the year 1959 saw abundant additional cause for Chinese outrage, especially Soviet policy toward the United States and India.

About the end of 1959 Peking adopted what may be termed a dual adversary strategy. In other words, it determined to conduct simultaneous ideological and political struggles against both American "imperialism" and Soviet "revisionism" (or "modern revisionism"). One of the first signs of this was an anti-Soviet propaganda offensive, stopping only just short of naming Khrushchev as the target of its wrath, that Peking launched in April 1960. It was probably to proclaim defiance of Soviet "revisionism" that the highly ideological Lin Piao, who was to become the classic exponent of the dual adversary strategy in 1965 (in his *Long Live the Victory of People's War!*), organized violations of the Soviet frontier by Chinese military personnel beginning shortly after he became defense minister in 1959.

A fairly frequent feature of Peking's anti-Soviet propaganda was the charge that the United States and the Soviet Union were "colluding" against China, in addition to "contending" against each other in some other respects. In addition to appeasing "imperialism," Soviet "revisionism" was alleged to be remiss in supporting the cause of world revolution. Peking seems to have been surprised, and was certainly infuriated, when Khrushchev retaliated by cutting off economic aid in the summer of 1960.

Peking soon came to perceive Albania as a useful ally and a point of leverage in the intensifying struggle. The trend of 1962 toward an improvement in Sino-Soviet relations was more than wiped out by Khrushchev's performance in the Cuban missile crisis. For nearly two years after that, until his fall, Peking vigorously opposed his efforts to convene another international conference of Communist parties and did its best to create anti-Soviet "Marxist-Leninist" splinter parties. It was outraged by the nuclear test ban treaty not only as an outstanding case of Soviet "collusion" with the United States but as a device to make it more embarrassing for China to develop nuclear weapons. Peking's raising of the Sino-Soviet territorial issue began in March 1963 following a taunting inquiry by Khrushchev as to why China, which had been so rough with India, tolerated enclaves of Chinese territory under the control of Western powers (Britain in Hong Kong, Portugal in Macao). This was a serious Chinese mistake, one that introduced a grave risk of war into the Sino-Soviet dispute.

Mao's campaign against Soviet "revisionism" had evidently come to seem indispensable to him not only as an aspect of his foreign policy but in his domestic struggle against his more moderate colleagues. It was therefore almost inevitable that he should reject Kosygin's offer of a pragmatic accommodation and the Soviet request for "united action" on Vietnam, as well as a Japanese Communist proposal of March 1966 along similar lines, and that he should use the term "Khrushchev revisionism" to describe the stand of Khrushchev's successors once they had resurrected (in March 1965) his project for another international conference of Communist parties. Some of Mao's colleagues, notably Liu Shao-ch'i, appear to have been considerably less hostile to the post-Khrushchev Soviet leadership than Mao was, and this difference was evidently one issue in the first stage of the Cultural Revolution. There is no doubt that even before Khrushchev's fall Mao had come to regard Soviet "revisionism" as the inspiration for at least

some of his domestic opponents and a possible source of ideological infec-
tion for China's youth; these were the problems that the Cultural Revolution was mainly designed to solve.

Peking, or at least the Maoists, was evidently not much impressed by the
Soviet military gestures of 1966. But it probably was concerned by a series
of powerful anti-Chinese articles in the Soviet theoretical journal *Kommunist,* which began in the spring of 1968 and were probably intended by
Suslov to give his colleagues an alternate target for their frustrations about
Czechoslovakia, the invasion of which he evidently opposed. The invasion,
followed by the proclamation of the Brezhnev Doctrine, which suggested
that the Soviet Union might try to do to China what it had just done to
Czechoslovakia, aroused much greater concern and created in Peking for
the first time a serious perception of an imminent Soviet military threat.
Chou En-lai began in November 1968 to try to improve relations with the
United States as the best available strategy, but in January–February 1969
Mao, probably at Lin Piao's urging, vetoed this approach for the time
being and cancelled an ambassadorial conversation with the United States
scheduled for 20 February at Warsaw.

Consistent with his simpleminded adherence to the dual adversary
strategy, Lin then appears to have planned a blow at the Soviet "social imperialists" that would also create an atmosphere of manageable crisis that
might be helpful to him at the forthcoming Ninth Party Congress, where he
was scheduled to be proclaimed Mao's heir. He probably reasoned that the
Soviet Union would be inhibited—both by its paper bear nature and by the
crisis over West Berlin in which it appeared to be involved—from
retaliating at a level genuinely dangerous to China. But the Soviet response
soon assumed massive proportions, and Lin was unable to prevent Chou
En-lai from stepping forward and entering into negotiations with the Soviet
Union, as well as showing some receptivity to the private overtures from
the Nixon administration that began to be made through intermediaries in
March 1969. There is no question that coping with the Soviet threat has
become Peking's most important single foreign policy objective.

Since Lin Piao's fall in September 1971, Peking has alleged that he was
pro-Soviet and indeed was killed in an airplane crash in the Mongolian
People's Republic (on the night of 12–13 September) while trying to defect
to the Soviet Union. The charge appears to be false and part of an extensive
"disinformation" campaign designed to blacken Lin's reputation. It is much
more probable that he interpreted Brezhnev's private offer of a nonaggression pact in February 1971 as evidence that the Soviet threat was
diminishing, that there was therefore no need to "tilt" toward the United
States, and that the dual adversary strategy could and should remain in effect. Chou En-lai, on the other hand, insisted successfully that Moscow was

still dangerous and untrustworthy and that there was no acceptable alternative to an opening to the United States. This issue was almost certainly a major factor in Lin's fall.

Peking has held the Soviet Union in play at the border talks while proceeding with great skill to construct a network of international relationships designed mainly to restrain possible Soviet pressures on China. The most important of these obviously is the relationship with the United States, and in particular the Nixon visit to China in February 1972. Other major achievements are the establishment of diplomatic relations with Japan (September 1972) and West Germany (October 1972). In addition to restraint, Peking is trying to exercise deterrence by modernizing China's conventional forces and creating a nuclear force that will be large enough to be effective and yet not so large as to be startling and provocative to Moscow; it appears that Peking is having considerable success in both respects.

While Peking and Moscow remain basically in a state of confrontation and are competing for influence in virtually every part of the world (including Western Europe, where Peking fears the Soviet Union is practicing a détente policy in order to be better able to turn against China), there have been some limited practical improvements in bilateral relations. Ambassadors were exchanged in October–November 1970 (they had been withdrawn in 1966), and a trade agreement was signed in November 1970. In November 1974 Peking gave the appearance of dropping a new boundary treaty from its list of demands on Moscow. On 27 December 1975, Peking released, with what amounted to an apology, the crew of a Soviet military helicopter whom it had been holding since March of the previous year on charges of espionage.

The death of the pragmatic and diplomatic Chou En-lai, on 8 January 1976, was followed by a period of ascendancy on the part of extreme anti-Soviet elements of the Chinese leadership. These were purged in October 1976, however, a month after the death of Mao Tse-tung. This important shift did not produce any observable change in Peking's anti-Soviet posture, for at least two reasons. In the first place, all Chinese leaders, radical or not, resent the bullying they have received at Moscow's hands since 1969 and the continuing threat posed by the massive Soviet forces near their border. Secondly, Peking seems to believe, correctly, that Moscow's price for a genuine Sino-Soviet reconciliation would include a return to something resembling the semisatellite status for China that existed in the early 1950s; this Chinese nationalism will not tolerate.

During 1978 and early 1979, Moscow perceived a series of developments that heightened its already grave concern over the behavior of its Chinese neighbor: a strengthened commitment to "socialist modernization" on Peking's part following Teng Hsaio-p'eng's return to office in 1977, accompanied by indications on the part of several industrial countries of interest in assisting this process; a new demand (in a speech by Hua Kuo-feng of 26 February 1978) that the Soviet Union reduce its military presence along the entire Sino-Soviet border; a Sino-Japanese peace treaty (12 August 1978) and a proliferation of commercial and technological ties between the two major East Asian states; the "normalization" of Sino-American relations (15 December 1978) and Teng's ensuing triumphant visit to the United States; and the Chinese attack (17 February 1979) on Vietnam, with which Moscow had signed a treaty of friendship as recently as 3 November 1978. In the spring of 1978 there was a flurry of Soviet excitement over the Sino-Soviet border, including a visit by Brezhnev and Defense Minister Ustinov. A year later, Moscow gave evidence of serious concern over the Chinese attack on Vietnam but also of a profound reluctance to intervene unless absolutely necessary; for its part, Peking made an obvious effort to limit its military operations so as not to precipitate Soviet intevention.

Japan and the Soviet Union

The Soviet Union is regarded in Japan as a traditional enemy and a current threat, and it regularly ranks in Japanese public opinion polls as the most disliked of foreign countries. This situation obviously limits very seriously Moscow's capability to acquire influence in and on Japan via conciliation. Moscow's capability for acquiring influence via pressure and coercion is drastically restricted by the American defensive commitment to Japan and by fear of pushing Japan into massive, and perhaps nuclear, rearmament. The situation is worsened by the usual, or more than usual, Soviet heavyhandedness, which in turn reflects Moscow's sense of frustration over its relationship with Japan: Soviet ships seize Japanese fishing boats and Soviet aircraft sometimes strafe them; provocative Soviet reconnaissance flights are conducted in the immediate vicinity of the Japanese home islands. All this had made it practically impossible for Moscow to exploit the various tensions in Japanese-American relations — over China policy, over security policy, and above all over economic relations — that have arisen since 1970.

The political clumsiness of the Soviet Union's approach to Japan is well illustrated in the history of its contacts with the Japanese Communist party, one of the oldest in Asia (it was established in 1922). For obvious geographic and cultural reasons, Chinese Communist influence on the party became significant at an early date. As the Sino-Soviet dispute came into the open about 1960 the JCP, like other Communist parties, had to choose sides or at least make a conscious effort to avoid doing so. The effects of the

Sino-Soviet dispute, combined with the JCP's own political maturation, have made the party increasingly and outspokenly independent of both Moscow and Peking over the long run. This in turn has contributed — together with the JCP's good organization and vigorous taking up of the issues most important to the urban population (inflation and pollution) — to making the JCP for a time the most rapidly growing party (in terms of electoral appeal) in Japan.

In 1963 the JCP, like the other major Asian Communist parties, tilted noticeably although not completely toward Peking. The main reasons were Khrushchev's anti-Chinese obsession and his seeming weakness in the face of American "imperialism." After his fall, Mao's rejection of a major effort by the JCP to bring about a Sino-Soviet compromise on the issue of "united action" over Vietnam in March 1966, together with Red Guard attacks on the JCP as "revisionist" during the Cultural Revolution, largely alienated the JCP from Peking but without pushing it much closer to Moscow.

The CPSU had angered the JCP by supporting a pro-Soviet splinter group, the Voice of Japan. Early in 1968, however, Suslov went to Japan prepared to stop this support in exchange for the JCP's participation in his plan for another international conference of Communist parties. But while he agreed to stop supporting the Voice of Japan (although this commitment was not fully kept), he was compelled to acquiesce in the JCP's refusal to take part in his proposed conference, which Peking was vigorously denouncing. The JCP was outraged by the invasion of Czechoslovakia and loudly attacked Moscow for it. In 1969 the JCP began to send the CPSU a series of quasi-diplomatic messages taking a strongly nationalist stand on the question of the northern territories, criticizing the continuing Soviet contacts with the Voice of Japan, and the like.

The rapid improvement of Sino-American and Sino-Japanese relations in 1972 startled Moscow into a somewhat more political approach to Japan, one aspect of which has been a renewed effort to improve relations with the JCP — for example, by something close to an actual break with the Voice of Japan.

The Japan Socialist party has never been as anti-Soviet, or as anti-Chinese, as the JCP has tended to become, although it too demands the return of all four of the disputed islands. But the JSP is not of much current interest to Moscow, except as a member of a hypothetical Popular Front, since it lacks both the "fraternal" status of the JCP and the hold on power of the ruling Liberal Democratic party.

In Moscow's eyes, if the Sato government (1964–1972) was too pro-American, the successor Tanaka government was far too pro-Chinese. Apparently it was precisely because of the moves by both Washington and Tokyo toward Peking that Foreign Minister Gromyko went to Japan in

January 1972. He agreed with his Japanese opposite numbers that negotiations on a peace treaty should start in September (the Soviet Union had not signed the San Francisco peace treaty in 1951) but made no concessions on the territorial issue, which the Japanese at that time were trying to link with the proposal to develop the Tiumen oil field.

The negotiations did not actually begin in September because Premier Tanaka, encouraged no doubt by the reversion of Okinawa to Japanese control the previous May, began shortly after his installation in July to make it clear that the return of the four disputed islands, or at least a promise to return them, was a prerequisite for starting the negotiations — even though the northern territories issue was far from possessing the importance in the eyes of the Japanese public that the Okinawa question had had.

Foreign Minister Ohira went to Moscow in October to discuss the problems of the peace treaty negotiations and the northern territories; he and the Soviet press subsequently disagreed as to whether Moscow had promised once more, at that time, to return Habomai and Shikotan as part of a peace settlement. It was agreed, however, that talks on these questions should continue in 1973.

Meanwhile Peking was loudly supporting Tokyo on the northern territories question, as it had done since a famous interview by Mao Tse-tung with a Japanese Socialist delegation in July 1964. In addition Peking was showing greater tolerance than before for the United States–Japanese security treaty and had committed itself (in the Chou-Tanaka communiqué of 29 September 1972) to negotiating a peace treaty of its own with Japan. These and other developments in Sino-Japanese relations were bound to have some effect on Moscow.

Tanaka, for his part, was looking for a way to improve his standing and that of his party after the setback suffered in the December 1972 election. Accordingly, in early March 1973, he wrote a letter to Brezhnev proposing resumption of talks on a peace treaty and the Tiumen oil project. Brezhnev gave this proposal a cordial reception and invited Tanaka to Moscow; he accepted, even though Brezhnev is not known to have promised any concessions on the northern territories. At present the Japanese government is somewhat divided on whether to link the two questions in the hope of getting concessions on the northern territories through Soviet eagerness for Japanese cooperation in the Tiumen project; Foreign Minister Ohira appears to favor separating the two issues, and in a formal sense they are being treated separately.

Since 1966 the Soviet Union has been expressing interest in Japanese cooperation in the economic development of Siberia and the Soviet Far East, and the most important of the projects it has in mind involves the Tiumen oil and gas reserves in Western Siberia. Japan for its part is enormously interested in the fossil fuels and mineral resources of Soviet Asia. Apart from the obvious drawback of distance, Japanese industry is greatly interested in the Tiumen project because the petroleum is known to be very low in sulfur. Also, the time and cost of transporting it from the Soviet Pacific port of Nakhodka (assuming the prior construction of a 4,400-mile pipeline, of course) would be far less than to ship oil from the Middle East, where in any case political conditions are notoriously unstable and the governments increasingly greedy in the matter of oil royalties.

Moscow has asked for Japanese financing, on the order of $1 billion, for the project and has given the Japanese to understand that they can expect 40 to 50 million tons of oil a year from the Tiumen fields (only a small fraction of total Japanese consumption, which was 200 million tons in 1970 and growing rapidly). Moscow has also shown some interest in American cooperation in this project, and two American firms have tentatively involved themselves in it.

Attractive though the Tiumen project is, it presents several serious difficulties from the Japanese point of view. Not only are the economic philosophies and organization of the two countries entirely different but so are their senses of priorities; the Japanese would prefer more emphasis on Eastern Siberia and the Far East, and less on Western Siberia. The Tiumen project obviously poses formidable problems of distance, climate, and so on, which are likely to eat into its profitability. The Japanese firms interested in the project want more technical data, access to the site, and guarantees on quantities and prices than Moscow has so far been willing to provide.

Soviet demands for large credits on easy terms, ideally with the participation of the Japanese government, have not gone down very well in Japan, where there are many alternate demands for capital. Tokyo is also concerned because Peking, although not necessarily opposed to Japanese activity in Soviet Asia, has qualms about the Tiumen project on the ground that some of the oil would go to the Soviet Pacific fleet (which is also regarded as a threat by many Japanese) and to Soviet forces along the Chinese border. Finally, some Japanese vaguely fear that Japan might become "dependent" in some sense on Tiumen oil and thereby place dangerous leverage in Moscow's hands.

Progress toward a Soviet-Japanese treaty of peace and friendship is currently being blocked by two main obstacles. One is continuing Soviet refusal, partly for strategic reasons (the importance of the Kuriles as a defensive barrier and an outward passage for the Soviet Pacific fleet) and partly for political reasons (the likelihood that yielding territory to one neighbor would whet the appetite of others) to return the four islands at the southern end of the Kurile chain that is a Japanese sine qua non for a treaty. The other is vigorous Soviet objections to Tokyo's eventual decision, after much Chinese prodding, to sign a similar treaty with Peking that would include an "antihegemony" clause, which Moscow correctly considers to be aimed (by Peking) at itself.

Korea and the Soviet Union

North Korea was a Soviet satellite from its creation in 1948 (or in reality from the beginning of the Soviet occupation in 1945) to 1950, to the point where it is inconceivable that the invasion of South Korea was undertaken without Stalin's approval, except that Kim Il Song may have moved the time up from midsummer to late June on his own initiative. In any case Moscow, like the other Communist regimes involved, seems to have drawn from this episode and its aftermath the conclusion that it would be most unwise to resort to large-scale violence in the Korean peninsula again.

Chinese intervention in the war, to which Stalin had evidently given his approval, obviously created the possibility that North Korea would become a Chinese instead of a Soviet satellite. That this did not actually happen was ensured by Chinese defeats suffered after December 1950, which opened the way to a steady process whereby Kim Il Song achieved his own unchallenged power over his colleagues — or in some cases ex-colleagues, since a number were purged at intervals — as well as his independence from Soviet or Chinese control. This happy situation both resulted from and contributed to Kim's ability to play Peking and Moscow against each other, especially as the Sino-Soviet dispute worsened. This was true even though he attempted, rather paradoxically and especially in the tense year 1969, to mediate the dispute.

As he grew in stature and independence, Kim created a towering "cult of personality" for himself, not only at home but abroad; he even held North Korea up as a model for Third World countries. Much as they disliked this, Peking and Moscow had no choice but to keep on as good terms with him as possible (except for a brief period of strain in Sino–North Korean relations caused by the Cultural Revolution); this involved, among other things, extending him economic and military aid in a more or less competitive fashion, beginning in 1953.

Kim evidently felt threatened by the military seizure of power in South Korea in May 1961 and was happy to be able to extract defensive alliances first from Moscow and then from Peking within the next several weeks. His growing objections after 1962 to Soviet "revisionism," and in particular to Khrushchev's vacillating policy toward the United States, moved him somewhat closer to Peking for a time after 1963, but he never went so far as to break with Moscow, as Peking in effect did.

Unlike the Chinese but like the North Vietnamese, for example, Kim continued to send delegates to Soviet Party Congresses, although all three boycotted the international conference of Communist parties held at Moscow in June 1969. Indeed a kind of tacit alliance emerged between Pyongyang and Hanoi with the aim of coping not only with American hostility but with allegedly inadequate Soviet and Chinese support. It is almost certainly not a coincidence that a period of strenuous although unsuccessful North Korean efforts to start a "people's war" in South Korea through armed infiltration coincided very closely with the most intense phase of the Vietnam War (1965–1969). Nevertheless Kim Il Song's domestic and foreign policies claimed to be, and to a considerable extent were, based on the principle of *chuch'e* (self-identity, or self-reliance), or in other words on an effort to go it alone as much as possible.

There is some reason to believe that Moscow was involved in the seizure by the North Korean navy of the American "spy" ship *Pueblo* in January 1968; certainly it was Moscow more than Pyongyang that benefited from the opportunity to examine the ship's equipment. On the other hand the shooting down of the American EC-121 (a reconnaissance aircraft) over the Sea of Japan in mid-April 1969 appears to have been a unilateral North Korean act. Soviet ships took part in the search for survivors, and Moscow gave signs of being perturbed by the immense buildup of American naval power in the region that ensued.

President Podgorny's visit to North Korea the following month was probably designed to discourage Pyongyang from further performances of that kind, as well as to give it at least moral support in a border dispute that it was having with Peking at the time (and that Peking dropped in 1970, no doubt mainly in order to prevent Moscow from benefiting from it). In the spring of 1970 Peking had a windfall when Pyongyang withdrew from an international oceanographic project for the Sea of Japan in protest against Soviet insistence on including Japanese scientists; the next several months witnessed some very energetic cultivation of the North Koreans by the Chinese, which Moscow was unable or unwilling to match.

Moscow had no reason to be surprised when the atmosphere of détente created by the improvement in relations between the United States and both the Soviet Union and China found a reflection in Korea. But much as Moscow prefers political to military approaches to Korean reunification, it must have been perturbed by the fervor with which Kim Il Song threw himself into the commencement of a political relationship with South Korea, and in particular by the extraordinary (for a Communist state) reference in the joint communiqué issued by Seoul and Pyongyang on 4 July 1972, to a "great national unity . . . transcending differences in ideas, ideologies, and systems." For the record, of course, Moscow had no choice but to approve this dramatic development.

The Soviet Union is likely to make some sort of response in the near future to South Korea's recently expressed interest in relations, mainly commercial, with "nonhostile" Communist states, a term that includes the Soviet Union since it was not formally involved in the Korean War. As in the case of other countries such as Thailand, South Korea's motivation appears to be both to seek a counterweight to Japanese commercial influence and to help ensure against possible Chinese domination in the aftermath of American military withdrawal from the region.

Peking's presence in the United Nations is likely to prove very valuable to Pyongyang in its struggle to terminate the United Nations' role in Korea and thus undermine the American military position in South Korea. Moscow cannot afford to let itself be too greatly outdone in this regard, as it showed when it gave crucial support to North Korea's admission to the World Health Organization on 17 May 1973, by successfully proposing that the vote be conducted by secret ballot.

In recent years Moscow has been considerably less energetic and successful than Peking in cultivating North Korean goodwill, although both of Pyongyang's allies agree to the extent of wanting few things less than another war in the Korean peninsula. The Soviet Union appears to favor, without being willing to propose openly, a "German" solution for Korea: two separate states enjoying de facto relations with each other and willing to refrain from attacking one another.

Conclusions and Outlook

On account of obvious geographic and geopolitical factors, notably the powerful military presence of the United States since 1945, East Asia has generally been an area of high risk and, except perhaps in the economic field, relatively little potential gain — except the avoidance of setbacks or disaster — for the Soviet Union. For a time the risks seemed to be greatly lessened, and the potential for gain enhanced, through China's "leaning to one side" after 1949. But this promise was soon wiped out and reversed by the rapid escalation of the Sino-Soviet dispute after 1959.

Except for the heyday of the Sino-Soviet alliance (1950–1953), the Soviet Union has not had much political influence on the countries of East Asia since 1945, political influence being normally derived for the most part from common interests; the Soviet Union's influence has come mainly from its economic and military strength — which it, like the United States, has found difficult to translate into political gains.

For the Soviet Union continues to be in East Asia but not of it. It lacks positive cultural and historic ties, as well as empathy, with the true regional states. It has a tradition of aggression in the region and a reputation for having been even more aggressive than it has been in fact; this was offset, but only for a time, by its good record against Germany and Japan during World War II.

The USSR also has a poor reputation for fair dealing with the states of the region, including the Communist ones. By its heavyhandedness, no matter how justified in its own eyes, it has helped to keep Japan more closely tied to the United States than would otherwise have been the case and has vitually driven China into the arms of the United States and Japan. The Sino-Soviet dispute, to whose emergence Moscow certainly made a massive contribution, has created valuable opportunities for the United States, and to a lesser extent for Japan. If the Soviet Union was once welcomed in China as a counterweight to and shield against the United States, its treatment of the Chinese has ensured, at least for a time, that it will not be equally welcome again anywhere else in the region.

Chinese opposition to the Soviet "collective security" proposal has not been balanced by strong support from any of the other Asian states, most of which in fact are distinctly cool toward it, in part on account of the Chinese objections. The Japanese are particularly put off by the reference to the "inviolability of frontiers," which clearly suggests an invitation to them to abandon their claim to the northern territories. Only if—in the context of an American withdrawal—China came to be perceived as more of a threat to the region than it is at present, would the Soviet Union stand much of a chance of gaining acceptance for proposals such as this or for itself as a counterweight to Peking. In the meantime the Asian states are likely to seek better relations with both Moscow and Peking, thus in effect playing them against each other.

The Sino-Soviet conflict has compelled each of the adversaries to strengthen its position, militarily in particular. While most of this increment is of course currently absorbed in the management of the conflict, it could become available for other purposes, especially if American military strength in the region continues to decline and if some sort of accommodation is reached between Peking and Moscow. The Soviet Union has attained strategic parity with the United States in recent years, and since 1969 its regional buildup has put it in a position, probably for the first time since 1945, to fight a major war in East Asia. This fact, plus for Japan the pull of Soviet Asia's resources, makes the Soviet Union a factor that must be taken more seriously in the region than ever before, whether as a threat or as a prospective partner. This will be all the more true when Moscow completes its Baikal Amur Main Line Railway to Sovietskaia Gavan on the Pacific and its naval base complex in Sakhalin and Kamohatka, which may rival the formidable one on the Kola Peninsula near Murmansk.

There is an obvious possibility that American disengagement will open the way for Soviet advances in East Asia. This Peking is particularly anxious to avoid; it prefers as an alternative the retention of a substantial American military presence in Japan and Korea as well as elsewhere in Asia, for the time being at least, and it has recently indicated a tolerant attitude toward a somewhat increased Japanese defense establishment as long as it does not become a genuine threat to China. The latter eventuality is most improbable; if anything, both the United States and Japan are trying to stabilize China so as to increase its powers of resistance to possible Soviet pressures.

The range of possibilities for the future relationship between the Soviet Union and China is obviously rather wide, but that of the probabilities is considerably less so. A Sino-Soviet war, in which the Soviet Union would presumably be the aggressor and the victor, is not very likely for a number of reasons; two of the most important reasons are the relationship of both countries with the United States and the nuclear deterrent that Peking is in the process of creating.

For the time being, meaning at least as long as Brezhnev remains in charge, the outlook seems to be for a continuation of roughly the current neither-war-nor-peace relationship. Thereafter, provided the Soviet Union does not apply military pressures, a trend toward accommodation seems likely since it is desirable on both sides on a number of practical grounds. It would presumably involve a defusing of the territorial issue, with or without a formal agreement, and would almost certainly require a substantial Soviet military withdrawal from the border region, just as the achievement of a positive political relationship between China and the United States was impossible as long as Peking felt threatened by the American containment policy. A restoration of the spirit of 1950 in Sino-Soviet relations, however, is highly improbable.

If this scenario materializes, and if the present trend toward a loosening of Japanese-American ties without a sharp break continues, a multilateral balance among the four major regional powers seems likely to emerge. If so, the effects on the stability of East Asia will presumably be beneficial, since neither the Soviet Union nor any other power will be able to dominate the region, even if it should feel inclined to try.

Notes

1. "The Origin and Development of the Differences Between the Leadership of the CPSU and Ourselves," *People's Daily* and *Red Flag,* 6 September 1963.

8

Southeast Asia

Bernard K. Gordon

The role of the Soviet Union in Southeast Asia in the 1980s will be more self-confident, more wide-ranging, and probably more effective than in any earlier period. Since at least the mid-1970s, Moscow has prepared the groundwork in this region for initiatives of a political, economic, and to a lesser extent a military nature, and Southeast Asia will now witness an active Soviet effort designed to capitalize on the investment. There are three main reasons for this. The first pertains to the Sino-Soviet relationship; the second to Soviet relations with the United States; and the third is independent of Moscow's policy toward any particular foreign state. It derives instead from the overall and general nature of Soviet foreign policy in this era.

Main Soviet Considerations and Issue Areas

In connection with the first—China—the Soviet aim will be to forestall Peking from achieving any position of exclusive advantage, or dependency on China, among any of the Southeast Asian nations. China is a main adversary, and it is in the Soviet interest to prevent where possible accretions to China's prestige and power. Second, and with reference to the United States, the USSR recognizes that there has been an American withdrawal from the most forward positions and postures the U.S. occupied in Southeast Asia during the period 1955–1975. Moscow expects that for a variety of reasons some of that American disengagement will continue, and the Soviet aim will be to have itself regarded as a substitute for some of the roles previously filled by the U.S., and in some of the same places. Finally, there is a general view among Russian leaders that the USSR is a global power, no less so than the United States, and Southeast Asia has assets of geography and resources that are important for any power with such universal pretensions. Accordingly, to make it unalterably clear that the

Soviet Union is a state with worldwide interests, Soviet trade, Soviet shipping, and the involvement of the Soviet Union generally will be projected
to this region where previously its presence was modest.

There may be a fourth reason, probably not essential to a heightened Soviet concern with Southeast Asia, but one that will reinforce the impetus for
the involvement provided by the first three. This is the growing role in Asia
generally, but especially in Southeast Asia, of Japan. Tokyo is already the
dominant economic force in the area, and the importance it attaches to
Southeast Asia underscores the significance that all major states give to this
region of 300 million. Its resources—rubber, oil, and tin, for example—
have long been considered of major importance, and increasingly Southeast Asia is recognized as a significant market. This stems from its fairly
successful economic development performance since the mid-1960s, especially among the five states grouped together in ASEAN, the Association of
Southeast Asian Nations.[1] The region has accomplished the highest rate of
economic growth among all developing regions; along with its good future
prospects and its large population, this has made Southeast Asia an already
attractive market for both the manufactured goods and many of the commodities of the industrialized states.

This factor would be of importance in any case to a Soviet Union that is
in an outward-looking phase; the newer consideration that the region has
become so exclusively Japan's economic domain will heighten that interest.
·For Japan is an old Soviet (and Russian) adversary, and it is today the
world's second-ranking economic power. The fact that Japan draws
significantly for its economic strength from its Southeast Asian base, while
it is politically aligned with the U.S. and increasingly cooperative with
China, will add to Soviet reasons for interest in Southeast Asia. In this case
the Soviet approach will be to project an alternative to those governments
already wary of too-heavy a dependence on Japan and apprehensive about
China's future policies. Concretely, Moscow will seek to offer attractive
commercial competition—as supplier, shipper, and as a market for Southeast Asian commodities.

It is, however, the political presence of the USSR with which we need to
be initially most concerned, and in Southeast Asia, Moscow has been led by
considerations of international politics and Soviet national security to break
new ground in the practice of its foreign policy. For example, in 1978 the
Communist-world economic group known as COMECOM, led by the
USSR, for the first time admitted to full membership a nation from Asia.
Only months later, in 1978, the Soviet Union signed a treaty with the same
Asian nation—Vietnam—that incorporates a clear mutual security provision.[2] This was the first time since the ill-fated treaty with China, almost
thirty years before, that the Soviet Union has implied this sort of formal

military commitment to an Asian state.

Similarly in 1978, the USSR dropped its long-standing policy of coolness, or outright opposition, to all "regional cooperation" arrangements among non-Communist nations. In a 180-degree reverse course, the USSR has begun to endorse ASEAN, the regional group in Southeast Asia that for ten years it had denounced as an American invention. And it was in 1977 that Soviet imports from the Philippines, which for years had been so insignificant that they had not been reported, reached the remarkable figure of $144 million. This was a figure almost *nine times* higher than they had been just two years earlier, in 1975.

Each of these developments—having to do with (1) Vietnam and Indochina; (2) with the ASEAN *group;* and (3) with certain ASEAN *members* who have been among the most "pro-Western" of all nations—suggests the extent to which there is a qualitative change in Soviet policy toward Southeast Asia. In the remainder of this chapter, I will take up each of these three issues. My goal will be to describe what has been the course of recent events, to explain the likely direction of future Soviet relations with the region, and finally to suggest the reasons for the now-evident change in Moscow's posture.

Beachhead in Vietnam

In Moscow on 3 November 1978, Leonid Brezhnev, general secretary of the Soviet Communist party, hugged Le Duan, general secretary of the Vietnam Communist party. The occasion was the signing of the Soviet-Vietnam Treaty of Friendship and Cooperation, and the symbols that this was a momentous occasion were much in evidence. Aside from Kosygin and Pham Van Dong, who signed as heads of government, also present were such figures as Suslov and Ustinov, and for the Vietnamese, chief of the army general staff Van Tien Dung. While it is proper that the event captured worldwide attention, and understandable why it was quickly denounced by Peking, it is less clear why it seemed to cause such surprise in Washington and Tokyo. It would have been more correct to recognize that in Vietnam the Soviet Union had at long last found what Brezhnev called "an important outpost for peace and socialism in Southeast Asia."[3]

Indeed the treaty had been presaged, as I have already indicated, by Vietnam's entrance into COMECOM the previous June—the first full member since Cuba joined in 1962—and the only Asian state in the Communist economic community. Both developments reflect a genuine convergence of interests between Moscow and Hanoi, for the Soviet Union has for years been aiming for just such an Asian outpost—with the requirement only that it front on the South China Sea or nearby. In the early 1960s (as the earlier edition of this book pointed out) there was widespread suspicion that a Soviet-built (but never completed) "oceanographic research institute" in Indonesia was intended as a submarine base,[4] and after that relationship soured, as I wrote in 1968, the Soviets appear to have entertained hopes for the use of Cambodian territory. Moscow had surprisingly named as ambassador to Phnom Penh the very senior diplomat Sergei M. Kudryavtsev, and with the port of Sihanoukville in mind I suggested, "the Soviet Union may have chosen Phnom Penh as the base for its expected effort to become involved again in Southeast Asia—an involvement that has not been evident since 1965, when relations with Indonesia so markedly cooled."[5]

The Soviet Union's insistence on staying-on in Cambodia probably cost it any possibility of developing a decent relationship with the very radical, and Chinese-supported, Khmers who took control in Phnom Penh after 1975. From that point on, and particularly to the extent that the Soviet Union was willing to support Vietnam's ambitions in Indochina, the relationship with Hanoi became increasingly close. For it has to be recognized that the leadership of Vietnam, despite numerous disclaimers, does see itself as the proper leadership for postcolonial Indochina. Its intentions were made clear—certainly insofar as Laos was concerned—in the summer of 1977. At that time Vietnam and Laos signed their own Treaty of Friendship, and its terms include so heavy a degree of Vietnamese "guidance" in Laotian affairs that the treaty represents a virtual Vietnamese annexation of Laos.

In all of this the Soviet Union's role, reflected in the presence of scores of Soviet technicians and significant road-construction projects in Laos, has been firmly supportive. Moscow, in other words, endorses Hanoi's plans for Indochina, for which the proper term is hegemony. Concretely, moreover, it has been only the Soviets who have been willing and able to provide the postwar economic assistance sought by the Vietnamese, despite Hanoi's ability during the war years (1965–1975) to obtain military assistance from both China and the USSR, and to stay on good terms with each. In the late stages of the war, particularly in terms of antiaircraft and other modern equipment, China was not in a position to be of as much help, and has been similarly unable (or unwilling) to provide the heavy industrial support related to Vietnamese "reconstruction." For this goal Vietnam sought U.S. assistance as "compensation," but the Congress refused that notion. Japan is the only other possible source, and it has been most reluctant to underwrite a major Vietnam aid program in Vietnam—in the absence of clear assurances that Hanoi has no further territorial or political ambitions in Southeast Asia.

Moscow has made no such demands, and according to a Soviet announcement, "already 170 large industrial, agricultural, and cultural projects have been built in Vietnam with Soviet assistance, and another 90 are in the stage of construction."[6] Independent sources indicate that the cost of the new projects, in the period 1979–1982, will come to at least $3 billion, of which at least half will be borne by the USSR, and the remainder by COMECOM's European states, principally East Germany.[7] The question arises, of course, why the USSR is willing to undertake such major expenses in Vietnam and to underwrite its foreign policies. There are two reasons, both having to do principally with Vietnam's location.

First, a strong and coherent Vietnam, especially one that also dominates Laos, assures that on China's southern border there is a political entity with a deep and long-standing interest in resisting the influence of China and the Chinese. The antipathy of all of Southeast Asia's indigenous peoples toward the *Nanyang* (South Seas) Chinese is the first fact of political learning when considering the affairs of this region, and Vietnamese attitudes are no different. In the case of Vietnam, moreover, this factor of modern history is reinforced by the fact that for ten centuries (111 B.C.–A.D. 939) Vietnam endured and smarted under an often harsh Chinese rule. As America's most sensitive historian of Southeast Asia has remarked, the Vietnamese emerged from that era "with a warlike tradition and with probably the most keenly developed patriotism in Southeast Asia. . . . The most enduring theme in Vietnamese history is that of struggle to preserve independence from China."[8]

From the perspective of the Soviet Union, this aspect of Vietnamese nationalism is a positive feature from which it would be foolish not to capitalize. A state that borders on China, is inclined to operate as a constant thorn-in-its-side, and is willing to develop intimate relations with the USSR, is obviously a state whose interests are convergent with Moscow's. The leadership of Vietnam, moreover, is a tough and tested group, buoyed by confidence after its victory over U.S. forces in 1975, and inclined to see Vietnam as in an ascendant stage. In late 1978, when the USSR endorsed Hanoi's successful effort to oust the China-supported Cambodian government, Vietnam's self-confidence was no doubt further encouraged.

While it need not be expected that Hanoi will seek physically to incorporate Cambodia (or even to exercise the same degree of influence in Phnom Penh that it has achieved in Laos), Vietnam did aim after late 1977 to bring about a change there. Its goal was to replace Cambodia's too-radical leadership with a group that would be less clearly dependent on China, and at the same time less of an irritant to Vietnam. For this purpose, Hanoi gave strong armed-forces support to another group of Khmers, the "Kampuchea United Front for National Salvation." Within hours of the fall of Phnom Penh to this Front on 7 January 1979 (a feat for which Vietnamese army regulars were essential), *Tass* exultantly described the ousted group as "a tool of the expansionist policy of the ruling circle of Peking."[9]

In whatever juridical form Hanoi chooses to exercise its new-found influence in Cambodia, it will at least make certain that no new pro-China government is emplaced there, and it has the ability to assure that goal throughout former French Indochina. For with its victory in South Vietnam in 1975, its special influence in Laos since 1977, and its decisive role in creating a new Cambodian regime in 1979, the government of Vietnam has succeeded to the position that France established in nineteenth-century Indochina. Today this is a region of more than fifty million, and in the creation of this new Hanoi-dominated political structure, the supporting role of the USSR was both highly visible and shows every sign of intensifying. That achievement — literally in China's backyard — is in terms of geography alone a considerable prize for the Soviet Union.

The second reason for the strong Soviet support for Vietnam is also based in geography, and derives from the continuing USSR interest in harbor facilities on or near the South China Sea. A decade earlier, this concern probably contributed to the heavy Soviet attention given to Indonesia. It should not be forgotten that so much of Moscow's military assistance in that period was to the Indonesian navy rather than to the politically much more important army of Indonesia. Later, the USSR also at least toyed with the notion of attempting to develop a special arrangement with Singapore; in 1970–1971 inquiries were made about arranging for "secure" facilities for naval vessels.[10] In the same era, it was long rumored that the Soviet Union was attempting to develop a special arrangement with India for port facilities on the Bay of Bengal (at Visakhapatnam).

All such speculation (including the possible interest in the port of Sihanoukville in Cambodia in the late 1960s) derived from a conviction that the USSR, especially since the mid-1960s, has sought some means by which to improve its capacity for naval activities in East Asia. It has to be recalled that except for Petropavlovsk, the USSR's own naval facilities border the Pacific front on the Sea of Japan and the Sea of Okhotsk. In all cases there are severe limitations on egress to the Pacific — either because of winter ice or because naval units must pass through straits adjacent to Japanese territory. In those cases, access to the safer operational environment of the Pacific Ocean is subject to monitoring and interdiction by the U.S. Navy *before* those ocean expanses are reached. Not too surprisingly, therefore, much attention since the end of the Vietnam War has come to Cam Ranh Bay, at roughly 12° north latitude, on the coast of South Vietnam.

Cam Ranh Bay is an outstanding safe anchorage for vessels of every size, on an all-year basis, and during the war it was the site of an extensive naval facility built by the U.S. Navy. Since 1976, at least, there have been recurrent reports that the USSR has sought, or even obtained, Vietnamese approval to make use of this location. While these reports are clouded by the fact that they often originate from Chinese sources, and have been denied both in Hanoi and Moscow,[11] there is some reason to give credence to the notion.

Japanese officials, for example, are very apprehensive that as part of the price Hanoi has had to pay for its largesse from Moscow, some facilities at Cam Ranh Bay will have to be made available to Soviet shipping or naval units. While Defense Agency officials with whom I spoke in Tokyo in 1977–1978 suddenly became quite silent when this issue was raised, the senior official responsible for defense policy was required to respond to a direct question in Parliament. He reported with certainty that "surface-to-air missiles have been deployed at Cam Ranh Bay," and gave as his source the commander of U.S. naval forces in the Pacific. He added only that "it is not clear whether they are Soviet missiles or Vietnamese missiles."[12]

What can be said with certainty is that the Soviet Union is actively engaged in augmenting Vietnam's own maritime capacity. Early in 1978, for example, it was reported from Vladivostok that "a group of specialists at the Primorskiy ship repair plant . . . has left for Vietnam to train their colleagues in repairing fishing and transport vessels."[13] Then in September, Hanoi reported that the "Haiphong seafoods factory" would receive ten trawlers "given by the Soviet Union as aid to Vietnam."[14] And at the end of the year, the U.S. Seventh Fleet shadowed the delivery, aided by two Soviet tugs, of "two Petya II class frigates to the Vietnamese navy." This report indicated that American sources would not disclose their final destination, but that the U.S. was "waiting to see whether there will be reciprocal payoffs at Da Nangh or Cam Ranh Bay."[15]

What can also be said with certainty is that the USSR, in connection with these activities in Vietnam, is building among its own naval and maritime personnel a body of knowledge and experience about operating conditions in the South China Sea, and in the coastal areas adjacent to Vietnam. That alone wil be valuable in an era in which the USSR is clearly embarked on a program of naval expansion, for under the influence of Admiral Gorshkov much of that expansion is focused on the Pacific, and in this light, the old Russian need for a "warm-water port" will have new urgency.

It is already clear that in its association with Vietnam the USSR has scored a political coup, and in connection with its support for Hanoi's successful invasion of Cambodia in 1978–1979, Moscow delivered a particularly sharp slap to China. But by virtue of the mutual-security provisions (articles 5 and especially 6) of the Vietnam-Soviet treaty of November 1978, the USSR has laid the groundwork for moving beyond that. With an already very large Pacific fleet of 755 ships (1,250,000 tons) that includes 21 missile-carrying cruisers and destroyers, and 125 sub-marines (50 of those nuclear-powered),[16] and with a growing political stake in East Asia, the Soviet investment in Vietnam has all the earmarks of reaching the payoff stage. We are likely soon to learn whether the invest-ment has in fact made Vietnam a "grateful client who would presumably be happy to allow Moscow to enjoy at Cam Ranh Bay those superb naval and air base facilities which Americans left behind. . . ."[17]

Policy Toward ASEAN

The unique advantage of Soviet diplomacy is that when it acts moder-ately and responsibly — or in ways that would be seen as no more than rea-sonable if it were some other nation — it receives applause. In no instance is this double standard more evident than in the case of recent Soviet attitudes towards ASEAN, and no more may be involved than attitudes. Japan, for example, while it annually buys $7 billion of the region's commodities, sells at competitive prices $6 billion of the goods ASEAN wants, and invests billions, is criticized in the region if it is slow to embark on a major aid pro-gram for ASEAN industrial projects.[18] Similarly with the U.S. and the EEC: both are anxious to buy and sell, but are criticized if they are slow to adopt "preferential" schemes for the region's products and commodities. The Soviet Union, in contrast, which historically has had very little trade in the region (and contributed nothing to its progress), has after a decade of criticizing or ignoring ASEAN now pronounced it a good thing — and the result is sighs of relief.

The reason for this reaction is the knowledge that historically, the USSR has always been cool to all efforts in "regional cooperation" not initially sponsored in Moscow. When ASEAN was formed in 1967, the Soviet atti-tude was consistent with that record. Though from the outset the organiza-tion has stressed (and shown) that its concerns are principally with eco-nomic improvement, the USSR was always skeptical. Moscow preferred to suggest that ASEAN was designed as a "political" body, with the intent to transform it into a new SEATO or military alliance. Given the fact that Thailand and the Philippines were SEATO members, and that Indonesia after 1965 was dominated by a bitterly anti-Communist military leadership (largely trained in the U.S.), some Soviet doubts about ASEAN were understandable if not justified.

Accordingly, when the USSR seemed to reverse its posture toward the group in mid-1978, and gave it Moscow's outright endorsement on the oc-casion of ASEAN's 11th anniversary in August, this was an event hard to ignore. Soviet commentators now argue that Moscow has always been supportive of ASEAN, and the tone of some recent remarks are worth repeating:

> In the past 11 years, ASEAN has made many achievements, as reflected in the member nations' economic development and their increasingly important role in the world. . . .
> ASEAN pursues a constructive international policy. Its 1971 proposal to establish a peaceful, free and neutral zone in Southeast Asia won support both in and outside Southeast Asia. The Soviet Union was the first to support this proposal. . . . On the 11th anniversary of the founding of ASEAN, all the people in the Soviet Union wish it new successes on this bright new road.[19]

There is as yet no reason to believe that this "support" for any aspect of ASEAN's activities will go beyond rhetoric, and there certainly is no sign that the USSR will be willing to participate in the development needs of the ASEAN states. Japan, for example, has offered to provide $1 billion in a special low-interest loan program to five ASEAN industrial projects, and there is no sign that the USSR has anything of that sort in mind. Nevertheless, the rhetorical shift is a shift, and there are three aspects to Soviet policy in the region that explain the change.

No doubt the principal reason has to do with Chinese policies. Soon after the American defeat in Vietnam, China began to make clear its hope that the event would not necessarily lead to further profound changes in the structure of East Asia's international politics. In particular, when the leaders of the ASEAN states trooped to Peking in the immediate wake of the Vietnam defeat (all but Indonesia have gone), Mao himself suggested that it would be best if U.S. military forces did not depart from the region altogether. The states in Southeast Asia, China warned, needed now to be on their guard against "the bear at the gate." For their part, ASEAN-state foreign ministers and heads of government stressed that they had no desire to remain alienated from China; they emphasized that they were aiming (partly through ASEAN) to reduce the region's vulnerability to great-power interventions.

China was quick to respond favorably to these overtures from the non-communist and essentially "pro-Western" states that comprise ASEAN. While insisting always that relations with local communist activists (and even terrorists) in the region are a party-to-party affair, Peking also made clear that it would respect the sovereignty of each of the ASEAN members, and that it endorsed their evident commitment to the development of ASEAN as a group. In a series of high-level visits to the region made in 1977, Peking underscored this posture, and by early 1978, as a Singapore spokesman put it, it was evident that "China, the biggest power in Asia, now supports ASEAN in no uncertain terms. Her problems with the Soviet Union could have contributed to this attitude. The USSR on her part has been vocal in criticizing ASEAN."[20]

It was not long after that April speech that both Soviet and Vietnamese policy toward ASEAN changed sharply (Vietnam's leaders, including Pham Van Dong, made impressive visits to the ASEAN capitals in this period).[21] The first clear sign of the Soviet shift came in June, on the occasion of the regular ASEAN foreign ministers' meeting. *Tass* gave that event quite dispassionate, even favorable attention, though it could not resist the temptation to warn that the U.S. and Japan seek "to involve the ASEAN countries in the orbit of the U.S.'s 'New Asian Doctrine'."[22] Then in August, as I have mentioned, the USSR sent warm eleventh-birthday greetings to ASEAN, and in September it sought to send Deputy Foreign Minister Firyubin on a first-time Soviet tour of the ASEAN capitals.

This was all too much attention for the group, and in what must have been quite an irritant to the USSR, the ASEAN states replied to Moscow that the planned visit by Firyubin would not be "opportune" at the time. China, of course, exulted in this rebuff; in a perfect illustration of *schadenfreude,* Peking trumpeted that the cancellation was "very embarrassing . . . since this diplomat of a superpower was all packed and ready to go." As the *People's Daily* in Peking put it, "Firyubin found the door slammed in his face because the ASEAN countries have come to understand the Soviet Union through protracted practice."[23]

From the Soviet perspective, the hostile relationship with China that is reflected in those bitter Peking remarks, reinforced by Moscow's knowledge that between the two it is the more distrusted in the region, is reason enough for the USSR to seek improved relations with ASEAN and its members. But to the extent the Soviet Union makes that effort it is liable to encounter a special skepticism, especially among some in ASEAN, because for ten years the USSR has been advocating its own form of Asian "regionalism." The issue for Moscow in Southeast Asia is how to relate the two, and this concern is the second factor—after the preoccupation with China—that explains the turnabout in Soviet attitudes toward ASEAN.

To put this into context, we need first to recall that in the spring of 1969 a prominent Soviet commentator first mentioned that the time was ripe for a "system of collective security" in Asia. Brezhnev then made this official when he touched on the subject in an important speech that summer. Since then, while Moscow has not pressed its proposal with very great energy (at least in public), neither has it abandoned it. The topic continues to be mentioned from time to time in Soviet commentaries, and there is adequate reason for believing that its "collective security" proposal is an idea that Moscow intends to keep alive.

At the same time, it is now evident to Soviet policymakers that ASEAN, which they sought to ignore or to dismiss for more than a decade, is probably here to stay. ASEAN in fact preceded the Brezhnev proposal by two years, and while its achievements have hardly been dramatic, its survival alone is something of an accomplishment. Since 1975 ASEAN has significantly intensified its internal economic and political content, and it has been given important external recognition by Japan (in the "Fukuda Doctrine" of 1977), by the U.S. in less dramatic but no less official ways, and in a very concrete manner by the EEC, which has established a special ASEAN consultative committee on trade issues. ASEAN, in other words, represents Asia's first moderately successful effort in indigenous regional cooperation, and the prospects for growth in its economic significance and political role are genuinely quite good.

Recognition of this reality, in the light of its unwillingness to abandon Brezhnev's concept for Asian regionalism, represents something of a dilemma for the USSR. It has sought to bridge this dilemma, again in tandem with Hanoi, by seizing on one aspect of ASEAN's foreign policy and seeking to transform it into something the USSR and Vietnam can endorse. That aspect is ASEAN's formal commitment to work for the development in Southeast Asia of a "zone of peace, freedom, and neutrality."

This proposal, introduced into ASEAN deliberations by Malaysia in 1971, has privately been regarded by the four others as not very likely of realization. It was nevertheless accepted, partly out of deference to Kuala Lumpur; partly because it was regarded as a probably harmless gesture to the nonaligned world; and perhaps also to signal ASEAN's nonhostility to Vietnam.

Though ASEAN was at pains each year after 1971 to repeat its commitment to the goal of Southeast Asia as a "zone of peace, freedom, and neutrality," no significant reciprocity from the Communist states ever resulted from these efforts. Indeed in the summer of 1977, at the meeting of nonaligned nations, Vietnam took the lead in excoriating ASEAN, and selected for particular criticism the Malaysian "zone of peace" proposal. In 1978, however, Vietnam suggested that it, too, stood for a Southeast Asia of "peace, *genuine independence,* and neutrality," and although that is importantly not the same as the original proposal, the thrust of the next stage in the joint Soviet-Vietnamese policy toward ASEAN may be deduced from the difference.

Other ASEAN leaders (most notably in Singapore) have been quick to point out that there is quite a difference between "freedom," as stressed in the original Malaysian-ASEAN proposal, and what might be meant by the Vietnamese substitute suggestion of the words "genuine independence." While at one point Vietnamese leaders visiting ASEAN sought to suggest that the difference was one only of terminology, the USSR has continued to endorse the original Vietnamese formulation. The most practical reason for this stress on "genuine independence" is that the phrase lays a basis for questioning the legitimacy of continued U.S. military assistance in the region (as in Thailand and less extensively in Indonesia), to say nothing of the U.S. bases in the Philippines.

A certain sensitivity to the Philippines installations has long characterized some in ASEAN (Malaysia recently and Indonesia in the past), and in the Philippines itself opposition to the bases has been allowed by the Marcos government to intensify and broaden. After more than three years of difficult bargaining, a new "bases agreement" was reached only in December 1978, and it calls for much earlier review and possible termination (after just five years) than has been the case before. Moreover, as I will mention again, the Philippines government has been the object of quite intensive wooing from the USSR throughout the 1970s; since the 1975 Vietnam defeat of the U.S., both Moscow's pace and the level of Filipino receptiveness have greatly intensified.

To put the point most bluntly, the continuing growth among the Manila elite of disaffection from the United States, combined with increased Filipino reluctance to continue hosting the only remaining U.S. bases in Southeast Asia (and the largest in the western Pacific), represents an attractive oportunity for the USSR.[24] Subic Bay and to a lesser extent Clark Air Force Base are very important U.S. military assets, and the navy regards Subic as essential because its facilities are the cheapest and largest facilities for full-scale ship-repair and maintenance in the Pacific west of Pearl Harbor. These must figure highly in Soviet strategic planning, and what should be expected is a patient effort both from Moscow and Hanoi to develop the view in Southeast Asia that these bases are inconsistent with ASEAN's commitment to a "zone of peace and neutrality."

To have these bases eventually closed down should be regarded as the most tangible goal of Soviet policy toward ASEAN, and it should also be recognized that it is not an altogether empty hope. The desire of the ASEAN states to "prove" their neutrality, and at the same time ultimately to attract the participation of the Indochina states in ASEAN is strong.[25] Vietnam in particular is likely to press the view that it can hardly be expected to join a regional body that houses military bases of the United States on the territory of one of its prominent members. Termination of the Philippines bases would in that light be the price demanded by Hanoi for membership in ASEAN. If that fails, both Moscow and Hanoi could then reasonably argue that others cannot properly object to the granting of "fraternal" maritime facilities to the USSR at Cam Ranh Bay—by a Vietnam in or out of ASEAN. In either event, the Soviet Union has much to gain and nothing to lose by the effort.

The less tangible Soviet goal in relation to ASEAN has to do with the conceptual, if not concrete, meaning of Moscow's Asian "collective security" proposal. This is clearly indicated in two Soviet statements in mid-1978. In the first, the embassy in Bangkok distributed a paper acknowledging that "ASEAN has become a reality to be contended with," but added that "this *should be broadened to include other countries* with different regimes, such as Vietnam, Laos, and Cambodia."[26] In the second, a lengthy *Radio Moscow* commentary took strong exception to an Indonesian newspaper's suggestion that the USSR should accept ASEAN and "withdraw its proposal on Asian collective security":

> It seems that newspaper writers are not very well informed about the Soviet stand on peace in Asia in general and in Southeast Asia in particular, because if they were they would know that the Soviet Union considers the proposals of creating a zone of peace, freedom and neutrality in Southeast Asia and of turning the Indian Ocean into a zone of peace *as being on a par with the Soviet proposal on creating a stable peace and lasting security on the entire Asian Continent.*
>
> . . . The attempt to compare a proposal dealing with all of Asia with one dealing with a particular region is unacceptable, because the proposals have deep-rooted links which are based on the Asian nations' experiences in struggling for peace, freedom and progress.[27]

The special significance of that statement is that it makes clear that Moscow still regards its "collective security" proposal as alive, and that it is envisaged as the proper umbrella concept for all other proposals for Asian regionalism. If Moscow can have its way, the place in this concept for ASEAN (now that it cannot be wished away) is that the group not serve any Chinese purposes, and the inclusion of Vietnam into an enlarged and altered ASEAN will achieve that. Similarly, the inclusion of Vietnam (and the resulting "neutralization" of ASEAN) would help bring about the dismantling of the U.S. base in the Philippines. Second only to the China-containment goal, the reduction of U.S. military capacities in the Pacific is the other side of the Soviet strategic coin in East Asia.

In pressing for the realization of certain of these goals, the USSR will be working with, and not against, the grain of much thinking in the region. For many, the fact that Vietnam, Laos, and Cambodia are not already in ASEAN is an unfortunate consequence of the ill-advised Indochina policy of the U.S. in the 1960s: a doomed effort to impose "cold war" thinking in Southeast Asia. It interrupted historically powerful forces of Asian nationalism and identity, and the enlargement of ASEAN to include Indochina will mean that the momentum of those forces has been resumed.

Even those in ASEAN who do not share that somewhat romantic view of the inevitability of Asian regionalism will be inclined, for another reason, to support Vietnamese membership in ASEAN. Like those Europeans who were anxious to see German participation in the EEC and NATO, it is strongly believed in Southeast Asia that it is better to deal with a potential troublemaker by including rather than alienating his energies. Malaysia, which prides itself on the "close ties" it believes it has established with Hanoi, and feels committed to the neutralization proposal it initiated, will take this view. Thailand, with its long border with Laos and Cambodia, will also reluctantly recognize that Vietnamese membership in ASEAN could be beneficial. And the Philippines—for reasons related mostly to its desire to stress independence from U.S. policy—would also support ASEAN membership for Vietnam.

The USSR appears to recognize these considerations as assets for the promotion of its own goals in the region, for even before its turnabout on ASEAN, Moscow had begun to seek closer bilateral ties with each of the members. It has given special emphasis to the Philippines, but its efforts in several of these states should be mentioned before concluding this essay.

Refurbishing the Soviet Image

Imelda Marcos, wife of the Philippines president and also holder in her own right of numerous government positions, has become in recent years a regular visitor to East Europe and the USSR. In one sense that is unexceptionable, since the Philippines has been anxious to reduce its heavy trade dependence on Japan and the U.S.—both as purchasers of its commodities and its new manufactured goods, and as the almost sole suppliers of its industrial imports. However, both the president and his wife have taken to singling out the COMECOM states for new trade ties if Washington and Tokyo are not more forthcoming. They did that in 1978, for example, when the U.S. Congress and Justice Department questioned aspects of a nuclear reactor sale to the Philippines. In that case, issues of human rights and allegations of bribery by Mrs. Marcos' family were prominently raised, and Manila's reaction was a scarcely concealed threat. The USSR was pictured as "waiting in the wings" with a nuclear-reactor offer of its own.

Some of that can be regarded with skepticism, for Philippines politics, both domestic and foreign, are often given to hyperbole and dramatics. But it is also true that Philippine foreign policy, especially below the level of the foreign secretary, is characterized by considerable inexperience and even amateurism. Moreover, and until there is strong and continuing evidence to the contrary, it must also be recognized that in the Philippines—more than almost anywhere else in Southeast Asia—many official favors, contracts, and seemingly small decisions can be bought or otherwise oddly influenced. Against that background, the USSR is making an effort to achieve an economic and other presence in the Philippines in ways never before experienced.

In commerce, for example, the recent changes are dramatic. As I indicated at the beginning of this paper, trade between the two countries before 1975 was so small as to be hardly worth reporting. In that year, USSR *imports* were $17.1 million, and Soviet *exports* to the Philippines were valued at only $600,000. In 1977, however, Soviet imports from the Philippines multiplied almost nine times, to $144 million, and exports quadrupled to $2.4 million.[28] One important ingredient was the remarkably large purchase of 600,000 tons of Philippine sugar.[29] There has also been sudden growth in East Europe's attention to the Philippines. This includes a series of high-level visits; the posting for the first time of commercial attachés; and the signing by Czechoslovakia of its first trade agreement with Manila. A CIA study shows that in 1976 the Philippines was the *only* non-communist state in East Asia extended any economic assistance ($5 million) by the East European states.[30]

Supplemented by strong East German efforts, the Soviet Union has sought to reinforce these developing economic connections with an array of "cultural" links. Filipino students and intellectuals are now being offered scholarships and tours, and the ties that Mrs. Marcos began to develop in the mid-1970s were capped, in the summer of 1978, by a week-long visit to the USSR. In her role as Honorary Chairman of the "Philippine-USSR Friendship Society," she was asked to attend the famous Tchaikovsky musical competition, and during her visit she met with Kosygin.[31] Probably the most important result came at the end of her visit when a formal agreement for "cultural cooperation" was signed. As a consequence, an extensive program for the distribution of Soviet books and periodicals will begin, and there will be "wide exchanges of scientists, cultural and art workers . . . aimed at expanding and strengthening friendly links between the Soviet Union and Filipino peoples."[32]

It is not likely that the main motive for this cultural offensive is to disseminate more knowledge of Soviet life among Filipinos, and it is for just that reason that in Thailand there continues to be resistance to a recent upsurge of similar Soviet efforts there. When a quite senior Foreign Ministry official was named as ambassador to Bangkok in mid-1978, his immediately announced goal was to develop closer relations "particularly in fields of culture and arts."[33] He proposed a formal long-term cultural agreement with the USSR (as had just been signed with Manila), and the Thai government just as quickly turned it down. A Bangkok editorial reflected the government's view perfectly:

> The Soviet Union will remember that Russian ballet troups have been here and a Thai classical dance troupe has visited the Soviet Union. Such cultural exchanges can take place without any difficulty and *without any necessity for an agreement.* . . . *Perhaps such an agreement will enable the Soviet Union to increase its personnel in the embassy, but we are not sure whether that is an advantage.* [34]

The USSR, no doubt aware of the skepticism with which its past diplomacy in Thailand has been regarded (there are still memories of a major espionage effort in the 1950s), will certainly adopt a much less heavy-handed approach than in the past. For one thing, the USSR is a much more attractive economic partner with Thailand than ever before, and its ability to promote exports of heavy-industrial goods (both its own and from several of the East European states) is a significant new factor. As *Pravda* points out, "for the first time Soviet welding and printing equipment and metal-cutting tools are being delivered," and the USSR "has increased sixfold its purchases of rubber, a traditional Thai export commodity."[35] As elsewhere in the region, the attractiveness of trade with the USSR is reinforced in the Thai case by growing irritation with Japan — and Soviet propaganda efforts ceaselessly emphasize the dominant Japanese role in Southeast Asia's economies.[36]

Aside from the Philippines, the other ASEAN state where the Soviet Union probably expects to make the most headway is Malaysia. The reason is not that Kuala Lumpur lacks an experienced foreign-affairs bureaucracy, for its standing in this respect is almost as impressive as that in Bangkok. Nor is it especially vulnerable to subversion, for the capacity of the Malaysian "special branch" remains high. And also unlike the Philippines, there is little disposition to create distance from the former metropole state, a factor which might otherwise make Malaysia especially receptive to Soviet efforts. What does, however, lead Kuala Lumpur to look with added interest to the Soviet Union, and to regard it as a potentially useful "counterbalancing" factor in Southeast Asia, is Malaysia's special concerns with China.

This derives, of course, from the always-tense coexistence in Malaysia among the Malays and Chinese, for the two communities are almost equally divided and mutually suspicious. This ethnic duality dominates every aspect of life in the country, and Sinophobia is always present among the Malay community. The government structure generally is dominated by Malays — in foreign affairs almost exclusively so. Among this group there is a belief that a higher Soviet posture in Southeast Asia is not necessarily bad for Malaysia; indeed it was the thought that a Soviet presence might be beneficial to regional stability that led Kuala Lumpur to propose the "neutralization" concept in the first place.

The same thinking is involved among those Malaysian leaders who would like greater national acceptance among the nonaligned group of nations, and who also want Malaysia to be more closely identified in world affairs with Muslim issues. Both considerations have encouraged a more receptive stance toward the USSR, and until its invasion of Afghanistan, Moscow was a successful champion of many Islamic (and Arab) causes in world affairs.

There will be tensions on this issue because the first-generation Malaysian leadership has been strongly anticommunist and very skeptical of Soviet motives, but that quite cosmopolitan group is passing from the scene. Tun Razak, the late prime minister, and Ghazali Schafie, the present home minister, are good examples. The newer generation of Malay leaders, however, has a different agenda, and they will be reinforced in their arguments by new economic considerations that the USSR is actively exploiting. The Soviet Union has long been an important buyer of Malaysia's rubber, and there has been a marked increase of economic activity in Malaysia by the other COMECOM states—Poland and East Germany especially. Malaysia, like the others in the region, is uneasy with its dependence on Japan for industrial imports, and the COMECON states are anxious to respond: "Renewed Soviet and East European initiatives to expand their exports to Malaysia were designed to offset their $250 million annual hard currency expenditures for natural rubber and tin."[37] A visit to Kuala Lumpur by Poland's foreign minister in late 1978 was designed to underscore Malaysia's potential for new trade patterns with East Europe.[38]

Soviet Designs and Prospects

I have sought to show in this essay that as the USSR looks at Southeast Asia, there is reason for Moscow to be optimistic. In the past, Soviet diplomacy in this region was clumsy at best: tales of overdressed and overweight Russians, perspiring in Bangkok's heat and Djakarta's humidity are still readily recalled. Deriving both from that period and from certain Soviet setbacks in the region, there is still resistance to the USSR in Southeast Asia. Thus, in 1978, Indonesia turned down a very large scale ($360 million) Soviet offer for the development of a 600,000-ton alumina project.[39] Part of the reason is the 1960s memories of too many Russian and East European "technicians" who lived apart, seemed unable to participate in the generally lighthearted openness of the Southeast Asian environment, and were always suspected of espionage, subversion, or both.

But the USSR today, especially as it looks forward to the 1980s, appears to be a far more sophisticated actor in these environs. Of course, not all of its recent commercial activities have been successful, as in the case of the Singapore branch of the Moscow Narodny Bank — where its practices were too flamboyant, seemingly unbusinesslike, and therefore suspect. But in such fields as industrial exports and especially in shipping, Soviet prospects are very bright. That is altogether another topic, and all that can be said here is that Soviet shipping has come on a scene in which for twenty years Southeast Asians have been seeking to loosen their dependence on the cartelized rate structure of the European Shipping Conference. The USSR has arrived with modern containerized vessels and has begun to outbid its competitors effectively. Obviously (as the traditional shippers have complained) the Soviet lines are subsidized, but from the vantage point of the import-export houses in Manila, Bangkok, and Singapore the more important point is that Soviet freight rates are lower and their port calls are on time.

In these and related economic fields, Soviet activity indicates a commitment not only to showing but to maintaining the flag: a commitment, in other words, to demonstrating (just as the United States has been saying about itself) that the USSR intends to "remain an Asian and Pacific power." Moscow has concretized this goal through its now close association and support for Vietnam, the new ruler of all of Indochina. From the vantage point of Soviet foreign policy, that Vietnam connection represents a long-sought and very important beachhead: it is the successful extension of Soviet prestige, power, and physical presence — over thousands of intervening miles — to a region of East Asia where before it was a lonely pariah. That presence is not likely to be fragile, nor is it analogous to the hopes the USSR entertained (by virtue of its relationship with similarly distant Cuba) for a significant Soviet role in Latin America.

Peking, in fact, never tires of warning that Vietnam is "Moscow's Asian Cuba," but that analogy is false and highly misleading. For, unlike Cuba in Latin America, Vietnam is a state whose size, energies, and ambitions within its region means that its aims and capacities have long been closely followed throughout Southeast Asia. This was true even before Hanoi signed its mutual security treaty with the USSR in November 1978 and before Hanoi's admittance to COMECON just before that. Vietnam's goals were already the principal security question among its neighbors in Southeast Asia, and the issue was of high concern to Peking and Tokyo as well. The new connection with the USSR strongly reinforces that concern.

The explanation lies in the fact that Vietnam is no ministate, and also lies in the fact that its leadership, after thirty years of struggle, is tough, hardened, and self-confident. As I wrote in another connection, "Vietnam's self-image is not that of an Asian medium-sized state, with something to be gained from cooperation with its similarly situated neighbors. Rather, it sees itself as an Asian model state, whose victory and vindication after thirty years give it a global stature well above its *comprador* neighbors. . . ."[40] Thus, when the Soviet Union chose Vietnam as its "outpost of socialism in Southeast Asia" it chose well indeed.

Notes

1. ASEAN was formed in 1967 and consists of Indonesia (135 million); Philippines (44 million); Thailand (45 million); Malaysia (13 million); and Singapore (2.5 million). The total, of 240 million, is of course the bulk of Southeast Asia's population.

2. The Mongolian Republic is the only other "Asian" state in COMECOM, but it is hardly independent from Moscow.

3. *Radio Moscow,* 25 June 1978, in FBIS, 25 June 1978.

4. Guy and Ewa Pauker, "Southeast Asia," in K. London, ed., *The Soviet Impact on World Politics* (Hawthorn Books, 1974), pp. 143–144.

5. Bernard K. Gordon, "Shadow Over Angkor," *Asian Survey,* January 1969, p. 68. To the consternation of Prince Sihanouk, who was deposed by the American-supported General Lon Nol in 1970, Moscow maintained its Embassy in Cambodia throughout the Vietnam War. Sihanouk went to China, and the USSR appears to have given up on Cambodia only *after* a firmly China-oriented group took power in 1975 (in the wake of the American defeat in Vietnam).

6. *Novosti Daily Review* (Moscow), 9 November 1978.

7. *Christian Science Monitor,* 27 October 1978. Russian oil shipments alone to Vietnam account for $300 million. East Germany, it is important to note, has also signed a "friendship and cooperation" treaty with Vietnam; Hanoi now has such arrangements with Laos and the USSR (from the Vietnamese army newspaper, *Quan Doi Nhan Dan,* 30 November 1978).

8. Lea E. Willians, *Southeast Asia: A History* (New York: Oxford University Press, 1976), pp. 42–43.

9. *Christian Science Monitor,* 9 January 1979.

10. If the inquiries were serious, Singapore authorities quickly threw cold water on them by warning that a Soviet vessel might have to berth alongside one from the United States.

11. One of the most detailed accounts appeared in the Hong Kong Communist newspaper *Wen Wei Po,* on 14 June 1978. It was stated there that interviews with Chinese who had been expelled from Vietnam had seen Soviet cruisers and destroyers at Cam Ranh Bay. European journalists were told the same thing by a former "Viet Cong" cadre of Chinese origin. One of many denials, in response to reporters' questions, came from the Soviet Ambassador to Thailand (*Bangkok Post,* 4 December 1978), who said simply that "The Soviet Union has no intention to have bases at Cam Ranh Bay."

12. *Tokyo Shimbun,* 5 July 1978.

13. From a broadcast by the Vladivostok domestic radio, 9 March 1978, in FBIS, 16 March 1978.

14. *Radio Hanoi* broadcast, 6 September 1978.

15. *Far Eastern Economic Review,* 22 December 1978.

16. From a report of the Japan Defense Agency's assessment, in *Yomiuri,* 18 July 1978. These figures are consistent with other responsible sources, though the reported number of nuclear-powered submarines deployed in the Pacific by the USSR varies.

17. Joseph C. Harsch, in *Christian Science Monitor,* 5 January 1978. The history-minded will note that the Russian fleet that steamed to its disaster at the hands of the Japanese in 1905 had stopped en route for provisions at Cam Ranh Bay.

18. For the levels of Japanese and American trade and investment in the ASEAN region see my "Japan, the U.S., and Southeast Asia," *Foreign Affairs,* April 1978.

19. *Moscow Radio Peace and Progress,* 8 August 1978.

20. A. Rahim Ishak, senior minister of state for foreign affairs, in Manila on 29 March 1978 (*The Mirror,* Singapore), 17 April 1978.

21. *Far Eastern Economic Review,* 15 September 1978.

22. *Tass,* 16 June 1978.

23. *People's Daily* (Peking), 14 September 1978.

24. Moscow is now actively exploiting the issue: "The American bases are a constant source of tension in the Philippines . . . the Filipino public considers [these extraterritorial rights] to be a direct violation of the country's sovereignty and territorial integrity" (*Tass,* 6 September 1978).

25. The overthrow of the Pol Pot regime in Cambodia by Vietnam will of course mute for a while any open receptivity to Vietnam as an ASEAN member, but assuming that Cambodia does not entirely disappear, the sentiment for Vietnamese and Indochinese participation will again surface fairly soon.

26. From a statement signed by N. Kudryavtsev, distributed by the USSR Bangkok Embassy, 7 July 1978, and reported by European press agencies (FBIS, 7 July 1978). Emphasis added.

27. *Radio Moscow,* 8 September 1978. My emphasis.

28. *Soviet Trade With Less Developed Countries* (CIA Research Paper ER 78-10326, May 1978).

29. *Communist Aid to Less Developed Countries of the Free World, 1977* (CIA Research Paper ER 78-10478U, November 1978).

30. *Handbook of Economic Statistics, 1978* (CIA Research Aid ER 78-10365, October 1978).

31. These events were reported in *Izvestiia,* 2 July 1978, and by *Tass,* 4 July 1978.

32. *Radio Moscow,* 6 July 1978.

33. *Bangkok Post,* 11 August 1978. Department Deputy Chief Kuznetsov was sent as Soviet ambassador.

34. *Nation Review* (Bangkok), 1 September 1978. Emphasis added.

35. *Pravda,* 14 November 1978.

36. "Under the capitalist economic system, the fortuitous gains made by ASEAN countries are 'eaten up' by the monopolies that prey on their junior partners . . . the

capitalist powers actually allow ASEAN only the choice of which yoke [Japanese or American] to place more firmly around its neck" (*Pravda,* 14 August 1978).

37. *Communist Aid to Less Developed Countries of the Free World, 1977* (CIA Research Paper ER 78-10478U, November 1978).

38. Particularly good terms were offered by Poland for the sale of machinery (*Agence France Presse,* 6 December 1978).

39. *Communist Aid to Less Developed Countries,* 1977, ibid.

40. "Japan, the United States, and Southeast Asia," *Foreign Affairs,* April 1978, p. 596.

9

South Asia

William J. Barnds

The Indian subcontinent, by virtue of its location and population, for many years has been a central arena of the great-power struggle for influence that characterized Asia in the wake of decolonization. Both the United States and the Soviet Union have used all the tools of contemporary statecraft to gain and hold a foothold in an area each regards as crucial to its interests. This struggle continued — partly from inertia and partly for more complex reasons — with the decline of bipolarity and the disarray of the Communist and Western alliance systems in Asia, although its intensity diminished during the 1970s as the full implications of the looser constellation of power that was evolving became apparent to political leaders everywhere. Both the Soviet Union and the United States have experienced periodic advances and setbacks in South Asia over the years, but the underlying trend has seen a rise in the Soviet role relative to that of the United States.

Soviet success is all the more remarkable in that its gains came about mainly since the mid-1950s. Before 1955 the USSR largely ignored the subcontinent, and its few ventures there either came to naught or backfired. Moscow made good use of its opportunities by giving top priority to the establishment of a firm and broadly based relationship with India as the key power in the area. The Soviets have benefited from the widespread Indian conviction of the importance of good relations with the USSR. New Delhi views the Soviet Union as an essential counterweight to the United States when Indo-American relations are strained, while good relations with Moscow are proof that India is retaining its nonaligned stance when relations with the United States are harmonious. Moscow's involvement with Afghanistan, Sri Lanka, and Nepal was for years managed in a manner that was acceptable to New Delhi as well as to the countries themselves. The April 1978 Marxist coup in Afghanistan opened new opportunities for the USSR to expand its influence in that backward country, but continual conflicts within the regime and growing popular hostility toward it led to a spreading insurgency that by late 1979 threatened the regime's power despite the presence of several thousand Soviet "advisors." Faced with this situation, the Soviet Union invaded Afghanistan in December of 1979, creating a military threat to the rest of South Asia and effecting an international crisis the implications of which will be appraised later in this chapter.

It is clear that Soviet gains over the years have not come easily or without cost. The intense nationalism of the newly independent countries, and their political, economic, and cultural links with the West, have presented continuing barriers to Soviet ambitions. Moreover, the centrality of the deeply-rooted antagonism between the Hindus and Muslims of the subcontinent, which has transformed into Indo-Pakistani hostility at partition, has presented obstacles as well as opportunities to Soviet leaders.

Nor should the striking continuity of Soviet policy since the mid-1950s be allowed to obscure periodic strains between New Delhi and Moscow, particularly in the late 1950s when Khrushchev was struggling to prevent the Sino-Soviet alliance from unravelling and in the latter half of the 1960s when his successors attempted to improve relations with Pakistan. Nonetheless, when forced to a choice, the USSR accepted the costs its support of India entailed in terms of its relations with China, Pakistan, and certain Middle Eastern countries which were friendly toward Pakistan. Moscow may face a more difficult problem in maintaining its links with India after its invasion of Afghanistan, although New Delhi's initial reaction demonstrated how reluctant it is to challenge the Soviet Union.

During the past twenty-five years the USSR has been forced to respond to a series of critical situations in South Asia, and the decisions it has made have determined its relations with and its impact on the subcontinent. These situations have sometimes involved a combination of domestic trends in the South Asian countries, their relations with each other, and the area's evolving position in world affairs—as well as changing conditions within the USSR and in its general foreign policy stance.

The Soviet position and prospects today are closely linked to its response to six different developments: (1) the United States involvement in the affairs of the subcontinent in the early 1950s, particularly the American alliance with Pakistan; (2) the emergence of the Sino-Indian conflict in the late 1950s; (3) the development of close Sino-Pakistani relations in the mid-1960s, which coincided with a time of political and economic disarray in India; (4) the 1971 upheaval in Bangladesh and the reemergence of a strong Indian government under Mrs. Gandhi; (5) Indian predominance in the subcontinent and reduced U.S. engagement in South Asian affairs during the 1970s; and (6) the establishment of a Communist regime in Afghanistan in 1978, which was unable to maintain its position without direct Soviet military action. Analysis of Soviet maneuvers in the varying circumstances involved will lay the groundwork for appraising the lessons the Soviet leaders have drawn from their experiences and the possible lines of future policy.

This analytical scheme does not mean that Soviet policy has been purely reactive. But the emphasis Moscow placed on consolidating rather than on expanding its position since the 1971 emergence of an India preeminent in a subcontinent that was no longer a focal point of American concern suggests that *past* Soviet policy toward South Asia was geared as much to the moves of others as to positive goals of its own. It should be noted, however, that the Soviets have until recently been operating in an international environment more responsive to U.S. power and influence than to Soviet maneuvers, which placed limits on the USSR's capabilities and its practical, as distinct from its ultimate, goals. If Soviet power were to surpass U.S. power—or U.S. determination—the opportunities available to Soviet leaders would expand and they would be likely to move to take advantage of this more favorable "correlation of forces." The Soviet move into Afghanistan may have been partly a response to such considerations. But before discussing past and future Soviet policies, a few comments on Soviet perceptions of South Asia and its position in Soviet strategy generally are necessary.

South Asia in Soviet Perspective

The USSR has always ranked the Indian subcontinent below Europe and East Asia in terms of its interests and concerns.[1] The West has been the principal source of modern Russian culture under the czars as well as their communist successors. At least since the time of Napoleon the principal threats to the security of the Russian state—especially its European heartland—have originated in the West, although the rise of first Japan and then China in the twentieth century have increased Soviet apprehensions about the security of their position in Siberia.[2]

South Asia occupies an intermediate position in the hierarchy of Soviet foreign policy priorities, below Europe, East Asia, and the Middle East but well above Southeast Asia or Latin America. No South Asian nation possesses the indigenous power to threaten the Soviet Union. However, the ability of certain countries (either out of fear of the USSR or their neighbors) to ally themselves with a major power hostile to Moscow periodically creates apprehension among Soviet leaders. In the early cold war period the principal source of such a danger was the United States, but later Soviet concern over China made Moscow particularly apprehensive about Peking's activities in the area. Quite apart from these specific concerns, Soviet leaders are aware that they cannot achieve their cherished ambition of being recognized as a global power without a strong position in the areas along their southern border from the eastern Mediterranean through the Indian subcontinent. Moreover, the Soviet leaders attach considerable importance to area and population in picking their friends.[3] This reinforced their initial tendency to accord top priority to relations with the largest regional power that was willing to cooperate—Indonesia in Southeast Asia, India in South Asia, and Egypt among the Arab states.

The Soviet Union also has a record of historical interest and cultural links with South Asia, although it is easy to overestimate the importance of such considerations today. Russia vied with Britain off and on during the nineteenth and early twentieth centuries in Central Asia, although Russia's spasmodic efforts in South Asia were partly directed toward influencing the British posture in areas in Eastern Europe that were more central to Russian interests. Such experiences kept the subcontinent on the agenda of Russian concerns after the Communists came to power, even if there was little the Soviet leaders could do in view of their pressing problems at home, in Europe, and in East Asia during their first two decades in power.[4]

Similar ethnic groups live on both sides of the Soviet border, and historically many of these peoples shared a common Islamic culture. But the links across the borders were sundered by the Soviet practice of sealing its citizens in and keeping foreigners of all varieties out, and the role of Islam has been steadily and sharply curtailed in the life of Central Asian Republics of the USSR. This isolation, as well as the obvious dominance of Russians within the USSR, has limited the impact on other Asians of the rapid material advances made in Central Asia. Moreover, Moscow's strongest links in recent decades have—excepting Afghanistan—been with Indians and Arabs rather than with peoples closer to the Soviet Union. Finally, the prominence of religion and caste in the politics and social structures of the subcontinent have been difficult for Soviet officials and scholars to understand and fit into a Marxist framework of analysis.

Checking the American Thrust

The cold war, which raged across Europe and the Far East following the defeat of the Axis powers in World War II, reached an uneasy stalemate in these areas after the Korean and Indochinese agreements in 1953 and 1954. But neither side thought a stalemate could long endure, and the competition shifted to a new arena. The new Republican administration (particularly Secretary of State John Foster Dulles) was convinced that the lands between Turkey and the South China Sea were too weak and inexperienced to deal with the Soviets and Chinese on their own, and that they presented too tempting a target for the Communists to ignore. In

Washington's eyes the withdrawal of the former colonial powers had created a vacuum, despite the insistence of Stalin and his underlings that the leaders of the newly independent nations were bourgeois "lackeys of the imperialists"—a charge echoed by Peking.

In the years before nuclear intercontinental missiles, American strategists wanted military facilities in areas around the periphery of the communist world to check Soviet and Chinese power. Thus the United States extended its containment policy by establishing anticommunist alliances—SEATO and the Baghdad Pact. American leaders saw Pakistan, deeply fearful of India and casting about for a major power protector, as the country that could provide the link between the Asian alliance systems.[5]

The Soviet leaders who succeeded Stalin first had to overcome the legacy of his policy toward the subcontinent. The failure of the Soviet policy in China in the 1920s, after local nationalists turned on their communist collaborators, left Stalin skeptical about the bona fides of Asian nationalists, although Soviet national interests required tactical accommodations at times. Therefore the 1920s and 1930s were devoted to building local Communist parties in the subcontinent, especially India. This was slow and frustrating, and by 1939 the Communist party of India (CPI) had only about 5,000 members. The CPI grew rapidly during World War II, reaching over 50,000 members by 1946. The party's gains, which also involved winning control of several mass movements, were made possible by two developments: (1) British legalization of the CPI as a result of the party's support of the Allied war effort after the German attack on the USSR in 1941; and (2) British repression of the Congress party and incarceration of its leaders for their unwillingness to support the war effort unless India's independence was assured.

These impressive gains came at a heavy cost. Indians now recognized that the CPI gave priority to Soviet needs rather than to nationalistic aspirations. Awareness of CPI subordination to foreign control was heightened when the party responded to Moscow's militant policy at the onset of the cold war by launching a revolutionary struggle, which in various forms lasted from 1948 to 1951. The party's exaggeration of the potential for revolution and its underestimation of New Delhi's ability to take forceful action to maintain its control led to a drastic decline in CPI strength—from 90,000 in 1948 to 20,000–30,000 in 1951.[6] Soviet attacks on Gandhi and Nehru further embittered many Indians.

The new Soviet leaders saw that the CPI was as much a hindrance as a help in influencing events. They also gradually recognized that Stalin had misjudged Asian nationalist leaders.[7] The opposition of Nehru to American efforts to create military alliances in his part of the world convinced the Soviet leaders, particularly Khrushchev, that the Soviet Union and India shared a common interest in preventing the United States from establishing itself firmly in South Asia. But any effort to exploit India's nonalignment policy required accepting it in the short term. The rapid postwar recovery of the Soviet economy made it possible to offer some economic assistance, more attractive trade arrangements, and military equipment that was obsolescent by Soviet standards. Moscow could also offer political support to one or the other party in regional quarrels — to India and Afghanistan in the Kashmir and Pushtunistan disputes with Pakistan — which would help it gain a foothold in the area.

Nehru searched for a means to counter the U.S.-Pakistani alliance, but his continued suspicion of the USSR led Moscow to conclude that a break with the past was essential. This would involve not only support for Indian nationalism, whatever the consequences for the CPI, but an attempt to move the party in a direction that would make its existence less of a concern to New Delhi by urging it to adopt a policy of "constitutional communism." This meshed with Nehru's approach of trying to draw the more moderate elements of the CPI into Indian political life while isolating, and when necessary repressing, its more radical elements.

It is a tribute to the imagination and flexibility of Khrushchev and his colleagues that despite their long years of subservience to Stalin they were able to cast aside his approach within a short time after his demise. The change in Indo-Soviet relations was only one element in a much broader shift in Soviet foreign policy, as Stalin's successors concluded that his harsh and inflexible policies were uniting rather than dividing the noncommunist world.

Indo-Soviet relations expanded rapidly as Moscow provided aid for India's industrialization program — especially state-owned projects — and support for its stand on Kashmir. Leaders of both countries exchanged visits and compliments although a note of caution was evident in Nehru's repeated comments stressing the dangers of any country interfering in the affairs of another. His uncertainty about the depth and the duration of the changes in Soviet policy was one reason India for many years continued to purchase its arms from the West, thereby limiting its links with the USSR. Such restraint was not possible for Afghanistan, for no Western power was willing to provide the arms its leaders felt were essential to enable the central government to control the country's restive tribes and to stand up to Pakistan.

It is easy to overstate the extent to which the Soviets were following a well-conceived and integrated strategy. They had no blueprint; there was uncertainty and experimentation. The new approach probably was abhorrent to orthodox communists and questionable to others, particularly those who remembered how Asian nationalists had turned on local communists in the past. But however good an *argument* the skeptics may have made, they suffered from one fatal weakness — the lack of a plausible alternative. Soviet failure to support those governments opposed to Western influence in the area would have made such opposition less effective, and could have led some to conclude that they had no real option but to cooperate closely with the West. Moreover, the advocates of the new approach were not without an ideological justification, for they could argue that the bourgeois-nationalist leaders would be unable to satisfy local aspirations for reforms and economic development without becoming increasingly radical. In such an environment, Soviet influence and the demonstrated success of the Soviet model would lead the Asian countries to adopt the socialist course.

The initial responsiveness of India, Afghanistan, and (after the Bandaranaike victory in 1956) Ceylon to the Soviet overtures, and the growing emphasis on socialism in many Asian countries, raised hopes in Moscow that events were moving rapidly along anticipated lines and that the United States had been effectively checked. But history moves in cycles as well as trends, and in time the Soviets recognized that their gains would not come as quickly or easily as once seemed possible.

An important obstacle to Soviet aspirations was that the United States never pushed its alliance with Pakistan to its logical — or illogical — conclusion. The United States stood behind Pakistan vis-à-vis the Communist powers, but gave Pakistan only qualified support in its quarrels with India and Afghanistan. The American insistence that its obligations to Pakistan did not include support against its noncommunist neighbors was a source of disappointment, but the lack of an alternate source of external backing at this time left Pakistan no choice but grudgingly to accept the American stance. The United States recognized that it had a stake in the stability and progress of India — as well as of the small South Asian states — and that if nonalignment prevented close Indo-American cooperation it could also set a limit on Indo-Soviet links. Therefore, the United States took care not to alienate India completely, and beginning in 1957 greatly expanded its economic aid program. Nor were Indo-Soviet relations without friction: Soviet actions in Eastern Europe (especially Hungary) in the mid-1950s made clear to South Asian leaders that there were limits to Moscow's respect for national independence, and Nehru's outspoken criticism of dogmatic ideologies annoyed the USSR and prompted a strong Soviet reply.[8]

But such differences were kept in check, for Moscow and New Delhi realized their need for each other. India's willingness to expand relations with the Communist countries enhanced their international stature and made other Asian countries more receptive to Soviet overtures. Soviet backing of India vis-à-vis Pakistan strengthened New Delhi's resolve to stand firm on Kashmir rather than seek a compromise, just as the alliance with the United States encouraged Pakistan to think it might succeed in pressuring India to be more accommodating. Thus within a decade of independence the two principal nations of the subcontinent were caught up in the cold war and in great-power politics. Although their involvement enabled them to extract material benefits from the cold war antagonists, it solidified their hostility toward each other.

The Chinese Challenge

The USSR's close relationship with China created no obstacles to its courting of India during the mid-1950s. While India had reacted negatively to Peking's absorption of Tibet by force rather than by negotiation in 1950, Nehru accepted Chinese sovereignty there—a position formalized in the 1954 Sino-Indian treaty. He directed India's efforts toward securing Chinese acceptance of New Delhi's special interests in the Himalayan border states of Nepal, Bhutan, and Sikkim, and to India's version of the alignment of the Sino-Indian border. But Nehru's method of doing so—by public proclamation stressing his belief in China's good faith and intentions while slowly and quietly building up India's border defenses—was unsuccessful, and when it failed he lost his hitherto unchallenged control of Indian foreign policy.

The growing divergence of Soviet and Chinese policies after 1957—Peking becoming more militant toward the noncommunist world, and Moscow more determined to emphasize peaceful coexistence—created strain and then hostility in Sino-Soviet relations. Part of the problem was simple misinterpretation. Mao imputed a passivity to Khrushchev's policy that the latter never intended it to have; he saw it as a less dangerous way to advance Soviet aims in a nuclear age. Similarly, the Soviets saw Mao as more belligerent and reckless than he actually was.

But even perfect understanding would not have held the two powers together in the face of their disputes about the locus of authority in the world communist movement, Soviet unwillingness to support Chinese territorial and nuclear aspirations, and the different policy imperatives that sprang from their vastly different stages of development.

These differences were exacerbated by a sharp deterioration of Sino-Indian relations. Widespread Indian criticism over the harsh measures taken by Peking against the Tibetans when they revolted in March 1959, and India's hospitality to the refugees who poured across the border, prompted increasingly strident Chinese accusations that India had a hand in the uprising. On 16 May the Chinese ambassador to New Delhi delivered a strong protest ending with an ominous warning that "you . . . cannot have two fronts."⁹ Nehru attempted to limit the damage to Sino-Indian relations, but he was caught between rising anti-Chinese feelings in India and Chinese attacks on his policies.¹⁰ He soon concluded that he could no longer leave the Indian public in the dark about the existence of a more serious Sino-Indian dispute. Therefore in August 1959 he publicly acknowledged that China contested some 50,000 square miles of Indian territory in the Himalayas, that China had built a road across the Aksai Chin section of Ladakh, and that Indian and Chinese patrols had clashed in the summer of 1959.¹¹ Such revelations inflamed Indian public opinion, intensified the divisions within the CPI, and posed a serious threat to the Soviet position in India.

Moscow had supported Peking's suppression of the Tibetan rebels in March without, however, echoing Chinese criticism of India. (The CPI had been more outspoken, condemning New Delhi while praising Peking.) New Delhi's removal of the Communist ministry from the Indian state of Kerala in July 1959 evoked only weak protests in the Soviet media even though Moscow had just extended a large loan to India. India's growing dependence on the West for aid had already led the Chinese to be more critical of India, but the Soviets decided they had to be even more forthcoming to maintain their position. The Sino-Indian border dispute forced Moscow to raise the ante once more lest India turn to the West for support against a united Communist world, however difficult it was not to support a Communist state involved in a quarrel with a bourgeois government. Moscow probably was also worried that automatic support of its Communist ally would have an unfavorable impact on other nonaligned states it was courting. Therefore, the USSR adopted what was essentially a neutral position early in September, and one implicitly critical of China.

Certain political circles and the press in Western countries recently opened up a noisy campaign about an incident that occurred not long ago on the Chinese-Indian border, in the region of the Himalayas. This campaign was obviously directed at driving a wedge between the two largest states in Asia, the Chinese People's Republic and the Republic of India, whose friendship has great importance in ensuring peace and international cooperation in Asia and in the whole world. Those who inspired it are trying to discredit the idea of peaceful coexistence of states with different social systems and to prevent the strengthening of the Asian people's solidarity in the fight to consolidate national independence.

. . . It would be wrong not to express regret that the incident on the Chinese-Indian boundary took place. The Soviet Union enjoys friendly relations with both the Chinese People's Republic and the Republic of India. The Chinese and Soviet peoples are tied together by indestructible bonds of fraternal friendship based on the great principles of socialist internationalism.

> Friendly cooperation between the USSR and India according to the ideas of peaceful coexistence is developing successfully.[12]

Soviet actions at a crucial moment enhanced India's ability to maintain its nonalignment. Nehru, with Soviet neutrality and Western sympathy, could stand firm against China and reject Pakistani president Ayub's conditional offer of joint defense of the subcontinent. Nehru next sought to turn Soviet neutrality into support; soon India was purchasing Soviet transport aircraft and helicopters for use along the frontier, and later MiG fighters — which Nehru hoped would serve as a warning to Peking.

There apparently was a price involved, although the evidence is circumstantial. The USSR, at least in 1960, was still hoping to prevent Sino-Soviet relations from completely unraveling, and urged Nehru to seek a negotiated settlement of the Sino-Indian dispute.[13] The most Nehru would agree to was a visit by Chou En-lai in April 1960. But his willingness to talk to the Chinese premier was, in historical perspective, much less significant than his refusal to accede to Chou's suggested compromise — Chinese retention of the Aksai Chin in return for Peking's recognition of India's claims in the northeast (the MacMahon Line). Moscow probably was unhappy, but the continued deterioration of Sino-Soviet relations and the improvement of Indo-American relations in the late Eisenhower and early Kennedy years led the Soviets to accept the Indian stance.

The challenge posed by the Sino-Indian conflict became acute once again with the outbreak of war in the Himalayas late in 1962.[14] Moscow, ensnarled in the Cuban missile crisis and uncertain whether or not it faced a major war, was reluctant to antagonize China further. A *Pravda* editorial of 25 October not only attacked the MacMahon Line but called upon India to accept the Chinese terms for a halt in the fighting.[15] It briefly looked as though nearly ten years of Soviet effort would be undone in a few weeks, as stunned Indians compared the Soviet desertion with the immediate Western response to India's plea for arms and support. Once the Cuban crisis subsided, however, Soviet policy reverted to its earlier stance, and in a *Pravda* editorial on 5 November Moscow retreated from its support of Peking.

Soviet leaders worked hard to rehabilitate their country's position in India, and soon became increasingly critical of Chinese policy toward India.[16] Their efforts were aided once again by Western ties to Pakistan, for Nehru calculated that the Western desire to retain its position in a Pakistan already furious over Western arms to India would limit British and American willingness to aid India's military buildup. He also saw that Western strategy for dealing with the USSR and China would lead Britain and the United States to press India to compromise on Kashmir so as to make joint defense of the subcontinent possible. When his judgments were proven correct, the value of India's links to Moscow again became evident to his domestic critics. Soviet willingness to meet India's arms requests — even after Nehru died in May 1964 — made it clear that Moscow saw a close relationship with India as essential to counter China as well as the West.

Broadening Options or Deepening Ties?

Once relations with India were again solidified, Khrushchev's stolid successors took a new look at their position in the subcontinent and in the world. Their efforts to effect a rapprochement with Peking were unsuccessful in the face of Chinese intransigence. Their position in Eastern Europe was again coming under challenge, and would in time lead to the Soviet invasion of Czechoslovakia and the enunciation of the Brezhnev Doctrine.[17] The Western alliance systems were weakening under the impact of De Gaulle's search for grandeur and American preoccupation with Vietnam, but Moscow found it difficult to turn such troubles to its advantage. Continued Western — and looming Chinese — involvement created barriers to further Soviet progress in Asia and Africa that lasted for ten years.

It was about this time that Moscow came to realize that conditions within the Third World countries posed obstacles to its ambitions as serious as those stemming from the efforts of other major powers. The overthrow of such leaders as Nkrumah and Sukarno, the periodic troubles with Nasser, and Nasser's stunning defeat by the Israelis in 1967 were painful lessons in the fragility of the Soviet position. The strength of nationalism in Asia and, to a lesser extent, in Africa, as well as the intractability of the economic and social problems in these countries, was increasingly seen in the late 1960s by the Soviet as a persisting fact of life that the USSR could affect only slowly and marginally.[18] Indeed, the Soviets showed considerable concern because their continued support for India was not preventing it from moving to the right in domestic affairs and toward the West in its foreign policy stance.[19]

India after the mid-1960s encountered a wide variety of troubles. Its international stature had declined after its military defeat at the hands of China. Poor monsoons sharply curtailed agricultural production and led to industrial slowdowns. More ominously, a serious weakening of the Congress party after its setback in the 1967 national elections raised questions about its basic stability. The Communist party of India, whose tenuous unity had been heavily dependent upon the external authority of a unified international Communist movement, fragmented as a result of internal disputes over the proper position to take on the Sino-Indian dispute and in

Indian politics generally. The CPI formally split in 1964, and while the "rightist" CPI remained oriented toward Moscow, the more radical CPI (Marxist) for a time looked to Peking for inspiration.[20] Indian Communists were thus unable to take advantage of the Congress party's troubles. While India's troubles did not lead Moscow to reduce its involvement there, Soviet leaders were forced to lower their ideological sights. Thus Moscow decided to consolidate its position in India rather than try to deepen Indo-Soviet ties.

Soviet leaders also saw that the declining intensity of the cold war, combined with sharpening regional conflicts involving Turkey, Iran, and Pakistan with their neighbors (in which these countries were able to secure only limited backing from their Western allies) offered an opportunity to establish a position in these hitherto hostile nations.

Moscow knew that overtures to Pakistan would be resented by India, but hoped New Delhi's need for Soviet support would temper its reaction. Indeed, a demonstration that the Soviet position in the subcontinent did not rest entirely on India might actually increase Soviet leverage in New Delhi. In any case, Pakistan's fury at the United States over the sending of American arms to India was not only weakening U.S.-Pakistani ties but also leading Ayub to look to Peking for assistance. China's eager response led to a rapid expansion of Sino-Pakistani relations. In such circumstances, Moscow could no longer depend entirely upon India to counter China in the subcontinent.

But it must be emphasized that the Soviet leaders had no intention of *shifting* their backing from India to Pakistan; they were only trying to work out *supplementary* links with Pakistan lest it move from the Western to the Chinese orbit. Soviet support for the Indian position on Kashmir disappeared from Indo-Soviet communiqués, and Moscow proclaimed its neutrality in the armed clash between India and Pakistan over the Rann of Kutch in April 1965. It took a similar position during the war between the two countries that began in August 1965, with *Pravda* asserting, "We would like Soviet-Pakistani relations, like our traditional friendship with India, to be a stabilizing factor in the situation in Asia and to contribute to the normalization of relations between India and Pakistan."[21]

But neutrality was feasible in the face of inflamed public sentiment in India and Pakistan only if their disputes could be kept in check. Moscow's efforts in the United Nations to promote a ceasefire lest China enter the fray, and the invitation to President Ayub and Prime Minister Shastri to avail themselves of Soviet good offices at Tashkent to work out a broader settlement, revealed a growing Soviet awareness of this fact. Premier Kosygin's success at Tashkent, limited though it was to achieving a disengagement of Indian and Pakistani forces and a statement of their intention to normalize relations, had a dramatic if ironic impact. As a British observer commented:

> Mr. Kosygin, whose ideology demands the fostering of chaos and disruption in non-Communist lands, finds himself doing his level best to calm down a Hindu under direct threat from China and a Muslim supposed to be on friendly terms with Peking, embroiled in a quarrel over the possessions of the mountain playground of the late British Raj.
> And, except for China, nobody minds.[22]

Ayub next tried to turn Soviet neutrality into support, but had only partial success. Between 1966 and 1968 he was able to secure Soviet agreement to provide military vehicles, helicopters, and finally a wider variety of arms. This was particularly important to his military-based regime, for the United States had ended its arms aid to Pakistan and India during the 1965 war, and Ayub did not want to replace his previous dependence upon the United States with complete dependence on China. He failed completely, however, to persuade the Soviet Union to halt or even reduce its arms deliveries to India.

Prime Minister Gandhi's cautious criticism of the new Soviet policy was irritating but tolerable to Soviet leaders. Fearful that an abatement of the cold war was leading to Soviet-American collusion, she hinted that Indian hostility toward China might be replaced by efforts to normalize relations. Although China continued to pour scorn on India, New Delhi's actions were a warning to Moscow that in time India might have some options of its own. New Delhi also refused to heed Soviet appeals that all nations sign the Nuclear Nonproliferation Treaty. India continued to expand its nuclear capabilities while maintaining it had no plans to create a nuclear weapons arsenal. New Delhi rebuffed Kosygin's offer to mediate the Indo-Pakistani dispute over the sharing of the waters of the Ganges River, and turned aside Brezhnev's call for an Asian collective security system. But in some cases New Delhi felt it had to accept Soviet proposals, and Mrs. Gandhi made only a pro forma protest over the Soviet invasion of Czechoslovakia. She also either ignored the activity of the Soviet navy in the Indian Ocean or, when that was not possible, passed it off as a response to Western naval activity. Nonetheless, the Soviets treated India brusquely in the late 1960s and relations, while formally correct, cooled considerably.

Moscow and New Delhi: Friends in Need

Beginning in 1969, trends in India, and more dramatically in Pakistan, called into question the Soviet attempt to move toward a balanced policy.

Mrs. Gandhi's move to the left created a split within the Congress party. If her gamble paid off, this would create a more promising political milieu in India, especially if her minority government became dependent on the Moscow-oriented CPI. If her right-wing opponents came out on top, there was a danger India would adopt a more conservative, pro-Western orientation. Thus Soviet hopes and fears both led Moscow to support Mrs. Gandhi and attack her antagonists as representatives of "reaction and imperialism."[23] Her smashing victory in the national elections in March 1971 ended any need for her new Congress party to rely on the CPI at the national level, but her utilization of Indian politicians friendly to the USSR in senior positions was encouraging to Moscow.

A more fundamental factor was the series of political upheavals Pakistan experienced following the overthrow of the Ayub regime early in 1969. Nationwide demands for representative government and a fairer distribution of Pakistan's economic growth were soon overshadowed by Bengali insistence on a radically new deal for East Pakistan. The Bengalis argued that their exclusion from political power and their exploitation by West Pakistan could only be remedied by a constitutional arrangement that guaranteed them complete provincial autonomy, a move that West Pakistanis felt would undermine the unity of the nation. The inability of Ayub's military successors to reach a compromise with the politicians who emerged victorious in the December 1970 elections—especially East Pakistan's Sheikh Mujibar Rahman—led to the outbreak of civil war in March 1971.[24]

Soviet leaders quickly moved to adjust their policy. President Podgorny's 3 April letter to President Yahya (which was immediately published) lashed out at the army's policy of "repression."[25] Moscow's criticism was made easier by growing Soviet disappointment about the difficulties it had encountered in its relations with Pakistan. In 1969 Pakistan had closed the American intelligence facilities in Peshawar directed against the USSR, but Moscow had been unable to curtail Sino-Pakistani ties. Pakistan continued to rely on China for arms; it rejected Brezhnev's call for an Asian collective security system (with its anti-Chinese overtones); and it turned down Kosygin's proposal for regional economic cooperation by India, Pakistan, Afghanistan, and Iran.

Such recalcitrance soured the Soviet leaders on Pakistan.[26] The 1968 Soviet-Pakistani arms agreement had called for three shipments of arms, but Moscow's displeasure led it to hold back on the third shipment.[27] Nonetheless, the Soviets did not want to give up on Pakistan, and when Yahya visited Moscow in 1970 they agreed to finance a one-million-ton steel mill.

Moscow's fear of Chinese involvement if a new Indo-Pakistani war broke out, and its concern for its position in the Muslim world—which generally supported the Yahya government's attempt to hold the country together—

also led it to call for a settlement acceptable to "the entire people" of Pakistan. Such phraseology created apprehension in India about Soviet unwillingness to alienate West Pakistan completely. But then the Kissinger visit to Peking by way of Pakistan raised the spectre of a U.S.-Chinese-Pakistani alignment. Soviet and Indian leaders alike were shaken, but their shared fears pushed them together and they soon responded with a dramatic move of their own — the signing of a twenty-year friendship and cooperation treaty on 9 August. Soviet arms shipments to India also rose dramatically.

When the third Indo-Pakistani war broke out in November 1971, Soviet vetoes in the United Nations Security Council neutralized that body, and the massive Soviet military forces on China's northern border served as a clear warning to Peking not to render more than verbal assistance to Pakistan. By the end of 1971 India's military victory had won independence for Bangladesh, Chinese and American ineptness left them with only a foothold in a truncated and embittered Pakistan, and the Soviet Union stood unchallenged as the ranking external power in South Asia.

Continuity and Consolidation

Moscow was faced with a basic policy choice after its dramatic success growing out of the 1971 upheaval. Should it commit Soviet prestige and resources to an attempt to greatly expand its influence in South Asia, or would its interests be adequately served by doing only what was necessary to maintain the position it had won? The Soviet course would be influenced by both its appraisal of conditions within the subcontinent and of the likely course of U.S. and Chinese policy.

The more ambitious course, if successful, would enhance the USSR's status as a superpower playing an increasing role in world affairs. But to make the effort worthwhile increased Soviet status would have to be accompanied by more tangible gains, such as regular use of naval facilities in India and Bangladesh and their support for Brezhnev's Asian collective security system. Neither India nor Bangladesh was willing to facilitate any substantial expansion of Soviet naval activity in the area. In 1971–72 Moscow tried to portray the Indo-Soviet treaty as an initial move toward fulfillment of the Brezhnev proposal.[28] But by 1973, the lack of Asian response was leading some Soviet officials to claim that these were two separate affairs.[29]

Thus it soon became clear to Soviet leaders that there were formidable obstacles that would make it difficult to succeed if it undertook a more ambitious course. India was determined to appear as well as be in control of its own destiny and thus resist any Soviet effort to expand its influence further. India's enhanced position in the subcontinent, while achieved partly as a

result of Soviet support, limited New Delhi's need for further Soviet backing. Prime Minister Gandhi's comment to *New York Times* correspondent
C. L. Sulzberger that "we are unable to display gratitude in any tangible
sense for anything" was a clear warning to Moscow not to press for a greater
role in the area.[30] Mrs. Gandhi's insistence that Indo-Pakistani problems be
handled bilaterally foreclosed any possibility that the Soviets would assume
the role of an outside mediator as they had done so successfully at Tashkent
in 1966. Finally, India's development of a heavy industrial sector reduced
its need for major Soviet aid projects. New Delhi utilized only about $20
million annually in Soviet project aid in the early 1970s, and at the end of
1976 about $475 million in Soviet project aid commitments remained un-
utilized.[31] India's opinion of Soviet technology declined as Moscow began
to seek Western and Japanese technology. India needed chiefly raw
materials and (periodically) foodstuffs, which Moscow would provide only
in emergencies, such as its two-million-ton wheat loan in 1973.

Soviet doubts about the gains that it could achieve by an expanded effort
were matched by an awareness that it need not adopt such a policy to protect its basic interests. Sino-Indian hostility remained unchanged, and
Peking could not play a significant role in Bangladesh as long as New Delhi
and Dacca were friendly. Pakistan had little choice but to maintain its links
with Peking, but their limits as well as their value were now apparent to
Pakistanis.[32] The United States showed no inclination to try to rebuild its
position in the subcontinent.

If India demonstrated its opposition to any substantial increase in the
Soviet role in South Asia, it was careful not to antagonize Moscow because
of its fears—which in time proved groundless—that a Sino-American-
Pakistani alliance might emerge and challenge India's hard-won position in
the subcontinent. Moreover, the Indian navy and air force remained
dependent on Soviet equipment, and the USSR was India's second largest
trading partner. The two countries signed numerous economic and scientific agreements, the USSR supplied India with heavy water for its nuclear
energy program, and Soviet missiles boosted Indian satellites into orbit.

Moscow did move quickly in 1972 to establish ties with newly independent Bangladesh, but was careful not to commit itself to open-ended
programs for the reconstruction or the economic development of that war-
ravaged and impoverished country. Sheikh Mujibar Rahman, the first
prime minister, was lavish in his praise for the USSR when he visited
Moscow in March 1972, and he agreed to hold regular political consultations with the Soviet Union.[33] The USSR provided Bangladesh with some
civilian and military aircraft, cleared sunken ships from two important
ports, and made economic aid commitments of $121 million between 1972
and 1975.[34] Nor did the USSR ignore such countries as Sri Lanka and

Afghanistan during the 1970s, which received economic aid credits of $57 million and $437 million respectively in 1975. The Soviet and South Asian political leaders frequently visited each other's capitals, but not even the most dramatic of these visits — that of Brezhnev to New Delhi in November 1973 — led to any significant change in the basic pattern of relationship.

The continuity of Soviet policy was demonstrated not only by its decision to consolidate rather than to seek a new breakthrough in its relations with India, but also by its decision to make renewed efforts to establish closer relations with Pakistan. Pakistan's location made it more important geopolitically than Bangladesh in Soviet strategy. Moreover, the dangers that could develop out of new wars probably led Soviet leaders to conclude the USSR would benefit by the regional stability that would follow the amelioration and eventual settlement of the deep-rooted Indo-Pakistan disputes.[35] But if Moscow was to exert any influence on such matters, it had to reestablish at least a modest position in Pakistan. Arms aid would alienate India, but trade and economic aid would not. Thus the Soviet leaders renewed their offer to finance a one-million-ton steel mill near Karachi, and agreed to provide $435 million in credits for the project.

Moscow also urged the South Asian countries to seek compromise settlements to their disputes, a course beneficial to all, but especially welcome to a weakened Pakistan, which feared that the Soviets would support India and Afghanistan in their disputes with Pakistan. Thus Moscow, while probably disappointed that it was not allowed a role in the process, welcomed the agreements dealing with the effects of the 1971 upheaval reached between India, Pakistan, and Bangladesh beginning in July 1972.[36] Similarly, Pakistani fears that the Soviets would urge Afghanistan to encourage disaffection and separation in a truncated Pakistan were alleviated by communiqués issued at the end of the Moscow visits of Pakistani Prime Minister Bhutto in October 1974 and Afghan Prime Minister Daoud in April 1977 urging that disagreements between the two countries over the status of the border people in Pakistan be settled by peaceful means.[37] Prime Minister Bhutto also worked to convince Moscow that Pakistan wanted better relations, and stressed that while Pakistan would not reduce its links to China these were not directed against the USSR.

By the mid-1970s, the trend of events in South Asia probably reinforced the conviction of Soviet leaders that they had been wise not to pursue a more ambitious policy. Yet the satisfaction they could take from such a conclusion was offset by a series of developments that threatened to erode their position. Rising frustration in Bangladesh over prolonged disorder, inflation, and corruption turned to anti-Indian sentiment in view of Dacca's close ties with and dependence on New Delhi. Moscow as well as New Delhi was alarmed when conservative forces overthrew Sheikh Mujib in

August 1975 and gradually began to move the country out of India's orbit, an action that offered new opportunities for the United States and China if they were disposed to play a more active role. The turmoil that grew out of the rigged March 1977 elections in Pakistan, which after several months resulted in a military takeover there, was also a cause of concern to Moscow. Soviet leaders had not trusted Bhutto, but they had welcomed his decision to follow a policy of accommodation rather than confrontation with Pakistan's neighbors and had praised the economic and social reforms he had carried out.[38] The strength of the pro-Islamic and anti-Indian political forces and the political ineptitude of the military establishment did not augur well for Pakistan's future or for South Asia's stability.

A more serious cause of Soviet concern was the trend of events in India. By 1974, it was clear that Mrs. Gandhi was unable to take advantage of her dramatic election victories in 1971–72, and the country was in turmoil as a result of ill-conceived policies, poor management of government affairs, and bad monsoons. The Soviet government as well as the Communist party of the Soviet Union repeatedly expressed strong support for Mrs. Gandhi's declaration of an emergency in June 1975 as an essential move against reactionary forces.[39] Shortly before the March 1977 national elections *Izvestia* insisted that "everything India has achieved during its thirty years of independence has been directly connected with the Indian National Congress."[40] Moscow was shocked and dismayed over the stunning upset of the Congress party by the newly formed Janata (People's) party, and its subsequent installation of the conservative and anti-Communist Morarji Desai as prime minister.

Soviet concern over the course of events was intensified by two other developments affecting South Asia. During 1976 India and China had finally moved toward a normalization of relations, thereby increasing New Delhi's room for maneuver. Equally ominous was the move of the newly elected Carter adminstration to adopt a more friendly posture toward India. Clearly a Soviet reappraisal of its position and policies in South Asia—especially India—was necessary.[41]

The Afghan Crisis

Soviet apprehensions about the erosion of their position in South Asia turned out to be greater than warranted. In part this was because of Soviet flexibility in dealing with the new Indian government. Soviet policy continued to be oriented toward—but not dominated by—its need to be the external power whose voice carried the greatest weight in New Delhi. This task became more difficult with the advent of the Janata government in March 1977. Moscow was worried by Prime Minister Desai's remarks that his government would follow a policy of "genuine" nonalignment, and would not let the 1971 Indo-Soviet treaty stand in the way of Indian friendship with any other country. Foreign Minister Gromyko hurried to New Delhi in April 1977 and came away reassured if not completely satisfied, for once in office, the new government gave a high priority to continuity in foreign policy. India was determined to work for improved relations with China and the United States, but not willing to substantially weaken its links with its only great power supporter. Indian Foreign Minister Vajpayee commented that "Indo-Soviet friendship had been a stable factor and was of mutual benefit."[42] Such language was more restrained than during Gandhi's time, but Gromyko responded with a new offer of the equivalent of $252 million in credits for heavy industrial projects, a move that was largely symbolic in view of past unused Soviet credits. Indian reaffirmation of the validity of the 1971 Indo-Soviet treaty during Desai's visit to Moscow in October 1977 further pleased the USSR.

The Soviet Union's concern about American—and Chinese—ability to take advantage of developments in the subcontinent also declined during the late 1970s. China continued to support Pakistan, but that country's internal weaknesses made it a less attractive partner, especially since Peking wanted to establish less hostile relations with New Delhi. Progress toward better Sino-Indian relations was made when ambassadors were finally exchanged after a hiatus of nearly fifteen years. Yet the Janata government appproached China warily. Indian Foreign Minister Vajpayee's visit to China early in 1979 was a cause of concern to Moscow, but the Chinese attack on Vietnam on 17 February caused him to shorten his stay as a protest against the Chinese action. Chinese comparisons of its action against Vietnam with its military moves against India in 1962 touched raw nerves in New Delhi, and provided an indication of the obstacles facing any fundamental Sino-Indian rapprochement.

Moscow's apprehensions about an enhanced U.S. role in the subcontinent also declined during the late 1970s. President Carter wanted better relations with India and visited that country in January 1978; however, India did not rank high in U.S. priorities. Moreover, the importance attached to nonproliferation by the new administration created problems in America's relations with both countries, and its human rights policies complicated its desire to maintain good relations with Pakistan. U.S. law required the administration to halt all economic aid—except foodstuffs—and all military credit sales to Pakistan in April 1979, when that country was discovered to be striving to develop a nuclear weapons capacity.

More significant than these developments, which essentially maintained the basic pattern of relationships between the great powers and the states of South Asia established during the 1970s, was the coup in Afghanistan on 27

April 1978. In order to appraise its significance in world affairs and its implications for Soviet foreign policy, however, a brief analysis of internal
Afghan political developments before and since the coup and of Afghanistan's international position is required.

Afghanistan, a deeply religious, primitive, tribal society with a long
history of fierce resistance to outside attempts to control the country, began
to move cautiously on the path toward modernization in the years after
World War II. The monarchy was the initial sponsor of this modernization
attempt, which was spurred by the government of Prime Minister Daoud
(a cousin of King Zahir Shah) during his years in office from 1953 to 1963.
He was able to take advantage of the cold war between the superpowers and
their competition for influence in the Third World, thereby extracting
relatively large amounts of aid from both the Soviet and Western blocs.
However, even in the 1950s when the United States was establishing
military pacts to contain the Soviet Union, Washington refused Afghan requests for military support. U.S. interests in the country apparently were
regarded as minimal, and the United States regarded Pakistan as a more
important country. Thus the United States accepted a situation in which
the USSR became virtually the sole supplier of arms to Afghanistan,
adopted a nonaligned stance, and took care not to offend the Soviet Union.

The efforts of the Afghan government to develop its economy and its
military forces created both a need for trained manpower and rising expectations among the newly educated. The rapid expansion of educational opportunities, combined with the frustrations inherent in any development
effort in a country such as Afghanistan, led some of the newly educated
people to turn to Marxism. King Zahir Shah's dismissal of the authoritarian Daoud in 1963 and subsequent halfhearted attempts to permit more
open political activity led Marxist elements to coalesce and found the People's Democratic party (PDP) in January 1965. The strength of the Marxist
elements gradually increased, but factional disputes based on personal
rivalries, cultural, and ethnic differences, and conflicts over how to respond
to alternating government tactics of repression and co-optation led to a
party split within a year, and to bitter hostility between the *Khalq* (Masses)
factions led by Nur Muhammad Tariki and Hafizullah Amin and the *Parcham* (Banner) faction led by Babrak Karmal.

In 1973 former Prime Minister Daoud, concerned about the drift in
Afghan affairs, seized power in a coup that overthrew the monarchy as well
as the government. While Daoud was supported by many younger, reform
minded elements — including those within the military — by 1977 he was
acting more like a traditional Afghan ruler than a modernizer. He became
more repressive at home, but also more friendly toward Iran and Pakistan,
thus alarming the Soviets and leading the *Khalq* and *Parcham* factions to

reunite in July 1977. The stage was set for the April 1978 coup and the emergence of a Communist government in Afghanistan.

This is not the place to describe in detail developments leading up to and following the coup.[43] The extent to which the coup was a reactive affair by those fearful of further repression by Daoud, and the extent of Soviet knowledge and encouragement, are matters about which those knowledgeable on Afghan affairs differ. What is clear, however, are three points: (1) the PDP regime attempted to push through a thorough reform of Afghan society, which alienated not only the religiously-oriented rural, conservative forces, but most moderates and many leftists as well; (2) the divisions within the PDP persisted after the seizure of power, and over the following eighteen months there were many purges and upheavals, including one against the *Parcham* leaders in July 1978 and another in September 1979 within the dominant *Khalq* faction, in which forces led by Prime Minister Amin (perhaps fearing he was about to be removed) ousted President Tariki, who died a month later; and (3) the Soviet Union gave the new regime strong support, and in October 1978 they signed a twenty-year treaty of cooperation that linked the two countries politically, economically, and militarily. Moscow's backing was essential to the narrowly based and internally divided regime, but the identification of Marxism with atheism and the regime's subservience to the traditionally hated Russians not only restricted its popular appeal but led to localized resistance a few months before the coup. The Soviets apparently were aware of the problems created by the regime's brutality and headlong rush to reform Afghan society, but were unable to persuade their local clients to be less dogmatic, broaden their base, or cease their factional struggles.

During 1979 the insurgency spread throughout the country. The government's authority hardly extended beyond the major cities and provincial centers, and did not last beyond sunset in some of them. The government's security forces, which probably numbered about 100,000 shortly after the coup, were cut in half by purges and desertions, the latter sometimes involving entire units that defected with their arms to the rebels. The latter, while steadily increasing in number and strength, remained constrained by their lack of any organizational structure at either the military or the political level. Repeated infusions of Soviet arms and the provision of several thousand advisors—often assigned down to the level of small units —were enough to slow the insurgency's growth but were not adequate to halt it, much less reverse the tide.

The deteriorating situation in Afghanistan and the poor prospects for reversing the trend confronted the Soviet leaders with a painful choice by late 1979. They could leave what was widely regarded as a Communist regime to its fate, which was likely to be its demise during the course of

1980, or they could intervene in such numbers and with such force as were thought to be sufficient to save their client. They chose the second course, and on 8 and 9 December began a rapid expansion of their troop strength in Afghanistan. This apparently was done with the agreement of—and possibly even at the request of—President Amin, who despite his desire to make his own decisions probably was well aware of his regime's need for additional Soviet support to offset the growing strength of the insurgents. However, once the Soviets had added several thousand men to their forces in Afghanistan during December they staged a coup on 27 December that resulted in the execution of President Amin and the installation of the strongly pro-Soviet Babrak Karmal as the new president. Tens of thousands of Soviet troops poured across the border—the first time that Soviet troops had moved beyond the lines between the Communist and non-Communist worlds that grew out of the defeat of Germany and Japan in World War II.

The possible motivations and implications of the Soviet invasion, and the international crisis it generated, will be discussed in the final section of this chapter. One point that is clear as of the end of February 1980, however, is that the Afghan insurgency will be far more difficult and costly for the Soviets to suppress than were its early military moves in Hungary in 1956 and Czechoslovakia in 1968. Assertions that Afghanistan will be the Soviet Union's "Vietnam" are much too facile and ignore important differences between the two situations. Nonetheless, the willingness of the Soviet Union to invade a nonaligned country, the determination of the Afghan people to resist foreign domination, and the widespread international condemnation of the Soviet move indicate that a new stage in the struggle between the Communist and non-Communist worlds has begun.

The Soviet Impact on South Asia: 1954–1979

Before turning to the likely course of Soviet relations with South Asia, it is useful to assess the Soviet position in the late 1970s, the impact of its past policies, and the lessons the Soviet leaders had drawn from their past experiences. It is by no means clear at this time which of these lessons will have continuing validity after the changes resulting from the Afghan crisis, but the efforts of twenty-five years are likely to have some enduring significance.

The Soviet Union won its position by working out an approach that combined strategic consistency with tactical flexibility. Its efforts have been centered on India but not confined to it; New Delhi has felt confident enough of Soviet support to make close relations with Moscow the touchstone of its foreign policy, but the occasional wavering of Moscow's stance has convinced New Delhi it must cultivate Soviet ties rather than take them for granted. The Soviet approach has naturally been less successful in Pakistan, but in recent years, at least, has led Pakistan to take Soviet interests into account when it made important decisions.

Moscow is now the major external source of arms for South Asia; its commitments to India and Afghanistan between 1954 and 1974 amounted to $1.4 billion and $490 million respectively.[44] (It has also occasionally sent arms to other South Asian countries—as when it provided military equipment to Sri Lanka to put down a leftist insurgency in 1971, demonstrating its concern about the uncertain outcomes of revolutionary upheavals that it feared might benefit China more than the USSR.) Such arms have been essential to Indian and Afghan efforts to build up their military forces. However, India's expanding defense industry and its improved strategic position during the 1970s limited New Delhi's dependence on Moscow, and led India to turn to Western Europe for some key weapon systems such as high performance aircraft. Nonetheless, a major Western military aid program for Pakistan in the 1980s could increase India's dependence on Soviet arms once again.

The great expansion of Soviet economic relations with South Asia since the mid-1950s has also played an important part in enlarging the Soviet role in the area, as shown in Table 9.1. Moscow's $1.9 billion in aid commitments to India from 1954–76 on relatively easy terms (supplemented by $487 million from Eastern Europe) have been directed overwhelmingly to the construction of large state-owned industrial enterprises, such as steel mills, machinery factories, and oil exploration. Although such aid is but a

TABLE 9.1
Communist Economic Assistance Extended to South Asia, 1954–76
(Millions in U.S. Dollars)

Country	Total	USSR	East Europe	China
	5,460	3,961	684	810
Afghanistan	1,364	1,251	40	73
Sri Lanka	326	95	73	153
India	2,430	1,943	487	--
Nepal	199	20	--	179
Pakistan	1,141	652	84	405

Source: Central Intelligence Agency, *Communist Aid to the Less Developed Countries of the Free World, 1976;* ER 77-10296, August 1977.

fraction of the more than $20 billion extended by Western nations to India—and Soviet disbursements are normally slower than Western deliveries—its concentration in areas regarded by Indians as essential to their eventual economic independence gives it a political impact much greater than such comparisons suggest. (Soviet aid to Afghanistan has been larger than that supplied by the United States.) Soviet technicians and training programs have increased the capabilities of the recipient countries. As Table 9.1 shows, however, China as well as the West has been an important competitor. Peking's aid exceeds that of the USSR in Sri Lanka and Nepal, and its aid to Pakistan is about two-thirds as much as Soviet aid.

Nor should the expansion of Soviet trade with the South Asian countries be overlooked. As Table 9.2 shows, Soviet and Eastern European trade expanded dramatically between 1955 and 1975. If the communist countries still occupy a secondary place in the trading patterns of countries of the subcontinent, it is no longer (except with Nepal) an insignificant place. The South Asian countries have benefited in a number of ways from economic ties with the communist countries. New industries have been established and existing ones expanded, and new markets for a variety of South Asian products obtained. These markets were initially for traditional products, but in recent years have included manufactured goods as well; by 1970 nearly half of India's exports to the USSR consisted of finished or semi-finished products.[45]

However, problems arise periodically and lead to complaints by the South Asians. For example, the Eastern European practice of reexporting some commodities (at discount rates) cuts into the direct sales of South Asian countries and thus limits the value they derive from these trade links. In addition, Moscow often drives a hard bargain over the prices of the goods it buys and sells. More generally, strictly bilateral trading arrangements (dubbed "taking in each other's dirty laundry" by economists) discourage the most efficient international division of labor, for one partner is sometimes forced to take unneeded products in order to balance its accounts with the other. A former high Indian official once told me his country's economic relationship with the USSR was particularly beneficial because it required little marketing effort; the Soviets had the responsibility of finding Indian products to import in order to be repaid for past loans. Such a procedure has its short-run attractions, but it ultimately works against the developing countries' interests by causing them to neglect the effort necessary to penetrate world markets generally. But despite these drawbacks, the developing countries' chronic shortage of capital and lack of assured access to the markets of Western nations make their economic relations with the Communist countries an important if limited benefit in an imperfect world.

TABLE 9.2
South Asia: Foreign Trade (Imports and Exports), 1955 and 1975

Country	1955 USSR & East Europe		China		Rest of World		1975 USSR & East Europe		China		Rest of World	
	U.S. $ Million	Per-cent	U.S. $ Million	Per-cent	U.S. $ Million	Per-cent	U.S. $ Million	Per-cent	U.S. $ Million	Per-cent	U.S. $ Million	Per-cent
India	25.9	1.0	19.7	.7	2,645.1	98.3	1,418.2	13.4	.9	0.0	9,142.8	86.6
Pakistan*	5.7	.8	31.9	4.4	684.1	94.8	153.0	4.8	67.2	2.1	2,959.9	93.1
Bangladesh	n.a.	n.a.	n.a.	n.a.	n.a.	n.a.	123.7	7.8	2.9	0.0	1,476.3	92.2
Afghanistan**	33.4	29.0	n.a.	n.a.	81.6	71.0	86.5	19.3	3.2	1.0	361.2	80.7
Sri Lanka	1.9	.3	42.3	5.9	669.7	93.8	62.1	5.3	87.3	7.4	1,027.3	87.3
Nepal***	n.a.	n.a.	n.a.	n.a.	n.a.	n.a.	1.5	2.0	2.0	2.7	71.3	95.3

*1955 data include trade of area not comprising Bangladesh.

**1955 data not available; 1956 figures used.

***1975 data not available; 1970 figures used.

n.a.—not available.

Sources: UN, IMF, IBRD: Direction of International Trade, Statistical Papers, Series T, vol. 10, no. 8 (New York, 1959). Annual Data for the years 1955–1958 and 1970–1975.

Bureau of Intelligence and Research, Department of State, Communist States and Developing Countries: Trade and Aid in 1971, RECS-3 (Washington, D.C., 15 May 1972), p. 27.

Another point warrants mention. Soviet emphasis on aid for state-owned projects and on government-to-government trade agreements has (with a minor assist from Soviet propaganda extolling the virtues of socialism) made it easier for the governments of many developing countries to move toward greater control over their economies. Many of them desired this on their own, and it has been necessary in some cases in view of the limited number and capabilities of private entrepreneurs able to develop and operate large-scale enterprises. Few of the countries have yet adopted anything resembling Soviet-style socialism. But this trend, given the inefficiency of many state-operated industries in countries such as India, although gradually diminishing, has probably been something of a handicap to their economic development efforts.[46]

The impact of Soviet military aid and diplomatic activities in the South Asia scene until 1980 is, in the first instance, rather easy to assess. It has substantially enhanced Indian military strength and international stature, and enabled India to maintain firm positions in its disputes with Pakistan and China. Its effects on Pakistan have been quite different. The primary responsibility for that country's destruction in 1971 rests with the short-sightedness of its West Pakistani rulers over a period of many years. Once the civil war erupted, the Bengalis probably would have eventually worn down and expelled the Pakistani army, but Soviet support of India sealed Pakistan's fate as a nation.

Would India have been more flexible in dealing with its two major neighbors if it had lacked such extensive Soviet support? Would its future as a nation be more promising if it had reached compromise settlements with Pakistan and China a decade or so ago, and thus been able to direct more of its resources and energies to economic development? Or did the ability to stand fast against external enemies, whatever the cost in terms of development, provide a crucial element of cohesion to a nation beset by many serious internal divisions? (Moscow's policies, it should be noted, have been directed toward amelioration of regional disputes at times — such as before 1962 regarding the Sino-Indian conflict, and most of the period after 1965 in the Indo-Pakistani dispute — just as it encouraged India to take a hard line toward Pakistan between 1955 and 1965 and toward China since 1962.) Unfortunately, historical alternatives cannot be programmed and played out in a computerized politico-military war game. Thus such questions are essentially unanswerable, but the very fact that they can be asked raises some doubts about the ultimate impact of Soviet support on India's prospects as a nation.

Finally, how much influence — and of what types — had the Soviet Union acquired in South Asia by the late 1970s? The term *influence,* while used constantly — and carelessly — by students of politics, is extremely difficult to measure with accuracy or confidence. Most Indians have denied that the USSR exercises any substantial influence in India. This overstates Indian ability to pursue its own course, but not by any great extent — to the frustration of Soviet officials.[47]

The pattern appears to be mixed. The Soviet political system had not been attractive to any of the South Asian peoples — at least until the leftist coup in Afghanistan in April 1978. Soviet writings on economic development have had little impact on Indian thinking.[48] The USSR has been handicapped by the lack of personal rapport between many of its officials sent to the subcontinent and the local people they deal with, and many South Asians sent to the Soviet Union for training have a negative reaction to the country.

At the same time, the Soviet presence had become part of the landscape in South Asia, and all of the countries saw value in a Soviet connection. All of them dealt with the USSR carefully, and tried not to oppose or offend it on matters Moscow considered important. If specific examples of positive Soviet influence beyond Afghanistan were difficult to discover and document, the reluctance of all of the South Asian countries to be openly at odds with their large northern neighbor assured Moscow that they would go to great lengths to avoid cooperating with the Soviet Union's enemies in schemes directed against it. This in itself represented a major Soviet gain compared to the situation in the late 1950s and 1960s, although its durability following the Soviet invasion of Afghanistan is uncertain.

Implications of the Soviet Invasion of Afghanistan

It is far too early, in March 1980, to assess with any degree of confidence the consequences of the Soviet invasion of Afghanistan, although government officials in many countries are already making decisions based upon their initial judgments of Soviet motivations and likely actions. What is possible at this time is to set forth the likely reasons behind the Soviet move, the initial reactions of the key countries of the area, and the factors and considerations that will influence the evaluation of this crisis. Once this has been done, a few comments on the possible long-term implications for the Soviet Union's position in South Asia may be possible.

There were probably several important reasons behind the USSR's invasion, beginning with the fear of the Soviet leaders that a *neighboring* Communist regime would collapse if Moscow did not intervene. This would have been a substantial setback for the Soviet Union in any circumstances, but the fact that it would have occurred in a country Moscow regarded as within its general sphere of influence would have increased the seriousness of such a reversal. Moreover, given the polarization of forces within Afghanistan, the Communist regime probably would have been replaced by militantly Islamic and anti-Soviet forces. Such an outcome, given the upsurge of Islamic fervor and disorder in Iran, would have been a matter of great concern to a leadership and people traditionally extremely sensitive to the security of their borders.

It is possible that Soviet leaders feared that an upsurge of Islamic military would have created problems for them among the rapidly growing Muslim population of Soviet central Asia. Speculation about a religious revival among Soviet Muslims has been supported by little factual evidence, but even the absence of positive signs of an Islamic revival inside the USSR would not mean Soviet leaders had no apprehensions about such a development.

A more difficult question is whether the Soviet invasion was essentially a defensive move or whether it signalled more ominous dangers for South Asia and the Persian Gulf? George Kennan argued that the Soviet action was an anomaly and basically a defensive move; he sharply criticized the U.S. government for speaking and acting as if the Soviet intervention were a prelude to further aggressive moves:

> In the official American interpretation of what occurred in Afghanistan, no serious account appears to have been taken of such specific factors as geographic proximity, ethnic affinity of peoples on both sides of the border, and political instability in what is, after all, a border country of the Soviet Union. Now, specific factors of this nature, all suggesting defensive rather than offensive impulses, may not have been all there was to Soviet motivation, nor would they have sufficed to justify the action; but they were relevant to it and should have been given their due in any realistic appraisal of it.[49]

A less sanguine view was expressed by Helmut Sonnenfeldt:

> For many years, the Soviet Union has used its growing military capabilities to assert its influence and establish its presence around the world. But apart from suppressing popular uprisings and pressures for liberalization in Eastern Europe by the actual use of military force, the Soviets have generally avoided injecting their own organized combat units into regional conflicts or domestic upheavals. . . .
>
> The events in Afghanistan in one sense represent the culmination of these trends, in that the Soviets are now unabashedly and directly using their own forces. They also represent a new departure because Soviet military power is being used for the first time since the 1940s in an effort to extend Soviet dominance beyond its precious perimeter on the Eurasian landmass by preserving a new addition to the "Socialist camp". . . .
>
> Whether the military options opened by the occupation of the territory of Afghanistan will come to be exercised by the Soviet rulers cannot be predicted

. . . But even if the military options arising from the military occupation of Afghanistan were not soon exercised, the strategic map of the world would nevertheless have been changed for the worse for all those concerned about the expansion of Soviet influence and power. . . .

Whatever the "defensive" rationale for the Soviet action — and acknowledging the importance of attempting to interpret Soviet reasoning as objectively as possible — the practical political-military results are nevertheless as indicated earlier in this article. In the end, a "defensive" set of motives may serve as a more powerful stimulus to action than the desire for pure aggrandizement. And, of course, once having invested blood, military power and prestige to maintain Afghanistan's orientation and to suppress resistance to its regime, it is not so farfetched a step for the Soviets to push beyond that country's borders in order to secure them against external incursions, real or imagined.[50]

No one can be certain which of these views is the more accurate, but several points can be made. Whatever the initial Soviet motivations, the serious difficulties they have encountered in Afghanistan suggest that it will be some months, if not longer, before they will be in a position to pose a major military threat to Iran or Pakistan. However, if they succeed in their Afghan adventure they will have advanced the frontiers of the Soviet bloc, and new opportunities for pressures on Iran and Pakistan — perhaps including open military moves — will have been created.

Finally, the stakes involved in these matters are tremendous. The gains that the Soviets would realize by a major military advance into as poor an area as Pakistan would be modest, and the costs would be substantial if such a move alienated India. However, a Soviet military advance to the Persian Gulf would be quite a different matter in view of the industrial world's critical dependence on oil from the area — a prize that could prove more attractive to the Soviet Union if its oil production declines as sharply as some petroleum specialists have forecast. President Carter has stated that the United States has vital interests in the area and would use military force to protect them, but U.S. ability to project military forces of any significant size into the Persian Gulf area will remain limited for the foreseeable future. The Soviet leaders now passing from the scene are not reckless men, but the course likely to be followed by their successors will be influenced and dependent upon the outcome of the Soviet adventure in Afghanistan as well as their perception of the trend of world affairs.

Thus the Soviet invasion of Afghanistan and the future course of Soviet policy cannot be considered apart from the general state of Soviet relations with the outside world, especially the United States. Soviet leaders probably were influenced by a combination of apprehensions and optimism. The United States had allowed its military power relative to that of the

Soviet Union to decline during the 1970s. It had been unable or unwilling to prevent the overthrow of Shah Pahlavi's pro-Western regime in Iran, and had been unable to obtain the release of its embassy officials in Tehran. Soviet support for Marxist regimes in such countries as Angola, Ethiopia, and South Yemen had generated only limited American responses. At the same time, Soviet leaders were clearly worried that the United States, Japan, and Western Europe were moving toward closer cooperation with China, and perceived a new and more dangerous form of encirclement developing. NATO had agreed late in 1979 to place new nuclear missiles in Western Europe. The Carter administration was moving toward a significant if moderate increase in its rate of defense spending. In view of prospects of Senate ratification of the SALT II Treaty, Soviet leaders may have felt they had little to fear from the United States if they moved into Afghanistan and little to gain from the United States if they refrained from such intervention.

Some observers of Soviet affairs have suggested that there may have been serious divisions within the aging and ailing Soviet leadership about whether or not to intervene in Afghanistan and that the Soviets may have seriously miscalculated the reaction to their invasion. While there probably are some differences in views among Soviet leaders, it would be a mistake to believe that there are "doves" and "moderates" who need to be encouraged by the West so that they can hold their own against the "hawks" and "hard liners." No Soviet leader defeated on a major policy issue like Afghanistan would be likely to remain in a position of power. Yet it is possible that the Soviets underestimated the difficulties they would encounter in subduing the Afghans, or did not expect as strong a reaction from the United States to their move into a formerly nonaligned country. We should not assume that greater difficulties than were anticipated will cause the Soviets to search for a way to withdraw from Afghanistan, for the USSR is tenacious and quite willing to spill blood—both Russian and Afghan—to achieve its objectives. They probably count on divisions within the West and the Third World, especially if the Afghan insurgency is reduced in scope, to lead a gradual acceptance of Soviet control of Afghanistan. The reluctance of most Western European countries to take actions that would seriously endanger the relations they had built with the Soviet bloc during the period of détente probably will sustain such Soviet expectations.

Soviet policy in the future will be influenced by the policies of the countries in the area. Pakistan and India reacted quite differently to the Soviet invasion. Pakistan was convinced that some seventy-five thousand Soviet troops in what had been a buffer state between the USSR and the subcontinent represented a direct threat to its security and even to its ability to survive as a nation. Its leaders felt that their country needed massive external support to enable it to meet the Soviet challenge. At the same time they feared that a firm stance could lead the Soviet Union to take harsh measures against Pakistan; thus the leaders probably wondered if they should not explore the possibility of reaching an accommodation with Moscow. Pakistan's convening of an Islamic foreign ministers conference in January and its success in persuading the foreign ministers to condemn the Soviet invasion suggest that it realizes the possibility that such an accommodation could encourage further Soviet pressures rather than satisfy the USSR. Yet Pakistan was far from convinced that the United Staets would be a consistent supporter over the long term if it accepted American backing, as its unwillingness to accept the initial U.S. aid offer demonstrates.

Pakistan's worries were heightened by Gandhi's initial reaction immediately after her remarkable political comeback in the elections of January 1980. India first publicly accepted the Soviet explanation that their intervention occurred in response to an invitation by an Afghan government struggling to defeat an insurgency supported by external forces. India soon changed the emphasis in its public statements somewhat, calling the Soviet move unjustified and urging the Soviets to remove their military forces as soon as possible. However, India's initial reaction created fears in Pakistan that Moscow and New Delhi might be moving toward joint action to partition Pakistan rather than see it strengthened by outside financial and military support. New Delhi's shifting statements reflect the conflict between its inability to reconcile its fears of an expanded Soviet military role in the area, its fear of a rearmed Pakistan backed by China and the United States, its dependence upon the USSR for arms and international political support, and its dependence upon the West for trade and aid.

India was particularly concerned that a Sino-American-Pakistani-Islamic alliance would develop as a response to the Soviet invasion. New Delhi felt it essential to remain on good terms with Moscow because of the widespread Indian belief that any arms sent to Pakistan are likely to be used by that country's military rulers to suppress their own people, or to threaten India. Chinese, American, and Pakistani efforts to convince New Delhi that each of them wanted to avoid anything that would threaten India's security will continue to encounter skepticism in New Delhi, for it is extremely reluctant to admit openly that Soviet troops in Afghanistan pose a serious security problem to Pakistan—and to the entire subcontinent.

India had no success in persuading Soviet Foreign Minister Gromyko to set forth a specific plan or timetable for Soviet troop withdrawals when he visited India in February, and New Delhi made no attempt to hide its differences with Moscow over this matter. At the same time, its public statements emphasizing the dangers that were being created by U.S. moves to build countervailing military strength in the area indicate that Indian foreign policy will continue to tilt toward Moscow. Underlying these moves is the Indian frustration over its awareness that increased great power involvement in the subcontinent will undercut Indian efforts to be the predominant power in the area.

The Afghan crisis could lead to a wide variety of developments, which would have quite different implications for the Soviet position in the subcontinent, but some variation of one of the following three scenarios would appear likely. The first would be a Soviet failure in its effort to subdue Afghanistan. Such a failure would involve Moscow's encountering such heavy costs within Afghanistan or in its relations with other countries, as to lead it to withdraw its troops from the country even if that meant establishing a noncommunist regime of one complexion or another.

It seems unlikely that Moscow will incur heavy enough costs in terms of its relations with the West or the Third World to lead to such an outcome. Given the costs of such a defeat to the USSR, and the latter's ability and willingness to pay a heavy price to succeed in its Afghan venture, such a development probably could result only if the Afghan people were willing to sustain heavy losses for a considerable period of time. The chances for such an outcome will depend heavily upon whether Moscow is able to reconstruct an Afghan government, police, and army that can win at least the sullen acquiescence of a sizable part of the population. So far the trend has been in the opposite direction. All these entities have been disintegrating, and are viewed as Soviet puppets by virtually the entire population. However, Soviet determination and ruthlessness might gradually lead more Afghans to conclude that cooperation is the only feasible course.

Such an outcome would hardly destroy the Soviet position in South Asia. India would still desire Soviet support and assistance, and Pakistan would have no reason to offend the USSR. Yet the aura of growing power and determination that Moscow has successfully sought to project would have been badly if not irreparably damaged, and all of the countries of the area would give much less weight to the views of a "superpower" that could not subdue fifteen million poorly armed Afghans.

A second possible outcome would be a stalemate. The essential difference between this scenario and the first one would be that Moscow would achieve enough in Afghanistan to be able to have a significant voice — perhaps even a veto — over the final outcome, but would still find its venture costly enough over a prolonged period so as to be willing to seek a compromise solution. The specific outline of such a compromise can hardly be determined at this point, but it probably would involve some form of guaranteed neutralization or nonalignment internationally and a coalition of diverse forces domestically.

The international aspects of such an outcome appear feasible, although

Moscow probably would move slowly to accept such a solution. However, the domestic component is hard to envisage, for the Afghan people are bitterly polarized between a few thousand Marxists and millions of militantly anti-Marxist tribesmen and townsmen in a country where blood feuds and revenge are matters of honor. In this atmosphere, moderates acceptable to both sides — if they have not already been decimated — have little if any political base. Yet conflicts do not always end with clear victors and vanquished, and a prolonged stalemate could eventually lead to at least some temporary accommodations.

Before Moscow would accept such an outcome it probably would be tempted to deal with its Afghan problem by striking at Pakistan and/or Iran. This could involve cross border attacks, especially against Pakistan, for Soviet officers in Afghanistan would almost inevitably tell Moscow that the reason they were not able to quell the insurgency was that it was benefitting from privileged sanctuaries beyond the borders. Moscow probably would also attempt to subvert dissatisfied groups, such as the Baluchis in Pakistan, in order to weaken the latter and force it to accommodate the USSR. In short, the dangers of wider conflicts and upheavals probably would increase substantially, and only if the countries of the area — and the West — were able to meet such challenges would a compromise become likely.

Such an outcome probably would, in general terms, leave the Soviet position in South Asia about like it was before its invasion of Afghanistan. Those suspicious of Moscow would have had their suspicions confirmed, and the Soviet need to find a compromise solution would reduce Soviet status. Yet those desirous of maintaining good realtions with the USSR would stress the willingness of the Soviet Union to compromise as evidence of its responsibility and maturity, while perhaps breathing easier because the limits of Soviet power had been demonstrated. Such a demonstration might even help Moscow by making cooperation — at arm's length — seem less dangerous once Moscow had retreated, although South Asian leaders would not overlook the precedent of President Amin's execution when considering cooperation with the USSR.

A third outcome would be Soviet success in subduing the Afghan insurgency and creating local political and military forces that were both loyal to Moscow and able to control the country with minimum direct Soviet involvement. Afghanistan, in such an event, would resemble Mongolia. Such a result could lead to closer cooperation among the states of the area and between these nations and the West, in order to confine Soviet power to Afghanistan. Given the deep-seated differences between the countries of the area and the demonstrated Soviet success in imposing its will on Afghanistan, the pressure, especially on Pakistan, to move toward accommodation with Moscow would be great. If such a pattern developed the Soviet Union might be willing to refrain from trying to manipulate Pakistani affairs for a few years. However, such an outcome probably would also subordinate Pakistan to India. This could so demoralize the key groups in Pakistan, who have yet to create a viable political system, that it would lead to great internal instability, or even national disintegration. Such upheavals would be likely to draw Moscow even deeper into the affairs of the subcontinent, although it might eventually bring Moscow and New Delhi into open contention. Even if such dramatic developments did not occur, by this scenario Moscow would have become the predominant external power in South Asia and all of the countries there would be wary of doing anything objectionable to the Soviet Union. Such a development could also increase the inclination of Middle Eastern countries to reach their own accommodations with Moscow, which would erode what remained of the Western position in much of the area from the eastern Mediterranean through the Indian subcontinent. In the event such developments took place a basic shift of the balance of power in world affairs would have occurred.

Notes

1. There is little point in an extended examination of the perennial question of the relationship between national interest and ideology in Soviet foreign policy. Most scholars have concluded that considerations of national interest take precedence whenever there is a conflict, but such a formulation of the issue is too simple. If a country's national interests were a discernible objective reality, readily apparent to its leaders and people, foreign policy would rarely be the source of domestic disagreements. Moreover "ideology" and "national interest" are not held in separate compartments of people's minds. Rather, people's concepts of the national interest are shaped to some degree by their ideology or values.

2. For an excellent discussion of Soviet views of the different parts of Asia, see Thomas P. Thornton, "The USSR in Asia," in Wilcox, Rose, and Boyd, *Asia and the International System* (Cambridge, Mass.: Winthrop, 1972).

3. Malcolm MacKintosh, "Some Aspects of Soviet Policy in Asia," in Hedley Bull, ed., *Asia and the Western Pacific: Internal Changes and External Influences* (Sydney: Angus and Robertson for the Australian Institute of International Affairs, 1975).

4. Soviet leaders focused briefly on South Asia in their negotiations with Nazi Germany over spheres of influence in the wake of the Soviet-Nazi pact in 1939. However, the negotiations centered on the future of Eastern Europe. Soviet efforts to seize a share of the spoils of the British Empire by gaining Nazi agreement that Soviet aspirations included the Persian Gulf as well as the Indian Ocean came to naught when the course of war went differently than anticipated. See John C. Campbell, "The Soviet Union and the Middle East: In the General Direction of

the Persian Gulf," parts 1 and 2, *The Russian Review,* vol. 29, nos. 2 and 3 (April and July 1970).

5. See William J. Barnds, *India, Pakistan and the Great Powers* (New York: Praeger, 1972), for an analysis of the motivations of the American leaders at that time.

6. The CPI also suffered many serious internal weaknesses, which continue to hamper the Indian Communist movement to this day. Its strength was confined to a few scattered areas, its lack of nationalist appeal led it to rely on the grievances of particular castes and linguistic groups, and it suffered from acute factional disputes. Its supporters were drawn heavily from the more politically aware and active Hindu community, which made it of little consequence in the areas that comprised Pakistan after the partition. For a survey of the development of the CPI and its relations with the Soviet Union see Gene D. Overstreet and Marshal Windmiller, *Communism in India* (Berkeley: University of California Press, 1959).

7. Stalin himself showed a few signs of recognizing this in his last year or so. India's criticism of the West at certain stages of the Korean War and its unwillingness to sign the Japanese Peace Treaty probably made some impression in Moscow. See Marshall Shulman, *Stalin's Foreign Policy Reappraised* (Cambridge: Harvard University Press, 1963).

8. Jawaharlal Nehru, "The Basic Approach," *AICC Economic Review* vol. 10, nos. 8 and 9 (15 August 1958), pp. 3–6; P. Yudin, "Can We Accept Pandit Nehru's Approach?" *World Marxist Review* (Toronto), vol. 1, no. 4 (December 1958), pp. 42–54.

9. Ministry of External Affairs, Government of India, *Notes, Memoranda and Letters Exchanged and Agreements Signed Between the Governments of India and China* (White Paper, 8 September 1959), pp. 73–76.

10. Peking was uncertain and vacillating in its appraisal of Nehru at this time. On 6 May, the *People's Daily* published a long article on India that referred to Nehru in a friendly manner, while criticizing him for certain aspects of his policy toward Tibet. See "The Revolution in Tibet and Nehru's Philosophy," in *Peking Review,* vol. 2, no. 19 (12 May 1959), pp. 73–76.

11. Two excellent short studies of the Sino-Indian dispute are Alastair Lamb, *The China-Indian Border: The Origins of the Disputed Boundaries* (London: Oxford University Press for the Royal Institute of International Affairs, 1964); and W. F. Van Eakelen, *Indian Foreign Policy and the Border Dispute with China* (The Hague: Martinus Nijhoff, 1964).

12. *Pravda,* 10 September 1959, in *The Current Digest of the Soviet Press,* vol. 11, no. 36 (7 October 1959), p. 14.

13. This is discussed in Harish Kapur, *The Soviet Union and the Emerging Nations* (London: Michael Joseph, Ltd., 1972), pp. 70–71.

14. The most detailed treatment of the events leading up to the war is in Neville Maxwell, *India's China War* (New York: Pantheon, 1970). But Maxwell's account must be treated with some caution in view of his tendency to give China the benefit of every doubt as far as responsibility for the conflict is concerned.

15. *Pravda,* 25 October 1962, in *The Current Digest of the Soviet Press,* vol. 14, no. 43 (21 November 1962), p. 17.

16. Koslov referred to Chinese "adventurism" at the Italian Party Congress held in December 1962, *London Times,* 4 December 1962. Similarly, *Pravda* lashed out at

China on 10 August 1963, p. 4.

17. Robert F. Byrnes, "Russia in Eastern Europe: Hegemony Without Security," *Foreign Affairs,* vol. 49, no. 4 (July 1971), pp. 682–97.

18. For a series of Western appraisals of the shifting Soviet viewpoint, see W. Raymond Duncan, ed., *Soviet Policy in Developing Countries* (Waltham, Mass.: Ginn Blaisdell, 1970). The essay by R. A. Yellon, *Shifts in Soviet Policies Toward Developing Areas: 1964–1968,* is particularly useful.

19. See, for example, G. Adhikari, "The Problem of the Non-Capitalist Path in India and the State of National Democracy," *World Marxist Review* (Toronto), vol. 7, (November 1964), p. 39; V. Yakunin, "Problems of India's Congress Party," *New Times* (Moscow), 2 March 1966; and P. Nikolsky, "Nehru's Party Without Nehru," *New Times* (Moscow), 11 August 1966.

20. The 1964 split was only the beginning of the fragmentation of the Indian Communist movement, for the ambivalence of the CPI (M) toward participation in state ministries led ultraradicals within that party to desert it in 1967 and 1968 and to form the violence-prone CPI (Marxist-Leninist) in 1969. See Marcus F. Franda, "India's Third Communist Party," *Asian Survey,* vol. 9, no. 11 (November 1969), pp. 797–817. For a more extensive discussion of the Indian Communist movement in this period, see Bhabani Sen Gupta, *Communism in Indian Politics* (New York: Columbia University Press, 1972).

21. *Pravda,* 24 August 1965, in the *Current Digest of the Soviet Press,* vol. 17, no. 34 (15 September 1965), pp. 15–16.

22. Edward Crankshaw, *The Observer* (London), 10 January 1966.

23. *Pravda,* 14 November 1969, in *The Current Digest of the Soviet Press,* vol. 21, no. 46 (10 December 1969), p. 15; P. Kretsobin, "The Indian Confrontation," *New Times* (Moscow), no. 47 (26 November 1969), pp. 6–8.

24. See G. W. Choudbury, *The Last Days of United Pakistan* (Bloomington: Indiana University Press, 1974).

25. *Pravda,* 4 April 1971, in *The Current Digest of the Soviet Press,* vol. 23, no. 14 (4 May 1971), pp. 35–36.

26. G. W. Choudbury, "The Emergence of Bangladesh and the South Asian Triangle," *The Yearbook of World Affairs: 1973* (London: London Institute of World Affairs, Stevens & Sons), pp. 66–68.

27. I am indebted to Ian Clark of the Australian National University for pointing this out to me. See his letter in *Problems of Communism,* November–December 1972, pp. 91–92, in response to my article, "Moscow and South Asia," *Problems of Communism,* May–June 1972, pp. 12–31.

28. The proposal's vagueness and implicit anti-Chinese focus led Asian governments to ignore or reject it. For respective Western and Soviet appraisals, see Ian Clark, "Collective Security in Asia: Towards a Framework for Soviet Diplomacy," *The Round Table,* October 1973, pp. 473–81; and V. Pavdovsky, "Collective Security: The Way to Peace in Asia," *International Affairs* (Moscow), July 1972, pp. 23–27.

29. J.D.B. Miller, "Summing up of Discussion," in Hedley Bull, ed., *Asia and the Western Pacific: Towards a New International Order* (Sydney, Angus and Robertson for the Australian Institute of International Affairs, 1975).

30. *New York Times,* 17 February 1972.

31. *Times of India,* 5 June 1977, Central Intelligence Agency, "Communist Aid to the Less Developed Countries of the Free World, 1976," ER77-10296, August 1977.

32. See William J. Barnds, "Pakistan's Relations with China: Durability Amidst Discontinuity," *The China Quarterly,* September 1975, pp. 463–89.

33. *Izvestia,* 26 March 1972, in *The Current Digest of the Soviet Press,* 19 April 1972, p. 18.

34. For an appraisal of Soviet-Bangladesh relations, see Bhabani Sen Gupta, "Moscow and Bangladesh," *Problems of Communism,* March–April 1975, pp. 56–68.

35. See Robert Donaldson, *Soviet Policy Toward India: Ideology and Strategy* (Cambridge: Harvard University Press, 1974), especially chapter 6.

36. See P. Kutsobin and V. Shurygin, "South Asia: Tendencies Toward Stability," *International Affairs* (Moscow), April 1973, pp. 43–48.

37. *Pravda,* 27 October 1974, in *The Current Digest of the Soviet Press,* 20 November 1974, p. 15; and *Pravda,* 16 April 1977, in *The Current Digest of the Soviet Press,* 11 May 1977, pp. 17–18.

38. *Pravda,* 11 March 1977, in *The Current Digest of the Soviet Press,* 6 April 1977, p. 20.

39. See *Pravda,* 2 July 1975, in *The Current Digest of the Soviet Press,* 23 July 1975, p. 12; *Izvestia,* 4 July 1975, in *The Current Digest of the Soviet Press,* 30 July 1975, p. 17; and *Pravda,* 13 July 1975, in *The Current Digest of the Soviet Press,* 6 August 1975, pp. 17–18.

40. *Izvestia,* 13 March 1977, in *The Current Digest of the Soviet Press,* 13 April 1977, pp. 15–16.

41. For a more detailed discussion of Soviet policy in the 1970s, see William J. Barnds, "The USSR, China, and South Asia," *Problems of Communism,* November–December 1977, pp. 44–59.

42. *Hindustan Times,* 25 April 1977.

43. Articles that describe the evolution of the Afghan scene and the development of the Marxist movement there prior and subsequent to the April 1978 coup include Robert G. Neumann, "Afghanistan," *Review of Strategic and International Affairs,* July 1978, pp. 115–118. Louis Dupree, "Red Flag over the Hindu Kush — Parts I and II," *American Universities Field Staff Reports,* nos. 44 and 45, 1979; Richard S. Newell, "Revolution and Revolt in Afghanistan," *The World Today,* November 1979, pp. 432–442; and Louis Dupree, "Afghanistan Under the Khalq," *Problems of Communism,* July-August 1979, pp. 34–50.

44. Bureau of Intelligence and Research, Department of State, *Communist States and Developing Countries: Aid and Trade in 1974,* Report no. 298, Washington, D.C., 27 January 1976.

45. L. M. Raina, "India–USSR: Widening Areas of Cooperation," *Indian and Foreign Review* (New Delhi), 1 September 1971, pp. 9–10; and Lev L. Klochkovsky, "USSR's Trade Patterns," (Geneva: International Trade Forum, December 1970), pp. 17–29.

46. To illustrate the complexities involved in any evaluation of Soviet economic activities, petroleum imports from the Communist countries probably improved India's bargaining position with Western oil companies over prices. But the availability of Soviet exploration teams (which have had only moderate success) probably

was one reason New Delhi insisted for many years on terms unacceptable to Western exploration firms for the important offshore areas, and thus until recently was deprived of modern technology in a crucial area.

47. For an analysis of this topic, see William J. Barnds, "Soviet Influence in India: A Search for the Spoils that Go with Victory," in Alvin Z. Rubinstein, ed., *Soviet and Chinese Influence in the Third World* (New York: Praeger, 1975).

48. See Stephen Clarkson, "The Low Impact of Soviet Writing and Aid on Indian Thinking and Policy," *Survey,* winter 1974, pp. 1–23.

49. *New York Times,* 1 February 1980.

50. Helmut Sonnefeldt, "Some Implications of the Soviet Invasion of Afghanistan for East-West Relations," *NATO Review,* March 1980.

10

Latin America

Leon Goure with Morris Rothenberg

The scope of Soviet relations with Latin America has been shaped by the geographic remoteness of that region from the USSR, by the East-West balance of power, and by the extent of the United States' influence over its southern neighbors.

Prior to the 1960s, Latin America was of only marginal interest to Moscow. The Soviet Union lacked the means to support an active policy in an area so distant and seemingly under firm U.S. control, a condition that gave rise to the concept of "geographic fatalism"—belief in the impossibility of successful revolutions in close proximity to the United States. This perception was fueled by the failure of various communist-led revolts and by U.S. reaction to Moscow's support of the Arbenz regime in Guatemala in 1954, which led to the latter's overthrow.

Throughout this time, however, Soviet leaders showed an interest—albeit not a very active one—in the potential of Latin America as an arena where growing nationalism and political ferment might weaken U.S. capitalism and divert Washington's attention from policies threatening the Soviet Union. For example, one Soviet assessment asserts that "from the beginning of the twentieth century, Latin America has become an active front in the struggle against imperialism, especially North American imperialism."[1]

But Soviet activities to exploit this struggle yielded little practical success. Until the late 1930s the Comintern's efforts to use the Latin American Communist parties for political subversion and abortive revolutions left a residue of suspicion and hostility toward native Communist parties as well as the Soviet Union. These activities undermined Moscow's efforts to establish diplomatic and trade relations in Latin America. With the dissolution of the Comintern and the shift of native Communist parties to a policy of cooperation with their respective governments, the Soviet Union did succeed in establishing diplomatic relations with thirteen Latin American countries. But most of these World War II gains did not survive the onset of the cold war.

Nevertheless, by the early 1960s this picture had changed significantly. The Cuban Revolution, notably the unexpected survival of Castro's regime in the face of U.S. hostility, loomed—in Moscow's view—as a momentous break in U.S. dominance of Latin America and appeared to open the way for an upsurge of pressures for political, social, and economic change on the continent. Events in Cuba were said to demonstrate that the United States was no longer able to slow down the revolutionary process in the Western Hemisphere, which it had long regarded as its own backyard. Soviet commentators ascribed to the Cuban Revolution a "tremendous role . . . in the development of the subsequent revolutionary process in Latin America."[2] The Cuban example was used to show that the United States had become more constrained in its responses to challenges to its interests in Latin America—and consequently that there was no longer any need to exclude the possibility of successful revolutions in the Western Hemisphere on grounds of "geographic fatalism." But Cuba's impact on the "revolutionary process" in Latin America proved far less than originally predicted.

Although the fortuitous events in Cuba provided the Soviet Union with a much-needed political and psychological windfall in its competition with the United States and its claim to leadership of the global national liberation struggle, they also confronted Moscow with a variety of unanticipated difficulties. From the Soviet point of view Cuba proved an important experiment in the problems of controlling, sustaining, and protecting a self-proclaimed Communist regime in a country geographically remote from the USSR, as well as a test of Soviet theories concerning the feasibility of rapid transformation of an essentially agrarian society into an industrial one.

During the Cuban missile crisis Khrushchev discovered that, while Washington was reluctant to resort to overt military intervention against Castro, it was determined to exclude Soviet military presence from the region and to impose severe limits on Soviet activities. Furthermore, while the Cuban example gave an impetus to the rise of a new radical Left in Latin America—a situation hardly welcomed by the orthodox Communist parties there—Moscow considered it inexpedient to follow Castro's lead in calling for violent revolution and guerrilla warfare on the continent.

Instead the Soviet Union found itself not only with a growing commitment to support the Cuban economy (which proved unsuited to rapid industrialization) but also, until 1968, in the position of competing with Castro's claim to leadership of the Latin American revolution. In the words of Cuba's foreign minister, Carlos Rafael Rodriguez, Cuban-Soviet relations were marked by "inevitable differences which on some occasions became acute."[3]

But by 1968 the failure of the Cuba-supported guerrilla movements on the continent, culminating in Che Guevara's death in Bolivia in 1967, proved the general validity of Moscow's policy line of seeking relations with the existing regimes in Latin America and urging a united front and a "peaceful road to power" strategy of the Left for most countries in that region. With the evidence of the inability of Castroism to repeat the Cuban success, and with increasing Soviet economic leverage on Havana, Castro was left no other option but to accept increasing alignment with Moscow and integration with the Soviet bloc.

No doubt Cuba provided the Soviet Union with a hard lesson in the difficulties of maintaining a client state in Latin America. Nevertheless, Moscow succeeded — albeit at considerable cost — in upholding in Cuba the validity of the Communist dictum concerning the "irreversibility" of successful revolutions. Above all, Cuba marked the beginning of a new stage in Soviet interest and involvement in Latin America.

This interest in Latin America has remained conditioned by two basic perceptions. The first is the Kremlin's belief that Latin America is becoming increasingly involved in the anti-imperialist and national liberation struggle — a struggle that, in its view, remains the most active form of Soviet competition with the West, and especially the United States, even under conditions of "peaceful coexistence," i.e., détente in East-West relations.[4] The second is the Soviet view of the strategic importance of Latin America for the United States and, consequently, as a factor in influencing the East-West balance of power.

If the decade following the Cuban Revolution included a succession of defeats for the "revolutionary process," such as the fall of the João Goulart regime in Brazil in 1964 and the U.S. intervention in the Dominican Republic in 1965, it nevertheless revealed a continuing upsurge of nationalist and reformist movements in Latin America. In the late 1960s, developments in the region (notably the emergence of "revolutionary" military regimes in Peru and Bolivia, followed in 1970 by the election in Chile of a Marxist president, Salvador Allende, and his Popular Unity government, headed by a coalition of the Socialist and Communist parties) led Soviet analysts to speak once again of an "intensification of the revolutionary process" in Latin America. By then the Soviet capability to play a more active role in the region had also increased markedly.

The challenges to U.S. interests in the 1960s and 1970s on the part of Peru, Panama, Ecuador, and for a time, Bolivia and Chile, and also the possibility that such other states as Venezuela and Argentina might pursue policies damaging to the United States, generated within the Soviet leadership an increasing interest in and, by and large, an optimistic view of trends in Latin America.

Although the anti-imperialist struggle was said to take diverse forms, it was recognized that, despite the Cuban example, only two have "proved to be the most effective" on the continent: the broad popular coalitions and the nationalistic military regimes that carry out "progressive" policies and impose restrictions on U.S. capital and the local oligarchies. Moscow attributed particular importance to the 1970 electoral victory in Chile of the Popular Unity coalition led by Allende, which Soviet commentators hastened to describe as "second only to the victory of the Cuban Revolution in the magnitude of its significance as a revolutionary blow to the imperialist system in Latin America."[5] Moscow was quick to assert that the lessons of Chile were of great significance for the rest of the continent and called on all "progressive" forces throughout Latin America to support the Allende regime and to follow the Chilean example.

Obedient to the call, the Communist parties in a number of countries — notably in Argentina, Bolivia, Uruguay, Ecuador, El Salvador, Colombia, Panama, Peru, and Venezuela — set out to organize united fronts, but none of these attained any significant political strength or gained power.

At first, Soviet comments also underscored the uniqueness of the Chilean case. Thus Brezhnev noted in his speech at the Twenty-fourth CPSU Congress that this was "the first time in the history of the continent" that such a government had come to power by constitutional means, while a specialist on Latin America quoted Lenin's sayings concerning the "extremely rare" and "extremely valuable" opportunities for revolution without armed struggle. Soviet commentators also recognized the precariousness of Allende's regime as it sought to consolidate its position and carry through the "revolutionary transformation of Chile" within the framework of the constitution and largely by legal means. Both the Chilean Communist leaders and the Soviet spokesmen warned that the revolution still needed to be made irreversible.

Prior to the coup that overthrew the Allende regime, Soviet analysts took a generally optimistic view of the attitude of the Chilean armed forces toward the regime. Much to their delight, the armed forces appeared willing to cooperate with Allende (to the point that senior officers joined his government and took ministerial posts) and to protect the regime against violence on the part of rightists as well as extreme leftist elements. Some experts came to the conclusion that the majority of the Chilean soldiers, like Chile's youth in general, supported the government and were unlikely to obey orders aimed at its overthrow.

This generally positive attitude toward the stance taken by the Chilean military, together with the rise of and turn to the Left of military regimes in Bolivia and Peru, brought a new and changed focus on Moscow's part to the issue of the role of the military in general, and in particular the military regimes in the so-called anti-imperialist struggle in Latin America. Initially, Moscow dismissed the military takeovers in Peru and Bolivia as just another few reactionary coups. But when these regimes nationalized U.S. oil interests and entered into direct conflict with Washington, Moscow changed its mind and somewhat gingerly proclaimed them to be "progressive" and worthy of support. Thereafter, this "new phenomenon," as Soviet ideologist Ponomarev termed it, underwent extensive scrutiny. "Simplistic anti-militarism"—perceiving the military as merely an instrument of the ruling class—was condemned and it was recognized that the military is a part of society and consequently responsive to socio-political developments.

Thus, it was said, as the officer corps of various armed forces comes to be recruited from the middle class and petty bourgeoisie, it identifies with their aspirations and becomes imbued with their nationalism and desire for change. When the officers have been taught at military institutions by instructors "who held progressive views," as in Peru, and there occurs a sharpening of the class struggle, the military men who take power may pursue truly "progressive" domestic and foreign policies.[6] Moscow also claimed in the early 1970s to see signs of restlessness and of "important changes" taking place in the political attitudes of various elements of the military in Argentina, Bolivia, Honduras, Nicaragua and "even in the armies as dependent on the Pentagon as those of Paraguay, Brazil and Haiti."[7]

The longer Allende survived and the leftward military trend seemed to be continuing, the more optimistic Soviet ideological pronouncements became. In April 1971 the resolution of the Twenty-fourth CPSU Congress stated that "the anti-imperialist struggle of the people in Latin America is growing even stronger."[8] This was followed by an all-union conference of Soviet Latin Americanists that concluded that "in Latin America, there exist objective and subjective conditions for the flowering of Lenin's theory of the transition of democratic agrarian revolution to socialist revolution, as it happened in Cuba and in other areas of the world."[9] Finally, the most detailed and authoritative overview of the Soviet perceptions of developments in Latin America in 1971 was given by Boris Ponomarev, CPSU Central Committee secretary and now candidate-member of the Politburo, who wrote in the October 1971 issue of the CPSU journal *Kommunist:* "The victory of the Popular Unity bloc in Chile, the progressive struggle in Uruguay and several other countries lead us to believe that *the revolutionary process there* [i.e., in Latin America] *is continuing to develop at a faster pace than in other parts of the non-socialist world.* This is truly a "continent in upheaval.'"[10]

Ponomarev justified this view on the ground of the deepening socioeconomic contradictions in and political polarization of Latin American society, which were said to generate a growing anti-imperialist and anti-capitalist mass movement; the presence of a relatively strong working class led by the Communist parties in some of the countries; and the region's traditions of "revolutionary liberation struggle."

These developments were perceived as a mounting assault on the U.S. presence and interests in Latin America, and thus as politically able to alter the global balance of power in favor of the Soviet Union. Thus, Ponomarev asserted that the upsurge of the revolutionary movement in Latin America was of "tremendous importance to the world revolutionary process" and that the changes taking place in that region "are having and undoubtedly will continue to have a strong impact on the further changes in the correlation of world forces in favor of the international working class and socialism."

According to Soviet analysts, Latin America bore the unique distinction of being characterized as the "strategic rear" of the United States—and thus presumably the point at which significant damage can be done to U.S. power and prestige. For example, an article in *Kommunist* asserted, "The U.S. ruling circles regard this region as their strategic rear, a sphere of vitally important interests. U.S. industry draws from there a considerable share of the raw materials it needs, including 40 to 100 percent of its imports of various strategic materials."[11]

Similarly, Boris Ponomarev wrote about the transformation of this "quite reliable rear" of the United States into a "tremendous hotbed of anti-imperialist revolution" whose particular significance is that it is "developing alongside the main citadel of imperialism, the United States." Other commentators went so far as to describe Latin America as "one of the most vulnerable sectors of U.S. imperialism's rear."[12]

The United States was said to no longer be in a position to "send the marines," and not even to "dare to use the Hickenlooper Amendment." Instead, it was said, the United States is being "compelled to go on the defensive with increasing frequency."[13] As was their wont, Soviet commentators ascribed this change first of all to the shift in the balance of power in Moscow's favor, which increased the Soviets' ability to frustrate U.S. attempts to "export counterrevolution," and to the growing unity of Latin American and global anti-imperialist forces. While some recognition was given to the possibility that this situation reflected a decline in the attention of the United States paid to Latin America, Soviet analysts hastened to add that this show of indifference on Washington's part was more apparent than real. "In reality," it was argued, "since Latin America remains one of the chief areas of concentration of U.S. imperialist interests, the USA has kept a watchful eye on it."[14]

In fact, the United States was also accused of attempting more indirect, subtle, and sophisticated methods of preserving its position and interest, including the instigation of plots to overthrow various regimes and an intensification of psychological and economic warfare. Soviet analysts warned that "the stakes of the U.S. monopolies in Latin America were too high for the U.S. to retreat without a fight,"[15] thus suggesting that Soviet leaders remained uncertain about the true extent of U.S. sensitivities to developments in that region.

Even at its most optimistic, Moscow had had tremors of concern about the military. In late August 1973, Soviet commentators had noted the efforts of rightist elements to "split the Chilean armed forces" and to encourage their "reactionary" officers to carry out a coup d'etat. In Peru and other countries Soviet analysts had been concerned that military regimes claimed that they made "unnecessary the existence of revolutionary Communist parties."[16]

The ambiguity of the Communist parties' position under such regimes was reflected in a statement by the general secretary of the Peruvian Communist party:

> As we see it, in Peru we are witnessing an anti-imperialist and anti-oligarchic revolution with anti-capitalist overtones. It is part of the Latin American revolutionary process, even though of a different level and with a different balance of class forces dissimilar to that of Cuba and Chile. The Communists are actively involved and working to deepen the revolution. Supporting the military government's progressive measures, we strive to impart to the masses an outlook favoring socialism.[17]

Even so, Moscow's mistrust of the military leaders and uneasiness as to their future course were evident in repeated warnings that these regimes are not a substitute for revolution and that their role in the national liberation movement in Latin America "should not be overrated, all the more so as one still must expect reactionary military coups to occur."[18]

Despite all its premonitions, however, the overthrow of Allende and the ease of the coup's execution caught Moscow by surprise. Less than a week before the coup, Moscow signed a new scientific and cultural agreement with Chile.

Preoccupied for some time with licking their wounds, Soviet and Latin American communists took several months before undertaking detailed postmortems. The first statement by a top Soviet leader did not come until June 1974, and then only as part of a broader article by Boris Ponomarev in the international communist journal *World Marxist Review*. Significantly, no definitive analysis of the "lessons of Chile" has ever appeared in Moscow's most authoritative newspaper, *Pravda,* or magazine, *Kommunist.*

Two recurring themes upon which all Soviet postmortems agreed were that, despite the fall of Allende, peaceful revolutions were still possible but that, in light of Chilean events, much greater emphasis had to be put on preparations for possible resort to violence.

Ponomarev, in his June 1974 article, conceded that the Chilean experience showed a leftist regime "can come to power in a constitutional way" but, more significantly, "that the events in Chile are a further reminder of the importance of maintaining revolutionary gains, of the tremendous importance of being prepared to promptly change forms of struggle, peaceful and non-peaceful, of the ability to repel the counterrevolutionary violence."[19]

Brezhnev, in his keynote speech to the Twenty-fifth Soviet Party Congress in 1976, put the same idea more succinctly: "The Chilean tragedy has by no means invalidated the communist thesis about the possibility of different ways of revolution, including the peaceful way, if the necessary conditions for it exist. But it has been a forceful reminder that a revolution must know how to defend itself."[20]

In addition to fuller discussions of these points, communist postmortems on Chile dwelled on such questions as the relationship between the communists and their allies on both left and right, the limits of parliamentarianism, the issue of reconciling economic policies catering to the proletariat with the political need not to antagonize the "middle strata," and how to handle elements of power not under leftist control.[21]

Following the fall of Allende, Soviet analysis became increasingly gloomy about Latin America as a whole. Chilean Communist exile leader V. Teitelboim felt obliged in March 1974 to reject "pessimistic claims" by unnamed people that imperialism should be conceded "our part of the world for another decade or two."[22] A Soviet analyst at about the same time revealed that events in Chile had "led to some moods of despondency" not only among "sections of the Latin American public" but also among those who "consider themselves revolutionaries."[23] Ponomarev warned in June 1974 that the "Chilean people's tragedy today is evidence of the reality of the fascist danger."[24] The June 1975 Latin American Communist party conference in Havana saw socialism coming only after a "whole period of intensive struggles and radical transformations."[25]

Soviet discussions in the next several years focused heavily on the nature of rightist authoritarian regimes in Latin America, implying an expectation that such regimes were a long-term feature of the Latin American scene.[26] One participant in a 1975 symposium suggested that such regimes "act as a basic long-term alternative to a revolutionary solution of the problems of crisis."[27] While Soviet propagandists were deriding the Brazilian model, this same commentator was grudgingly conceding the "counterrevolutionary effectiveness of this model."[28]

New looks were taken at the military in general. Communists were advised that more determined efforts were needed to infiltrate armies of Latin America in order to "democratize" them. An international communist symposium in 1974 declared that "the depth of revolutionary spirit in the army should not be overrated even with a military regime that favors reform."[29] The need was also suggested to arm the workers as a counterforce to the army. "But," one Soviet commentator asked rhetorically, "wouldn't such an attempt have given this old army the necessary pretext for an uprising at earlier stages?"[30]

The turn to the right in Peru in the late 1970s intensified Soviet caution about the revolutionary potential of the Latin American military. In a 1977 symposium by *Latinskaia Amerika* on the army issue, one Soviet ideologist confessed that "many of our research assistants (I count myself among them) manifestly exaggerated the possibility of the military's progressive role."[31] He suggested that Peruvian developments reaffirmed that the Latin American military was heterogeneous and that in Peru key elements of the military "came to be terrified by the danger of social revolution." Other participants claimed that "only a few people experienced these illusions" about Peru, but conceded that there had been "a kind of euphoria" about developments in Peru (and Portugal) which had been overtaken by events.[32] A later article declared somewhat wistfully that the military in Peru saw themselves as the saviors of society and "regarded the communists not as allies but as rivals."[33]

While discouraged about the prospect for radical transformation in which the Latin American communists would play a decisive role, Moscow and its supporters saw new hopes in the growing nationalism which, in the Latin American context, necessarily took the form of anti-Americanism or at least efforts to loosen ties with the United States. In communist parlance, this meant that the main focus of the Soviets and communists should be on the struggle against "imperialism," that is, the United States. This orientation was spelled out with utmost clarity at a meeting held in June 1975 in Havana, attended by twenty-four Communist parties.

The very title of the final document, undoubtedly drafted with Soviet help, indicated current priorities: "Latin America in the Struggle Against Imperialism, For National Independence, Democracy, People's Welfare, Peace and Socialism." Although reaffirming that their ultimate aim was the establishment of socialism, the document declared that this "will become feasible in all Latin American countries only after a whole period of intensive struggle and radical transformations." Moreover, it went on, even progress well short of the final goal required "eliminating the oppression on the part of U.S. imperialism and the domination of transnational corporations."

Accordingly, it proclaimed:

> Since U.S. imperialism is our main and common enemy, the strategy and tactics of revolution in Latin America for those whose final objective, like ours, is socialism, should be anti-imperialist in character. Therefore, we Communists judge the political positions of other Latin American forces mainly by their attitude to this enemy. Therefore, while continuing the struggle for democratic rights and for new structures inside our countries, we Communists are ready to support and encourage the stand of those Latin American governments who come out in defense of our natural resources or strive to frustrate the transnational companies' efforts to maintain and extend their domination over economies.[34]

Based on this criterion, Moscow saw Latin American countries as covering a wide spectrum. One Soviet Latin Americanist, in apparent imitation of Western social science methods, worked out a table classifying twenty Latin American countries according to their level of pro-imperialist or anti-imperialist activity from 1974–1976 based mainly on their foreign policy attitudes.[35] Generally, Soviet discussions divided Latin America into three categories: "progressive" regimes such as Peru and Panama; "nationalist reformist" regimes such as Venezuela, Mexico, and Colombia; and rightist regimes, such as Chile, Uruguay, Nicaragua, Haiti, and Paraguay. Venezuela, following its nationalization of oil, sometimes was deemed to be progressive, Brazil at times was considered in a class by itself. Obviously these lists undergo constant changes, depending on specific developments.

Between 1975 and 1979 Moscow seized on a number of issues — relations with Cuba, the Panamanian question, and the question of a "new economic order" — as evidence of growing Latin American independence of the United States. Changes in U.S. policy took the sting at least out of the first two issues, but the third issue has remained the focus of major Soviet attention.

In the early seventies, the decision by several Latin American countries to establish trade or diplomatic relations with Cuba, despite earlier Organization of American States (OAS) decisions against such actions, was seen by Moscow as a particularly significant gesture of defiance of the U.S. When, however, the United States itself acceded in July 1975 to an OAS resolution leaving it up to each country to make its own decision on Cuban recognition, Moscow interpreted this as a decision made "under duress" because the United States did not want "to pit itself once again against the overwhelming majority of Latin American countries and thus trigger more criticism on their part of the OAS." Moreover, the United States was seen as a double loser, since there remained "fierce opponents" who "fear the influence of the Cuban Revolution and a curtailment of the American presence on the continent."[36]

In this connection, while Moscow continues to point to Cuba as an inspirational example, it has put more emphasis on Cuba's role as a focal point for encouraging other Latin American governments in anti-U.S. positions. Thus *International Affairs* wrote:

> The prestige of the first socialist state in the Western Hemisphere has become as it were a catalyst for the increased activity of a wide movement among the Latin American peoples to restructure inter-American relations on the basis of the principles of peaceful coexistence and the recognition of the right of countries with different social systems to exist, dispose of their own natural resources, do away with the domination of the multinational monopolies, and establish independent economies.[37]

Moscow took delight in reporting the increasing number of Latin American institutions that now included Cuba, with special emphasis on the Latin American Economic System (SELA), established in 1975, which Soviet media pointedly noted "include[s] Cuba but not the United States."[38] While uncertain about how significant SELA would be in practice, Moscow was clearly pleased by the symbolism of the action, which it also saw as part of the progressive weakening of the OAS. According to the 1975 Latin American Communist declaration, the OAS "created by Washington essentially as a colonial departure for Latin America is losing any factual effectiveness for imperialism."[39] The authoritative *Kommunist* in August 1978 concluded that "starting with the 1970s, a situation developed within the OAS in which, ever more frequently, the United States is in the minority and, occasionally, stands alone in the solution of one or another political or economic problem."[40]

A related area where the Soviet Union has seen significant gains is the declining ability of the U.S. to control Latin America in the world arena, reflected by the breakup of the Latin American voting bloc in support of U.S. policies in international organizations. Moscow has noted with satisfaction the increasing tendency of Latin American countries to side with the nonaligned nations and their increasing participation in nonaligned meetings.

In the absence of a revolutionary situation, the basic Soviet prescription for communist strategy and tactics called for the formation of broad popular fronts, the nature of which were to depend on specific conditions. As a leading Soviet theoretical journal succinctly put it late in 1978: "The struggle for the unity of anti-imperialist forces is the key problem of the strategy and tactics of communist parties in the countries of Latin America."[41]

This journal divided Latin American regimes into two main categories: (1) right-authoritarian fascist, and (2) "comparatively democratic" regimes. In the first, communists were said to aim for an "anti-fascist front" of the "broadest type," focusing on such issues as amnesties, the right to organize, and defense of small business against big monopolies. In the second group of states, more emphasis was put on support for "progressive" steps such as oil nationalization in the case of Venezuela.

While Soviet focus since the ouster of Allende has been on the foreign policy of Latin American states, there were indications in the late seventies that Soviet attention might shift back to domestic opportunities as a result of changes it perceived in several Latin American countries. According to Sergo Mikoyan, the editor of *Latinskaia Amerika,* "The counter-offensive launched by the reactionary and fascist forces in the 1970s did not affect the whole of Latin America. This stage in its history was of relatively short duration. Today, when we have entered 1979, it is clearly ending. And, judging by everything, a new upsurge of the revolutionary movement is about to begin."[42]

To bolster his contention, Mikoyan particularly noted various maneuvers by military regimes to restore civilian rule or give a broader base to their governments. "It sometimes happens," Mikoyan wrote, "that such maneuvers, conceived as pure demagoguery, trigger off a democratic process contrary to the wishes of their organizers." In this connection he cited Bolivia (where, among other things, a ban on the Communist party was lifted), correctly predicted comparable developments in Brazil, and noted that "even the military-fascist regimes in Chile and Uruguay are resorting more to political camouflage."

Argentina he found still "complex and contradictory" but "Central America at present is a zone of storms." In this connection, Moscow devoted continuing attention to the growing movement against Somoza in Nicaragua as well as against right-wing governments in Guatemala and El Salvador. After initial reticence, Moscow came out increasingly in support of the Sandinista movement in Nicaragua. *Pravda* on 3 September 1978 saw events in that country as part of a "movement for liberation [which] is gathering force throughout Latin America."[43]

In Nicaragua and elsewhere in Latin America, Moscow saw the United States more and more caught by sharpening dilemmas. In Nicaragua, this dilemma was seen as a choice between a desire to retain its position in that country and fear that the alternative to Somoza might be a radical Marxist regime. Moscow saw Somoza's fall in July 1979 as salutary evidence of declining U.S. influence and growing leftist trends in Central America. The USSR and Nicaragua established diplomatic relations on 19 October 1979.

More generally, Moscow appeared somewhat nonplussed by the Carter administration's emphasis on human rights and the impact it had on relations between the United States and various regimes in Latin America. Especially after the fall of Allende and for the next several years, Moscow considered right-wing regimes as the chosen instruments and most faithful allies of the United States. Thus, while the 1975 members of the symposium on right-wing authoritarianism in Latin America argued considerably over various domestic aspects of the problem, no one took issue with the statement that "neither nationalist declamations, an expansionist policy, conflicts with this or that monopoly, nor individual contradictions with the imperialist states can change the main point: conscious and unconditional support of U.S. imperialism in all strategic questions and subordination to its fundamental interests represent the basis of the right-wing authoritarian regime's foreign policy."[44]

Moscow's first impulse and that of the Latin American communists was to dismiss the Carter human rights program as "attempts to carry out imperialist policies with the aid of more subtle methods."[45] Sergo Mikoyan in 1979 conceded, however, that this human rights campaign "not only encouraged the liberals but somewhat frightened the dictators," resulting in friction between the United States and Brazil, Chile, Uruguay, and Argentina. In the end, he claimed this campaign petered out and proved essentially meaningless.[46]

Nevertheless, it was recognized that the human rights campaign did have an impact domestically on some regimes, which communists were advised to use. Writing in Moscow's Latin American journal, Rodnei Arismendi, Uruguay party chief and a favorite Soviet source on the continent, cautioned against any illusions about the U.S. motives and urged that "everything that punches a hole in the fascist structure can be used — on condition that we will be capable of doing so — for enhancing the struggle and strengthening the unity of the democratic and patriotic forces."[47]

Soviet Political Relations with Latin America

In recent years Soviet efforts to expand relations with Latin America have benefited from the progressive détente in East-West relations, the region's increasing self-assertion and search for new markets, and the improved Soviet economic and scientific-technological capabilities to develop trade and aid contacts with distant countries. As a result, after the mid-1960s the Soviet Union was largely successful in its efforts to establish or renew diplomatic relations with the countries of Latin America. At the height of the cold war in the late 1950s and early 1960s Moscow enjoyed diplomatic relations only with Argentina, Brazil, Cuba, Mexico, and

Uruguay, which were joined in 1964 by Chile. After 1967, however, the political climate became more propitious. Despite their continuing distrust of Soviet motivations and intentions, and some persistent fear of Communist subversion, the majority of the South American countries established relations with the Soviet Union: Colombia in 1968; Peru, Ecuador, and Bolivia in 1969; Venezuela and Guyana in 1970; Costa Rica in 1971; Trinidad and Tobago in 1974; Surinam in 1975; Jamaica in 1977; and Nicaragua in 1979. Soundings were made in 1978 about establishment of relations with Panama. In response to the overthrow of the Allende regime, the Soviet Union broke diplomatic relations with Chile on 21 September 1973. Chile thus joined Paraguay, Panama, Haiti, and Honduras as countries in Latin America without diplomatic relations with the Soviet Union.

Soviet commentators have chosen to interpret these developments as an indication of the Latin American drive for independence from U.S. tutelage and a gesture of defiance of Washington's efforts to isolate them from contacts with the Communist bloc. Brezhnev has acknowledged that the question of establishing relations with the Soviet Union is a politically sensitive issue for many less developed countries, but he argued that they learn from experience that "friendship with the Soviet Union facilitates their successful struggle against imperialism and for genuine independence."[48]

Soviet propaganda in Latin America sought to exploit the May 1972 Moscow summit agreements and to assert that the principles of "peaceful coexistence" stand in direct contradiction to "the policy of blocs" organized against the "so-called danger of communism or the threat from the Soviet Union." The governments of the region have been urged to further expand their relations with the Communist countries in that light.

Indeed there has been a marked increase in recent years in the visits by Latin American officials to the Soviet Union. Beginning with Castro in the 1960s, top Latin Americans have included Allende in 1972, Mexican president Echeverria in 1973, Trinidad and Tobago premier Williams in 1975, Venezuelan president Perez in 1976, Guyana premier Burnham and Mexican president Lopez Portillo in 1978, and the Jamaican premier Manley in 1979.

No doubt Latin American willingness to establish relations with the Soviet Union has been motivated in part by the general nationalistic and, at times, leftist trends in that region. The continent has also taken its cue from shifts in Western and especially U.S. policies and attitudes vis-à-vis the Soviet Union, and from Washington's apparent lower sensitivity to Soviet diplomatic and trade activities in that region. Not only has Latin America's fear of the Soviet Union declined, but its attitude toward the native Communist parties also has changed. By comparison with the radical Left and

the Castro-inspired guerrilla movements, the pro-Soviet Communist parties—with their "peaceful road to power" programs and united front
strategy—appear "conservative" and nonrevolutionary. However, the
Communist parties remain either banned or in a semilegal status in many
countries of South and Central America.

Above all, however, the principal motivation has been economic, as
many of the countries in the region search for new markets for their
agricultural surpluses and manufactured goods and for new sources of technology and development investments. In some cases, such as Chile and
Peru, disputes with the United States over nationalization policies have encouraged a look to Moscow as a possible alternative for losses in U.S. investments, especially since the Soviet Union has supported their position
against Washington.

But various incidents indicate that Latin American suspicions of Soviet
intentions and activities are easily aroused and have led to repeated charges
of Soviet interference in the internal affairs of various countries as well as
the expulsion of a number of Soviet diplomats. Expulsions have occurred in
Argentina, Bolivia, Colombia, Ecuador, and Mexico, where Soviet representatives were accused of engaging in various subversive activities. A
number of Latin American countries have also shown sensitivity to the
considerable size of the Soviet missions on their territory, which appear
disproportionately large for the actual level of Soviet diplomatic and trade
activities. But it is noteworthy that, in contrast to the past, the various incidents have not resulted in a rupture in relations with the Soviet Union.

Insofar as Soviet political activities are concerned, Moscow has championed Latin America's sovereignty and independence and the countries'
right to control their own natural resources—which allegedly are being
"plundered" by the United States. Thus Yakov Malik, the Soviet representative at the U.N. Security Council meeting in Panama City in March
1973, assured the Latin Americans that "the USSR supports the demands
of the Latin American countries in regard to their sovereignty and natural
resources." He also said that the Soviet government "is opposed to every attempt to exercise direct or indirect pressure" on them, obviously referring
to Washington's threat of economic sanctions against countries that nationalized U.S. businesses without compensations.

Moscow's propaganda has been loud in its support of the nationalization
policies of Chile under Allende as well as Ecuador, Peru, and Venezuela,
and of Panama's demands for sovereignty and control over the Canal Zone.
But Soviet support was less emphatic in the dispute of Ecuador and Peru
with the United States over tuna fishing and their claims—as well as those
of several other Latin American countries—to 200 miles of territorial
waters, a claim Moscow itself did not recognize until 1977. Moscow also

resisted accession to Protocol II of the Latin American Nuclear Free Zone treaty until May 1978, when it finally did so, but with a number of reservations, during the visit of Mexican president Lopez Portillo.

While asserting that the might of the Soviet Union is an important factor in deterring the United States from attempts to reimpose its dominance in Latin America by force, Moscow also has been careful not to commit itself explicitly to any action, political or military, in the event that the United States were to try to reimpose itself. Even Cuba, which became a full member of Comecon in July 1972, does not have a formal defense treaty with the Soviet Union.

Soviet support of the Latin American Communist parties generally appears to be routine. The Kremlin is undoubtedly well aware of the fact that for the most part these parties are small, split by internal dissent and purges, and have only limited popular support. Except in Argentina, they have relatively little control over local labor unions, although they have some influence among the intellectuals and students. However, at times their influence exceeds their size — because the parties are more disciplined and have a more experienced leadership than other groups on the Left and because they can count on some financial assistance from the Soviet Union. The USSR has underscored its interest by sending various high-ranking CPSU members to attend some of the Latin American Communist party congresses, notably those of the Chilean party, prior to the 1973 coup, and has to some extent attempted to woo actual or potential allies of these parties, such as the Chilean Socialist party. Beyond this, however, Soviet policy gives indications of not being overly concerned with the interests of the local Communist parties, while giving priority to efforts to develop relations with and influence among the existing regimes.

A special target of Soviet and Communist party propaganda is the Latin American military, whose role, as noted above, is believed critical to the national liberation and anti-U.S. struggle. The Communist parties have been trying to reassure the military groups that they do not advocate their dissolution, as happened in Cuba, but on the contrary are in favor of maintaining the regular armed forces and, far from being antimilitary, defend the professional interests and welfare of these forces.

While in power, Allende sought to neutralize the Chilean armed forces and prevent a military coup by raising military pay and providing other benefits. But the main Communist line, as described in Soviet sources, is to exploit the dissatisfaction of Latin America's military with U.S. restrictions on the sale of sophisticated arms. Beginning in the early 1970s, the Latin American military began to look for alternate sources and also undertook "the accelerated development of a national military industry."[49]

The Soviet Union has used the low-key approach of encouraging — when the military has been amenable — visits of various military delegations to the Soviet Union and Cuba where they can inspect Soviet arms and equipment and, in the latter case, see evidence of Soviet generosity in providing in excess of $2 billion worth of military assistance to its Cuban client. Since 1970 such visits have become increasingly frequent, involving not only delegations from Chile and Peru but also from a number of other countries. Side by side with this, Soviet and Communist propaganda has been campaigning for the closing of all U.S. military bases and facilities in Latin America, charging that they constitute an infringement of sovereignty and a form of U.S. domination.

Despite known Soviet military aid offers to a number of countries (Argentina, Colombia, Ecuador), its only significant breakthrough has been in Peru. In late 1973, Peru purchased a limited number of Soviet T-55 medium tanks while in 1976 Peru put in an order for $250 million worth of jet aircraft. In 1977, Peru took delivery of 36 SU-22 fighter bombers, the most advanced aircraft yet delivered to Latin America. Other deliveries in 1977 included helicopters, transports, and tanks. In April 1978, however, Peru had to ask the USSR to reschedule the debt for these purchases, to which the USSR agreed.[50]

Latin America's military leaders have proved themselves suspicious of Soviet blandishments and have shown a marked preference for U.S. and Western European arms and equipment, which do not pose the same political and technical problems as similar purchases from the Soviet Union. Nevertheless, Moscow keeps trying and its arms sale to Peru may provide it with an opening for larger sales to that and other countries in the region in the future.

The possibility of such a development has been viewed with some uneasiness, if not alarm, by the more conservative regimes, notably those of Brazil, Bolivia, and Chile. One may also note in this connection that, although the increased Soviet naval activities in the Caribbean and the Soviet efforts to develop a submarine base at Cienfuegos in Cuba evoked little reaction in Latin America, suspicions concerning Soviet military intentions are reflected in the persistent rumors and occasional press reports (despite emphatic denials by the respective governments) that several fishing ports being built with Soviet assistance in Peru, and earlier in Chile as well, were intended to serve as Soviet naval bases.

Finally, Soviet propaganda has continued its practice of criticizing and denouncing Latin American tours and fact-finding trips by high-ranking U.S. officials as well as all of Washington's proposals for developing new kinds of relationships with the countries of the region. Thus Secretary of State William P. Rogers's tour of Latin America in May 1973, and his proposals to place U.S. relations with the countries of that region on a more bilateral basis tailored to their individual wishes and needs, were described in the Soviet media as a U.S. attempt to divide the united anti-U.S. front of the countries "even before it has gained strength" in order to benefit Washington.[51] Almost identical comments greeted visits to the continent by Secretary Kissinger in 1975, Secretary Vance in 1977, and President Carter to Mexico in 1979.

Similarly, Moscow played down the significance first of the signature in September 1977, then of the ratification in April 1978, of the Panama Canal Treaty. Evidently unwilling to condemn the treaty as long as Panama accepted it, Moscow instead attacked Senate efforts to "emasculate" it through amendments and the U.S. in general of "exerting gross pressure" on Panama throughout the ratification process.[52]

Soviet and East European Economic Activities

The Soviet diplomatic and political drive in Latin America has been paralleled by an expansion of Soviet economic relations with the countries of the region. These activities became especially notable after 1969, when developments in Latin America not only offered Moscow opportunities for such an expansion but also generated pressures on it to assist the new "progressive" regimes.

While Cuba remains the predominant recipient of Soviet aid and trade, this expensive experience has not deterred Moscow from extending substantial offers of aid to other Latin American nations wherever it deemed this to be in the Soviet political interest. Until recent years the modest level and slow growth of Soviet aid and trade in Latin America appeared to support the thesis that the "lesson of Cuba" had convinced the Soviets to avoid making large economic commitments to countries in that region.

But more recent experience indicates that, given the importance Moscow attributes to the anti-imperialist struggle in Latin America, it is aware that political endorsement of this struggle and of emerging "progressive" regimes unavoidably entails providing them with economic support. Therefore the earlier low level of Soviet economic activities in the region was more indicative of a lack of opportunity than a fundamental unwillingness to assume the burden. It would appear, however, that the Soviet leadership has learned from its earlier foreign aid programs to be more cautious about supporting the rapid industrialization of developing countries, to be more selective in its choices of assistance, to avoid overcommitments, and to pay more attention to the cost effectiveness of projects it is asked to support. At the same time it should be recognized that the case of Cuba is probably unique since it is highly unlikely — given the resources of the continental South American countries — that any one of them would become "another Cuba" in terms of similar dependence on the Soviet Union for aid and as a market.

That Soviet economic aid and trade in Latin America reflect predominantly Soviet political interests and objectives is evident from the fact that the Soviet Union buys few of the "strategic" materials produced there and maintains a substantial deficit in its trade with the region, importing mainly goods that are not of major significance for the Soviet economy at the present stage.

Moscow is careful to avoid any indication that it is prepared to completely replace the capitalist countries as a source of investments, aid, and technology. But it persistently asserts that, by expanding economic relations with the Soviet bloc, the less developed countries (including those in Latin America) can escape economic and political domination by the Western monopolies, and thus from a neocolonial status, and attain independence. Of course it is argued that Soviet aid, in contrast to that of the United States, is disinterested, has no political strings, and is designed to benefit all parties.

Prior to 1967 the Soviet Union had granted significant commercial credits for the purchase of Soviet machinery and equipment only to Argentina ($45 million) and Brazil ($85 million). The other East European countries had provided $231 million in credits, also predominantly to Brazil. Soviet aid policies thereafter reflected both the expansion of relations with Latin America and Moscow's response to the political changes taking place in the various countries. Thus in 1967 the "reformist" Christian Democratic government of President Eduardo Frei of Chile was granted $55 million in Soviet credits. In 1968 Moscow gave $2 million in credits to Colombia, and in 1969 a total of $20 million to Uruguay. In the same time period the other Communist countries provided a total of $36 million in credits to Argentina, Chile, Ecuador, and Uruguay. By the end of 1969 the Soviet Union had issued a total of $207 million in credits and loans to five Latin American nations (aside from Cuba), and other members of the bloc had provided a total of $267 million to six countries, representing increases over 1967 of 12 and 9 percent, respectively.[53]

The next two years saw a sharp increase in Communist credits and loans, primarily in response to political developments in Bolivia, Chile, and Peru. In 1970 the Soviet Union granted the Torres regime in Bolivia $28 million for the purchase of Soviet equipment, and a similar amount to Peru, while Costa Rica received $10 million. That same year Eastern Europe provided a total of $51 million, of which Peru received $25 million.[54] In 1971, the Soviet bloc began a policy of support of the Allende regime in Chile. The Soviet Union renewed the $55 million credit it had granted the previous government, which had remained unused, and provided an additional credit for the purchase of Soviet equipment to the amount of some $36 million. At the same time the other members of the bloc increased their credits and loans to Chile from $5 million in 1970 to $100 milllion in 1971. Communist China also began to provide development credits to Latin America with a grant of $2 million to Chile in 1971.[55]

In 1972 Soviet credits to Chile increased by $168 million to a cumulative total of $259 million for the purchase of complete plants as well as machinery and equipment. In addition it appears that in the course of the year Moscow granted Chile some $100 million in short-term credits, possibly in convertible currency, to finance imports of food and critical raw materials.[56] The other East European countries increased their credits to Chile by some $20 million to $120 million; Peking expanded its credits and loans to $65 million; and North Korea granted Chile a credit of $5 million. Thus the cumulative total of all Communist credits and loans to Chile rose to $449 million by the end of 1972, which represented an increase of 750 percent in two years. Moscow was also reported to have offered the Chilean state foreign trade agency, Corfo, $40 million for Communist credits to private enterprises.

In that same period Communist credits to Peru also increased. Starting with only $6 million in East European credits in 1969, Peru received a total of $53 million in Communist credits in 1970, a further $86 million in 1971, and some $100 million in 1972 for a cumulative total of some $245 million.

In the case of Peru, however, Soviet credits increased by only $8 million during that two-year period, apparently reflecting Lima's hesitations as to how to spend these credits and Moscow's uneasiness about the political character of the ruling junta. Nevertheless, Soviet credits in 1972 included an agreement to finance a preliminary survey of the Olmos irrigation and hydroelectric power project—which the Soviet Union had refused to assist in 1969 despite the urging of the Peruvian Communist party—whose total cost has been estimated at $375 million.[57]

During the next six years (1973–1978), the USSR and Eastern Europe extended another $1159 million in credits to Latin America, of which $923 million went to Argentina and Brazil. Of this, $420 million was extended during the trip to the USSR and Eastern Europe of Argentine economics minister Gelbard. Another $200 million credit for export financing was extended by the GDR to Brazil in 1978. Otherwise during this period, the USSR offered only $54 million in credit (including 30 to Jamaica, 8 to Colombia, and 1 to Bolivia), and Eastern Europe offered $191 million divided among nine countries (in descending order: Colombia, Jamaica, Mexico, Guyana, Bolivia, Costa Rica, Uruguay, Ecuador, and Peru).

Cumulative Soviet credits and loans to Latin America (exclusive of

Cuba) therefore increased from $207 million in 1969 to $301 million in 1971, $565 million in 1972, and $964 million in 1978. At the same time, comparable figures for the entire communist world stood at $431 million in 1967, $474 million in 1969, $1.3 billion in 1972, and $2.7 billion in 1977.[58]

The Soviet Union has shown particular interest in participating in major hydroelectric projects in Latin America. By 1977, it had $175 million in power contracts in hand with Argentina for the supply of turbines for the Salto Grande project. During the same year, it signed an agreement with Colombia for Soviet involvement in the Alto Sinu hydropower project scheduled for completion in the mid-1980s, at an estimated cost of $400 million. The USSR made an offer for the $700 million Boruca hydroelectric project in Costa Rica, which, however, it did not pursue.

Most Soviet and other Communist credits and loans are repayable in goods rather than hard currency, including manufactured goods, which Latin American countries are eager to sell. The long-term credits provide for low interest rates and long repayment periods, usually ten to twelve years. With Soviet credits, the interest rates are usually 3 percent for the state sector and 3.5 percent for the private sector; in the case of Chile under Allende, however, the interest rates were 2 to 2.5 percent for the state sector, reflecting the country's special status as a "progressive" state. The intrusion of China as a lender into Latin America has brought pressure on Moscow to increase its aid and provide favorable terms, especially as Chinese credits are for the most part interest-free and repayable over twenty years.

The granting of Soviet and other Communist credits does not necessarily mean that the recipient countries are willing to utilize them. This was particularly true prior to 1969 and Moscow blamed it on the "opposition of reactionary circles." The utilization of Soviet credits was prevented not only by the opposition of such circles but also by Latin American suspicions about the suitability of Soviet equipment and the availability of spare parts, as well as reluctance to send technicians to be trained in the Soviet Union or to accept large numbers of Soviet technicians at home. From 1958 to 1977, only $525 million of the $2.4 billion offered were drawn. When used, the Communist credits are applied primarily to strengthen the state economic sector and in projects for which Western financing is difficult to obtain, such as the construction of fishing ports in Chile and Peru. The aid includes the purchase of complete plants as well as machinery and equipment for various projects and technical assistance in electrification, mining, transportation, health and education, prospecting for oil and minerals, fisheries, and so on.

There is no reason to assume that Soviet bloc credits reflect a coordinated policy or effort in all areas. Unlike the Soviet Union, the other communist countries appear to have a genuine need for imports of various minerals and raw materials from Latin America. Chile under Allende, however, appears to have been an instance of a joint effort by the Soviet bloc under Moscow's leadership to assist industrial development and make available technical assistance to replace that previously provided from U.S. sources. Although the Allende regime was faced with a sharp decline in Western aid and investments, Soviet bloc aid to Chile did not bear the character of an economic "rescue" effort as it had in the Cuban case when the United States severed relations with Havana. In fact, Moscow appears to have been either reluctant or unable to fully satisfy Allende's urgent need to overcome Chile's serious shortages in food and consumer goods, although it did provide some short-term credits for this purpose and shipped a certain amount of wheat to Chile (124,600 tons in 1971).

At the same time, however, the Soviet bloc did show its willingness to assist Chile's economic development in an effort to strengthen the position of the Allende regime. Central Committee Secretary Ponomarev asserted that "the CPSU, as always, is giving practical support to the revolutionary struggle of the Chilean people" with the aim of accelerating that country's economic development.[59] It was further specified that "Soviet-Chilean trade and economic links have the task of giving all possible support in this respect to the anti-imperialist policy of Allende's government." This being the case, President Allende was assured in December 1972 that the Soviet Union was "prepared to give further political and economic support" to Chile.[60] Chile also was given special signs of Soviet favor, such as the sending of Soviet volunteer youth brigades to work on construction projects and the provision of fishing boats and crews to augment Chile's catch — distinctions Chile shared with Cuba. Another distinction was the institution in 1972 of a Soviet passenger air service to Chile and of regular maritime shipping service with ports of call in Chile and Peru. In practice, however, few of the Soviet bloc credits were used prior to the fall of the Allende regime and Communist bloc aid had no significant impact on solving the problems of Chile's economy.

The Soviet Union and the other communist countries have made a considerable effort to conclude various trade and most favored nation agreements with Latin American countries. But, despite the existence of a substantial network of such agreements, the total volume of Soviet trade with the region, exclusive of Cuba, has remained relatively small, both in absolute amounts and in comparison with the size of Soviet credits. This appears to reflect, among other factors, the hesitation of the countries to make use of these credits, their suspicions concerning the poor quality of Soviet goods, the slowness of Soviet deliveries, and Moscow's disinclination to buy substantial amounts of such traditional Latin American exports as bauxite, copper, and tin.

During the sixties, Soviet trade turnover with Latin America was extremely erratic, rising in 1962, falling in 1963 and 1964, rising in 1965 and 1966, falling in 1967, rising in 1968 and 1969, falling in 1970. The trend in the 1970s has been strikingly different, rising annually from a low of a 78.7-million-rubles turnover in 1970 to 910.9 million rubles in 1975 and falling every year until 1978. Except for a drop in 1976, Soviet exports have increased every year from 1970 to 1978, while Soviet imports follow almost the same trends as total turnover, rising steadily until 1975, falling in the next two years but rising again in 1978. In contrast to its trade with the less developed countries as a whole, the Soviet Union has incurred a significant deficit with Latin America (exclusive of Cuba) every year, reaching a high point of 624.5 million rubles (or about $900 million) in 1975.[61]

In an effort to reduce its deficit, the USSR has pushed oil sales to Brazil and sought to bring pressure on it to draw on existing credits. In Argentina, the USSR has put in bids for additional power projects. In 1978, however, it reduced its deficit with Brazil by sharply curtailing imports but the deficit with Argentina reached its highest point ever as a result of large Soviet grain purchases.

The volume of Soviet trade has been dominated by and has fluctuated primarily in response to Moscow's trade with the two largest countries in the region, Argentina and Brazil. It constituted, in 1977 for example, about 80 percent of Soviet trade with Latin America (excluding Cuba). Trade with the "progressive" countries through 1970 was negligible; the volume of Soviet trade with Chile never exceeded $1 million, and that with Peru $1.5 million. In 1973, however, the volume of trade with Chile rose to 28.6 million rubles, while in 1975 Soviet trade with Peru reached 118.5 million rubles as a result of large Soviet sugar purchases.

Although the volume of Soviet trade with Latin America has remained relatively modest, Moscow has derived some political benefits from it. Many countries in the region see the Soviet bloc and China as an enormous potential market for their surplus agricultural products and for manufactured goods they are unable to sell to the West.

Large numbers of official and private Latin American trade delegations have been traveling to the communist countries seeking to arrange such sales, and Moscow has taken advantage of this situation. By buying surplus coffee, bananas, and other produce, it has won some goodwill for itself in a number of countries. Thus the purchase of surplus coffee from Costa Rica in 1969–1970 led that country to establish diplomatic and trade relations with Moscow and also led to public expressions of gratitude by its president, which Soviet propaganda was quick to exploit.

Because of some countries' serious problems in disposing of their surpluses, such Soviet purchases generated some competition among them.
For example, when Guatemala sold some coffee to the Soviet Union in
1971, Costa Rica expressed concern that this might adversely affect its own
sales to Moscow, and an editorial in an Ecuadorian newspaper warned that
"competition from other countries which can offer Eastern Europe the same
agricultural products that we are able to sell is very strong, and these countries have a flexible system of negotiaion, which we do not have in our
country."[62] Obviously such competition provides Moscow with some opportunities to exploit its political advantage. The changing attitude toward
China also resulted in a rush by Latin American governments in
1971–1972 to establish diplomatic and trade relations in the hope of opening up another market.

East European trade with Latin America has been consistently larger
than that of the Soviet Union, but it, too, has on the whole been operating
at a deficit. The volume of such trade rose from $305.5 million in 1969 to
$1874.3 million in 1977.[63] In this case also, the main trading partners have
been Argentina and Brazil but they also include Colombia, Mexico, and
Peru. China's volume of trade with Latin America increased from $7.8
million in 1970 to $519.9 million in 1977. China has been buying large
amounts of fishmeal in Peru and copper in Chile. Overall, the communist
countries' trade with Latin America, while smaller than their trade with
other less developed regions, has grown steadily.

While communist trade is said to reduce the dependence of Latin
American countries on the Western powers, it is highly unlikely that either
the Soviet Union or the bloc as a whole will become a major trading partner
of that region or, for that matter, that they will become the sole economic
support of select countries—i.e., "other Cubas."

Even so, Soviet and communist economic activities are having some impact. They serve to strengthen the state sectors of the economies of the recipient countries, to provide to some extent for their industrial growth, and
to help various projects, such as the construction of fishing ports, for which
these countries may not be able to obtain support from other sources. To
some degree they help buttress the "progressive" regimes and give some
credibility to Moscow's assertions that governments that defy the United
States are not without friends and supporters. Fundamentally, of course,
trade and aid are indispensable parts of the USSR's total effort to expand its
presence and influence in Latin America.

That same purpose is also served by cultural, scientific, and technical cooperation agreements that the Soviet Union and Eastern European coun-

tries have negotiated with a number of Latin American governments. These have generated an ever increasing flow of exchanges of visits by all sorts of official and private delegations and groups, Soviet scientific and technical exhibits, tours by theatrical and dance troops, increased availability of Soviet publications in Latin America, and various joint scientific undertakings such as the use of Soviet oceanographic ships to survey the coasts of Chile and Peru and the use of Chilean observatories by Soviet astronomers.

The cultural exchange agreements also provide for scholarships for Latin American students and specialists to study and train in the academic and technical institutions of the USSR and Eastern Europe. Such scholarships also are offered unofficially to students in countries that lack formal agreements with the Soviet bloc. The number of students from Latin America attending academic institutions in the Soviet bloc countries has been steadily increasing. There were 2,425 such students in 1970, 2,650 in 1971, 3,005 in 1972, and 4,650 in 1978.[64] Aside from Cuba, the largest groups of students in 1978 came from Colombia, Peru, Costa Rica, Ecuador, Bolivia, El Salvador, and Nicaragua.

But it must be noted that a Soviet education does not necessarily open many doors to Latin American students, even in the "progressive" countries. For example, in a speech during his tour of the Soviet Union in 1972, Allende complained that Chilean academic institutions did not recognize Soviet degrees. On the other hand, such graduates are less likely to seek employment in the United States and Western Europe than those who receive their training in the West.

Some Implications of Current Trends

Although rapid and still accelerating social, political, and economic changes in Latin America may culminate in new "progressive" regimes, for the time being the keynote of Moscow's policy is "anti-imperialism" and in this respect the trend in Latin America is favorable to Soviet objectives. In pursuing these objectives, Soviet policies appear unencumbered by heavy ideological baggage as Moscow seems content to try to ride the wave of nationalism sweeping the continent, especially insofar as it erodes U.S. positions and influence. Consequently, at the present stage at least, any regime can qualify for Soviet support if its policies conflict with those of the United States, especially if it establishes diplomatic and trade relations with Moscow, nationalizes or restricts U.S. business interests and investments, demands the withdrawal of U.S. military bases or installations from its territory, supports Soviet positions on various international issues, and gives indications of willingness to establish or strengthen relations with Cuba.

Although old fears and mistrust of communism and the Soviet Union persist, expansion of relations with communist countries is now the order of the day for most of Latin America. In this connection, Cuba's increasing acceptance by the rest of Latin America gives Moscow a potent supplementary means for exerting influence on the continent. The consolidation of a communist regime in Cuba guarantees a continuing Soviet role in Latin America. With Cuba as a base for the operation of the Soviet navy and air force, the USSR has staked out a permanent presence for exerting influence in Latin America. While Cuban involvement in Africa initially aroused apprehensions and revived general fears of communist expansion in Latin America, notably in Brazil, these appeared to subside, especially in the absence of comparable Cuban attempts in Latin America. Indeed, Cuba's assumption of a world role may have raised its prestige in Latin America and indirectly that of the Soviet Union as well.

When Cuba is included, the evidence of major Soviet interest and investment in Latin American policy is quite impressive. As a relative newcomer to the Latin American continent — where it must overcome suspicion as to its motives and intentions, fear of domination by a great power, and active opposition by conservative forces and to some degree by the United States — the Soviet Union has scored significant gains in a short time. The foreseeable trends in Latin America make it highly likely that Moscow will continue an active policy in the region.

The rapid increase in the past decade in Soviet credits to Latin America, exclusive of Cuba, is indicative of Moscow's willingness to accept new economic burdens and even to establish a client relationship where opportunities arise for significant political gains. By trying to give the impression of offering Latin American countries an alternative to dependence on the United States and by encouraging them to nationalize U.S. business or restrict U.S. investments, the Soviet Union unavoidably implies commitments for continued support. Furthermore, criticism from the radical Left and competition with growing Chinese activities in the region also put pressure on Moscow to expand its involvement and, in particular, to help assure the survival of the regimes it endorses.

However, the Chilean experience, the volatility of Latin American regimes, and the lower priority of the region as compared to other parts of the Third World operate as constraints on Soviet policy. The meagerness of Soviet aid to Guyana and Jamaica, two regimes whose ideological stance would seem to merit Soviet support and whose low priority for the U.S. would seem to reduce the risks, suggests continuing Soviet caution about incurring the costs of a second Cuba.

Moscow has been careful to avoid becoming involved in intra–Latin American disputes such as those between Honduras and El Salvador or Venezuela and Guyana. However, the Soviet emergence as a major supplier of arms to Peru could be an important disruptive factor in Peru's disputes with Chile leading to increased Soviet involvement on the continent.

Nevertheless, for the present at least the Soviet intrusion into Latin America, aside from Cuba, has been on too small a scale and with too low a profile to significantly affect the politics of the region. Although the upsurge in Latin America of militant nationalism, with its anti-U.S. expression, has provided the Soviet Union with the opportunity to expand its relations in the region, the same nationalism is likely to prove a major obstacle to Soviet efforts to gain real political influence in Latin America. Despite the seeming intractability of many Latin American social and economic problems, communist forces have not proved themselves capable, except for Cuba and temporarily in Guatemala and Chile, of capitalizing on the situation to the point of achieving power.

Soviet policies in the region will also be influenced by the state of U.S.-Soviet and Soviet-Cuban relations. No doubt the Soviet Union would like to exploit opportunities in Latin America with a minimum of risk of confrontation with the United States. At the same time, Soviet competion with the United States in less developed regions of the world, including Latin America, has been consistently and unequivocally excluded by the Soviet leadership from all restrictions imposed by the principles of coexistence on relations among the great powers. Moreover, the establishment of a client state in Cuba willy-nilly gives the USSR an interest in Latin America it did not have before.

In the first decade of Castro's rule, Soviet policies toward both Latin America and the United States were disputed by Havana. Since approximately 1970, however, the two have appeared to operate in tandem, as Castro has come around both on the question of proper tactics in the current stage in Latin America and on the value of the Soviet approach to détente with the United States. The differing perspectives of the two countries suggests the possibility of future divergences that could influence Soviet calculations. Meanwhile, however, Soviet and Cuban actions have been mutually reinforcing.

In absolute terms, the Soviet Union still represents a relatively minor, if growing, factor in the affairs and activities of Latin America. From the standpoint of foreign influence and presence as well as hard power, the U.S. remains the colossus, even though its position has eroded. Consequently, the future nature of U.S. policies and U.S.–Latin American relations will carry far more weight than those of Moscow in the region.

Notes

1. V. V. Zagladin, *Mezhdunarodnoye Kommunisticheskoe Dvizhenie: Ocherk Strategii i Taktiki*, 2nd ed. (Moscow: Politizdad, 1972), cited in Joint Publications Research Service (JPRS), *The International Communist Movement: Sketch of Strategy and Tactics*, vol. 2 (Washington, D.C.: U.S. Department of Commerce, 18 September 1972), p. 239.

2. Boris Ponomarev, secretary of the CPSU Central Committee, "Topical Problems of the Theory of the Revolutionary Process," *Kommunist*, no. 15 (October 1971), p. 59.

3. Speech at the Moscow Conference of the World Communist and Workers' Parties, June 1969, reported in *Prensa Latina* (Havana), 12 June 1969.

4. For a general Soviet view, see F. D. Kohler, et al., *Soviet Strategy for the Seventies: From Cold War to Peaceful Coexistence* (Coral Gables, Fla.: Center for Advanced International Studies, University of Miami, 1973).

5. V. G. Spirin, "USA Imperialism and Latin American Reality," *SShA: Ekonomika, Politika, Ideologiia*, no. 8 (August 1971), p. 33.

6. Kh. Kobo and G. I. Mirskii, "Concerning the Peculiarities of the Evolution of the Armies on the Latin American Continent," *Latinskaia Amerika*, no. 4 (July–August 1971), pp. 49–52; A. F. Shulgovskii, "Latin America: The Army and Politics," ibid., pp. 7–41.

7. *Radio Moscow*, 16 February and 24 April 1973.

8. *Pravda*, 10 April 1971.

9. A. F. Shul'govskii, "Urgent Problems of Latin American Studies," *Vestnik Akademii Nauk* [Herald of the Academy of Science of the USSR], no. 8 (August 1971), p. 108.

10. Ponomarev, "Topical Problems," p. 59 (emphasis added). See also the speech by Politburo member V. Grishin on the occasion of the fifty-fourth anniversary of the October Revolution, *Radio Moscow,* 6 November 1971.

11. A. Aleksin, "The 'Quiet Intervention'," *Kommunist*, no. 10 (July 1970), p. 93.

12. V. Vasilyev, "The United States' 'New Approach' to Latin America," *International Affairs* (Moscow), no. 6 (June 1971), p. 43.

13. S. Gonionsky, "Latin America: The Struggle for 'Second Liberation'," *International Affairs* (Moscow), no. 11 (November 1972), p. 43. See also Spirin, "USA Imperialism," pp. 33, 35; B. Antonov, "Latin America Versus U.S. Domination," *International Affairs* (Moscow), no. 8 (August 1971) p. 52; V. Gantman, "A Policy that is Transforming the World," *Kommunist*, no. 7 (May 1973), p. 34.

14. Gonionsky, "Latin America," p. 38.

15. Antonov, "Latin America Versus U.S. Domination," p. 52.

16. Jorge Texier, "General and Distinct Features of the Liberation Process," *World Marxist Review*, April 1972, p. 109.

17. Jorge del Prado, "The Revolution Continues," *World Marxist Review,* no. 1 (January 1973), p. 65.

18. Antonov, "Latin America Versus U.S. Domination," p. 50.

19. B. N. Ponomarev, "The World Situation and the Revolutionary Process,"

World Marxist Review, no. 6 (June 1974), p. 10.

20. *Pravda,* 25 February 1976.

21. For a fuller discussion of all these issues, see L. Goure and M. Rothenberg, *Soviet Penetration of Latin America* (Coral Gables, Fla.: Center for Advanced International Studies, University of Miami, 1975), pp. 107–20.

22. V. Teitelboim, "Prelude to Future Victories," *World Marxist Review,* no. 3 (March 1974), p. 89.

23. V. Bushuyev, "Revolution and Counterrevolution in Latin America," *International Affairs,* no. 5 (May 1974), p. 32.

24. Ponomarev, "The World Situation and the Revolutionary Process," p. 9.

25. *World Marxist Review Information Bulletin,* no. 12–13 (1975), p. 42.

26. See, for example, "On the Problem of Contemporary Rightwing Authoritarian Regimes," *Latinskaia Amerika,* no. 6 (November–December 1975), pp. 97–122, and no. 1 (January–February 1976), pp. 98–133; and "Facism in Latin America: Origins and Features," *World Marxist Review,* April 1978, pp. 103–15.

27. "On the Problem of Contemporary Rightwing Authoritarian Regimes" (1975), p. 97.

28. Ibid., p. 98.

29. "Whom Does The Army Serve," *World Marxist Review,* no. 4 (April 1976), p. 57.

30. M. O. Karamanov, "The Experience of Chile and the Revolutionary Process," *Rabochii Klass i Sovremenny Mir,* no. 6 (November–December 1974), p. 133.

31. The Army and Politics in Contemporary Latin America," *Latinskaia Amerika,* no. 3 (May-June 1977), p. 69.

32. Ibid., p. 71.

33. S. M. Khenkin, "Certain Problems of the Policy of Working Class Alliances in the Countries of Latin America," *Rabochii Klass i Sovremenny Mir,* no. 6 (November–December 1978), p. 83.

34. For the text of this document, see *World Marxist Review Information Bulletin* (Toronto), no. 12–13 (1975), pp. 18–61.

35. E. V. Levykin, "On the Question of the Methodology of Forecasting Interstate Relations," *Latinskaia Amerika,* no. 1 (January–February 1978), pp. 125–35.

36. A. I. Kedrov, "New Trends in the Foreign Policy of Latin American Countries," *Novaia c Noveishaia Istoriia,* no. 4 (July–August 1977), pp. 68–82.

37. D. Lozinov, "The Liberation Struggle in Latin America," *International Affairs,* August 1977, p. 39.

38. Ibid.

39. *World Marxist Review Information Bulletin,* p. 36.

40. V. Busheyev and Yu. Kozlov, "Latin America: New Role in International Relations," *Kommunist,* no. 12 (August 1978), p. 115.

41. Khenkin, "Certain Problems of the Policy of Working Class Alliances," p. 80.

42. Sergo Mikoyan, "Winds of Change," *New Times,* no. 3, (January 1979), p. 4.

43. Aleksandr Serbin, "The International Week," *Pravda,* 3 September 1978.

44. *Latinskaia Amerika,* no. 6 (November–December 1975), p. 102.

45. "Meeting of Communist Parties of the Caribbean," *Granma,* 2 May 1977; also V. Selivanov, *op. cit.,* p. 72.

46. Mikoyan, "Winds of Change," p. 3.

47. Rodnei Arismendi, "The Contemporary State of the Liberation Movement," *Latinskaia Amerika,* no. 5 (September–October 1977), p. 23.

48. From his speech on the fiftieth anniversary of the USSR, *Pravda,* 22 December 1972.

49. "The Army and Politics in Contemporary Latin America," *Latinskaia Amerika,* no. 3 (1977), p. 81.

50. See Central Intelligence Agency Report, *Communist Aid to the Less Developed Countries of the Free World, 1976* (ER 77-102976, August 1976) and Ibid., *1977* (ER 78-10478U, November 1978).

51. R. Tuchnin, "A Troubled Trip," *Izvestiia,* 18 May 1973.

52. T. Kolesnichenko, "Treaties with Panama Ratified," *Pravda,* 20 April 1978.

53. U.S. Department of State, *Communist States and Developing Countries: Aid and Trade in 1969,* RECS-5 (Washington, D.C., 9 July 1970), p. 3.

54. U.S. Department of State, *Communist States and Developing Countries: Aid and Trade in 1970,* RECS-15 (Washington, D.C., 22 September 1971), p. 3.

55. U.S. Department of State, *Communist States and Developing Countries: Aid and Trade in 1971,* RECS-3 (Washington, D.C., 15 May 1972), p. 3.

56. Luis Corvalan, "Two Years After—What is Happening in Chile," *World Marxist Review,* no. 11 (November 1972), pp. 16, 19; The Economist Intelligence Unit, *Quarterly Economic Review: Chile* (London), no. 1 (1973), p. 19; *New York Times,* 22 December 1972; *Radio Moscow,* 5 May 1973.

57. *Unidad* (Lima), 4 January 1973; V. Listov, "Tunnel Through the Andes," *Pravda,* 11 January 1973; *Radio Moscow,* 6 February 1973.

58. CIA Report, *Communist Aid 1978* (ER 79-10412U, September 1979), p. 9.

59. Ponomarev, "Topical Problems," p. 61. See also Soviet-Chilean joint communiqué in *Pravda,* 30 May 1971; Soviet-Chilean joint communiqué on the occasion of President Allende's visit to the USSR, *Pravda,* 10 December 1972.

60. *Pravda,* 10 December 1972. The Soviet-Chilean joint communiqué of 9 December 1972 provided for Soviet assistance in a wide range of industrial, mining, power, chemical, agricultural, fishing, and other activities.

61. *Vneshniaia Torgovlia SSSR* for 1961–1977, "Mezhdunarodnye Otnosheniia," (Moscow, 1962–1978).

62. *El Tiempo* (Quito), 22 April 1971.

63. World Bank, International Monetary Fund, *Direction of Trade Annual,* 1969–1973; 1971–1977.

64. U.S. Department of State RECS-3, p. 15; RECS-10, Table 8; CIA Report ER 79-10412U, Table 8, p. 11.

11

The United States

Charles Burton Marshall

In the physical realm, impact — denoting force communicated between colliding objects — can be computed theoretically by factors of mass, velocity, and angle of incidence, or one can take its practical measure by comparing the state of an object to what it was before the collision. Here the term is figurative for effects on an organized society's awareness and conduct attributable to the circumstance of a particular other organized society's contemporaneous existence on the same planet. The phenomena are in history's realm where, in James Gould Cozzens' phrase, "The Nature of Things abhors a drawn line and loves a hodgepodge, resists consistency, and despises drama."[1] Causation is obdurately multiple, complex, and equivocal; events are convoluted; results are diffuse and ambiguous.

How different would the U.S. situation have been in recent times, and be now, with the Soviet Union's existence expunged? Legend — which is history untangled and compressed for quick comprehension — readily volunteers answers to questions like that, even as it puts tabs on causes, catalogs results, and explains epochs in catchwords. History would not tell even under torture; such an inquiry would only lead into endless surmise. What if an integrated Germany had not materialized to upset Europe's traditional strategic balance and precipitate World War I? What if an overreaching German general staff had not improvidently contrived Lenin's return from exile to engineer a Bolshevik takeover of distraught Russia? What if the once defeated Germans, hypothetically wise enough to have resisted Hitler's charisma and foregone a second try, had avoided the second defeat, which drew the Soviet Union's forces into Central Europe? What if invention had not produced guided missiles and unlocked the atom?

The first sixteen years of coexistence between the United States and the Soviet Union were marked by distant animosity. The two governments were not in official communication and not very much in each other's way after a brief U.S. involvement in a hapless military intervention ending in

263

1919. The eight years from 1933 were little different save that the two governments were formally in touch. Thereupon for four years, 1941–1945, the two were allies — not very close or mutually confiding, but awarely and actively interdependent — in history's most pervasive war. Then a multiplicity of circumstances, some long in unfolding and others immediately connected with the upshot of that war, converged to place the two in the uppermost rankings in a scale of nations rated according to considerations of scope, material resources, and psychic energy for attempting large policies in international relations.

Whatever history's hidden alternatives might have been, the configuration of power in the sequel to World War II was not surprising. The world had long been put on notice. In 1790 Melchior Grimm had foreseen Russia's and America's joint emergence as superpowers; he added, "and we, the people in between, shall be too degraded, we shall have sunk too low, to know, except through vague and incoherent tradition, what we have been."[2] Similar musings were reported from Napoleon in his last exile. Heinrich Heine, Alexis de Tocqueville, Adolphe Thiers, Henri Martin, and Henry Adams, among others, pondered the prospect from various vantage points.

The Soviet Union's emergence into a position of enormous importance in world affairs became an assured prospect upon the rout of the German Sixth Army at Stalingrad in late 1942. U.S. policymakers during World War II clearly anticipated the development and gave considerable thought, although not equal percipience, to management of relationships with an aggrandized Soviet Union in the sequel to victory. Such policymakers, in the main, were scarcely prepared psychologically for the effects as materialized and were impelled into a broad revision of expectations and intentions. To that extent, and in terms of consequences as distinguished from the new configuration of power itself, the development did prove surprising.

Lines from Jean Giraudoux's drama *Tiger at the Gates*, about an ancient rivalry between Greece and Troy, are appropriate to the ensuing diplomatic epoch: "When destiny has brought up two nations, as for years it has brought up yours and mine, to a future of similar invention and authority, and given to each a different scale of values, the universe knows that destiny wasn't preparing alternative ways for civilization to flower."[3]

In a miscellany of decisions not necessary to recount here, the United States undertook to apply its resources for purposes, including strategic deterrence, countering what were perceived to be the Soviet Union's purposes. Strategic concerns became a settled and continuing element of national awareness and practice for the first time in U.S. experience. The shift in outlook and habit was promptly reflected in a revival of military conscription, which had lapsed with the end of hostilities, and in a proliferation of bureaucratic acronyms symbolizing institutions unknown in peacetime, presumably for giving strength and coherence to multifarious undertakings to affect the vast realm external to national jurisdiction. No one can say which of these new institutions—NSC, DOD, JCS, CIA, NSA, AEC—would have been created if the Soviet Union had not existed. Ever since, and this is a point both certain and pertinent to our theme, the principal exterior factor in strategic calculations underlying U.S. approaches to the external realm has been the Soviet Union.

The new epoch has been chronicled and theorized about in profusion to match, if not excel, any other era in diplomatic history. A voluminous literature affords no end of answers concerning the epoch's nature, the causes, the moment of origin, determinations of culpability and justification, questions of whether and when the epoch ever ended, and even the source of its figurative name—the cold war. Retelling the multifarious events and rehearsing the issues would be impracticable and supererogatory, but something may be gained by pondering the interplay of hopes and perceptions at three stages in relationships between the United States and the Soviet Union: as allies against the Axis in World War II, as adversaries at the apogee of the cold war, and at the present juncture.

A reminiscence in Werner Heisenberg's *The Physicist's Conception of Nature*, concerning a discussion among German students caught up in civil turmoil in the sequel to World War I, is pertinent. One student said simplistically that "only force could lead to a real settlement of our conflict with the others." A theological student retorted that "in the final analysis even the question of what was meant by 'we' and 'the others,' and what distinguishes the two, would obviously lead to a purely spiritual decision"—no simple matter at all.[4] That distinction—basic to and an endless concern of all politics—lies at the root of every problem of order and conflict. "We" and "they"—collaboration and adversariness—are mutually contingent, almost symbiotic.

The process of distinguishing is integral to devising strategies, to conducting wars, and to every undertaking to establish conditions of peace. Those who count in large concurrences may be rich in information or overburdened with illusion, and their performance may be wise or improvident. Nations and states subsist or fail according to which it may be. Whether wisely or improvidently conceived, policy hinges on determining—stage by stage, according to circumstance—who are we and who are they.

The question of who are we and who are they seems to have lain lightly on national awareness and concern in early epochs. Such a generalization is offered with diffidence, for most Americans in times long past probably did not ponder international politics, and some among the ponderers undoubtedly shared Alexander Hamilton's pessimistic thought that, having achieved independence, the United States was fated to share in the vicissitudes that were the common lot of nations. In the prevailing appreciation, however, the nation was a special creation — and one aspect of its specialness was an inherent prerogative to choose sides in the world as a matter of sentimental preference only, with no thought to strategic entailments.

In self-image, Americans were a nonstrategic nation. In its sense of a larger pattern for matching means and ends in conducting war, strategy was a mode of thought and action only intermittently relevant for occasions when outright war interrupted normality. The concept of peace and war as correlated variations across a continuum, with strategy as pertinent to maintaining one as to waging the other, was no part of the national outlook. The war business was for other countries far away.

A desire to live outside the ambit of European military rivalries was one of the considerations that prompted settlement in Britain's North American colonies. The experience of being drawn into international hostilities as a consequence of British involvement in the Third Silesian War contributed to the urge for independence. The withdrawal of European powers from the American environs in the Napoleonic epoch increased the sense of apartness and exemption.

George Washington articulated that sense in his farewell address. The young Abraham Lincoln embellished it in a boast about national invulnerability: "All the Armies of Europe, Asia, and Africa combined, with all the treasure of the earth (our own excepted) in their military chest, with a Bonaparte for a commander, could not by force take a drink from the Ohio or make a track on the Blue Ridge in a trial of a thousand years."[5] Strategic security was bestowed. A nation so situated — needing a navy only to suppress piracy and foster trade in remote regions and an army with tactical proficiency only for tribal pacification and frontier order and contingently for ensuring domestic tranquility — had no intelligence apparatus, war colleges, general staffs, and the like.

Attitudes characteristic of that time persisted long after the United States, in the late nineteenth and early twentieth century, at last produced a strategic theorist in Admiral Alfred Thayer Mahan, began to develop a more formidable navy, and established armed services institutions for strategic study and direction.

In the persistent outlook, lack of strategic concern was interpreted as a virtue. Circumstances enabling Americans to afford that virtue were overlooked. Attributed to goodness rather than to mere good luck, the virtue was to be exemplified to the world from which the United States stood strategically apart. Reinhold Niebuhr wrote in *The Irony of American History* of a national past marked by "the innocence of irresponsibility" when "we had a religious version of our national destiny which interpreted the meaning of our nationhood as God's effort to make a new beginning in the history of mankind."[6] The virtue of being nonstrategic was an essential element in that aspiration.

The idea was summoned up by Woodrow Wilson on being called upon to give a lead in establishing conditions of peace to follow World War I. In Wilson's conception, the cause of World War I lay in the failure of a strategic concept, the balance of power. Hence the necessary goal was to provide a drastically different arrangement on which to rely.

Wilson's project for a nonstrategic world of nonstrategic nations — all free of the need to differentiate among friendly, indifferent, and hostile elements in contemplating the vast external realm — was to be achieved by faith and conversion. Every nation-state was to be pledged to honor and defend every other state's autonomy, and every state made secure by the power of promises to restrain even would-be promise-breakers. In Wilson's somewhat circular logic, "When all unite to act in the same sense and with the same purpose all act in the common interest and are free to live their own lives under a common protection."[7]

World War II renewed the urge to arrange preventive measures. In Franklin D. Roosevelt's conception, which was widely shared among Americans, World War II was an aberration attributable to general default on Woodrow Wilson's aspiration as institutionalized in the League of Nations. The United States' own rejection of League membership was taken as a principal and probably even decisive factor in that failure. This time a default on creating a world organization would be impermissible. The winning coalition must be perpetuated as that organization's nucleus.

A motif in the American nonstrategic tradition was emphasized anew. Secretary of State Cordell Hull prophesied to Congress in 1943, "There will no longer be need for spheres of influence, for alliances, for balances of power, or any other of the special arrangements through which, in the unhappy past, the nations strove to safeguard their interests or to promote their security."[8] In identical terms President Roosevelt depicted the prospective postwar world to a joint session of Congress in early 1945[9] following the Yalta conference, where, among other matters, structural principles for the new world organization and a decision to go ahead with it had been affirmed by the U.S., British and Soviet leaderships.

Harry Hopkins, Roosevelt's confidant and sometime surrogate, would recall about the height of collaboration at Yalta, "We really believed in our hearts that this was the dawn of the new day we had all been praying for and talking about for so many years."[10]

The dream was plausible from the standpoint of power. Times when the prospect of defeat had confronted the three allies represented at Yalta were long past. The common purpose of overcoming the Axis was prospering. President Roosevelt and Marshal Josef Stalin, with British Prime Minister Winston Churchill in auxiliary attendance, epitomized a global condominium—an unprecedented combination with sway over military factors, production and supply, and the future of polities in most of the world. If durable—a large and imaginative "if"—such a collaboration might indeed have banished strategic issues and anxieties to what Roosevelt and Hull called the unhappy past.

American perceptions in that phase of making common cause are pertinent. War, on vast scale and for immeasurable stakes, was the paramount circumstance. Edmund Burke's thought that "refined policy has ever been the parent of confusion" applies especially in times of such wars.[11] Issues must be simplified into good versus evil. Billboard language, not fine print, must be the idiom. Hitler's evil genius provided a standard by which to make gross moral judgments easy: Whoever was against that side was on the right side.

The Soviet Union's losses in havoc sustained and casualties suffered— twenty million killed—were awesome and disproportionate. That such huge attrition was due to factors of time and space and enemy strategic plans rather than to voluntary sacrifice was immaterial. The magnitudes were heroic. Time for the Western allies was purchased at a price in Russian lives and territory. Awareness of this fact impelled psychological amends and, as Charles Bohlen observed, "led to a guilt complex in our relations."[12]

Fighting for dear life, the Soviet leadership, besides dissolving institutional connections and controls affecting Communist parties in other countries, played down Communist characteristics and watchwords domestically and appealed instead to Russian national traditions. These gestures made it easier for outsiders, if not to expunge, then to forget at least temporarily the closed society, the Communist party monopoly of public life, Stalinist purges in the 1930s, the 1939–1941 collaboration with Hitler, and so on.

The war entailed huge marshaling of resources, expenditure of energy, and focusing of effort—a sharp contrast to the ambiguous, nagging, marginal conflict experienced in a later American generation. For many people the phenomena encouraged tendencies to think big, to believe in a future transcending the past. Minds stimulated in that direction reached for a precept and raised America's allies to a pinnacle of perfection. This approach—I wonder whether it is peculiar to the American psyche—was readily humored. Hollywood, the press, and radio rallied to depict the Soviet Union as a stout companion for the dawn of a new day. In general the reigning euphoria varied inversely to knowledge of the Soviet Union. Doubt was disproportionate among those in official life with a background of service in the U.S. embassy in Moscow.

Attitudes at the apex of authority counted most. President Roosevelt, seconded by Hopkins, was the central policymaking figure. Roosevelt and his surrogate, as Bohlen's memoir recalls, were preoccupied with present tasks, not recollections. The paramount purposes were to get the war won rapidly and then to enter a secure new era of peaceful trust. Soviet collaboration all the way was indispensable to both aims. Any issues involving strategic dispositions must be subordinated to that overriding consideration. The organized peace ahead would afford time to rectify imperfection. The approach put a premium on placating the Soviet ally.

The insights of Roosevelt and Hopkins into the Soviet Union were scant. Roosevelt's friend, Secretary of Labor Frances Perkins, recalls his recurring remark about Russians: "I just don't know what makes them tick."[13] Roosevelt assigned his similarly unknowledgeable friend to gather and digest instructive information about the Russians. Bohlen's memoir includes a telling detail from the conference at Teheran fourteen months before Yalta. At a mention of India, Roosevelt volunteered an opinion favoring reform there "from the 'bottom,' somewhat on the Soviet line." Bohlen comments: "He undoubtedly viewed the Bolshevik coup d'etat as a genuine revolution. He did not realize that the Bolsheviks were a minority who seized power during a period of anarchy."[14]

Without much background in Russian history, Marxist-Leninist dogma, or Soviet practice, Roosevelt, as the intuitive sort of politician he was, saw relations with the Soviet ally in a personal equation. Achieving rapport with Stalin seemed to require playing down the British collaboration. Bohlen, who was there, comments disdainfully in his memoir on Roosevelt's endeavor to that purpose at Teheran. Roosevelt's own detailed recollection, relayed by Frances Perkins, is unintentionally ironical: Stalin was "correct, stiff, solemn, not smiling, nothing human to get hold of," even though "I had done everything he asked me to do. I had stayed at his embassy, gone to his dinners, been introduced to his generals. . . . I had come there to accommodate Stalin. . . . I had to cut through this icy surface." In a wakeful night, Roosevelt planned a maneuver.

At the next meeting, taking pains to appear "chummy and confidential," Roosevelt whispered a remark about Churchill's matutinal crankiness, saw Stalin smile vaguely, felt himself to be on the right track, and, according to his own account, "began to tease Churchill about his Britishness, about John Bull, about his cigars, about his habits. . . . Winston got red and scowled, and the more he did so, the more Stalin smiled." A Stalin guffaw encouraged perseverance. Roosevelt's account continues: "I kept it up until

Stalin was laughing with me, and it was then that I called him 'Uncle Joe.' He would have thought me fresh the day before, but that day he laughed and came over and shook my hand." The ice broken, they "talked like men and brothers."[15]

Roosevelt virtually spiritualized his image of Stalin, according to the Perkins account. He was intrigued by Stalin's student years in a theological seminary before becoming a revolutionary. "Roosevelt wondered about that," Perkins wrote. "Two or three times he asked me, 'Don't you suppose that made some kind of a difference in Stalin? Doesn't that explain part of the sympathetic quality in his nature which we all feel?'"[16]

After a depiction of Marshal Stalin as combining "a tremendous relentless determination with a stalwart good humor" and being "representative of the heart and soul of Russia," Roosevelt added a prophesy in a 1943 Christmas broadcast: "I believe that we are going to get along very well with him and the Russian people — very well indeed."[17]

Roosevelt's reported reply to a warning from William C. Bullitt, former U.S. ambassador to Moscow, for vigilance against the Soviet dictator's craftiness invoked "a hunch that Stalin isn't that kind of a man" and an assurance that "if I give him everything I possibly can and ask for nothing in return, he won't try to annex anything and will work with me for a world of peace and democracy."[18] Similarly, Roosevelt said to Frances Perkins, "You know, I really think the Russians will go along with me about having no spheres of influence."[19]

Roosevelt misjudged the man who to him personified the Soviet state. In a manner not peculiar to him among statesmen, Roosevelt also romanced about his personal capacity to work great changes in general affairs. Whether he ever pondered how basic and how disorganizing a change in Soviet character and conduct would be entailed to fulfill his image of the future is questionable.

Roosevelt postulated "that by patience, proofs of good will and fair purpose, the mistrust of the Soviet authorities could be subdued, and they could be converted into good partners for the benefit of all mankind." In this regard Herbert Feis concludes in *Roosevelt-Churchill-Stalin:*

> To this purpose he held to the last breath. It could not have been easy in the face of the negative answers he had been getting from Stalin on so many questions. Nor, toward the end, could it have been wholly unaffected by the opinions being pressed upon him that the Soviet government was not to be led along the proper path merely by friendship or generosity, but that it had to be opposed, and dealt with on the basis of punishments and rewards.[20]

Roosevelt, as David Rees observes in *The Age of Containment,* "failed to discern the deep ideological content of Soviet foreign policy and also deliberately divorced United States political and military objectives," whereas Stalin, in contrast, "saw war as an extension of politics."[21]

In shifting from Roosevelt's postulates and seeking to apply strategic consideration reciprocally in dealing with the Soviet Union, did U.S. policymakers overlook the Soviet Union's inherent defensiveness and fancy an aggressive bent where there was none, even persuading themselves of the existence of a Soviet timetable for global conquest? Did they further err by unduly stressing Soviet capabilities as distinguished from intentions, discounting the Soviet ruling group's preoccupation with national interests as distinguished from revolutionary goals, and taking at face value the leadership's ceremonial professions of believing in Marxist-Leninist dogma? The short answer is no, although such propositions, often put forward as scholarly or journalistic hindsights, are not disprovable. Sound grounds for discounting them do exist and should be briefly indicated.

A double answer is appropriate for the postulate that U.S. policy was based on erroneous ascriptions of an aggressive potential to an inherently defensive regime. First, as a generality, to disjoin defensiveness from a disposition to aggression is questionable in analysis of international affairs just as it is in the field of individual behavior, for insecurity is a trait likely to give rise to pushiness. Second, Soviet defensiveness was recognized as a heritage from Russia's long experience of vulnerability. The urge underlying processes by which the ancient duchy of Moscow had expanded to imperial dimensions reflected chronic fearfulness about perimeters. The old apprehension, joined to communist distrust of differentiated societies, had been made acute by recent experience of invasion on a vastly destructive scale.

Circumspection is called for in applying definitional distinctions between intentions and capabilities in social and political analysis. Intentions are not fixed abstractions. They are mutable. They are lines of action susceptible of being affected by variables of opportunity and resources—a point true of the United States, true in human affairs in general, and applicable to the Soviet Union. Arguments citing Soviet intentions as given and immutable — and as revealed to the adducer — are not impressive. Probably no one in a responsible position in U.S. policy ever surmised the existence of any such thing as a Soviet timetable for conquest of the world's troubled countries. To question the existence of such a timetable, however, is not equivalent to supposing the Soviet rulership to have no preferences for the future, no ambition to push those preferences in external affairs, and no interest in taking advantage of pertinent opportunities.

The premised paramountcy of national interest over revolutionary purposes has merit, but only relative merit. No one I ever knew or heard of in the U.S. policy nexus was ever inclined to reverse that order, assuming that the Soviet ruling group would be inclined to sacrifice national interest in deference to revolutionary purposes elevated to absolute supremacy. Here are the prevailing assumptions as I recall them. The Soviet Union in a general way, as a Communist regime, abided by a precept in the *Communist Manifesto*: "The Communists everywhere support every revolutionary movement against the existing social order." Where feasible, national interests and revolutionary purposes were pursued concurrently as mutually reinforcing objects. In pinches requiring choice, the ruling group would give precedence to national considerations, and in particular to the regime's continuity.

I regard as a more significant point for analytic comment the perceived relevance to Soviet policy of Marxist-Leninist theories — I purposely avoid that frayed word, "ideology" — regarding historic laws and human motivations. This matter is sensitive because it is intellectually *de rigueur* now to deny linkage between belief systems and intentions in a Soviet context. Scholars and publicists who would not question such links elsewhere will shake their heads at any suggested connection between creed and deed in Moscow. That inhibition and its source are immaterial here. What is pertinent is that the belief system prescribed and enforced in the Soviet Union was in the main taken seriously by U.S. policymakers — although not necessarily at face value.

The distinction between taking seriously and taking at face value may be clarified by examining the words "believe in." That phrase denotes a mind's function in ascribing a quality to a corporeal or abstract object. The quality in a particular case can be inferred from context. To believe in angels is to ascribe reality; in judgment day, inevitability; in drawing to an inside straight, prudence; in astrology, predictability; in papal infallibility, truth; in women's liberation, justice; in the doctrine of executive privilege, authority; and so on. That the Soviet rulers believed in Marxism-Leninism strikes me as indisputable. Whether they ascribed historic inevitability to its triumphs, and whether they accepted the tenets as devoutly, say, as a practicing Christian Scientist subscribes to his faith, are immaterial considerations.

The ruling group believed in Marxism-Leninism in the sense that it provided them, to use Nathan Leites' expression, an operational code — a frame of rationalization by which to justify every deed or misdeed.[22] However credulously or cynically the ruling group may have regarded the utopian promise of eventual deliverance from diversity in a harmonized world of classless societies, the creed provided a rationale for a closed system of dominance set off against differentiated societies regarded as inherently hostile.

Recounting facts of the time is easy enough a generation later. Correlation of facts — that is, truth — is less easy. To call up cogently the spirit of that juncture now is most difficult, in part because ambivalence — a mixture of trepidation and self-confidence — characterized the major adversaries.

The Soviet regime's inherent anxieties undoubtedly were increased by the sudden disclosure of atomic capability, a strategically momentous achievement worked out by the United States in secret collaboration with Britain and Canada. U.S. policy conceivably missed fortune's tide by not willingly sharing the new technology with its Soviet ally without insisting on elaborate institutional safeguards — a point ably although not conclusively argued in Lisle A. Rose's *After Yalta*.[23] We shall never know. The systematically, compulsively secretive regime felt itself pressed to choose among submitting to conditions antithetic to its domestic tenure, acquiescing to indefinite strategic subordination, and striving to become an atomic rival to the United States at whatever cost to be exacted from a populace that had suffered ruin, privation, and enormous casualties.

At the same time the Soviet Union, as a major agent of victory, enjoyed enhanced prestige in the war's aftermath. Multiple outright annexations had aggrandized its strategic base. Beyond what it had annexed, the Soviet rulership was imposing its image over a sphere of influence comprising a diversity of Eastern European countries and part of Germany brought under its military sway by the tides of victory. Its forces stood in Austria, Manchuria, and a major portion of Korea. Soviet auxiliaries in Communist parties in a multiplicity of countries beyond Soviet control were comporting themselves as prospective heirs to power.

Impoverishment and faltering confidence pervaded Europe. Germany, divided into mutually exclusive and unfriendly zones of victor occupation, was in political eclipse. Defeated Japan, then under U.S. occupation and tutelage, was an economic ruin. China, its chronic demoralization acutely intensified, was under a government deficient for coping with a threat imposed by indigenous Communist forces. Southeast Asia was in civil turbulence.

While not identifying the Soviet Union as a ubiquitous malefactor, the United States did find itself in a conflict relationship with the USSR over what to do about such unsatisfactory circumstances. U.S. policymakers formed intentions of halting a drift of events into directions likely to redound to Soviet advantage and to open political opportunities for the Soviet Union in areas beyond its span of dominance.

The shift from Roosevelt's postulates to strategic polarization under what came to be known as the containment policy, far from being a sudden shift, was a gradual process involving changes of perception, stage by stage, within many minds. I once discussed with Bohlen the question of fixing the point of departure. He felt the turn had occurred at Secretary of State James F. Byrnes' staff conference on a day in late February of 1946, focusing on then current Soviet initiatives to partition Iran. Previously a persistent exemplifier of the Roosevelt approach, Byrnes now took a different direction and disavowed placation as futile. He attributed Soviet suspiciousness, obduracy, and truculence to deliberate design rather than misunderstanding. He concluded on a need for recognizing the Soviet Union as an opponent to countervail rather than a partner to woo. Bohlen recalled that as the first occasion of hearing such views from someone so high in authority—a juncture as appropriate as any for marking conscious entry into the cold war. Four and a quarter more years would pass and many events transpire—notably establishment of Communist rule over mainland China and the Soviet Union's first nuclear explosion—before the U.S. government, in a National Security Council study known as NSC-68, systematically attempted to correlate means and purposes in a comprehensive strategic policy.

As an underlying assumption in the strategy undertaken, no combination of nations without U.S. participation could marshal factors of strength sufficient to alleviate anxiety and provide a cogent basis for resistance to Soviet pressures—and alleviation of anxiety was a psychic requisite for economic recovery and political recuperation.

The United States was at that time unchallengeable in naval power and military aviation and had the advantage of a considerable headstart in nuclear technology. Singular among nations of considerable magnitude, the United States' capital plant was hugely expanded and improved, rather than impaired, in consequence of the war. The United States was the world's sole large source of supply and credit in international commerce and commanded huge preponderance in maritime shipping.

Essentially what the United States undertook was, by applying such elements of strength, to bolster needy countries and pari passu to foreclose political opportunities exploitable for communist purposes. The undertaking entailed altering perceptions of probabilities pertinent to contingencies of war in the minds of those affecting policymaking within the Soviet realm and in diverse lands beyond.

Such perceptions—for lack of a better generic term let us call them strategic images—merit a moment's elucidation. They consist of composite estimates of what would happen in respect of interacting dimensions of warfare if hypothetical war should become actual. What countries would be drawn into hostilities? Which ones, while standing aside, might tilt to one side or the other—and to which? What would be the theater of hostilities? What sort of weapons would be used—in what environments, over what duration, at what intensity, to what consequence in material havoc wrought, with what result measured in damage to ability to persevere or in dissipation of civil will on the respective sides, and to what final outcome? Strategic images also include counterpart estimates in putative enemies' minds and their perceptions of how they are being perceived—and so on in a notional pattern akin to a conceptual hall of mirrors.

From such strategic images, potential enemies derive their assumptions concerning thresholds of hostilities, their sense as to when in prudence to temporize or to accommodate on differences, and their grasp of how far it is safe to press a particular issue. Security for one side is calculable in terms of perceived risk on the other. Strategic calculation, however, affords only relative certainties, never perfect ones, and its equations always rest on postulates of having opponents capable of perceiving and calculating rationally. A moderately adept theorizer could easily think up dozens of permutations in pondering effects of interacting strategic images in international relationships involving some degree of opposition and tension. Three situations suffice here:

Situation A: Both sides make similar assumptions of the accrual of a clear advantage to one and the same side in the hypothetical event of war. Each side correctly perceives the other's estimate. One side is in a position to press its preferences, and the other side is constrained to accommodate. The probability of war is slight.

Situation B: In both sides' estimates, clear advantage in the hypothetical event of war would accrue to neither side. Each side correctly perceives the other's estimate. Neither side is in a position to press its preferences far or under constraint to accommodate all the way. The probability of war is slight.

Situation C: Both sides feel sure of having an advantage, or one side feels thus assured and the other perceives a standoff, in the hypothetical event of war. Their estimates are discrepant but each side assumes the other side's estimate to be like its own. The danger of bringing on war unintended by either side is appreciable.

As an assumption basic to strategy worked out in support of the containment policy, the relationship between the strategic images held respectively by the United States and the Soviet Union corresponded to Situation A, weighted to the U.S. advantage. That advantage was mitigated by an inclination to avoid risks of precipitating showdowns. Assurance of being able to prevail in the extremity of war was offset by rational calculations of costs of fighting over, and risks of rigorously pursuing, many desiderata that were attractive in abstract. These considerations did not gainsay the inherent advantage once accruing to the United States.

U.S. policy sought to preserve that situation as an end, while at the same time employing it as a means. Both as means and as end, the advantages of that situation related to efforts under the containment policy to bring

within the scope of assurance provided by the situation certain other countries, which without U.S. support, would find themselves in Situation A
weighted to their disadvantage.

The pertinent measures, focused at the outset on the Soviet Union and
designed to provide security for the part of Europe lying beyond Soviet
dominance, also were applied vis-à-vis continental China after the Nationalist regime's retreat to insular Taiwan and the 1950 attack on the portion of Korea beyond Communist control. The instrumentalities have included an array of bilateral and multilateral alliances contracted from the
late 1940s through the mid-1950s and encompassing most noncommunist
European and Asian countries and all of the Americas; tendering of
military equipment and training; and deployment of U.S. forces abroad
where considered necessary to make guarantees sufficiently dissuasive to
adversaries and persuasive to allies. In the Korean and Southeast Asian instances, direct engagement of U.S. forces against indigenous Communist
forces in wars of large scope and great duration have been considered
necessary because — to those in charge of U.S. policy — confidence in U.S.
guarantees in general hinged upon making containment work even in
peripheral situations where Communist forces bore presumptive vicarious
relationships to the Soviet Union or China.

In a typical expression of the mood, John F. Kennedy, while a senator,
said: "I believe the central task of American and Western military policy is
to make all forms of Communist aggression irrational and unattractive."[24]
In that spirit, and in a twinkling of history, the United States entered into
strategic commitments of a scope and variety unprecedented in its own or
any other nation's experience.

The epoch in U.S.–Soviet relations that thus began involved international politics as conceptual warfare, a contest of will and purpose bearing
on military factors but not spilling over into direct hostile military operations. This concept would fit in with Karl von Clausewitz's oft-quoted
aphorism about war as a continuation of politics by other means, and with
Oswald Spengler's logical corollary identifying politics as a continuation of
war by other means.[25] According to a similar idea expressed in Sir Keith
Hancock's *Four Studies of War and Peace in This Century*, "We make a mistake
by thinking in chronological slabs, here a slab of peace, there a slab of war,
so many years of peace, so many years of war. Defence and opulence, war
and peace, are with us all the time as alternative ends of policy, alternative
activities of government, alternative postures of society."[26] In this view
peace and war are complementary variables occurring across a continuum.
Conducting policy under conditions of rigorous strategic competition in
keeping with such a view would prove a vexatious as well as novel experience.

Launching into an incalculable term of conceptual warfare, a departure from norms familiar to the American past, was a highly speculative venture. Observations from an excellent book about an earlier strategic confrontation, namely, E. L. Woodward's *Great Britain and the German Navy,* are appropriate to the juncture concerned:

> The limits of human capacity . . . are too often ignored by those who possess after-knowledge of events. The force of circumstance is noticed in tragedy, and is a general theme of play-acting; yet it is forgotten or underestimated in the popular verdict upon the actors in public affairs. We, who do not know to-morrow, assume that the men of yesterday knew to-day and that every sower can forsee every harvest.[27]

According to a myth of recent origin — and a myth it definitely is — those involved in shaping U.S. policy undertook the course in a mood of pugnacity and unmitigated presumption. In *After Yalta* Rose provides a proper corrective to that idea. The mood, as he says, was mixed.[28] Essentially it was one of reluctance, even of apprehension.

An illustrative recollection from a night session in the State Department Policy Planning Staff after months of work on NSC-68 comes to mind. One member asked whether the envisaged course was soundly based in premising greater inherent resiliency and stamina for a contract society, with an accountable government and free flow of information, over a long haul in strategic competition with a totally administered society under a despotic regime exercising a monopoly on general information within its domain. In his estimation, the undertaking was based on sentiment rather than sensibility, and benefits to flow from strategic deterrence would be negative. What evils might be prevented — at great expense and with many unforeseeable vicissitudes — would never be demonstrable. The American society, as a whole alien to strategic considerations, would tire before the adversary, he ventured to conclude — and none present challenged the thought.

I recall, in contrast, instances of assurance that, in retrospect, seem utterly romantic. When, for example, someone at a National Security Council staff session raised a query about hypothetical monetary effects, a State Department economist answered — with a Treasury man unequivocally concurring — to the effect that, for as far ahead as one could rationally calculate, in a prospect as nearly absolute as a mind could venture to conceive in general affairs, the dollar rated at thirty-five to an ounce of gold would remain the universal yardstick in international commerce.

Self-doubt and self-assurance were then, as ever since, dialectical components of U.S. policy. The optimistic strain was perhaps linked to the circumstance of following so closely after World War II, which had occasioned tremendous proofs of national efficacy in concentrating on external goals. Moreover, as Paul Seabury has observed in *The Rise and Decline of the Cold War,* of all the belligerents "only the United States had devised a programmatic set of universal goals to guide its aspirations and to undergird its own wartime actions."[29]

The war had left the United States with huge inventories of unconfirmed slogans and unfulfilled aspirations about transforming international relations. The concept of the Free World—as a partly real, partly impalpable community opposing the Axis version of the future in World War II had been called—was renovated and given embodiment in a miscellany of more or less organized societies regarded as more or less disposed not to be run from Moscow. A multiplicity of common civic aspirations concerning the good life, prosperity, and development of personality was psychologically imputed to that aggregate.

So again, in Seabury's words, "as in all major previous conflicts in American history, populist idealism quickly invested this spacious yet limited conflict with universal messianic justification."[30] Once again, also, statesmanship professed to discern transformation ahead. Strategic aims plausible in themselves were rationalized as elements of a program by which to vindicate universal aspirations professed as purposes of the war last in memory.

Such an end would require not only that the Soviet Union be strategically deterred but also that the adversary undergo conversion and be brought to a reordering of values, expectations, and purposes. By being foreclosed from opportunities conducive to a Marxist-Leninist triumph, the Soviet Union supposedly would be impelled rationally to alter its preferences—its image of the future—and guided toward moderation, tractability, and cooperation.

As a counterpart goal on the Soviet side, noncommunist states, including emphatically the United States, must be dissuaded from policies offering resistance to revolutionary purposes. States as states, communist and noncommunist alike, must enter into universal concord, with those communist in orientation, including preeminently the Soviet Union, left free in their Communist embodiment to prosecute their enmities against differentiated social orders.

In a fashion prevailing in recent years, a past tense is used for referring to the cold war. By implication, the conflicted purposes between the major strategic adversaries in the sequel to World War II have been resolved and relegated. It is in point to consider the evidence for that assumption. Wariness is called for in such an inquiry in view of the multiplicity of the junctures when tidal changes in U.S.-Soviet relations have been discerned, analyzed, and hailed. The 1930s brought two such episodes. A dozen or so turning points were alleged during World War II. An even larger number of such junctures giving rise to optimistic prognoses punctuated the quarter century following. In a comprehensive average, turns for the better in U.S.-Soviet relations were sighted at a rate of one per year between the early 1930s and the late 1970s.[31]

That record provides a basis for being skeptical concerning a basic amelioration in the superpower rivalry. Yet to dismiss with a shrug of *déjà vu* the pertinent developments since the early 1970s is not sufficient. The volume and variety of U.S.-Soviet accords formally arrived at during that interval are unprecedented for so brief a span in the history of diplomatic relations between the two countries concerned and indeed hard to match in the annals of bilateral diplomacy between any two countries. If the character of the future is determined by documentary promises, then what has been accomplished must be rated as stupendous, fulfilling former president Richard M. Nixon's appraisal — a transformation from an era of confrontation to an era of negotiation — given in 1972 after the first of his three summit meetings with the Soviet Union's Leonid Brezhnev.[32] In Nixon's version conveyed to the Congress, what had been accomplished was the institutionalization of détente, but the key pertinent accord echoed the Soviet phraseology, "peaceful coexistence." Inferentially, the two concepts had become interchangeable.

A point of reference by which to test that implicit assumption is provided by a follow-on agreement — it was subscribed at the second Nixon-Brezhnev summit a year later — obligating the two superpowers to keep each other informed regarding any incipient threat to peace whenever occurring and to cooperative measures to counter any such threat. The Soviet Union's subsequent actions have included surreptitious provisioning of the Yom Kippur attacks on Israel in 1973, unilateral initiatives toward direct intervention after a shift in the tide of battle against the Soviet Union's Arab clients, the abetting of the petroleum embargo by the Arab oil-producing states, and utmost efforts, though in vain, to get the embargo prolonged. The score card includes Soviet efforts to impede the United States' step-by-step efforts to abate the Arab-Israeli quarrel, and prompting of the North Vietnamese in the overrunning of South Vietnam in 1975 in violation of the Paris accords of 1973 signed by the Soviet Union as a guarantor. The pertinent record includes unilateral Soviet intervention in the Angolan civil war in 1975 in scornful repudiation of the U.S. Secretary of State's entreaties. The meaning of peace and of the promotion of peace — such is the conclusion supported by that accord — continues to diverge profoundly as between the United States' and the Soviet Union's respective operational codes. That divergence continues to bear on the transactional relationship between the superpowers.

The "clear and straight-forward aim" the ruling figures in the Soviet Union "assert from every forum in which they talk to each other about the future"—I quote Foy Kohler, a former United States ambassador to Moscow on the point—is

> to achieve conditions in relationship with the capitalist states, particularly the United States, which will, on the one hand, maximize the opportunities and capabilities of the Soviet Union to prosecute a relentless struggle against the capitalist states by all means short of war; and, on the other hand, minimize the chances that the capitalist states will make effective use of their resources and power in defense of their interests, and ultimately of their existence, in the face of relentless and ever-broadening and intensifying Soviet pressures and advances. . . . The leaders openly reject any notion that respect for the Western powers' vital interests, or anything in the way of "live and let live," is implicit in the policy of peaceful coexistence.[33]

The supersedence of adversariness by mutual amity is a fancy entertained on only this side.

Strategic factors remain the centerpiece of the relationship. There the changes since earlier phases are profound, the main one being the recession of the United States' one-time palpable preeminence in strategic strength, so telling in a succession of episodes such as the Korean War, the quarrels over accesses to Berlin, and the Cuban missile crisis.

The response within this country to the last-named episode has special pertinence. At high levels within the government, as well as among the wider public, success in bringing the United States' strategic nuclear superiority to bear, along with local superiority in conventional military strength, produced a mixture of self-congratulation and abashment. Wishfulness nurtured a notion of the allaying, once and for all, of dangers of a nuclear confrontation between the superpowers. Nuclear competition—so the supposition went—had proved to be too perilous a business for rational nations to engage in. The possibility of a Soviet resolve never again to be caught in the predicament of being second best in a showdown was scarcely entertained. Instead, a Soviet reconcilement to strategic inferiority was fancifully assumed. A Soviet decision to opt out of strategic nuclear competition, reflecting a recognition of having lost out in it, was happily reported by the U.S. Secretary of Defense in 1965. "There is no indication that the Soviets are seeking to develop a strategic nuclear force as large as ours," he added for emphasis.[34]

Thus implicitly assured of a permanent hold on Situation A weighted to its own advantage, the United States desisted from further important advances in nuclear strategic capability. Subsequently, with the Soviet Union's persistence in development of strategic nuclear strength at a rate and to a level incompatible with that optimistic premise, the official interpretation here shifted to an assumption no less wishful: to wit, that the Soviet endeavor was only to catch up. With strategic nuclear parity thus achieved between the superpowers, a foundation would be in place for Situation B. It would be necessary then only to document the circumstance in a superpower contract, and thereupon strategic nuclear factors would be neutralized and eliminated from international politics.

That aspiration — it is Wilson's old dream at Versailles and Roosevelt's at Yalta, with a new twist — is the core of the United States' purpose in the strategic arms limitation talks (SALT) under way with the Soviet Union since 1969. It is feasible only to note the asymmetry of purpose between the superpower participants, for the decade of negotiations with their concurrent connections to armament policies pursued by the respective governments cover a course too intricate for recounting here. Mr. Nixon's claims about a transformed future, during the signature stage of the first round at Moscow in 1972, have surely proved hyperbolic. The same fate will probably overtake claims for the product of the second round. What is patent is that the SALT outcome of itself can scarcely fulfill the United States' initial hopes either in codifying a nuclear strategic equilibrium or in neutralizing nuclear strategic power as a factor in international politics. The United States' and the Soviet Union's negotiating aims are simply not complementary. In effect, while the United States has sought terms to ensure a strategic standoff, the Soviet Union's intent has been to ensure terms to facilitate its succession to strategic preeminence.

Soviet reciprocation of the United States' willingness to settle for strategic equilibrium would amount to substantiation of détente — that is to say, a sure sign of a winding down of the cold war on terms upholding the basic purposes of U.S. foreign policy from the outset of the troubled epoch. On the other hand, Soviet perseverance in quest of strategic preeminence — that is, of Situation A weighted to Soviet advantage — would be essentially in keeping with the Soviet Union's preferred version, as heretofore expressed, concerning configurations of power in succession to the cold war.

In international relations, purposes are affected by opportunity. I should not venture to specify what purposes the Soviet leaders, once in irreversible strategic circumstances, might choose to activate. For such a shift in strategic circumstances to make no difference in their conduct would indeed be surprising. They would, I should guess, seek to accomplish many things that strategic constraints have heretofore blocked. A Soviet hierarch's reported words to a visiting United States congressman in the spring of 1978 — perhaps a little prematurely — adumbrate the mood: "The United States has always been in a position where it could not be threatened by foreign powers. That is no longer true. Today the Soviet Union has military superiority over the United States, and henceforth the United States will be threatened. You had better get used to it."[35]

I do not mean to imply that the Soviet Union would gear up for attacking the United States or any other particular target. Soviet goals would, in high probability, be projected as aggregated results to be realized through multiple small incremental modifications — with none to be regarded by a disadvantaged opponent as worth precipitating a showdown involving the risk of war, and perhaps none even susceptible of being made an occasion for challenge. Policymakers in many other capitals would perceive the trend and make adaptations accordingly. Little by little the array of alliances contracted and maintained by the United States would lose cogency and relevance — a process already under way to some extent. National policy would at last be put in the position — to paraphrase Machiavelli — of having kept no friends and lost no enemies.

On the other hand, those determining policy for the United States might be loath to reconcile themselves to the consequences of being put in a strategically disadvantaged position. Their refusal might take the form of holding onto — and acting on the basis of — presumptions of strategic parity no longer evident to others, especially the Soviet Union. Alternatively the United States might find itself constrained at some juncture to stem the momentum of adversity by invoking audacity — deliberately attempting an ostentatious display of willingness to propel issues toward war in a situation of high contention, inciting crisis in expectation of impelling an advantaged opponent to shy away from risks. Such courses would be charged with the dangers of precipitating unintended wars in the pattern previously depicted as Situation C.

In Samuel Huntington's words, "As American hegemony recedes, it seems clear that the United States would feel insecure and would hence *be* insecure if any other power or combination of powers acquired global preeminence comparable to that which the United States is now losing."[36] The central question is how to avoid that configuration of power. The SALT process will not do the job for this country. It can be done only by the United States itself, irrespectively of the SALT outcome. The course will be difficult, for the drift of the times is strongly against any case based on strategic considerations. The foreign policy of the times of unequivocal cold war has substantially lost its constituency — and a considerable reversion to nonstrategic outlooks prevalent in the long past has occurred — both within the government and among the generality of Americans.

I am loath to lay claim to knowing why such indubitably profound changes in national mood have occurred, for lines of causation in such matters are inherently elusive. Misadventures in trying to apply the containment concept in Southeast Asia have surely been an aggravating circumstance. The nexus between means and ends in terms of U.S. national security proved too subtle and complex to command sufficient and enduring public affirmation. The Vietnam War dragged along too long. Successive high-level strategic pronouncements were too consistently unprophetic. The fact of the Soviet Union's existence in the background was surely an essential consideration in precipitating the U.S. interposition in Southeast Asia. Anxiety to avoid magnifying hostilities by drawing in the Communist metropole impelled extreme wariness in prosecuting the intervention. The struggle developed into a contest of attrition — the worst sort for troops. Having precipitated its forces into the conflict, the American society then proceeded to put in doubt the legitimacy of the mission — a demoralizing thing to do to military forces. Huge damage was done to the American military profession, and to the strategic component in American consciousness, by an unwon and disowned war. A war fought under such hobbling necessities probably should not have been undertaken in the first place. Such is the disconsoling lesson to be drawn. The deplorable outcome enters into an accounting of the Soviet impact on the United States, for cold war considerations impelled the intervention and the Soviet Union's existence in the background contributed to its failure.

"We are by all standards, the strongest country in the world, as we have been since the end of World War II," Ray S. Cline has observed. "Yet we have lost our self-confidence and our self-esteem."[37] Walter Laqueur compares the United States to Britain on the eve of World War II: "a country adrift, confused, and misguided, whose people, good-humored and peace-loving, are willing to be pushed around and lied to both at home and on the international scene."[38] Whatever the causes, contemporary phenomena include, as noted by Huntington, "fundamental changes in American culture and opinion in an anti-military direction" coupled with disintegration of "the domestic basis for American foreign policy" and "trends toward demilitarization and withdrawal which now dominate the American scene."[39] Those appraisals of the national mood — all by judicious observers — seem to confirm the late Ambassador Bohlen's glum expectations: "Unhappily, the United States is not ready for the continuous struggle of wills and never-ending diplomatic crises that we face with the Soviet Union. . . . It is therefore pertinent to ask whether the United States is capable of leading the free world. . . . There is doubt that as a people we possess the discipline and patience to prevail."[40] Yet the causes appear not to lie in consciousness of weakness and vulnerability or to be linked to cultural despair. Rather, as Laqueur has observed, the root is a notion, lingering on from the long past, of the country's being "so secure that no outside danger can possibly threaten it."[41]

Notes

1. James Gould Cozzens, *Guard of Honor* (London: Longmans, 1949), p. 572.

2. Denis de Rougemont, *The Meaning of Europe* (New York: Stein and Day, 1968), pp. 103–4.

3. Jean Giradoux, *Tiger at the Gates* (New York: Samuel French, 1956), p. 66.

4. Werner Heisenberg, *The Physicist's Conception of Nature* (New York: Harcourt, Brace, 1958), p. 54.

5. Albert J. Beveridge, *Abraham Lincoln, 1809–1858,* vol. 1 (Boston: Houghton Mifflin, 1928), pp. 227–28.

6. Reinhold Niebuhr, *The Irony of American History* (New York: Scribner's, 1952), p. 4.

7. James Brown Scott, ed., *President Wilson's Foreign Policy: Messages, Addresses, and Papers* (New York: Oxford, 1918), p. 254.

8. Cordell Hull, "Address by the Secretary of State Before Congress Regarding the Moscow Conference," Department of State *Bulletin* 9, no. 230 (18 November 1943), pp. 341, 347.

9. Franklin D. Roosevelt, "Report on the Crimea Conference," Department of State *Bulletin* 12, no. 297 (4 March 1945), p. 361.

10. Robert E. Sherwood, *Roosevelt and Hopkins: An Intimate History* (New York: Harper and Row, 1948), p. 870.

11. W. J. Bate, ed., *Edmund Burke: Selected Works* (New York: Random House, 1960), p. 111.

12. Charles E. Bohlen, *Witness to History, 1929–1969* (New York: Norton, 1973), p. 123.

13. Frances Perkins, *The Roosevelt I Knew* (New York: Viking, 1946), p. 86.

14. Bohlen, *Witness to History,* pp. 140, 146.

15. Perkins, *The Roosevelt I Knew,* pp. 83–85.

16. Ibid., p. 142.

17. Franklin D. Roosevelt, "Address by the President on Christmas Eve," State Department *Bulletin* 10, no. 236 (1 January 1944), pp. 1, 5.

18. William C. Bullitt, "How We Won the War and Lost the Peace," *Life,* 30 August 1948, pp. 83, 92.

19. Perkins, *The Roosevelt I Knew,* p. 382.

20. Herbert Feis, *Churchill-Roosevelt-Stalin: The War They Fought and the Peace They Sought* (Princeton, N.J.: Princeton University Press, 1957), p. 586.

21. David Rees, *The Age of Containment: The Cold War, 1945–1965* (London: Macmillan, 1967), p. 12.

22. Nathan Leites, *The Operational Code of the Politburo* (New York: McGraw-Hill, 1951).

23. Lisle A. Rose, *After Yalta* (New York: Scribner's, 1973), pp. 83–85.

24. John F. Kennedy, untitled review of B. H. Liddell Hart's *Deterrence of Defense,* in *Saturday Review,* 3 September 1960, p. 17.

25. Oswald Spengler, *The Decline of the West,* vol. 2 (New York: Knopf, 1950), p. 474.

26. W. K. Hancock, *Four Studies of War and Peace in This Century* (Cambridge: Cambridge University Press, 1961), pp. 22–23.

27. E. L. Woodward, *Great Britain and the German Navy* (Oxford: Clarendon Press, 1935), p. 17.

28. Rose, *After Yalta,* pp. 86–112, 183.

29. Paul Seabury, *The Rise and Decline of the Cold War* (New York: Basic Books, 1967), p. 38.

30. Ibid., p. 87.

31. The occasions prompting various official or unofficial pronouncements detailing turns for the better in U.S.–Soviet relations:

17 November 1933 — establishment of U.S.–Soviet diplomatic relations and Soviet pledge to desist from propaganda in the U.S.;

5 December 1936 — promulgation of a "democratic" Soviet constitution with a secret ballot and guaranteed civic rights;

1 October 1941 — first protocol on U.S. aid to the Soviet Union;

1 January 1942 — formalizing of anti-Axis coalition and formal Soviet endorsement of the Atlantic Charter;

11 January 1942 — signing of Master Lend-Lease Agreement;

6 May 1943 — Stalin's declaration anticipating friendly postwar relations with a free, independent Poland;

23 May 1943 — formal dissolution of the Third International nominally ending Soviet domination of world communist movement;

19 October–1 November 1943 — the Moscow conference of foreign ministers and agreement to perpetuate the anti-Axis coalition as the core of postwar organization to maintain world peace;

28 November–1 December 1943 — the Teheran summit conference;

21 August–27 September 1944 — the Dumbarton Oaks Conference on structure of postwar world organization;

7–12 February 1945 — the Yalta summit conference;

30 April–6 June 1945 — the San Francisco Conference, with the U.S. and the Soviet united in acceptance of UN Charter;

17 July–2 August 1945 — the Potsdam summit conference;

8 August 1945 — Soviet entry into war against Japan;

29 July–14 October 1946 — the Paris conference on peace terms for Italy, Rumania, Hungary, Bulgaria, and Finland;

12 May 1949 — lifting of the first Berlin blockade;

5 March 1953 — death of Stalin;

26 July 1953 — the Korean armistice;

12 May 1944 — the Austrian State Treaty;

18–23 July 1955 — the Big Four summit conference in Geneva;

4 December 1955 — the U.S.–Soviet package deal for admission of 16 new member states to the UN General Assembly;

25–27 September 1959—the Eisenhower-Khrushchev summit conference at Camp David;

3–4 June 1961—the Kennedy-Khrushchev summit conference at Vienna;

14 March 1962—opening of 17-nation Disarmament Conference under U.S.-Soviet joint chairmanship;

28 October 1962—resolution of the Cuban missile crisis;

20 June 1963—establishment of Washington-Moscow "hot line";

23 July 1963—accord on neutralization of Laos;

5 August 1963—the limited test-ban treaty;

16 March 1967—U.S.-Soviet consular agreement;

23–25 June 1967—Johnson-Kosygin summit conference at Glassboro;

1 July 1968—the nuclear nonproliferation treaty;

17 November 1969—opening of SALT I;

12 August 1970—"normalization" treaty between West Germany and Soviet Union;

22–30 May 1972—the first Nixon-Brezhnev summit conference at Moscow;

17–25 June 1973—the second Nixon-Brezhnev summit conference at Washington;

27 June–3 July 1974—the third Nixon-Brezhnev conference at Moscow;

23–24 November 1974—the Ford-Brezhnev summit conference at Vladivostock;

30 July–1 August 1975—the conference at Helsinki on normalization in Europe;

18 June 1979—signing of SALT II at Vienna.

32. Richard Nixon, "The Moscow Summit and New Opportunities in U.S.-Soviet Relations," Department of State *Bulletin* 66, no. 1722 (26 June 1972), pp. 855–59. For pertinent treaties and agreements in the first Nixon-Brezhnev summit—covering limitation of offensive and defensive strategic nuclear weapons and cooperation in environmental protection, medical science and public health, space exploration, science and technology, and safety at sea—see ibid., pp. 918–27. For additional treaties and agreements incident to the second Nixon-Khrushchev summit conferences—covering principles for strategic negotiations and prevention of nuclear war; cooperation in peaceful uses of atomic energy, agriculture, ocean studies, transportation, cultural exchanges, and aviation safety; problems of overlapping taxation, the establishment of a joint chamber of commerce, and provision of commercial facilities—see ibid., 69, no. 1778 (23 July 1970), pp. 158–73. For treaties and agreements incident to the third Nixon-Brezhnev summit—covering further limitations of defensive strategic nuclear weapons and underground nuclear tests; economic, industrial, and technical cooperation, and cooperation in energy, housing, and heart research—see ibid., 71, no. 1831 (29 July 1972), pp. 213–23.

33. Foy D. Kohler, "Peaceful Coexistence as Currently Seen from Moscow: An Overview," manuscript report prepared for the Center for Advanced International Studies, University of Miami, Coral Gables, Florida, 1972, pp. 2–2a; quoted with author's permission.

34. "Is Russia Slowing Down the Arms Race? An Interview with Secretary of Defense Robert S. McNamara," *U.S. News and World Report* 58 (12 April 1965), pp. 52–56.

35. Marshal of the Soviet Union, First Deputy Minister of Defense N. V. Ogankov to Representative John Breckenridge, quoted in "Soviet Defense Leader

Says USSR Has Military Superiority," *Defense-Space Business Daily*, 27 April 1978, p. 329.

36. Samuel P. Huntington, "After Containment: The Function of the Military Establishment," *The Annals of the American Academy of Political and Social Science* 406 (March 1973), pp. 1,4.

37. Ray S. Cline, "A New Grand Strategy for the United States," *Comparative Strategy* 1, nos. 1–2 (October 1978), p. 2.

38. Walter S. Laqueur, "The Psychology of Appeasement," *Commentary* 66, no. 4 (October 1978), p. 49.

39. Huntington, "After Containment."

40. Bohlen, *Witness to History*, p. 540.

41. Laquer, "The Psychology of Appeasement."

Part 3
The Role of Soviet Armed Forces

12

Soviet Military Strategy and Force Levels

Robert L. Pfaltzgraff, Jr.

In no other major state do military factors occupy so prominent a position, relative to the other ingredients of statecraft, as in the Soviet Union in the late twentieth century. In nearly all indicators of power, except military, the Soviet Union lags substantially behind the United States and its principal allies, notably Western Europe and Japan. It is not communist ideology per se, but instead the possession of a strategy[1] for the maximization of available capabilities—sometimes against a militarily superior adversary—that has contributed decisively to the growth in influence the Soviet Union has experienced since the end of World War II. The capacity of Moscow to exercise control has coincided, as in the East-West divisions in Europe, either with the territories occupied by the Red Army or with the establishment of the Soviet Union as a principal arms supplier to a country, as in the case of Egypt until the early 1970s, or the equipping and backing by Moscow of proxy forces—as in the case of North Vietnam and the Viet Cong, or the Cubans fighting in support of Soviet objectives in Africa.

An analysis of Soviet military strategy and capabilities is fraught with many problems. There exists an abundant Soviet literature on military strategy, but not on Soviet force levels. The purpose of Soviet strategic literature is the education of the political-military elites of the Soviet Union, rather than the dissemination of ideas to a mass audience, either in the Soviet Union or abroad.[2] Soviet military literature thus serves a fundamentally different purpose in the Soviet Union than military literature does in the United States. In sharp contrast to the Soviet Union, the American strategic affairs community consists, in large part, of civilian analysts who have no direct relationship to the U.S. government. Thus it is pluralistic to an extent impossible in the Soviet Union, although there are said to have been occasional debates[3] in the "closed" Soviet system on matters of military policy, which are reflected in the literature published for limited, selective distribution in the Soviet Union. Furthermore, Soviet writings on military strategy can be compared to Soviet R&D and to actual weapons deployments for whatever insights they may produce. But knowledge about Soviet capabilities, dependent as it is upon Western intelligence sources, does not yield precise conclusions about the intentions of the Soviet Union. Taken together, military doctrine and force levels can narrow the gap in uncertainty about this important dimension of Soviet policy.

The Soviet view of military doctrine, and of military capabilities, differs greatly from that prevalent in the United States and the Western world in many ways. For example, there is no evidence that the Soviet political leadership, in sharp contrast to a substantial portion of Western thought, views military power as having little or no military or political utility. Instead, the Soviet Union has been engaged in a vast armaments effort. Although there is controversy among Western strategic military analysts, moreover, as to *how* sharp a divergence separates the strategic-military thought of the Soviet Union from that prevalent in the United States, there was widespread agreement, especially by the late 1970s, that the differences are of major proportions. To be sure, the Soviet leadership, by the late 1960s, when the Strategic Arms Limitation Talks (SALT) were initiated, may have concluded that an essentially stable strategic military balance then existed. If there was a form of "mutual deterrence," the Soviet Union saw the need, nevertheless, to make continuing military efforts perhaps, as at least one writer has suggested,[4] to attain at a level comparable to the United States.

Such a view accords with the notion prevalent in the 1960s that the Soviet Union, however much it differed from the United States in conceptions of military doctrine, would embrace, later if not sooner, such ideas as mutual assured destruction. As Fritz W. Ermarth has suggested: "We understood the problem of keeping the strategic peace on equitable and economical terms — or so we thought. As reasonable men, the Soviets, too, would come to understand it our way."[5]

American conceptions of strategy have often been based upon a quest for technical solutions to problems that, like the weapons systems themselves, are considered to be primarily scientific in nature. Hence the solutions, like science itself, supposedly have transnational applicability — to the Soviet Union as well as the United States. But strategy in the Soviet conception is, first and foremost, a political concept related, as Soviet writers have emphasized repeatedly, not to the natural sciences but to an unfolding reality interpreted in Marxian dialectical terms and grounded in the political objectives of the state. Hence, for the Soviet Union to embrace technical solutions to problems of strategy and arms, including arms control, would conflict with the essence of strategy itself, which from the Soviet perspective, to paraphrase Marshal Grechko, must always be designed in support of state policies.

In the United States, moreover, the rationale for mutual assured destruction strategy, and for its eventual acceptance, it was hoped, by the Soviet Union, was based on the view of strategic-nuclear forces stated by Secretary of Defense McNamara in the 1960s, namely, that their "only realistic role is deterrence of all-out nuclear or non-nuclear attacks since it is now impossible for either the United States or the Soviet Union to achieve a meaningful victory over the other in a strategic-nuclear exchange."[6]

Not only have Soviet strategists consistently failed to be "educated" by their Western counterparts, but they have repeatedly rejected, for their own purposes, both in word and deed, the doctrinal statements and force planning assumptions of the United States that it was hoped they would eventually embrace. Soviet military writers hold that nuclear weapons represent a change in warfare as fundamentally important as the introduction of gun powder. Hence traditional concepts and assumptions about the conduct of war must be revised. In the Soviet view, nuclear weapons are to be used in engagements where interests deemed vital to the Soviet Union are at stake. Therefore, Soviet forces on the long frontier with China and in the Warsaw Pact are equipped, and receive extensive training, to operate on a nuclear battlefield.[7] Soviet strategists reject the Western notion, prevalent especially in the McNamara era in the U.S. Department of Defense, that there would necessarily be a conventional phase in a major conflict before escalation to the nuclear level—the assumption contained in NATO flexible response strategy. Not only do Soviet and American strategic conceptions differ in this important respect, but also in the notion that a condition of strategic nuclear parity is stabilizing, as articulated by McNamara in the 1960s. Instead, the military programs of the Soviet Union since the 1960s have exceeded the expectations of a large number of Western defense planners. In fact, an analysis of the respective levels of the U.S. and Soviet military effort reveals a continued underestimation of the magnitude of the Soviet arms buildup, especially during the 1960s and early 1970s.[8]

The purpose of Soviet military strategy and force levels is apparent: it is to support a foreign policy that, in progressive stages since World War II, has become global in scope. Soviet military power is to provide the cutting edge of Soviet diplomacy. In the Soviet conception, military power casts before it a political shadow. The military capabilities available to the Soviet Union are not necessarily even to be used *militarily* in support of Moscow's objectives; they will have served Soviet interests well if they can induce opponents to take policy positions in accord with Soviet interests.

The late Marshal Sokolovskiy set forth in succinct form the relationship between strategic forces and political objectives. He stated the tenet, central to Soviet doctrine, that nuclear weapons constitute the most important capability in affecting the outcome of warfare and shaping modern military strategy for political purposes:

> Modern strategic means of armed conflict . . . are located in direct subordination to the high commands, and make it possible to achieve decisive results in gaining victory in war, often without utilizing the forces and means of the tactical and operational element . . . Thus, strategy, which in the past was nourished by the achievements of tactics and operational art, now is given the possibility to attain, by its own independent means, the war aims regardless of the outcome of battles and operations in the various areas of armed conflict.[9]

Soviet strategy is based on the principle enunciated by Clausewitz that warfare is always an extension of politics — that it is subordinated to the political objectives and the foreign policy interests in a "grand strategy" established by the Politburo. Military power is part of a political arsenal that includes a variety of nonmilitary capabilities as well.[10] According to Marshal Sokolovskiy: "The acceptance of war as a tool of politics also determines the interrelation of military strategy and politics, which is based on the principle of the full dependence of the former on the latter."[11]

In keeping with the injunctions of Clausewitz, whose writings deeply influenced Lenin, the greatest utility of military power inheres in its relationship to the other components of statecraft and, specifically, in the ability of its possessor to achieve his objectives without actual resort to force. This idea has been central to the strategic thought of Lenin and his successors. It accorded with a "correlation of forces" that for much of its history did not favor the Soviet Union. As the inferior party in a power relationship, the Soviet Union had to maximize whatever political leverage existed in limited military power, and by means of the possession of a superior *strategy,* to prevent an adversary from effectively using its superior capabilities. A recognition of this problem suffuses the writings of such theorists and practitioners of revolutionary warfare as Mao Tse-tung and Che Guevara. Therefore, it would be unusual indeed if the Soviet leadership did not postulate, and appreciate in ample measure, the relationship between military strategy and capabilities — between military power and political objectives. Thus it is possible to conclude that military power itself, in the Marxist-Leninist conception, "is not and should not be the driving element in world politics."[12] Instead, military *power* related to military *strategy* is a crucially important element not only in accelerating the inevitable forces of history, but also in holding in check military capabilities such as those of the United States, which might otherwise be tempted to utilize military force to thwart the unfolding course of history.

Soviet military strategy and capabilities are designed to underwrite a global political conception in which noncommunist industrialized states are weakened relative to the Soviet Union by the gradual loss of positions of influence and power, particularly in the Third World, and by the detachment of allies on the rimlands of Eurasia, especially European NATO members and Japan, from their close ties with the United States. The relationship between Finland and the Soviet Union has been cited by at least one Soviet analyst as providing an appropriate model for relationships between Moscow and West European states. Hence the Soviet interest in the dismantling of NATO and the gradual disengagement of American power from an increasingly neutralized Western Europe. Hence also Soviet support for "wars of national liberation" and for "progressive states engaged in the anti-imperialist struggle" in Third World states and even where feasible Moscow's encouragement of "revolutionary and progressive forces" within capitalist states themselves. Again, the Soviet conception of military power is related inextricably to a view of history — in the case of the Third World, a progression of revolutionary forces working against the West and to Moscow's favor, in which military power can be usefully employed to accelerate change that is held to be inevitable.

The sustained growth of military power is designed to permit the Soviet Union, first and foremost, to protect the Soviet homeland from attack and then to provide the basis for hastening the weakening of the West both in the Third World and on the rimlands of the vast Eurasian land mass. The Soviet Union, as the leading land power of Eurasia, stands juxtaposed to the United States as the leading maritime state. As Colin Gray has suggested: "Soviet foreign policy may usefully be characterized in terms of a maximum-minimum principle, namely to seek the maximum gains with minimum risks. Geopolitically, Soviet leaders probably believe that time is on their side; the Soviet Heartland power is permanently a Eurasian power, while the United States . . . may come to forget that the Eurasian rimlands are forever the American security dike."[13] Vast Soviet land forces are deployed principally against Western Europe, as discussed later in this chapter, and along the 5,000-mile frontier with China.

The emergence of the Soviet Union as a leading maritime power second only to the United States ranks as an achievement of major proportions for Moscow over the past generation. Since the United States is linked to its allies on the periphery of Eurasia by maritime routes and the airspace over them, the capacity of the Soviet Union to interpose military capabilities marks, for the Soviet Union, an advance of historic significance. Once again, this extension of Soviet influence into regions from which Russia historically was excluded and far from the Eurasian land mass itself, has been, and is being, achieved largely be means of military power, especially in this case naval deployments, but also as a result of the ability manifested increasingly by the Soviet Union to ship amounts of arms and to use proxy forces such as the Cubans in support of Soviet interests, notably in the Horn of Africa and in southern Africa.

Deterrence and Defense: The Soviet Conception

In the Soviet conception, war with capitalist states has been transformed from the inevitable prospect postulated during Lenin's time and until nearly the end of Stalin's rule to, in the late twentieth century, a possibility if capitalist states choose to resist the tide of events running in favor of the Soviet Union. Against this contingency the Soviet Union must be prepared in its military planning. Hence, one of the purposes of Soviet strategic-nuclear power is to deter an attack that might be mounted by the United States, lashing out against the Soviet Union in a last-ditch effort to forestall the inevitable triumph of communism—a theme of considerable prominence in Soviet military literature. In this sense, the Soviet Union has always had in its strategic-military doctrine an element of deterrence, first against a superior noncommunist world and more recently against adversaries, principally the United States (whose military power allegedly is declining relative to the Soviet Union). A central component of this aspect of Soviet military doctrine has been the development of a capability to defend against a U.S. attack by means of air defenses and a civil defense program of considerable magnitude and scope.

Especially when viewed in this context, deterrence occupies a position fundamentally different in the Soviet conception, as contrasted to U.S. strategic thought. As John Erickson has pointed out, in Soviet literature the term *oborona* (defense) is used to convey "deterrence," a distinction that reflects the deep substantive, rather than merely semantic, differences between Western and Soviet strategic-military concepts.[14]

In the United States, as Erickson notes, the terms "deterrence" and "defense" have been viewed as somehow separate phenomena. What has been deemed to be adequate for deterrence would not necessarily suffice for defense. If war is unthinkable, it is sufficient to deter, or prevent, its outbreak. What may be deemed adequate to deter the onset of war would not necessarily be sufficient to fight a war to a successful conclusion. But if war is unthinkable, as postulated often in the United States and Western Europe, a deterrence, rather than a war-waging and war-winning capability, will be considered to be adequate. In contrast, the Soviet logic holds that the possession of a war-waging, war-winning capability is the necessary prerequisite to the deterrence of an adversary. What it takes to prevail in war is what is necessary for the exercise of deterrence. In the Soviet conception, therefore, deterrence and defense are, for all practical purposes, one and the same.

The Soviet commitment to defense as integral to deterrence connotes a willingness to consider the possibility of nuclear warfare and to eschew the notion that nuclear warfare is unthinkable — an assumption central to much of Western thought, especially the concept of "mutual assured destruction." If nuclear war is "thinkable," it must be viewed in terms of its winnability, and thus the capacity of one or the other combatant to survive. For this reason, Soviet writings usually reject the idea of mutuality in assessing the destructive potential inherent in nuclear warfare or suggest, in effect, that mutuality of destruction should be superseded by a condition in which the Soviet Union is better able than the United States to withstand the effects of a nuclear war. In the event of a nuclear conflict, Soviet forces must be configured in such a way as to ensure the survival and, indeed, the ultimate victory of the Soviet Union. The objective postulated in Soviet military writings is not the deterrence of *both* sides, but rather the deterrence of the United States, and in the event of war the victory of the Soviet Union. Moreover, the Soviet Union seeks to deter the escalation of warfare from a regional conflict, as in Europe, to a nuclear exchange between the Soviet Union and the United States. Here again, Soviet military doctrine differs substantially from that of the United States, which has stressed the likelihood of escalation from the European battlefield to the superpower strategic-nuclear level. The United States has emphasized the link between our strategic-nuclear force, in keeping with its conception of deterrence, and the likelihood of escalation in Europe, while the Soviet Union has sought to decouple the U.S. strategic-nuclear force from European security, a theme considered in greater detail in a later section of this chapter.

The idea that has been central to much of Western strategic thought, especially mutual assured destruction — that each side is somehow more secure the more vulnerable it becomes (especially its urban-industrial centers) to a nuclear attack — finds no place in Soviet thought. For the Soviet Union it is essential, first and foremost, to deter an attack by the United States against the Soviet homeland. Hence a strategic posture that enhances the vulnerability of the Soviet Union to such an attack would be unacceptable. Soviet strategic-military literature rejects the notion that Soviet cities should be held hostage as postulated in a mutual assured destruction strategy. Therefore, as noted elsewhere in this chapter, the Soviet Union attaches considerable importance to active and passive defenses, and specifically to air defense and to civil defense.

Soviet military doctrine differs fundamentally from Western conceptions in its emphasis upon the dynamic nature of military capabilities and in the changing correlation between opposing forces and the ensuing implications for the political-diplomatic positions of the possessors of weapons. If history consists of an unfolding series of dialectical relationships in which conflict is an inherent element, it follows that conflict can, and often does, serve a constructive purpose in leading history from one stage to a higher stage in accordance with the Marxian dialectical view of history. The dynamic nature of power relationships is linked inextricably to the role of power, and specifically military power, in accelerating the trends toward a new, and higher, stage in history—even though Lenin cautioned repeatedly against the use of military power in any way that would endanger the longer-term prospects of the Communist party and, in 1918, concluded the Treaty of Brest-Litovsk with Germany on terms territorially disadvantageous to the Soviet Union. Caution, and even tactical retreat, were deemed necessary on occasion to safeguard broader strategic purposes.

This concept is central to Lenin's thought on the relationship between the Communist party as the vanguard of the proletariat and the necessity to mobilize power—to organize—for the achievement of the historical advances inherent in the Marxian dialectic. On a worldwide scale, Soviet military power allegedly serves a similar purpose in accelerating those forces making for change that is deemed to be constructive for the Soviet Union, but in a way that minimizes the direct risk to the Soviet Union itself, especially in those periods when the Soviet Union was demonstrably inferior to the West.

It follows, therefore, that the conception of strategic-military stability so widely held in the West is largely alien to the Soviet Union. Strategic-military stability is consistent with a status quo conception of world politics. From the Soviet perspective, détente viewed in the West as a form of strategic-military-political stability cannot be regarded as a permanent condition, but only as a temporary stage reflecting a particular "correlation of forces," subject to change as Soviet military power grows relative to its adversaries. If détente in the West is a process containing a series of confidence-building measures conducive to stability, in the Soviet view it is a process whereby the Soviet Union is enabled to strengthen its position and thereby to hasten those forces making for change. Similarly, it follows that the side that is committed to change, in contrast to a belief in the efficacy of the status quo, is likely to hold a sharply different view of the nature, the attainability, and the meaning of strategic superiority. This contrasts sharply with the notion expressed by Robert McNamara in the 1960s and widely accepted in the United States even in the late 1970s: "Unlike any other era in military history, a substantial numerical superiority of weapons today does not effectively translate into political control or diplomatic leverage. While thermonuclear power is almost inconceivably awesome and represents virtually unlimited potential destructiveness, it has proven to be a limited diplomatic instrument."[15] In the Western conception, moreover, strategic superiority is potentially destabilizing and hence undesirable — if not meaningless and perhaps even unattainable — because allegedly it leads the opponent to engage in an arms race designed to catch up, resulting in the so-called "action-reaction" syndrome in armaments competition. From the U.S. perspective of the 1960s, once the Soviet Union had reached a condition described as strategic parity with the United States, strategic stability would supposedly ensue, since the Soviet Union would have less reason to fear the possibility of an attack by the United States. Such a conception, however logically consistent with a commitment to a strategic-military status quo, is at odds with a view of military power as the indispensable ingredient in a diplomacy designed to achieve change — to give impetus to the revolutionary forces that allegedly abound, from a Marxist-Leninist prespective, in the world of the late twentieth century. A commitment to the exploitation of such forces in which military power plays a central role leads almost inevitably to the conclusion that a form of military superiority is not only desirable but even indispensable to the unsuccessful pursuit of foreign policy objectives.

If nuclear war is both thinkable and winnable, as Soviet literature maintains, Soviet strategy must contain concepts and provide for force levels designed to maximize for the Soviet Union the element of surprise. This concept is linked directly to the idea, stated explicitly in Soviet literature, that nuclear weapons will be employed as required by the dictates of battle, rather than in behest of abstract principles of "deterrence." In the Soviet view, the use of nuclear weapons in the initial stages of battle will facilitate surprise. Thus the advent of nuclear weapons has not altered the objective postulated in Soviet military doctrine: namely, to destroy an enemy's potential for the conduct of warfare. Instead, nuclear weapons are perceived as making possible the achievement of this objective without prior tactical or operational measures and warning. Thus nuclear weapons provide a potentially decisive means to influence the outcome of conflict. Similar doctrinal importance is attached to other means of mass destruction, notably chemical weapons, discussed later in this chapter.

The idea of surprise contained in Soviet doctrine applies at both the strategic-nuclear level and on the battlefield. As noted in the analysis of Soviet–Warsaw Pact doctrine later in this chapter, in the former case, Soviet literature contains essentially two scenarios: in the first, the Soviet Union preempts a U.S. first strike; in the second, the Soviet Union launches a first-strike attack against the United States. Both scenarios contain surprise as a decisive element. In both, the Soviet Union makes use of counterforce capabilities to destroy as much of the U.S. retaliatory forces as possible, especially the fixed, land-based component, as well as heavy bombers on the ground and nuclear submarines in port at the time of attack. In both scenarios, the Soviet Union anticipates that it would have to defend against an attack by surviving elements of U.S. strategic forces. The effect of this attack by surviving elements of U.S. strategic forces, Soviet writers postulate, can be reduced in magnitude by active and passive defensive measures. Some analysts have suggested that the possession by the Soviet Union of a counterforce capability that could destroy all or even a large part of the fixed, land-based component of U.S. strategic forces would give to Moscow potentially important political leverage in the event of a future crisis situation between the superpowers. Under such circumstances the United States, in response, could threaten to attack Soviet cities with its residual forces, notably the SSBNs on board the nuclear-powered submarines, including the Trident I scheduled for deployment in the early 1980s.

None of these systems possesses sufficient accuracy or throwweight to pose a threat to certain important categories of hardened Soviet targets. To destroy targets in the Soviet Union that have been hardened on the order of several hundred pounds of overpressure per square inch (psi), U.S. SLBMs would have to contain accuracies and/or yields far greater than those possessed by existing generation systems, including the Trident C-4 SLBM. After a U.S. second-strike, therefore, the Soviet Union would possess a residual capability for the destruction of remaining targets in the United States. The fear has been expressed that the mere contemplation of such a scenario, together with the cost-exchange ratios disadvantageous to the United States, might give the upper hand to the Soviet Union in crisis diplomacy. It might reduce the options available to the United States to the stark alternative of (1) a strategic nuclear strike with the knowledge that the Soviet Union could respond with superior residual forces, or (2) acquiescence by the United States to Soviet demands as a means of terminating a crisis on Moscow's terms without necessarily firing a shot.

The differences between U.S. and Soviet doctrine are also reflected in their respective strategic force configurations. The United States has maintained its fixed, land-based strategic missile arsenal at the level of 1054 since 1967 in the belief that such a force, together with the other components of the triad—strategic bombers and submarines with nuclear missiles (SSBNs)—would be adequate to preserve a deterrent relationship with the Soviet Union. In contrast, the Soviet Union has mounted an effort to develop, test, and deploy a series of new strategic systems far beyond the needs of deterrence postulated in U.S. doctrine. In 1975 the Soviet Union began deployment of the SS-17, SS-18, and SS-19, all of which possess far greater throwweight than the U.S. Minuteman. The greater throwweight potential of Soviet missiles gives the Soviet Union a capacity to deploy more or heavier warheads on a single MIRVed missile. The prospect of a Soviet counterforce capability—that could destroy all or a major portion of the fixed, land-based strategic force of the United States—looms as a possibility in the early 1980s as a result of superior throwweight combined with substantial anticipated improvements in the accuracy of Soviet delivery systems.[16]

Apprehension about a Soviet counterforce potential against the U.S. fixed, land-based strategic force has arisen from a projection or respective U.S. and Soviet strategic posture during the 1980s. With or without a SALT II treaty, the Soviet Union could deploy at least 300 SS-18s and about 500 SS-19s and SS-17s. The SS-18 has a payload of about 16,000 pounds, while the SS-17 and SS-19, respectively have payloads of 7,000 and 8,000 pounds. These missiles can be contrasted to the most advanced in the U.S. inventory, the Minuteman III, whose payload does not exceed 2,200 pounds. The Minuteman III carries three MIRVed warheads. A total of 550 Minuteman IIIs have been deployed, with no additional such deployments planned by the United States. Thus the United States will continue, during much of the 1980s at least, to have a total deployment of MIRVed ICBM warheads of 1,650—three times the number of Minuteman III missiles (550) deployed. A change in this situation must await the deployment by the United States of a follow-on missile well after 1985. The so-called M-X (Missile-Experimental) could not be deployed until the late 1980s, even if agreement could be reached on the controversial issue of deployment mode. Similarly, the deployment of technologies with major new accuracy improvements, the Advanced Inertial Reference System (AIRS), could probably not take place until after 1985. In contrast, the Soviet Union by the mid-1980s could have available an aggregate throwweight in its MIRVed ICBM force as great as 13,000,000 pounds, in contrast to about 3,000,000 pounds for the United States. In numbers of ICBM warheads, the Soviet Union could have as many as 9,200, while the United States figure will probably not exceed 2,150.

A second major focal point of the Soviet strategic-nuclear buildup has been SLBMs. By 1979, the Soviet Union had deployed as many as 250 of the SS-N-8 SLBM with a range between 4,200 and 5,600 nautical miles aboard nuclear submarines. First tested shortly after the signing of the SALT I Interim Agreement in 1972, this missile is comparable in range to the U.S. Trident II that will not begin to be deployed in the U.S. weapons inventory until the late 1980s. In 1978, the Soviet Union tested a new class submarine, the Typhoon. This submarine, which can carry between 20-24 SLBMs, is clearly comparable to the U.S. Trident class.

In addition to its formidable land-based MIRVed force, the Soviet Union possesses two MIRV-capable SLBMs. These include the SS-NX-17 and the SS-NX-18, the latter of which is being deployed on Delta III submarines. Thus, by the early 1980s, the Soviet Union will enjoy a quantitative edge in nuclear missile submarines, as permitted originally in the SALT I Interim Agreement, together with substantial qualitative gains relative to the United States. In some areas, notably warhead range and MIRV, the Soviet SLBM force will have a considerable advantage over the United States.

In the third element of the triad of strategic forces, the heavy bomber, the United States has been without equal. By 1979 the United States had about 300 operational strategic bombers, contrasted to 135 for the Soviet Union. However, the Soviet Union has at least 1000 bombers designed specifically for missions against targets in Western Europe, China, and Japan. Such systems could be used against the United States if they refueled during these missions. The Backfire, one of the controversial problems of SALT II, is being added to the Soviet bomber inventory. The Backfire is a supersonic aircraft with a range, in one version, as great as 6,000 miles. Although it may be designed principally for use against targets in Western Europe, China, and Japan, the Backfire could strike the United States and, with aerial refueling, for which the Backfire B version is equipped, it could even fly two-way missions without landing in a third country. The growing Soviet emphasis on the bomber leg of a triad of forces contrasts with the U.S. cancellation of the B-1 and the continued reliance by the United States upon its aging B-52 force, some of which will be equipped with cruise missiles.[17]

The question of the efficacy of the heavy bomber in the strategic arsenals of the superpowers is related to the role accorded to air defense. After the ratification of the ABM Treaty in 1972, the United States dismantled for the most part its continental air defense system. Thus the United States, by the late 1970s, maintained no surface-to-air missile (SAM) defenses, and had only a small force of six squadrons of F-106 interceptors whose missions are to patrol U.S. air space under peacetime conditions. The downgrading of such a capability accords with the U.S. conception of mutual assured destruction but, as in many other aspects of strategic doctrine and force planning, it diverges sharply from the Soviet Union. Air defenses are deemed to be important in the Soviet view: at least 12,000 surface-to-air missile launchers and nearly 3,000 interceptor aircraft are deployed in the Soviet Union, and considerable emphasis is placed on the modernization of air defenses.

Similarly, the Soviet interest in civil defense as a central element of strategy represents an asymmetry of fundamental proportions with respect to the United States, and specifically a strategic concept based on mutual assured destruction. If the Soviet Union anticipates a potential U.S. retaliatory strike in response to a Soviet attack against the fixed, land-based component of the American strategic force, it follows that Soviet defensive efforts must be directed against such a contingency. In civil defense, the Soviet Union appears to emphasize the protection of those individuals, institutions, and industries deemed most important to ensure the survival of the Soviet state and the communist political and economic system. Soviet literature on civil defense suggests that its goals include: "protecting the population from weapons of mass destruction; preparing national economic installations for work stability under conditions of enemy attack; and conducting urgent rescue and emergency restoration operations at sites of destruction."[18] This literature sets forth, in explicit form, the procedures to be used as well as the preparations and training considered essential to its effectiveness and the organizational structure for Soviet civil defense.

According to Leon Goure, civil defense has been steadily increasing since the mid-1950s as a component of the Soviet program for war survival. It has gained in importance especially since 1961, when it was placed within the Soviet Ministry of Defense. In Goure's view, the civil defense organization includes tens of millions of people. It provides for pre-attack urban evacuation and population dispersal, shelters and fallout cover, the location of a large number of new industrial plants in small towns, the dispersal and hardening of critically important industrial infrastructure, the duplication of sources of energy and critical production facilities, the stockpiling of food, spare parts, fuel, and raw materials, and the organization of production so as to increase regional and local post-attack self-sufficiency.[19]

There has long been a debate within the U.S. strategic affairs community focused not so much on the existence of a Soviet defensive effort, but instead on its scope, magnitude, and effectiveness. Those who stress the importance attached by the Soviet Union to civil defense point to the 1976 appointment of General A. A. Altunin, head of the civil defense program, to the Central Committee of the Communist party of the Soviet Union, a move that has been regarded as an important indicator of the increased priority attached to civil defense in the Soviet Union. Those who minimize its importance have emphasized the problems that supposedly would confront the Soviet Union in undertaking a vast civil defense effort, including those related to ensuring their survival in a post-attack nuclear environment, or under conditions in which several nuclear exchanges had taken place. The evacuation of Soviet cities would give warning time to the United States, since presumably such action could not be undertaken clandestinely. In response to such contentions, the ability of the Soviet Union to demonstrate resolve in a crisis situation by evacuating some or all of its cities, if the United States possessed no comparable capability as part of a civil defense program, might affect the outcome of crisis bargaining even without the actual use of nuclear weapons.

Closely related to civil defense is the Soviet conception of active defense.[20] This includes existing generation capabilities as well as new technologies (the so-called beam weapons discussed later in this chapter) that might become available within the next 10–20 years and perhaps even sooner, although there has been considerable controversy in the U.S. scientific and strategic-military communities about their feasibility and the timeframe in which, if they are technologically possible, they might be deployed. Fundamental to a discussion of strategic defense is an understanding of defense priorities as seen by the Soviet Union. What types of potential targets in the Soviet Union are deemed most important by the Soviet leadership? In Soviet literature, a distinction has been drawn between two separate categories of defense protection priorities: (1) war-fighting and war-winning assets; and (2) the post-attack recovery base. The specific strategic defense priorities, in some cases, are included in both categories because of their importance in both. The Soviet literature identifies as priority-protection military targets those forces that are deemed necessary for: (1) war-fighting; (2) leadership and command, control, and communications assets; and (3) transportation networks and forms of energy needed to sustain the war effort, including defense-related industries. In addition, Soviet military writings stress the protection of those military units essential for internal security in wartime both in the Soviet Union itself and in other territories under Soviet control.

In the second category — post-attack recovery — the Soviet Union emphasizes protection of reserve stockpiles, including raw materials and foodstuffs, and mineral resources and processing facilities for raw materials (for example, the electrometallurgical complex and mining works near Kursk in the Ukraine). Among the economic capabilities and installations of importance to the Soviet Union for post-attack recovery are electrical power generation, steel production, petroleum, motor vehicles, chemicals and fertilizers, machine tools and cement, and important junctions of roads and railways, as well as airports and communication facilities and nodal points. Governmental and military control constitute target protection priorities for the Soviet Union.

It follows that the number of target protection priorities that could be met is a function of the level of technological sophistication of Soviet defensive capabilities. As of the early 1970s the United States maintained an impressive lead over the Soviet Union in ABM technologies. This is said to have accounted in large part for the Soviet interest in the ABM treaty signed in May 1972 as part of the SALT I. In according the United States the option to protect one ICBM site and granting the Soviet Union the protection of one urban complex, the ABM Treaty symbolized the difference discussed earlier between their respective strategic doctrines. The United States could protect an ICBM site against a Soviet first strike and the Soviet Union could gain the potential for protection against a U.S. retaliatory counter-city attack.

There is general consensus in the strategic-military affairs community that, compared to the United States, the Soviet Union attaches greater importance, both in doctrine and in practice, to active defense. This is evident in the substantial allocations of resources to the air defense forces (PVO Strany). The question that is unresolved is related to the current level of Soviet R&D effort and the potential for the rapid deployment of an ABM capability from technologies now under development. This includes the possibility that the Soviet Union could upgrade the SA-5—a fixed-site, surface-to-air missile system that is effective to about 100,000 feet—to an ABM system. The SA-5 could be improved to counter older U.S. reentry systems such as the Polaris, but would not be effective against the Poseidon or Minuteman reentry systems. However, the so-called Soviet ABM-X-3 has been tested with an interceptor of the U.S. Sprint class. This could give the Soviet Union a capability against all U.S. reentry systems now deployed or contemplated, with the exception of MARV, for which the United States now has no deployment plans. It has been suggested, moreover, that the Soviet Union may be developing another long-range exospheric interceptor equipped with an infrared homing sensor system. Such an interceptor, together with the ABM-X-3, could provide the Soviet Union with an in-depth ABM using two different sensor systems. Last but not least, the Soviet Union has become concerned with the problem of defense against the U.S. cruise missile. For this purpose, the Soviet Union is testing a new SA-10, which is a high-speed missile using continuous wave radars scheduled for deployment in the 1980s. Its potential effectiveness against cruise missiles is uncertain.

Since the mid-1970s there has been increasing evidence that the Soviet Union is engaged in the development of laser and directed energy technologies, although there is disagreement in the United States about the likelihood of, and the timeframe required for, a breakthrough in these areas. The Soviet Union is said to be undertaking various types of beam research, including laser development and accelerator physics for application to particle beams. The Soviet Union appears to find exotic weapons concepts appealing, especially those that promise to "leapfrog" existing technologies for defense. There has been extended discussion of laser and particle beam work in the scientific literature of the Soviet Union.

In sum, current generation Soviet defense capabilities fall far short of the requirements for an "impenetrable" defense against all elements of an attack by U.S. aircraft and ballistic missiles. At the same time, the Soviet Union, in keeping with its emphasis on a doctrine designed to survive a nuclear attack, is giving substantial support to programs whose purpose is to provide for a more effective defense. Thus, the possibility of Soviet breakthroughs to new and exotic technologies for this purpose cannot be ruled out.

Soviet–Warsaw Pact Military Doctrine

The Soviet conception of nuclear weapons as usable instruments of warfare under conditions in which Soviet vital interests are at stake is fundamental to Soviet–Warsaw Pact doctrine in Europe. Nuclear weapons form a part of a "combined arms concept" integrated into a broader offensive in Soviet–Warsaw Pact strategy. Not only are such weapons an integral part of Soviet force levels in Europe, but they may be used on the battlefield without necessarily escalating to a strategic-nuclear exchange with the United States. The possession by the Soviet Union of strategic-nuclear forces, in the Soviet view, can play a decisive role in neutralizing the strategic-nuclear capabilities of the United States. Under such circumstances, the implications for conflict at a regional level, as in Europe, are of profound importance. The capacity of the Soviet Union to prevail in a NATO–Warsaw Pact war depends upon its possession of superior forces on the battlefield. According to Marshal A. A. Grechko, "No matter how significant might be the role of strategic-nuclear weapons, they cannot solve all of the problems of war. Therefore, great efforts are being directed, as before, toward the creation of new—as well as the improvement of existing—conventional types of weapons."[21] At the same time, the Soviet Union emphasizes the development of theater nuclear weapons, which are still regarded as the decisive means by which to influence the outcome of warfare in Europe.

In the past decade Soviet deployments of modern battlefield nuclear weapons have coincided with a major increase in conventional capabilities. The increased accuracy, range, and overall technological sophistication of battlefield weapons, both at the conventional and nuclear levels, has led some Western military analysts to discern in Soviet–Warsaw Pact capabilities, and perhaps also strategy, an evolution toward a form of flexible response. New generation Soviet nuclear-capable systems, including the SS-20, with greatly improved accuracy and lower yield, provide the option of a more discriminate use of nuclear weapons against targets in Western Europe. Such a targeting capability does not necessarily mean that the Soviet Union equates the term "selective" with "limited" or "fewer," but instead implies the utilization of larger-scale nuclear strikes to limit damage without sacrificing basic military objectives.[22] At the same time the growth of Soviet–Warsaw Pact conventional forces, both in qualitative and quantitative dimensions, enhances the flexibility of their options with respect to the use of weapons against Western Europe. The question has been posed whether the Soviet–Warsaw Pact forces are approaching a level in which an attack could be mounted against Western Europe without resort to nuclear weapons. If such weapons could be held in reserve by the Soviet Union, the onus for first use would be placed on NATO.[23]

There exists an extensive Soviet literature on the conduct of battlefield military operations. As at the strategic-nuclear level, Soviet doctrine places great emphasis on surprise and speed. Warsaw Pact strategy is based on the need for rapid maneuver utilizing a combined-arms concept, massed mechanized and armor formations, and a sustained offensive combat capability designed to seize and occupy territory and to overrun all or the major part of Western Europe quickly and decisively. According to Colonel A. A. Sidorenko, "The essence of the offensive consists of having the troops that are conducting it destroy the enemy with all available means and, exploiting the results obtained, advance swiftly into the depth of his disposition, destroy and capture personnel, armament, combat equipment belonging to the enemy, and seize specific territory."[24]

Central to Soviet–Warsaw Pact strategy is the capability to use surprise to minimize NATO warning time, to overrun forward NATO positions in the initial phase of a conflict, to cut vital supply lines to U.S. and other NATO forces on the central front, and to prevent resupply from the United States, Canada, or Great Britain. Major objectives of Soviet–Warsaw Pact forces would be the destruction of ports needed for resupply, the severing of maritime supply lines by means of large-scale deployments of attack submarines, and the use of airpower, for example the Backfire bomber, to destroy surface shipping.[25]

If attack—the offensive—constitutes the most important feature of Soviet–Warsaw Pact combat, the practical application of this concept provides for an assault against the NATO central front, with the northern and southern flanks having been neutralized by demonstrably superior military forces and by political trends, especially on the southern flank that make concerted NATO action difficult, if not impossible. A variant of the frontal assault is the so-called envelopment option, in which an initial surprise offensive would be mounted across NATO's northern flank either prior to or at the same time as a strike against the central front. Such an attack would be designed to enhance the Soviet capacity to control the coastal waters of Northern and Western Europe, and especially the strategically important Greenland–Iceland–United Kingdom gap and the North Atlantic sea lines of communication.

Soviet–Warsaw Pact strategy is designed to strike NATO forces before they can be reinforced to maximum strength, since in the initial stages of a conflict in Europe the Soviet–Warsaw Pact forces would enjoy a quantitative, and increasingly even a qualitative, edge over NATO forces, which must be reinforced from outside continental Europe. Hence, Soviet–Warsaw Pact attack plans are said to include: (1) a commitment of at least 50 unreinforced divisions in the decisively important first three-to-four days of battle based presumably on minimal NATO warning time of about 48 hours; (2) a partially reinforced Soviet–Warsaw Pact attack option that would allow the Soviet Union to deploy more than 75 divisions in eight days, affording NATO several days warning time; and (3) a fully reinforced Soviet–Warsaw Pact attack that would give the Soviet Union at least 94 divisions in two weeks, with NATO having no more than eight days' warning time.

The central question confronting NATO is the warning time available to reinforce and take other appropriate measures in advance of a Soviet–Warsaw Pact attack. A "worst case" analysis contains the assumption that NATO warning time might not exceed forty-eight hours. This stems from the deployment of a first strategic echelon of Warsaw Pact forces at a level of combat readiness so as to be able to move with only a few hours notice. The Soviet–Warsaw Pact emphasis on mobility, including the massive utilization of tanks, armored personnel carriers, and tactical air power, is illustrative of a commitment, noted above, to a doctrine based on the offensive and upon rapid movement and surprise. Thus the Soviet Union enjoys a substantial lead in tanks over the United States (42,000 to 6,400) and in other important categories of equipment, including combat vehicles (USSR, 41,900; U.S., 13,000), artillery (USSR, 19,000; U.S., 5,200), and combat aircraft (USSR, 9,400; U.S., 7,300). Only in antitank guided missiles does the United States presently maintain a lead over the Soviet Union (72,000 to 6,000).

Thus, NATO's main concern is whether, and under what conditions, the Warsaw Pact would be able to launch a surprise attack without prior reinforcement, and therefore with little or no warning time. The consensus is that the Warsaw Pact does not presently have such a capability,[26] although trends in its force structure point toward the possible eventual possession of such a capability.

Soviet Airpower

Of fundamental importance in Soviet military literature is the achievement of air supremacy as the prerequisite to victory on land and at sea. Control of air space is indispensable to command of terrestrial space.

Hence air power has been assigned essentially five major missions in Soviet military planning: strategic air defense; strategic attacks against the homeland of an adversary; antishipping and antisubmarine warfare; air lift; and support of land combat offensive operations, such as might be envisaged by Soviet–Warsaw Pact forces against Western Europe, or by the Soviet Union against China.

It has been noted elsewhere in this chapter that air defense constitutes one of the asymmetries between U.S. and Soviet strategic doctrine and force planning. The Soviet Union is said to have about 500,000 military personnel, together with at least 2,500 aircraft, assigned to air defense of Soviet territory in the PVO-Strany, the strategic air defense force. Aircraft designed for air defense include the MIG-17 Fresco; MIG-19 Farmer, MIG-23 Flogger, MIG-25 Foxbat, SU-9 Fishpot B, SU-11 Fishpot C, SU-1f Flagon, YAK-28 Firebar, and TU-28 Fiddler.[27] These capabilities accord with Soviet doctrine emphasizing defense and war survival. They would be used principally in the defense of the Soviet Union itself as well as Soviet military units. According to Colonel Sidorenko: "Armed conflict on the scale of all troop elements represents a uniform and simultaneous process of struggle against the ground and air enemy. Consequently, the grouping of PVO (air defense) forces and means designed to repulse enemy air attacks comprises an inalienable part of the troop combat formation of any scale."[28]

A second major element of Soviet air power is strategic strikes against an adversary. A generation ago, both in doctrine and R&D for force planning, the Soviet Union chose to place almost exclusive emphasis on the development of strategic rocket forces. According to Sokolovskiy, writing in the early 1960s, strategic missiles "are a decisive force in the hands of the high commands since it is primarily they who will be entrusted with achieving the main war aims: destruction of strategic and operational means of enemy nuclear attack throughout his territory, disrupting war economy, disorganizing the government and the military leadership, disrupting communications, and defeating the strategic reserves."[29] This view has been altered to encompass advanced generation bombers, notably the Backfire and in all likelihood, by the mid 1980s, a larger strategic bomber more fully comparable to the B-1 that was cancelled by the Carter administration in 1977. Thus, aircraft such as the Backfire would provide a component of the Soviet strategic force capable of missions against Western Europe and China, and perhaps even the United States. The Backfire, as noted earlier in this chapter, possesses ranges more suitable for striking targets in Western Europe and China, although, especially in its most advanced version, the Backfire could be employed against the United States if refueled in air or if it landed in a third country such as Cuba after an attack.

The Soviet Union places great emphasis in its conception of air power upon antishipping and antisubmarine operations and for maritime reconnaissance missions. Land-based aviation could locate and destroy surface ships and submarines in large expanses of the oceans. Such aircraft could identify maritime targets of high value such as aircraft carriers and merchant ship convoys, the latter especially vital in a resupply effort from the United States to Europe, or in an Asian-Pacific contingency in which the United States and the Soviet Union were at war. The identification of such targets by air power engaged in reconnaissance would be followed by the use of long-range maritime strike aircraft together with Soviet naval units, especially submarines, where appropriate against enemy surface units.[30]

The extension of Soviet influence into regions far beyond the historic confines of Russian interest has had as an indispenable element Soviet military power in the form of arms transfers. In turn, this has been dependent on sealift and airlift capacity. By 1979 the Soviet Union had developed an airlift capability that could move large numbers of military personnel and/or their equipment quickly to third countries, as demonstrated by the Soviet invasion of Afghanistan. The Soviet airlift fleet includes several categories of aircraft, such as the AN-12 Cub, the AN-22 and the IL-76 Candid, as well as transport helicopters. The Soviet civil airline Aeroflot, like the airlines of the United States and its allies, represents an important adjunct to military aircraft that would be available in a crisis situation.

Finally, the Soviet Union has placed increasing emphasis in the last decade on the development of tactical air power. In the 1970s the role of tactical air power underwent a change in Soviet doctrine from an emphasis principally upon the support of Soviet ground forces, to which it was traditionally subordinated, toward an offensive capability designed to secure control over the skies far behind enemy front lines. This use of air power accords fully with Soviet–Warsaw Pact doctrine based on the primacy of the offensive. The roles attached to Soviet frontal aviation have evolved substantially since 1957, when Khrushchev envisaged the missile as replacing the manned aircraft even on the battlefield. By the 1970s, Soviet thought had been altered to the extent that frontal aviation had become the largest component of the Soviet air force. According to one analysis: "In any plans for *conventional* confrontation with NATO forces, frontal aviation may well emerge as the peer among peers in Soviet combined arms doctrine."[31] Such capabilities would be used to neutralize NATO tactical air power in the opening stages of a conflict through strikes on airfields, and to destroy NATO command posts, communications centers, nuclear weapons stockpiles and delivery systems in addition to aircraft, and concentrations of ground forces.

Chemical Warfare

Among the capabilities increasingly available to the Soviet Union is chemical warfare. As in the modernization of conventional and nuclear forces, the Soviet Union is gaining unprecedented options in the utilization of various forms of warfare to achieve its political objectives. A Soviet decision to use chemical weapons is not considered in Soviet literature to be equivalent to the employment of nuclear capabilities. In fact, a Soviet decision to resort to chemical warfare would confront NATO with a dilemma of fundamental proportions: Since NATO, in sharp contrast to the Warsaw Pact, lacks either a high level of protection against chemical agents or an effective retaliatory capacity, the principal remaining option might be the use of tactical nuclear weapons. Here NATO faces a formidable array of modern Warsaw Pact battlefield nuclear capabilities. Although Soviet interest in chemical weapons dates from the military collaboration with Germany of the early 1920s, the Soviet Union has developed in the last decade a large stockpile of such capabilities, together with training for military personnel, as well as armored vehicles and uniforms, decontamination facilities, and delivery systems. Soviet–Warsaw Pact forces have deployed a large number of dual-capable systems that provide for the use of nuclear or chemical and/or biological agents — although biological agents have no apparent priority in present Soviet planning.

Chemical agents can be delivered by air-to-surface or surface-to-surface missiles or by artillery shells. Such capabilities have become an integral part of Soviet ground, air, and naval forces; they are said to be a part of every Soviet command and to include some 70,000–100,000 full-time personnel.[32] Units for the use of chemical warfare exist at the company level of all groups of Soviet ground forces. Soviet tanks and armored personnel carriers contain protective equipment against the effects of operations in a chemical warfare environment. These include detection and warning systems, alternative oxygen systems, and decontamination gear. The chemical agents available to the Soviet Union consist of blood, nerve, and mustard agents. They are said to include such chemical agents as phosgene, hydrogen, cyanide, and soman.

The substantial growth of Soviet–Warsaw Pact chemical warfare capabilities gives to the Soviet Union the increased option to strike targets without necessarily destroying them. Chemical agents could leave intact certain installations, including parts of cities, factories, and other infrastructure deemed important to the Soviet Union in a post-attack, or post-war, phase. Populations could be incapacitated or destroyed, as deemed appropriate by the Soviet Union. Conceivably, conflict could be waged for a longer period in a conventional phase with chemical agents. Certain areas, especially the urban complexes of Western Europe, could be cleared of resistance — military and paramilitary — to advancing Soviet–Warsaw Pact units. Critically important NATO command and control facilities, ports, and staging areas could be attacked with chemical warfare capabilities in the initial phase of a conflict.

Soviet Maritime Strategy and Capabilities

Only since the late 1960s has the navy become an important component of Soviet military power with the development of a "blue water" fleet capable of operating in any of the world's seas, symbolized by the multi-ocean exercises, OKEAN-70 and OKEAN-75, that have been conducted by the Soviet Union. Thus the emergence of the Soviet Union as a superpower with global interests coincided with the attainment by the Soviet Union of a navy second only to the United States. Naval capabilities not only enhance the Soviet capacity for the projection of influence to distant parts of the world, but because the Soviet Union faces adversaries on two fronts — Western Europe and China — its naval forces also provide a potential means for outflanking opponents from the sea. In this respect naval forces complement the huge land forces arrayed in the western and eastern regions of the Soviet Union.[33] As a land power, the Soviet Union, like tsarist Russia before it, traditionally relegated naval capabilities to missions in support of ground forces and to coastal defense. These were the principal missions of the Soviet navy in World War II, although they are mentioned in a contemporary context for two specific contingencies: support of Soviet ground operations after a strategic attack against an adversary, or strategic defense of the Soviet Union.

This view, like much of the Soviet literature on naval strategy, is the product of the thought of admiral of the fleet of the Soviet Union Sergey Gorshkov, widely considered to be the architect of the modern Soviet navy. Gorshkov's analysis of Soviet naval capabilities has been based upon a basic notion common to other students of naval power, namely, that the nature of any country's navy is set by geography, economics, and the character of its leadership.[34] According to this thesis, naval capabilities, including a large merchant marine, are vital to a state's position as a great industrial power. By the 1970s the Soviet Union had become not only a major naval power in the military dimension, but had also built a merchant marine comparable to that of the United States. Because the Soviet Union is a superpower, Gorshkov maintains, it must have a navy capable of protecting its interests on a global scale. According to Michael MccGuire, "The common thread that links all of Gorshkov's arguments about the role of navies in war and peace is that each of them justifies a stronger navy, not only in terms of numbers, but in the broadest sense of a properly balanced fleet, with a sufficient diversity of ship types and adequate afloat support."[35]

The missions given to the Soviet navy in the late twentieth century include, first and foremost, strategic nuclear strikes against the United States. In his *Sea Power and the Soviet State,* a major treatise on Soviet naval power, Admiral Gorshkov identified strategic attack as the priority mission, since the purpose of military power, in his view, must be not only the destruction of the military forces of the enemy but also his economic infrastructure, including defense industry, administrative centers, and electrical power systems.[36] This emphasis has been reflected in the development of Soviet ballistic missile submarines of the Yankee and Delta classes. The Yankee class SSBNs deployed off the eastern seaboard of the United States, together with those in the Pacific, can attack targets at any point in the United States with the 1,600-mile Mod 2 SS-n-6.[37] The Delta class, which displaces about 10,000 tons when submerged, is the world's largest submarine in service as of 1979. It could strike targets in any part of North America, Europe, and a large part of China from the Greenland and Norwegian seas. As noted earlier, the Soviet Union has under construction a new generation of submarines called the Typhoon, that will rival in size the U.S. Trident submarine at about 18,000 tons submerged.

The growth of the all-oceans navy has stemmed in part from an extension of the traditional conception of the "battle against the shore" to the use of the navy both in offensive and defensive missions against enemy targets on land. In the case of offensive missions, the Soviet Union would need naval forces both to interdict sea lines of communications to thwart U.S. resupply efforts to NATO in the event of a Soviet–Warsaw Pact attack, and to attack the United States directly.[38] Such a capability would be needed because the United States, by virtue of its geographic position, lies beyond the reach of the land forces of the Soviet Union. For the Soviet Union, the projection of political influence and military power makes necessary a naval capability in support of Soviet diplomacy. The peacetime operation on a regular basis of Soviet warships in the world's major oceans—the Atlantic, the Mediterranean, the Indian Ocean, and the Pacific—provides for Moscow a military presence that is deemed useful for political purposes.

Soviet naval capabilities can be, and have been, reinforced rapidly in crisis situations. For example, in October–November 1973, the Soviet Mediterranean fleet was increased from its normal strength of 40–45 ships to 96 naval units.[39]

The October War was illustrative of another important dimension of Soviet maritime power—sea-lift capabilities. At the outset of this chapter the use by the Soviet Union of military power, in the form of arms transfers

to the Third World states and to proxy forces such as the Cuban merce-
naries operating in Africa, was noted. The vast Soviet merchant fleet serves
this purpose, especially in the supply of arms that are not considered to be
time urgent. The largest part of the 2,000 tanks supplied to Arab states
after the outbreak of the October War, as well as many other types of
military equipment, came by Soviet merchant ships. Such shipping was
used in conjunction with airlift capability, treated elsewhere in this chapter,
in support of Soviet interests.

Of great, and probably decisive, importance to the United States and its
allies is control of sea lines of communication, especially in the maritime
dimension of conventional warfare of long duration. From the Soviet
perspective, the severing of sea lines of communication is, as Admiral
Gorshkov has indicated, "one of the most important of the [Soviet] Navy's
missions."[40] For NATO, with its flexible response strategy, the ability to
transport military supplies across the Atlantic — much of them by ship —
would probably be indispensable, especially in light of the advantages that
the Warsaw Pact might enjoy at the outbreak of conflict. The dependence
of industrialized states, and most Third World states, upon the oceans for
oil, raw materials, and other commerce enhances their vulnerability to supply interruption. The capacity of the Soviet Union even to threaten to interdict shipping vital to the security of other states provides a potentially
important form of political leverage.

The Soviet navy has been configured not as a "mirror image" of Western
naval forces, but instead to serve the objectives set by the Soviet Union.
Thus, the Soviet navy differs substantially in types of ships from that of the
United States. Although Soviet naval vessels are usually smaller in tonnage
than those of the United States, they place emphasis on speed and fire-
power. The Soviet Union has attached greater priority than the United
States to submarines and cruise missiles, both of which would have as their
missions the destruction of enemy surface fleets and merchant shipping,
perhaps in a preemptive attack designated to decimate U.S. naval power at
the outset of a war. Similarly, land-based long-range Soviet aviation, including at least one-half the Backfire aircraft now deployed, is assigned missions against surface shipping.

Conclusion

The emphasis in this chapter has been on the Soviet conception of
military doctrine, and the relationship between strategic concepts and force
levels. No effort has been made to examine, either in great detail or on a
comparative basis, the respective force levels of the United States and the
Soviet Union. The data about force levels included in this analysis are il-

lustrative only of some of the most important dimensions of and trends in Soviet strategy and capabilities. Nor has an analysis of the adequacy of Soviet military strategy and force levels to achieve the political objectives posited in Soviet foreign policy been attempted.

The basic conclusion that emerges from an analysis of Soviet military strategy and force levels relates to the differences between the Soviet Union and the United States in conceptions of deterrence, the role of military power in relation to other capabilities for the achievement of political objectives, the conception of nuclear weapons as deterrence and war-fighting instruments, the threshold, or "firebreak," between conventional and nuclear warfare, the meaning and implications of strategic-military superiority, and the importance attached to offensive and defensive capabilities. Perhaps the most important differences are those that separate the superpowers in their conceptions of strategy itself. What remains unanswered, and unanswerable at this stage, is which conception of military strategy and force levels — Soviet or American — will be adequate to support the foreign policy interests and objectives of the superpowers in their ongoing competition in the remaining years of this century.

Notes

1. According to Marshal A. A. Grechko: "Strategy is a component of military art and is its most important sphere. It encompasses questions of the theory and practice of preparing the Armed Forces for war, of planning and waging war, of using Services of the Armed Forces and directing them. Strategy is based on military doctrine and relies on a country's economic capabilities. *At the same time, it stems directly from a state's policy and is subordinated to it.*" Marshal A. A. Grechko, *The Armed Forces of the Soviet State: A Soviet View* (Moscow, 1975) translated and published under the auspices of the United States Air Force (Washington, D.C.: U.S. Government Printing Office), p. 279 (italics added).

2. Jacquelyn K. Davis, Robert L. Pfaltzgraff, Jr., and Uri Ra'anan, "The U.S.-Soviet Strategic Balance: Emerging Trends" (Paper presented at the Conference on the Emerging Strategic Environment: Implications for Ballistic Missile Defense, sponsored by the Institute for Foreign Policy Analysis, Inc., 8-9 March 1978 in Washington, D.C.), pp. 33-34.

3. Raymond L. Garthoff, "Mutual Deterrence and Strategic Arms Limitation in Soviet Policy," *International Security*, vol. 3., no. 1 (summer 1978), esp. pp. 115-17. See also Dennis Ross, *Rethinking Soviet Strategy Policy: Inputs and Implications,* ACIS Working Paper no. 5 (Center for Arms Control and International Security, University of California, Los Angeles, June 1977). The author suggests that a minority of Soviet writers seemingly accept, and "indirectly [italicized in original] argue that strategic superiority is unattainable, that counterforce strikes are at best futile and at worst destabilizing, and that nuclear wars are not winnable" (p. 17). These are said

to include A. Karenin, G. A. Trofimenko, V. M. Kulish, and George Arbatov, the director of the USA Institute in Moscow.

4. Garthoff, "Mutual Deterrence," p. 112.

5. Fritz W. Ermarth, "Contrasts in American and Soviet Strategic Thought," *International Security*, vol. 3, no. 2 (fall 1978), p. 140.

6. Robert S. McNamara, *The Essence of Security: Reflections in Office* (New York: Harper and Row, 1978).

7. C. G. Jacobson, *Soviet Strategy–Soviet Foreign Policy: Military Considerations Affecting Soviet Policymaking* (Glasgow: The University Press, 1972), pp. 21–25.

8. Albert Wohlstetter, "Is There a Strategic Arms Race?" *Foreign Policy*, no. 15 (summer 1974), p. 5. See also, by the same author, "Rivals, but no 'Race,'" *Foreign Policy*, no. 16 (fall 1974), pp. 48–81.

9. V. D. Sokolovskiy, *Soviet Military Strategy*, 3rd ed., 1968 trans. Harriet Fast Scott (New York: Crane, Russak and Company, 1975), p. 12.

10. Richard Pipes, "Why the Soviet Union Thinks it Could Fight and Win a Nuclear War," *Commentary*, vol.. 64, no. 1 (July 1977), p. 27. According to Clausewitz, "It is clear, consequently, that war is not a mere act of policy but a true political instrument, a continuation of political activity by other means. What remains peculiar to war is simply the peculiar nature of its means." Carl von Clausewitz, *On War*, ed. and trans. Michael Howard and Peter Paret (Princeton: Princeton University Press, 1976), p. 87.

11. Sokolovskiy, *Soviet Military Strategy*, pp. 14–15. Furthermore, Sokolovskiy writes: "In his remarks on Clausewitz' book, *On War*, V. I. Lenin stresses that 'politics is the reason, and war is only the tool, not the other way around. Consequently, it remains only to subordinate the military point of view to the political,'" ibid., p. 14.

12. Garthoff, "Mutual Deterrence," p. 146.

13. Colin S. Gray, *The Geopolitics of the Nuclear Era: Heartland, Rimlands, and the Technological Revolution* (New York: Crane, Russak and Company, Inc., 1977), p. 46.

14. John Erickson, "The Chimera of Mutual Deterrence," *Strategic Review*, spring 1978, p. 11.

15. McNamara, *The Essence of Security*, p. 59.

16. See, for example, *Is America Becoming Number 2? Current Trends in the U.S.-Soviet Military Balance*, Committee on the Present Danger, Washington, D.C., 1978; and John M. Collins, *American and Soviet Military Trends Since the Cuban Missile Crisis* (Washington, D.C.: The Center for Strategic and International Studies, Georgetown University, 1978), esp. pp. 75–141.

17. For a study of the cruise missile, see Robert L. Pfaltzgraff, Jr. and Jacquelyn K. Davis, *The Cruise Missile: Bargaining Chip or Defense Bargain?* (Cambridge: Institute for Foreign Policy Analysis, 1977). See also Hans Ruhle, "Cruise Missiles, NATO and the 'European Option,'" *Strategic Review*, fall 1978.

18. P. T. Yegorov, I. A. Shlyakhov, and N. I. Alabin, *Civil Defense: A Soviet View* (Moscow, 1970), translated and published under the auspices of the United States Air Force (Washington, D.C.: U.S. Government Printing Office), p. 6.

19. Leon Goure, *War Survival in Soviet Strategy: USSR Civil Defense,* Monographs in International Affairs, Center for Advanced International Studies, University of Miami, 1976, esp. pp. 1-19.

20. This analysis draws upon *The Soviet Union and Ballistic Missile Defense: A Conference Report II* (Summary of a conference held in Washington, D.C., 10-11 May 1978), Institute for Foreign Policy Analysis, Cambridge, Massachusetts, and Washington, D.C., 1978.

21. Grechko, *The Armed Forces of the Soviet State,* p. 153.

22. Joseph D. Douglass, Jr., "Soviet Nuclear Strategy in Europe: A Selective Targeting Doctrine," *Strategic Review,* fall 1977, p. 19.

23. Air Vice Marshal Stewart W. B. Menual, "The Shifting Theater Nuclear Balance in Europe," *Strategic Review,* fall 1978.

24. A. A. Sidorenko, *The Offensive (A Soviet View)* (Moscow, 1970), translated and published under the auspices of the United States Air Force, (Washington, D.C.: U.S. Government Printing Office), p. 1.

25. For a recent analysis of Soviet Warsaw Pact strategy and force levels, see Jacquelyn K. Davis and Robert L. Pfaltzgraff, Jr., *Soviet Theater Strategy: Implications for NATO,* USSI Report 78-1 (Washington, D.C.: United States Strategic Institute, 1978), pp. 7-10.

26. One notable exception to this view is that of the Belgian general, Robert Close, *L'Europe sans Defense?* (Brussels: Editions Arts et Voyages, 1976).

27. Robert P. Berman, *Soviet Air Power in Transition* (Washington, D.C.: The Brookings Institution, 1978), p. 9.

28. Sidorenko, *The Offensive (A Soviet View).*

29. Sokolovskiy, *Soviet Military Strategy,* p. 246.

30. Berman, *Soviet Air Power in Transition,* p. 12.

31. Lieutenant Colonel Lynn M. Hansen, "The Resurgence of Soviet Frontal Aviation," *Strategic Review,* fall 1978, p. 78 (italics in original).

32. Amoretta Hoeber and Joseph D. Douglass, Jr., "The Neglected Threat of Chemical Warfare," *International Security,* vol. 3, no. 1 (summer 1978), p. 60.

33. John R. Thomas, "Political-Strategic Framework for Soviet Oceanic Policy," in *Soviet Oceans Development,* Committee on Commerce, U.S. Senate (October 1976) (Washington, D.C.: U.S. Government Printing Office, 1976), p. 29.

34. John G. Hibbits, "Admiral Gorshkov's Writings: Twenty Years of Naval Thought," in Paul J. Murphy, ed., *Naval Power in Soviet Policy, Studies in Communist Affairs,* vol. 2, published under the auspices of the United States Air Force (Washington, D.C.: U.S. Government Printing Office, 1978), p. 4.

35. Michael MccGuire, "The Evolution of Soviet Naval Policy: 1960-1974," in Michael MccGuire, Ken Booth, and John McDonnell, eds., *Soviet Naval Policy: Objectives and Constraints* (New York: Praeger Publications, 1975), p. 538.

36. Ibid., p. 7.

37. Captain John E. Moore, *The Soviet Navy Today* (New York: Stein and Day, 1976), p. 31.

38. Thomas, "Political-Strategic Framework for Soviet Oceanic Policy," p. 29.

39. *Understanding Soviet Naval Developments,* Office of the Chief of Naval Opera-

tions, Department of the Navy (Washington, D.C.: U.S. Government Printing Office, 1978). The 96 Soviet naval units in the Mediterranean during the October War included: 5 cruisers, 14 destroyers, 6 escort ships, 2 Nanuchka-class missile ships, 9 amphibious ships, 6 intelligence ships, and about 25 submarines, several of which were nuclear powered. Soviet ships carried surface-to-air missile launchers and several ships and submarines had auto-shop missiles.

40. Quoted in *Understanding Soviet Naval Developments,* p. 10.

Part 4

An Overview of
Soviet Foreign Policies

13
Summaries and Conclusions
Kurt London

I

When the great powers met at Vienna in 1815 to pull a new order from the post-Napoleonic shambles, they agreed upon a code of international behavior. These regulations remained in force, more or less, for a hundred years; indeed the "fin de siècle" saw the International Court of Law established at The Hague. Not long thereafter World War I broke out, jolting traditions and producing two types of government basically inimical to the Law of Nations: the Marxist-Leninst state that became the Soviet Union and, just a few years later, the Nazi-Fascist states of Germany and Italy. World War II wiped out the latter and elevated the former to a world power.

As a result of these events there developed a chasm between "traditional" and "revolutionary" states:

> Traditional nations consider policy problems within the ethical framework of established principles. . . . Contrariwise, revolutionary states recognize no such limitations. They reject the principles of international relations developed by traditionalists, claiming that such principles are established in the interest of the "ruling classes" and do not, therefore, constitute the legitimate aspirations of the people. They tend to become ideological empires and like the medieval church, acknowledge no limit to their aims.[1]

With evangelical zeal for reaching ideological objectives, revolutionary nations tend to expect that they will be victorious, like virtue over sin, in the end. Soviet leaders, seeking to control all aspects of life in their country, concentrated all power upon themselves and appointed themselves saviors of downtrodden masses everywhere. In short, they became totalitarians.

It is of major importance to recognize the basic totalitarian aspects of Soviet foreign policy, as Professor Schapiro penetratingly demonstrates in Chapter 1. The Soviet leaders who best personify the totalitarian aspects of an ideological empire make full use of their dictatorial advantages: They formulate policy as they see fit and order its implementation. That there is now more of a collective leadership makes little difference. Always one man among them is, as George Orwell put it, more equal than the others.

The guiding principle of Soviet foreign policy is the contention of legality, based not on Western international law, but as Bernard Ramundo points out, on a "new" international law, that of peaceful coexistence.[2] If it is true that consent is the theoretical basis of the validity of international law, how is it then that Moscow has succeeded in achieving consent from the West in various treaties?

Does this mean that Soviet intentions have radically changed? Has the Soviet Union become a "traditional" nation-state and relinquished its revolutionary aspirations? Is it true, as so many Western optimists declare, that a new era has begun in light of Soviet aggression in Afghanistan?

The optimists, I fear, fail to understand the difference between Communist strategy and tactics. Strategy, from the Soviet point of view, means fundamental, long-range planning toward the achievement of the ultimate goal. It has never perceptibly changed. Tactics are the ways and means, however un-Marxist, employed to achieve this goal.

The Soviet leaders, unwilling to provoke a war that could destroy their country and their system, must have come to the conclusion during the post-Stalin years that they could not achieve their goal by military means but rather by political warfare. When by the end of the 1960s no progress had been achieved, their tactical measures became a far more important element of action than ever before. Moreover, the conflict with Peking called for adjustment with Western Europe, which Moscow has always regarded as a matter of primary concern.

Thus began a series of events that appeared to be out of Soviet character and therefore, in the eyes of many Westerners, indicative of a radical change in Soviet behavior and possibly the end of the traditional ideological underpinning of the Soviet state. An increasing number of observers in the West, particularly in the United States, no longer regard the Soviet state as revolutionary.

To determine whether or not the USSR has actually changed, it is necessary to look at its domestic conditions; there we find very little difference. The regime is as harshly Leninist as ever. To be sure, Brezhnev is better than Stalin, but one need only look at the Kremlin's treatment of disaffected intellectuals or even a giant like Solzhenitsyn to realize that the KGB's strong-arm methods still keep the population cowed. The concentration camps still exist.

Is it possible to assume that this Communist-ruled country has mellowed because of the application of a pragmatic policy abroad? There has been no evidence that the men in the Kremlin have retreated from their political philosophy. But they seem to have recognized that few "revolutionary situations" exist and that they therefore must proceed more slowly and cautiously. They believe, as Schapiro put it, that "world socialism is now to be achieved by subversion, political warfare, and military preponderance." And yet, as Adam Ulam points out cogently, here is a state that enjoys all the appurtenances of "normal" statehood and membership in the community of nations at the same time that its professed aim and ideology are to subvert all other existing forms of government. Even more extraordinary: "The USSR claimed, and what is rather amazing, achieved a special status in international relations. It was to be treated as a regular member of the community of nations, yet unlike other states its rulers never made a secret of the fact that they sought and hoped for an overthrow of other forms of government."

Although Soviet armed forces are in a high state of readiness, the Soviet leaders have recognized that the outbreak of a major conflict most likely would entail the use of nuclear weapons. By adopting a pragmatic approach, Soviet foreign policy has achieved more, in just a few years, than it would have with threats. Still, one must agree with Schapiro that "there is nothing to indicate that the main aim has ever been abandoned." I might add that such an abandonment is impossible so long as the Soviet system continues to dominate the USSR and its satellite nations.

The very soul of Soviet communism is internationalist, and since it is doubtful that a "socialist" can prevail forever in an ocean of nonsocialist states, Moscow will continue its efforts to save its camp from slipping into international isolation. The system is self-propelled, a fact that is hidden behind the benevolent smiles of Soviet leaders while they are visiting other countries.

I do not mean to imply that we should refuse to deal with the Soviets. But in dealing with them it is essential to recognize the nature of their system, which is irreconcilably hostile to ours. If we understand that and *match their strength with ours,* it is conceivable that peaceful coexistence, at least in Soviet-Western relations, could afford us a fairly secure period of peace *provided* we keep our powder dry.

II

The Communist leaders never cease to attack imperialism. But following World War II they became more imperialistic than the old-fashioned empires. The East European land grabs were undertaken without any respect for ethnic minorities—or for that matter, majorities. The states of Eastern Europe had passed through unhappy years before they came under Soviet control; that they eventually did is not only Stalin's making. The Western allies, negotiating with Stalin in Teheran and Yalta, must assume their share of guilt. It is saddening to read Charles Bohlen's account of these conferences, in which he participated as interpreter.[3] Be that as it may, Stalin annexed the Baltic states and gradually extended his control over the states of Eastern Europe from the Baltic to the Black Sea.

Soviet policy required, in Professor Seton-Watson's words, "that in each country there should be a pocket-sized Stalin with direct access to the Boss" — men like Rakosi, Gottwald, Dimitrov and Chervenkov, Bierut, and Gheorghiu-Dej. But the Soviet system, politically and economically, was hardly applicable to these small countries. There were deviations in Hungary and Czechoslovakia, but not even the trend to polycentric communism, which spread after 1956, could break the chains (with one glaring exception: Yugoslavia, which had the good fortune of not being contiguous to Soviet territory).

Seton-Watson vividly describes the consequences of the satellite status in these countries: the abject political and ideological subordination, the injection of the Russian language and culture in the educational systems, the throttling of bonds with Western culture. The *Comintern Journal* was set up to provide official guidance on interpretation of Soviet policy and prescribed attitudes toward the West. There were differences in the treatment of the individual vassals, but all of them were subjected to economic exploitation (through the Council for Mutual Economic Assistance), were forced to become part of the Soviet eastern defense system (in the Warsaw Pact), and had to follow Soviet direction in foreign policy (with some deviation by Romania). Later, in the sixties, Albania — noncontiguous to the USSR — dropped out of the Soviet security belt to align itself with Communist China, whose revolutionary fervor it sought to imitate. Khrushchev, in the Albanians' view, had become a "revisionist."

Soviet interest in Eastern Europe is not new; the tsars had long fixed their covetous attention on that area. The Soviets came to regard this region as a vital *cordon sanitaire* and a strategic sphere of interest (as well as a possible strategic jumping-off point). Also, they wanted to extend their ideological empire and bind these countries as closely as possible to their heartland.

The extent to which they were willing to go to prevent any weak links from loosening the grip was shown in the interference in the Berlin unrest of 1953, the Hungarian revolution in 1956, and the Czechoslovak invasion of 1968. Dubček's Czechoslovakia, from the Soviet point of view, infiltrated a dangerous element into the Soviet body politic — of which Eastern Europe was a part.

Berlin and Budapest were sudden violent outbursts, quickly subdued. But the Prague Spring was the beginning of a new development of a socialism freed from the ideological strait-jacket of Marxism-Leninism. It was to be a humane socialism. This could not be tolerated; Czechoslovakia was a vital part of the Soviet security system and Dubček's ideas could filter into the other satellites and even into part of the USSR. Thus the invading forces consisted not only of Soviet troops but also of units of the Warsaw Pact nations; the leaders of the satellite states were afraid of losing such power as they possessed and thus participated in the invasion.

If anyone had doubts about the Soviet position vis-à-vis Eastern Europe, the so-called Brezhnev Doctrine dispelled them. It was made clear to the world that the nations in the socialist camp would not be permitted to pursue their own road to socialism (as Togliatti had wished). Very minor deviations, such as in economic matters, were permitted. Romania's tough internal Communist rule made possible a somewhat enlarged activity in foreign affairs. But none of the deviations would be permitted if Soviet interests were hurt. Most East European states were caught in the net of Soviet dominance, and the Brezhnev Doctrine made it clear that no further attempts to gain more freedom will be tolerated.

It would be erroneous, however, to assume that these countries would adopt Western forms of government or become "capitalist" if they had a choice. They would remain socialist, albeit in a revisionist manner, and only gradually free themselves from the fallacies of the Soviet system. Nevertheless, as long as the Soviet version of Marxism-Leninism remains Moscow's rationale, no such development can be foreseen. The attempts by certain Western groups to "liberate" Eastern Europe are ill-advised and damaging to the captive states.

It is perhaps useful to look back to the negotiations between President Roosevelt (later Truman), Churchill, and Stalin at Teheran, Yalta, and Potsdam. The Yalta agreement on Poland was not kept by the Soviets. In his memoirs Charles Bohlen wrote, "Poland was just one of the areas where the Soviet Union was acting like an enemy and not like an ally. In Romania, Hungary, Bulgaria, and elsewhere, the Soviets were showing that the Declaration of Liberated Europe meant nothing."[4]

I do not believe that Lenin actually dreamed of a Soviet hegemony over non-Soviet Communist-ruled states; his writings mention no such ambition.[5] But Stalin, once the European part of World War II was won, had no intention of letting go of Eastern Europe. And Stalin's successors had no intention of changing this policy. The hopes expressed during the period of polycentrism and the apparent loosening of Soviet rule were futile. The USSR persisted in what Seton-Watson poignantly calls "national humiliation" of its satellites. That is indeed what Soviet rule amounts to, and while it is not consciously recognized as such in Moscow's vassal states (their national pride forbids it), it has not endeared Soviet rule to these countries.

III

Western Europe was the major battlefield of World War II; when the war was over, it was a shambles. Without U.S. help it would have collapsed politically and economically and the Communists would have taken over. The Soviets would have liked that, and the United States knew it. Thus, with an enormous effort and colossal amounts of money, American reconstruction and rehabilitation were undertaken.

The Germans were grateful to a degree, but the French disliked being on the receiving line, especially when it became clear that the German Federal Republic was not destined to occupy an inferior position (the French had hoped to become the most influential power in Western Europe). The Soviets did not help at all, not even in East Germany, where they dismantled factories and carried away as much as they could.

Among the most important results of the postwar differences between East and West were the division of Germany, the establishment of the North Atlantic Treaty Organization (NATO), the permanent stationing of an American army in West Germany and the rearmament of that nation, the creation of the Common Market, and the origin of the cold war. Moscow violated agreements signed in Teheran and Yalta and generally did its best to hinder European reconstruction beyond the Iron Curtain. It prodded the Communist parties in Italy, and especially in France, to foment strikes, riots, and civil disobedience.

The Bolsheviks held genuine peace to be inimical to their aims, and the West, especially the United States, had to establish ways and means to counter Soviet policies. During these years the cold war became a daily fact of life.

It should be remembered that the Communist parties in Western Europe experienced two shattering blows that weakened their political charisma. The first was the slaughter of Budapest (1956) and the development of polycentric communism, whereby the individual parties hoped to achieve a greater degree of independence from Moscow; heretofore they had followed Soviet party orders implicitly. The second was the invasion of Czechoslovakia (1968), which alienated many parties outside the Soviet bloc. Moreover, the outbreak of the Sino-Soviet conflict in 1960 had a disturbing influence on these parties; in the eyes of extreme leftists the images of Khrushchev and Brezhnev paled next to Mao's.

In other words, without the impact of Soviet policy, neither the division of Germany and the Western security measures (clearly directed toward the USSR) nor the involvement of the United States could have happened. Nor could the erection of the wall isolating East Germany and cutting Berlin to pieces have occurred. Thus evolved an awareness in the United States that

Moscow's reckless policies required counteraction so as to meet the needs of national and international security.

It was only after the arrival of Willy Brandt in the Bonn chancellery that gradual changes occurred in German-Soviet relations. In France, General De Gaulle tried to conduct a "normal" foreign policy toward the USSR; he never put much credence in the role of Marxism-Leninism. While it must not be forgotten that he stood firmly on the side of the United States during the Berlin and Cuban crises, on the other hand he expelled American NATO troops and installations from France and thus, when he visited Moscow in 1960, believed that he appeared to be a free agent vis-à-vis the Kremlin. Paradoxically, he knew, of course, that he could not do without the American nuclear umbrella, his "force de frappe" notwithstanding.

The attempts of De Gaulle and Pompidou to formulate their foreign policy regardless of the position of their Western allies failed for the simple reason that Soviet interest in France is only a negative one—that is, as a thorn in the side of NATO in general and the United States in particular. From the Soviet point of view the entire Western camp falls under one category, namely, Western imperialism. Any disagreements among the Western European nations or between the United States and Western Europe will be welcomed as a force serving to weaken NATO. The creation of a politically and economically united Western Europe would set up a formidable roadblock against any Soviet attempt to subvert or attack such a bloc. The combination of a united Western Europe with the United States would establish a virtually unbeatable power grid. It is regrettable that this goal could not be reached mainly due to the narrow nationalism of France.

The Soviets had been hostile toward West Germany ever since it was established. This is understandable because German-wrought destruction during the war was monstrous. Even the creation of East Germany under Communist control did not entirely eliminate ill feelings toward the population in that satellite; after all, these people were German, too.

It appears that in the late sixties the Politburo under Brezhnev recognized that its policies toward Germany had become stale, that Soviet influence in Western Europe should be enhanced, and that—in view of the Chinese danger—Moscow's eastern frontiers should be secured. This meant an opening toward the West, beginning with West Germany. General De Gaulle once expressed the (futile) hope for a "Europe to the Urals." Brezhnev reversed this dictum. Thus Willy Brandt's *Ostpolitik*—conciliation with the USSR and Eastern Europe—came in handy for the Kremlin. It made sense for the Soviets to make political peace with Germany, determine definitive frontiers, and establish a reliable status quo.

Brandt did not invent *Ostpolitik*. Former Chancellor Kurt Georg Kiesinger had suggested it, unsuccessfully, because he wanted a quid pro quo.

Brandt rather hastily sought to carry out his policy and so his treaties with
Moscow were not really reciprocal. Politically, he got little, apart from a
better arrangement for West Berlin. Economically, he fared somewhat better so that West Germany became a leading non-Communist trading partner. However, the Soviet prime target remained West Germany and when
Moscow failed to prevent the Federal Republic's rearmament and military
integration into NATO, Moscow became receptive to Brandt's *Ostpolitik.*
He was willing to recognize the new territorial and political status quo in
Europe, renounce nuclear weapons and provide the USSR with extensive
credits and valuable technology; he also improved West German–East German relations.

Professor Rubinstein reminds us that France remained an important
Soviet target. However, "Moscow has not been able to surmount the con-
tradiction in its policy of trying to improve relations with both Paris and
Bonn."

Clearly, Western Europe remains the most important focus of Soviet
foreign policy and Moscow, Rubinstein notes, "intends its stress on détente
in Europe to enable it to play on intra–West European rivalries. It hopes
that the inner contradictions within NATO and EEC will keep the West
divided enough for Moscow's military ascendancy to have political consequences, namely, to gain tacit acceptance for Soviet rule in Eastern
Europe." It should be added that the Soviet military buildup cannot help
but cause doubts about long-term Soviet strategic objectives.

Returning to Brandt's *Ostpolitik:* By means of these treaties and arrangements the Soviets achieved what they wanted—a giant step toward
making friends and influencing people in Western Europe. At the same
time they insisted on a European security conference in which they were
planning to intensify their influence by injecting themselves into the high
councils of the participating countries.

Since they realized that Western Europe was *nolens volens* tied to the
United States, they serenaded Washington with considerable success.
Their overtures were so successful that President Nixon went to Moscow.
(He also went to Peking, which unquestionably made the Soviets somewhat
nervous and probably even more intent on détente; the thought of an improvement in Sino-American relations was not desirable.) Thus Brezhnev,
when he returned Nixon's visit, smiled as he had never smiled before. The
treaties signed in Moscow and Washington were marginal but looked good
enough for the world to take notice. If Moscow wished to acquire greater
influence in Western Europe, it had to have the United States tuned in.

Contrary to the majority opinion, I regarded the *Ostpolitik* as unfortunate
mainly because it could make it too easy for the Soviets to achieve their
strategy of infiltrating Western Europe. Furthermore, the spirit of détente

afflicted the U.S. Congress, many of whose members, especially in the Senate, seemed to believe that real peace with the Soviet Union was right around the corner. Would that this were true. Instead, as Rubinstein points out in Chapter 4:

> Soviet hostility toward NATO remains a constant of Soviet policy. However, in practice, Moscow has pursued priorities: for example, to forestall Western Germany from acquiring nuclear weapons; to prevent nuclear weapons from being based in Norway or Denmark; to exploit vestigial French suspicions of Germany's military resurgence. In theory, Moscow would like to see all American troops withdrawn from Europe. But the probable alternatives—including a nuclear Germany—has led Moscow to downplay this course. Indeed, if one looks at the MFR talks in Vienna as a litmus test for Soviet policy objectives and preferences, one gains the impression that Moscow is not dissatisfied with the existing situation in Europe, which is characterized by a massive Soviet military presence in Central Europe and NATO seemingly willing to accept the Soviet Union as the major military power on the continent of Europe.
>
> Soviet diplomacy succeeded at the Helsinki conference of July 1975 in obtaining formal Western recognition for the territorial status quo in Europe—a prime Soviet objective since 1945. The Western countries generally favor expanded trade with the Soviet bloc, and believe that economic interrelationships will help keep the political climate from heating up. The Soviet military buildup, however, continues to cause gnawing doubts about long-term Soviet objectives. Through MFR Moscow hopes also to check the growth of the Bundeswehr.
>
> At a minimum, Moscow intends its stress of "détente" in Europe to enable it to play on intra–West European rivalries. It hopes that the inner contradictions within NATO and the ECC will keep the West divided enough for Moscow's military ascendency to have political consequences, namely, to gain tacit acceptance for Soviet rule in Eastern Europe, and to ensure that no policies are taken by the West European countries that threatens Soviet preeminence on the continent.
>
> Finlandization may well be a long-term Soviet foreign policy objective. But reality is more complex than any theory, and if Finlandization should come to pass it would be primarily because of the weaknesses and loss of resolution of Western Europe and the United States and not because of anything that Moscow did. The prognosis for the coming decade is a continuation of the trends that emerged in the 1970s.

IV

Active Soviet interest in the Middle East dates back only to the early 1950s. After the Baghdad Pact and NATO were established, Moscow concluded an arms agreement with Egypt to counter what it saw as the growing collective security threat to its southern frontier.

After the British withdrew from what is now the state of Israel, a political vacuum developed and the USSR eagerly hoped to fill it. Yet even after years of interest in the Middle East it is doubtful that the Soviets gained an appreciation of the Arab mentality. As a result, progress has been slow and Arab suspicion of communism has remained high.

The Suez crisis — that monument to faulty American policy — accelerated Moscow's activities in the area but with minor success. The Arab defeat in 1967 probably prompted the Soviets to recognize their mistakes to some extent. Presumably they realized that they had overvalued Arab numerical superiority and undervalued the strength of the state of Israel. Anti-Semitism — the Soviets euphemistically call it anti-Zionism — may have blinded their eyes and led them to conclude that it was safe to persuade Egypt to provoke war with Israel. The Politburo must have been severely jolted when Egypt expelled Soviet troops and advisers in 1972.

Soviet military investments in the Middle East, mostly in Egypt, are very great. So strong is Soviet interest in the area that even the expulsion of Soviet forces in 1972 did not trigger any visible Soviet reactions or stoppage of military aid. Soviet propaganda carefully avoided antagonizing the Muslim Arabs; perhaps the fact that the USSR in the past had made no attempts to infiltrate the region created a more receptive atmosphere.

One may argue that nowhere else have the Soviets been so cautious in their diplomacy and propaganda as in the Middle East. Prior to the fourth Arab-Israeli war in October 1973, the Soviets were careful to avoid major entanglements such as the Six-Day War with Israel, into which they apparently goaded the Egyptians. There always had been limits to Soviet involvement, especially after Egypt expelled the Soviet forces. The expulsion actually served to relieve Soviet fears of Russian casualties and preserved, to some extent, Moscow's freedom of action in the area. Although the Soviets take a dim view of "Arab socialism" without openly condemning it, they were and are cautious about mouthing the communist ideology. They realize perhaps that "Arab socialism" is really a type of nationalism consisting of elements of pan-Arabism, Islam, and, in some cases, traditional national feelings. Moscow also appreciates that several Arab countries have largely artificial frontiers and are still struggling to free themselves from colonial subjugation. Their nationalism is new and to some extent revolutionary.

Having lost all equipment given to Egypt prior to 1967, the USSR nevertheless inundated the area with weapons to replace material Egypt had lost. Before they were ordered to leave Egypt, some 17,000 Soviets were in the country; elements of the Soviet navy had moved into the eastern Mediterranean to signal Soviet presence to the U.S. Sixth Fleet and to prevent a possible outflanking by CENTO, which had replaced the Baghdad

Pact. Expelled by Egypt, the Soviets turned to Syria and, as later became evident, with more success than could have been suspected. A developing country, Syria is ruled by a highly volatile party that pretends to be both nationalist and socialist. The Soviets did not seem to mind.

The outbreak of the Yom Kippur War in October 1973 demonstrated the extent to which the Soviets have provided Egypt and Syria with the most modern weapons and had successfully instructed the Arabs how to use them. While for centuries the Arabs have been feuding with each other, this war has brought them together — Jordan being the only exception. Iraqi, Moroccan, and Algerian units joined the Syrians. It is probable that Arab air forces were strengthened by Libyan Mirages — purchased from France under the condition they be used only for the defense of Libya.

When the initial Egyptian and Syrian surprise successes faded and the fortunes of war turned favorably to Israel, Moscow continued its arms deliveries begun in October, but, fearful that the Arabs might be defeated, pressed for a cease-fire with forces in situ. Later the Russians seemed on the verge of military intervention, which was averted by an energetic U.S. alert. An armistice was virtually imposed upon the warring armies by United Nations fiat, supported by the United States and the USSR.

The position of the United States is not determined by Israel exclusively but also by the military capability of Soviet forces vis-à-vis NATO in the Mediterranean. A combination of Arab and Soviet forces, permitting Moscow to establish a permanent foothold in the area, would pose a formidable threat to NATO forces, especially the U.S. Sixth Fleet now based in Athens, and constitute a mortal danger to the existence of Israel.

Initially there was some doubt that the Arab states, including Saudi Arabia, would use oil as a weapon against Israel and its friends. But the (temporary) unity of the Arabs produced an oil embargo that, for a while, appeared to have changed the political map. This was exactly what the Soviets wanted. Although there exists no official evidence that Moscow goaded the Arabs into the embargo, there seems to be agreement among Western observers that Moscow welcomed some aspects of the Arab decision. The embargo was rescinded in March 1974 by the majority of Arab states despite heavy Soviet propaganda against lifting it. In view of the disarray the embargo had created in the West, particularly among the NATO nations, the Soviet policy had paid off handsomely, for the embargo created economic disruptions in Western countries and Japan while at the same time the price of oil skyrocketed. There is also the danger that the Arabs might continue to exert pressure with their "money weapon"; any major withdrawal of the enormous sums accumulated in the West could cause a financial avalanche.

Thus the impact of Soviet policy on the Middle East is considerable and hardly helpful to the advancement of peace. The flow of arms to generally irrational and unreliable peoples creates potential dangers to world peace, particularly as the Arabs are having difficulties adapting themselves to new political realities. Although the Soviets, despite their labors, have been unable to really "get through" to the Arab leaders, we can be sure that they will not give up. They regard this area as strategically vital to their interests and are loath to acknowledge successful American peacemaking efforts. They would rather see the Arab oil embargo perpetuated. But, as Galia Golan reminds us in Chapter 5, there is a factor limiting Soviet aggressiveness: the risk of superpower confrontation, which Moscow wants to avoid. Dr. Golan further suggests that

> with the decline and then loss of opportunities in Egypt, Moscow tried to fill the gap with Syria, and, to a lesser degree, Libya. Even in the 1960s the overall thrust of Soviet strategic interests in the area was, however, south-southeastward as the focal point of possible Soviet-American confrontation shifted to the deep-seas, in this region, the Indian Ocean. In the 1970s, coupled with a deterioration of its position in the Arab world, this overall strategic thrust prompted a slight shift in Soviet priorities from the area of the Arab-Israeli conflict to the Persian Gulf–Indian Ocean peripheral states.
>
> Ideological interests were subordinated to the strategic goals obtainable on a state-to-state basis, although extreme left-wing activity was supported when the opportunity appeared promising, American intervention seemed unlikely, and, in some cases, such as Sudan in 1971, competition with China forced the Communists to act. Economic interests in the region lay primarily in the Persian Gulf Area, i.e., with the states able to pay for Soviet goods — including arms procured for the Arab confrontation states in the Arab-Israeli conflict. While not in need of Middle East oil, the Soviets have sought (with only partial success) influence amongst the oil-producing states — primarily as a political goal designed to increase Soviet power vis-à-vis the Western countries and Japan which are dependent upon Middle Eastern oil.
>
> Given the somewhat declining Soviet interest in the confrontation states, precipitated in part by Moscow's failure to achieve significant influence over these increasingly independent states, plus the increasing danger of Soviet-American confrontation in the Arab-Israel context, the Soviets have lately demonstrated an interest in settlement of the Arab-Israeli conflict. Provided the Soviets could be party to such a settlement, primarily as coguarantors, they might be able to stem their enforced retreat from the region both by means of international recognition of their interest in the area and internationally agreed upon rights to even a physical presence (for the purpose of guaranteeing the settlement). No longer dependent upon the goodwill of this or that Arab government, unable in any case to compete economically with the United States, greater stability and permanence might be achieved for their presence without the risks involved in an ongoing crisis.

V

Regarding Soviet policy in Africa, Professor Gutteridge (Chapter 6) summarizes his views as follows:

The events of 1978 tended to confirm the already widely held view that the Soviet Union's involvement in Africa was the result of a deliberate strategy. In spite of a range of setbacks, the USSR seems over twenty years to have learned how to exploit tensions and divisions in Africa on a pragmatic basis. In a sense a new scramble for Africa is taking place, but for influence and the control of resources rather than for the occupation of territory.

Experience in the early days of African independence after 1960 convinced the Russians gradually that to look for the establishment of Marxist-Leninist states in the Soviet image was futile: neither Guinea nor Ghana, for example, was likely to become an African "Cuba." Presidents Sekou Touré and Nkrumah had their own characteristic views of Africa's destiny, and institutionalized communism did not seem to them an appropriate means for realizing it.

The role of China and the obvious importance of Nigeria served to make inevitable a practical approach to relations with Africa not overrestricted by the requirements of ideology. Progressively the Soviet Union sought to establish in African minds the impression that Russia was their friend who could be called on in times of conflict. Errors of judgement in the Congo (now Zaire) and the Sudan in Africa, and especially the invasion of Czechoslovakia in 1968, revived doubts, but gradually Soviet willingness to sacrifice the aims of socialist revolution to the immediate interest of her foreign policy made for smoother progress toward confirming Western influence.

From 1971 onward the commitment to overthrow white supremacist regimes in southern Africa was clear but further north the Sudan and Somalia proved increasingly treacherous ground and a period of low-key activity followed. However, before the situation in the Horn of Africa came to a head the Soviet Union made its boldest bid for an influence in intervening, apparently decisively, in Angola and sought to exploit South African involvements to its advantage, in OAU circles generally. Even so, in Angola, as subsequently in Ethiopia, the USSR displayed, alongside strength in providing military assistance in time of war, undoubted ineptitude in consolidating post-conflict peace by economic assistance.

The daring shown by Moscow in Angola was a calculated challenge to the West, directly related to the importance attached to the resources of Southern Africa in a potential global confrontation. Without it, but perhaps also in future as a result of it, the West might have been able to turn the tables on Russia by identifying her as the new imperialist power. On the other hand, both in Angola and the Horn in Africa, the Soviet Union has insured herself against a Vietnam-type enmeshment by using the Cubans as a willing sur rogate. It is the readiness to supply practical military assistance to governments or liberation movements, rather than ideological sympathy, that has given, and is likely to continue to give, Russia predominant influence in Africa. The only proper response the West, and in particular the EEC, could make would be in the form of real incentives to economic development. At the time, however, when the USSR is becoming more pragmatic, the West is tending to be afflicted by ideological constraints that lead to a depreciation of the undoubted advantages to it stemming from the economic orientation of most significant African states, which above all need fair trading partners.

The dependence of the West on southern African mineral resources, and to some extent on sea and air communications around and across Africa, is a source of vulnerability only if the Soviet Union is continually allowed to take the initiative. The self-sufficiency of some Warsaw Pact countries, as contrasted with the dependency of NATO states, is seen on both sides as critical, but generally without regard for the self-interest of African states in the region and of those in Zimbabwe and Namibia that will come into being. For both Russia and the West the critical factor remains African independence.

I might add the following observation:

Whether or not the Soviet presence in Africa will become permanent is by no means certain. It remains to be seen whether the Soviets can contribute to the continent's economic and political development. They might — if they could hide their ideological goals, which seems rather doubtful. The adoption of a Soviet application of Marxism-Leninsm to African tribesmen, notably those not Western educated, is extremely questionable. The struggle of Africans for freedom and recognition is outside the Soviet psychological range of understanding and eventually the Africans will appreciate this. But, alas, it may then be too late and they may fall from one type of slavery into another.

VI

It has been stated by Soviet leaders that Europe ranks highest on Moscow's list of priorities. This is understandable because Europe has overwhelming industrial power, enormous scientific know-how, and a key geopolitical position. In fact, up to now, the fate of the modern world has been decided on European battlefields. Whether this situation will hold true in the future is hard to foresee and to a great extent will depend on the triangular relations between Moscow, Peking, and Washington. Asia may well play an increasingly important role in world politics, but for the time being China is still number two on the Soviet priority list, followed by the Middle East and the smaller Asian countries.

The history of relations between Moscow and Peking has been amply researched and written about. The memory of tsarist imperial claims on China remains fresh in Peking even today. These memories were sharpened after Mao's victory when the Soviets did not return the border regions, which the Chinese claim were taken by Russia through "unequal" treaties. Only some of these complaints — Manchuria, for example — were adjusted during the few years of entente cordiale between Mao and Stalin. On China's northern border Outer Mongolia remains part of the Soviet camp.

But border questions are basically negotiable. Indeed, there have been long negotiations but no agreement has yet been reached. It is doubtful that all Chinese claims will ever be adjusted to Peking's complete satisfaction. Scholars seem to agree that the border dispute is not the main factor in the war of words between the two Communist powers that has been under way, with varying intensity, since 1960 when the conflict was made public.

The verbal war has been rough, yet we must remember that Communist verbiage is less inhibited than that of Western diplomacy, which seeks at least the appearance of politeness. In the West, invectives such as those used by Peking and Moscow would have resulted in a complete break of relations. But among Communists such verbal brawls come and go and are not necessarily an impediment to eventual conciliation when vital national interests coincide.

Most Western observers, failing to make a distinction between the dispute itself and its eventual outcome, regard the Sino-Soviet conflict as incurable. However, as Ambassador Bohlen put it, "While the dispute is real, it would be sheer madness for the United States to count on a permanent split between Moscow and Peking."[6]

True, the revolutionary comradeship of the early fifties cannot be expected. China has changed and so has the Soviet Union under Stalin's successors. But friendship is not necessary for an arrangement of cooperation that might pose serious problems to the West.

For the time being, however, the war of invectives is being backed by military forces on both sides. It has been estimated that the USSR has at least a million men and plenty of missiles poised along its frontiers. Conversely, the Chinese have strenghened their armies to possibly thirty-five to forty-five divisions. China also has made considerable progress in developing nuclear arms and the means for their delivery. Peking unquestionably does not want war but is taking all necessary precautions nevertheless. Both sides seem to be trying to avoid major military incidents. Besides, China is waging a strong diplomatic offensive: it has agreed to a rapprochement with the United States and signed a treaty with Japan. Interestingly, China now supports European unity and NATO because it does not want the Soviets to decrease their military might in Europe and thereby be able to strengthen their capabilities along their frontiers facing China.

Both sides must be aware of the consequences of a Sino-Soviet war. A Chinese victory is unlikely. But the size of its population, more than 800-million strong, would mean protracted guerrilla warfare. At best the USSR might succeed in establishing a Peking government with Soviet sympathies. However, much speaks against such a war; I doubt that the Soviet army would attack and the Chinese would hardly fire the first shot, for China would have too much to lose. A Sino-Soviet war almost certainly is not in the cards.

Hinton believes that the Soviet Union has never had much political influence on the countries of East Asia because they did not have common interests. (But didn't North Koreans fight Stalin's war?) The Soviet Union, Hinton observes, "continues to be in East Asia but not of it."

Russia's lack of understanding of these peoples pertains to Japan as well: A heavyhanded behavior, lacking empathy, "has helped to keep Japan more closely tied to the United States than would otherwise have been the case and has virtually driven China into the arms of the United States and Japan." Peking does not want to see a complete disengagement by the United States in Asia until Sino-Soviet relations are stabilized — if that ever happens.

On balance it is obvious that Soviet policy has had an enormous impact on Asia, mainly on China and North Korea, perhaps less so in Japan because of that country's close relations with the United States. East Asia has changed its political face and the changes are directly or indirectly the result of Soviet policies and activities. Without the Russian Revolution and the establishment of a Bolshevik Soviet Union, the Chinese Revolution might not have happened or might have taken a very different course — which would have been affected by the Japanese aggression and the initially close relations with the United States. As it turned out, Moscow's goal of gaining a dominating position in China and Japan has not been reached. On the contrary: Hua Kuo-feng demanded in a speech that the Soviets reduce their military presence along the Sino-Soviet border; in August 1978 a treaty of peace and friendship was concluded between China and Japan; relations between China and the United States were normalized and Teng Hsiao-p'ing's visit to the United States was most successful. Finally, the Chinese attacked Vietnam, a close ally of the USSR. Moscow was most reluctant to come into the fray and China very soon ended its military operations (which were undertaken to "teach Vietnam a lesson" for Vietnam's invasion of Cambodia, a Chinese ally) so as not to provoke the USSR too seriously.

VII

Next to East Asia, Southeast Asia has been very much in the forefront of the political and military interests of Washington, Peking, and Moscow.

Earlier, the Soviet attempt in Southeast Asia to establish Moscow's influence in Indonesia failed because the Indonesian Communist party and then Sukarno turned toward Peking, antagonized by what they perceived as Soviet betrayal of the world revolution. But the Indonesian episode provided the Soviets with valuable military experience: testing SA-2 missiles under tropical conditions; adapting Soviet ships to the tropics; and gaining operational experience far from the home base. Financially, the Soviet move in Indonesia was a catastrophic failure.

In Laos a Soviet presence had been established early in the 1960s with an airlift from Hanoi into Pathet Lao territory. But after the 1962 Geneva agreement the Soviets were anxious to maintain a presence in Vientiane, supporting the neutralist government of Souvanna Phouma in quiet cooperation with the American ambassador.

Generally, Soviet policy in Indonesia and Laos had three different aspects: an attempt to counter American influence; development of countervailing forces against the Chinese; and development of targets of opportunity for the expansion of Soviet influence—not only "against" other powers but as an early manifestation of Soviet determination to become a genuine superpower with global positions of strength. While Indonesia had to be written off as a total loss, Indonesia's friend Malaysia permitted diplomatic relations with the USSR to be established in 1968 and welcomed Brezhnev's 1969 proposal for an Asian collective security system. (Singapore's attitude toward Moscow is strictly businesslike.)

Other Southeast Asian countries such as Burma, Thailand, and the Philippines tend toward neutralism. The USSR is not viewed as an accepted ally but Soviet trade is acceptable. An excessive Soviet presence is held undesirable. However, the USSR seeks to achieve a more successful presence in Southeast Asia during the coming years. Professor Gordon (Chapter 8) suggests three reasons for this policy. First of all, the Soviets will try to prevent any increase of China's prestige and power; second, the USSR will attempt to substitute itself for the role previously played by the USA; and third, Moscow wishes to demonstrate its position as a global power and "reduce the near-exclusive economic dominance of Japan in Southeast Asia, for Japan is strategically allied with the USA and is cementing very large-scale economic ties with China."

Dr. Gordon also suggests the ways by which Moscow may try to improve its influence in Southeast Asia. First of all, the USSR has been quite successful in establishing close ties with Vietnam. Not only did Vietnam become a member of the East European COMECON as the only Asian state but also the USSR and Vietnam signed a Treaty of Friendship, containing important military provisions. As Gordon points out, "Vietnam represents a beachhead in Southeast Asia, and along with its East European allies, Moscow is underwriting Vietnam's economic development needs." Possibly in the near future, Moscow will obtain from Hanoi the rights of a naval base for Soviet ships operating in the South China sea.

Concerning ASEAN, the Soviets are now endorsing this organization and have revived Brezhnev's 1969 promotion of an Asian "collective security system." "Neutrality" in Southeast Asia is recommended, presumably directed against U.S. naval and air bases in the Philippines. At the same time, the Soviets are seeking more trade with the Philippines and seek better relations with Malaysia and Thailand.

Altogether, Soviet prospects in Southeast Asia are brighter than ever.

VIII

South Asia, particularly India, has been an important strategic area in Soviet thinking even though not a high-priority item on Moscow's list of foreign policy objectives. William Barnds points out that although none of the countries of South Asia threatens the USSR, Soviet leaders are aware that they cannot achieve their cherished ambition of being recognized as a global power without a strong position in the areas along their southern borders from the eastern Mediterranean through the Indian subcontinent.

Soviet policy toward South Asia has been consistent yet flexible. This approach, however, returned little in the case of Pakistan. In the competition for India's favor, the Soviets won out over the Americans. For some time there has been a rather close relationship between Moscow and New Delhi wherein Soviet help is taken for granted. Indeed, whatever India tried to do in the wars with Pakistan, it did better because of Soviet help; that is, India was able to advance its interests because of its close relationship with the USSR.

Moscow is now the major external source of arms for South Asia, Barnds writes, citing State Department sources that claim that during 1971 the Soviets gave India and Afghanistan arms valued at $1.1 billion and $450 million, respectively. India also received the lion's share of Soviet economic aid to South Asian countries. There has been considerable expansion of Soviet trade with these countries. It is therefore understandable that Western influence has lost its paramount position in the area.

India, thanks to Soviet aid, has enhanced its military position vis-à-vis China. This stance makes India the leading power of South Asia. Moscow must derive considerable satisfaction from this situation; there have been no setbacks as in some other Asian and African countries. In fact, Soviet relations with New Delhi have deepened. These developments are slower than the Soviets want, but they seem content nevertheless, particularly after the signature of the Indo-Soviet treaty of November 1973.

Barnds emphasizes that the Soviet link with India has been viewed as extremely valuable by New Delhi, largely because it has helped India to accomplish goals it was seeking in any case. This is not to suggest that New Delhi has not had to accommodate Moscow; it deals with the Soviet Union very carefully, especially in its public statements. But during the past twenty years Moscow has been able to advance its interests by supporting India's efforts and, broadly speaking, this obviously has played an important role in keeping the relationship on a generally even keel.

The invasion of Afghanistan in 1979, however, created a threat to the rest of South Asia and raised questions in India even though New Delhi was reluctant to challenge the Soviet Union. The return to power of Indira Gandhi, who had championed good relations with Moscow, had helped to overcome periodic strains between Moscow and New Delhi; Gandhi's rather tardy condemnation of the Soviet invasion did not carry strong conviction.

Barnds presents a picture of Afghanistan's political development and of Soviet reactions to the establishment in 1978 of a Communist regime in Kabul unable to maintain power without Soviet help. Moscow's belief that U.S. power (an important factor in Soviet foreign policy considerations) had been superseded by Soviet power may have played a role in the decision to invade Afghanistan.

After dedicating considerable reflection on the relations between Moscow, New Delhi, and Peking, Barnds describes the development of the Afghan crisis that began in April 1978 but had its origin much earlier when former Prime Minister Daoud overthrew the government and the monarchy. In July 1978 Afghanistan and the Soviet Union signed a twenty-year treaty establishing close political, economic, and military relations.

In 1979 insurgency spread throughout Afghanistan. The Soviets could not prevent the regime's brutality in imposing reforms unacceptable to the majority of orthodox Muslims. In view of the increasing difficulties of maintaining an essentially Communist regime they decided to intervene. Unwilling to permit the downfall of an ideologically related regime, the Soviets crossed the border in considerable strength to create a new regime after having had former President Amin executed.

Barnds raises several interesting questions regarding future Soviet policy toward the subcontinent. Will Moscow, for the time being, remain content with its successes even though they are slow-moving, or will it try to expand its role in the future, especially since American policy has given India a lower priority? But India certainly does not enjoy priority rating on the Soviet list either. However, there is Moscow's preoccupation with China to consider. Peking's lack of sympathy for India may have been enhanced by the important role the USSR plays in the subcontinent.

In order to strengthen the defensive position of South Asia against China, the USSR will try its best to promote a settlement between India, Pakistan, and Bangladesh. If a parallel with Europe is permissible, one might suggest that the American support for a unified Western Europe pursues similar objectives to guard against possible Soviet encroachment.

Thus Moscow's future India policy will be influenced by the development of relations between New Delhi and Peking. But it would be a mistake to assume that India is putty in Soviet hands. For example, India has rejected Brezhnev's proposal, made in 1972 and 1973, for a collective security system in Asia. Nor would India like to be drawn into the Soviet camp with more formal treaties than it has already signed.

Pakistan has links with China and the United States, which makes it a much more important target than, for example, Bangladesh. In its attitude toward Pakistan, Moscow has used soft and harsh lines, presenting a rather confused picture. But there can be little doubt that Moscow wants to build a stronger position in that country, presumably through economic assistance.

India has been a relatively stable nation for some years. Communist elements, sympathizing with either the USSR or China, have not had sufficient strength to attempt an overthrow of the central government. It would be very difficult for the Soviets to radicalize the Indian government, and they have been careful not to try to do so. But this has not prevented them, from time to time, from issuing rather harsh statements about India's so-called "bourgeois" government. However, as Barnds points out, their avowed aim now is peace rather than the disturbance of India's stability.

What is the significance of the Soviet invasion of Afghanistan? Barnds suggests the probable reasons for this aggression: the Soviet fear of a collapse of the Communist regime and the possibility that the Islamic forces in Afghanistan could have succeeded in establishing a new regime opposed to Communism. Perhaps one of the most important questions is whether the Soviet move was merely defensive or the beginning of a dangerous aggressive trend toward South Asia and the Persian Gulf.

Whatever the answer to these questions, the Soviets may have underestimated the difficulties they have encountered in Afghanistan but they are unlikely to abolish their objective. They may also await the reactions of the countries of the area. Afghanistan's neighbor Pakistan is clearly worried, particularly by the attitude of India and the fear that the USSR and India may join in a common cause at the expense of Pakistan. India, on the other hand, is fearful that great power involvement in the area could undercut India's efforts to become the predominant power in the area.

Even if Soviet losses would make Moscow's enterprise too expensive, Barnds does not believe that the Soviet position in South Asia would be endangered. Even a stalemate would secure an important voice for Moscow and permit Soviet leaders to accept a compromise solution, perhaps in the form of neutralization and nonalignment. Barnds suggests that before accepting an accommodation, Moscow may strike at Pakistan and/or Iran. Such a development could be prevented only if both the countries of the area and the West were able to meet this challenge.

Another result of a Soviet success in Afghanistan could be Moscow's ability to dominate Afghanistan with a minimum of Soviet involvement; Afghanistan would then be in a position similar to Mongolia. This, in turn, could lead to a closer cooperation of the countries in the area. While such a situation may save Pakistan for the time being, it might lead to its national disintegration with India as the *tertius gaudens*. It could also lead to a confrontation between Moscow and India—which both powers would like to avoid.

If the Soviets should succeed in becoming the predominant power in South Asia, it could initiate a gradual rapprochement of Moscow with Middle Eastern states. In turn, such a development might signify a shift of the balance of power in world affairs.

IX

In his discussion of the impact of Soviet foreign policy in Latin America, Dr. Goure notes that until recent years the Soviet Union lacked both the capability and the opportunities to conduct an active policy in Latin America. Although a number of Communist parties sprang up there in the 1920s, Latin America's geographic remoteness from the USSR, the social-political conditions, and the weight of U.S. influence precluded any successful Soviet extension of influence to that region. Yet precisely because many countries in Latin America were in the intermediate stage of capitalist industrial development and because of the area's economic and strategic importance to the United States, this region has been and continues to be of particular interest to the Soviet Union.

The Cuban Revolution opened the door to Soviet penetration into the Western Hemisphere, although Moscow's experience with Castro demonstrated the high cost and difficulties of sustaining and controlling a Communist regime so far from the Soviet Union and showed that such regimes tended to develop their own autonomous doctrines and policies that at times clashed with Moscow's.

The growing trend toward globalism in Soviet foreign policy—which was made possible by the significant shifts in the East-West balance of power and an increasing Soviet economic capability — coincided with a sharp upsurge in Latin American nationalism and a search for social, economic, and political changes that carry with them strong anti-U.S. overtones.

In the Soviet view this circumstance has transformed the region into an active and highly successful "front" of the global "anti-imperialist struggle" where, in the opinion of Boris Ponomarev, party secretary and alternate Politburo member, the "revolutionary process is continuing to develop at a faster pace than in other parts of the non-socialist world."[7] At the same time Latin America is given the distinction of being identified as the "strategic rear" where the loss of U.S. economic and political influence could help further shift the East-West balance in favor of Moscow.

The present Soviet line rejects the radical Left's call for an immediate socialist revolution and the establishment of the dictatorship of the proletariat, arguing that the existing social-economic conditions require most of the Latin American countries to pass first through a "people's democratic" stage of considerable duration where power would be shared by united fronts of "progressive" proletarian and petty bourgeois parties.

This flexible approach has allowed Moscow simultaneously to endorse such diverse regimes as Castro's self-proclaimed Communist rule, the now defunct Popular Unity government of Salvador Allende in Chile, and the "progressive" military juntas in Peru, Panama, and Ecuador. The Soviet Union and the local Communist parties are in effect ready to collaborate with and support representatives of other parties and social strata, including the military — if they are in power and carry out anti-imperialist reforms, i.e., if they conduct policies hostile to U.S. public and private interests.

In accord with the general current Soviet line promoting united front strategies in the noncommunist world, Moscow was quick to endorse Allende's Latin American "progressive" parties. At the same time the critical role of the armed forces in facilitating or hindering the "revolutionary transformation" of the continent is fully recognized and, consequently, so is the importance of the local Communist parties in attempting to radicalize the military. The fall of Allende was a bitter disappointment to Moscow.

As a relative newcomer to Latin America and still lacking significant political or military influence in the region, the Soviet Union is attempting to exploit and exacerbate the current wave of nationalism and anti-U.S. sentiment and policies sweeping the continent and to expand its diplomatic, economic, and cultural relations with the countries of the region. This approach has been facilitated by the détente in U.S.-Soviet relations and by Latin America's search for new markets, sources of technology, and assistance in its industrial development. As a result the Soviet Union has been notably successful in recent years in establishing diplomatic relations with all South American states except Paraguay.

On the economic side, despite its Cuban experience, the Soviet Union has shown its readiness to provide considerable development credits and loans to "progressive" regimes and to encourage similar investments by the other European Communist states. Thus Soviet credits and loans to Chile, which in 1970 amounted to only $55 million, grew to some $360 million by the end of 1972. (It is doubtful that Moscow will honor unused Chilean credits after Allende's demise.) Total Communist credits, including $65 million from China, came to exceed the half-billion dollar mark by the end of 1972, representing a 900 percent growth in two years. Peru has also received an increasing amount of Soviet and other Communist credits. Thus cumulative Soviet credits and loans to Latin America, exclusive of Cuba, have grown from $185 million in 1971 to approximately $565 million in 1972, while total Communist credits stood at $431 million in 1967 and now exceed $1 billion, according to Goure.

At the same time, the Latin American governments have been progressively overcoming their mistrust and making increasing use of these credits. It may be noted that total Soviet economic aid to Latin America, including Cuba, for 1959 to 1972 exceeds that total of such Soviet aid to the Middle East for the period 1954 to 1972, thus giving some indication of the overall Soviet involvement in the Western Hemisphere. Soviet–Latin American trade also has been expanding, although more slowly ($220 million in 1972). Soviet political interest in Latin America is evident from the fact that, although imports from that region are only of marginal importance to the Soviet economy, the Soviet Union persists in this trade even though it has consistently incurred a substantial deficit in its balance of trade with the region (exclusive of Cuba).

While Soviet investments and trade in Latin America are relatively modest in comparison to those of the United States, Western Europe, and Japan, they exert some influence because they serve to strengthen the state sectors of the economies of the recipient countries, promote their industrial growth, provide for technological transfer, and help various projects for which these countries were unable to obtain credits elsewhere, such as the construction of fishing ports in Chile and Peru. To varying degrees they help buttress the "progressive" regimes and give some credibility to Moscow's assertions that governments willing to defy the United States and nationalize U.S. businesses do not stand alone but have a powerful and allegedly disinterested friend.

Although concern is shown by some conservative elements in Latin America about the growing Soviet influence in the region, Goure feels that the degree of influence is still too limited to seriously alarm the countries or affect their mutual relations. This picture could change if the Soviet Union succeeds — as it attempted to do in Chile while Allende was still in power — in becoming a major supplier of armaments to one or more countries on the continent. At the same time, however, the Soviet Union and the orthodox Communist parties benefit from the fact that they appear increasingly "conservative" and "responsible" in comparison with the violent and romantic radicalism of the many new Left parties and groups in Latin America.

The foreseeable trends in Latin America make it highly likely that Moscow will continue to pursue an active policy in that region and that the scope of its involvement will expand even further. Yet, as in other Third World regions, Moscow may find it very difficult to translate its support of essentially nationalistic-reformist regimes into solid and lasting influence and to develop such regimes into reliable allies of the Soviet Union.

X

Ever since the United States recognized the Soviet Union de jure, its existence has preoccupied Americans. The regimes of the tsars were never popular but that of the Bolsheviks was, to the American mind, upsetting and deeply disturbing. The dualistic policies carried out both officially through the Soviet embassy and unofficially through Communist channels were not sufficiently understood by either Washington or the rest of the country.

Though assurances have been given, during the negotiation for recognition, that the Soviets would not interfere in the domestic affairs of the United States, this promise was broken almost immediately, a fact that contributed to the distrust and dislike of the Soviet Union in the United States. Thus the impact of Soviet foreign policy made itself felt, from the outset, first indirectly and then directly.

Events since World War I have increased Soviet-American friction. The Stalin regime, which was essentially responsible for the instigation of the cold war in 1945, hardly contributed to an improvement of relations. After the dictator's death, hard feelings persisted, relieved from time to time only to relapse during the many crises in the fifties and sixties. In the early seventies, for reasons already outlined, a relaxation of tensions was promoted. But this did not eliminate the basic and deep contradictions between the two countries that had been destined to become the most powerful superstates in the world.

It is probably fair to say that, without the existence of Soviet power and ideology, America today would be a very different country with a very different foreign policy. The impact of Soviet behavior on the United States after World War II was enormous. It compelled Washington to play a larger role in world politics — a role it was slow to accept.

Security responsibilities of the highest order were involved. The cost of security raised the hackles of many men in responsible positions, all the more so because it took nearly a quarter-century to reach even some understanding of the Soviet mind — an understanding that still has many gaffs. Pragmatic Americans experienced difficulties in recognizing the importance of the socio-political philosophy of the Soviet government and party.

Americans as a whole were reluctant to assume the responsibilities of Western defense. It was and is a heavy load on the taxpayers, and certain congressional leaders still appear to believe that the United States should not have assumed responsibility for the "free world." I believe that many Americans have never reconciled themselves to the need for the United States to bar the way against a Soviet-led world revolution. Yet without American help Western Europe might today be a Soviet-dominated area. Americans also felt that some degree of recognition was due them; they got little from most West European nations and little, in particular, from France.

As a people, Americans are optimistic and dislike pessimistic estimates. Thus observers who are familiar with Soviet affairs and take a dim view of Moscow's designs are unpopular because they cannot, with the best of intentions, presage a rosy future.

Charles Burton Marshall skillfully describes how, after seventeen years in official noncommunication and seven in formal — albeit cool and wary — diplomatic contact, the United States and the Soviet Union were thrown together as allies in 1941.

Then for four years, under President Franklin D. Roosevelt's guidance, U.S. policy toward the Soviet Union was persistently placative. Roosevelt's paramount aims were victory first and then preservation of the prevailing coalition as the foundation for a world security system so preponderant in scope and power as to be beyond challenge. Both aims entailed wooing the Soviet Union. Roosevelt rationalized the approach by perceiving unmitigated virtue and reservoirs of goodwill in the Soviet ally. The American nation as a whole concurred.

The Yalta conference in early 1945 marked the apogee of this propitiatory approach. A year later — with World War II over — the premises were dissipated. The upshot of the war had placed the United States and the Soviet Union as the top two in a scale of states ranked according to capacity to conduct strategies and undertake policies of wide scope. No combination of states adequate to cope with the Soviet Union strategically was feasible without the United States; no combination of states capable of posing a serious threat to U.S. security was possible without Soviet participation.

The two giants had divergent images of the future. Their brief alliance was superceded by pervasive rivalry over conditions of peace. Strategic considerations became a regular, exigent, and continuing element of policy for the first time in U.S. experience. The Soviet Union was the primary adversary factor. The relationship has persisted for a generation. Thus the principal aspect of the Soviet Union in American national awareness is its role as strategic rival.

Diverse theories may be invoked to explain what the conflicted relationship is, when and how it came about, and whether or not it is over. From the onset both sides have professed regret, and both have undertaken to propound conditions for getting the adversary relationship over with — each defining the conditions that befit its own preferences.

"Détente" is the expression generally used in the United States and among its cold war associates. On the Soviet side the favored term is "peaceful coexistence." The first envisages a tamed Soviet Union reconciled to pragmatic collaboration and no longer prone to sponsor revolutionary purposes in world affairs. The second envisages pragmatic collaboration — but subject to abandonment of opposition to Soviet sponsorship of revolutionary aims. No error in international affairs is more basic than the common one of equating these opposed prescriptions for moving beyond the cold war.

The question of terms on which the conflicted relationship — the cold war — is settled is inherently connected with the U.S.-Soviet strategic equation. U.S. policy is presently intent upon settling for equilibrium in warmaking potential in succession to the inherent advantage in strategic strength that accrued to the United States in earlier phases of the cold war. Whether such an outcome is illusory or in prospect depends on Soviet intentions; so far there is no empirical indication of Soviet reciprocity. On the contrary, mounting evidence indicates a Soviet intention to replace the United States in strategic ascendancy. U.S. hopes for a protracted strategic standoff, coupled with détente, may well prove as ephemeral as the concord at Yalta.

XI

The Soviet leadership does not regard détente with the West as a condition permitting either internal liberalization within the Soviet Union or relaxation of military preparedness to deal with what are perceived by Moscow as external threats to Soviet security. This being the case, it seems likely that the military ingredients of Soviet policy will continue for the foreseeable future to carry undiminished weight in the Soviet Union's behavior in the arena of world politics.

For example, despite undeniable Soviet interest in obtaining the détente benefits of greater economic and technological interchange with the West, one of the guiding principles of Soviet conduct in world affairs appears to remain that epitomized by a recent commentary on peaceful coexistence and security in the Soviet military daily, *Red Star*: "The greater the combat might and readiness of the Soviet armed forces and the armies of the fraternal socialist countries . . . the more secure is peace on earth . . . and the broader are the opportunities for consolidating the successes of the policy of peaceful coexistence."[8]

To sum up some of the salient military policy considerations and issues that loom large on the Politburo's agenda, one may begin with the question of whether the Soviet leadership still feels that the primary military threat to Soviet interests is posed by the Western "imperialist" coalition, led by the United States, or whether Communist China has moved up to the number one position as a potential threat to Soviet security.

This is not an easily answered question; perhaps the Soviet leaders themselves are not sure whether priority in the allocation of defense resources and military planning should continue to be directed in accordance with traditional Marxist-Leninist imperatives against the United States and its allies in the capitalist camp or whether circumstances now dictate shifting priority attention to military preparations against a rival Communist power in Asia.

Such a shift would without doubt constitute one of the ruder ironies of history. While the Soviet leaders had hoped that after Mao's death the opportunity might arise to patch up Soviet relations with China, their expectations on this score have not been heightened by the Tenth Party Congress in Peking, at which the Soviet Union was again labeled a worse enemy of China than the United States, and moreover was accused of contemplating a surprise attack against the People's Republic of China.

Thus, whatever course Sino-Soviet relations may take in a post-Mao environment, it seems safe to conclude that Moscow will not find it expedient to lower the level of military preparations and vigilance it has mounted in the past few years along its Asian borders, while at the same time strengthening its military might along its European borders far beyond defensive needs.

With regard to Soviet military policy toward the United States, the various ongoing negotiations on the balance of military power between the Soviet Union and the United States have as yet produced no conclusive evidence that the Soviet leadership is now prepared to stabilize its military power relationship with the United States on a lasting basis of "equality" and "no unilateral advantage" to either side, as implied in joint statements issued at successive summits in Moscow in May 1972 and Washington in June 1973.

In fact, as Dr. Pfaltzgraff notes, the evidence has mounted that the Soviet Union is striving for strategic-military superiority. Both in its military literature and in the configuration of its strategic-nuclear forces, the Soviet Union is developing the means to destroy all, or a major part, of the U.S. fixed, land-based force. During the 1970s the Soviet Union attained strategic parity with the United States — a status that was codified in the SALT I Agreement of May 1972. At that time, the United States enjoyed major qualitative advantages over the Soviet Union in its strategic-nuclear force, in particular in warhead design and accuracy. Therefore, the Soviet Union was conceded a quantitative edge in numbers of launchers permitted in the SALT I Interim Agreement. At a rate and level far in excess of what was anticipated by the United States at the time of SALT I, the Soviet Union developed and deployed its so-called fourth generation strategic systems. These systems — in particular the SS-17, SS-18, and SS-19 — have throw-weight far in excess of that possessed by the Minuteman, which constitutes nearly all of the land-based strategic force of the United States. In addition, the Soviet Union began the deployment of a MIRV capability greatly in advance of the dates for the entry of such a system into the Soviet inventory anticipated by the United States at the time of SALT I.

In short, within the framework established by SALT I, the Soviet Union proceeded to develop a strategic-nuclear capability that has created for the United States what has been termed a "window of vulnerability" in the early 1980s. Because of the threat posed by Soviet strategic deployments to the most accurate portion of the American strategic-nuclear force — the fixed, land-based Minuteman — the decade of the 1970s was a period of growing difficulty for the United States in its ongoing efforts to preserve strategic stability at the superpower level. As a result of trends outlined above and elsewhere in this volume, the United States enters the 1980s with the Soviet Union having attained a position of superiority in the throw-weight potential and in numbers of missiles as well as MIRVed reentry vehicles. This condition will exist for at least several years until the United States is able to deploy compensatory systems.

It may be argued that the ABM treaty — a part of the SALT Accords of 1972 — contributed to the vulnerability of the Minuteman force and to a possible Soviet preemptive first strike. This treaty effectively precluded the United States from deploying a point defense around all or most of the Minuteman force. At the time of the ABM treaty the United States had a technologically superior system that could have been deployed to protect its land-based strategic force. For this reason it may be argued that the Soviet Union was the net beneficiary of this treaty. There is evidence that the Soviet Union has had a R&D program since the early 1970s designed to produce breakthroughs in technologies for strategic defense. Because of the importance attached by the Soviet Union to the defense of its homeland from strategic attack, it must be anticipated that the Soviet Union will press ahead with new programs intended to produce capabilities for strategic defense.

Just as the Soviet Union has made major gains in its strategic-nuclear forces relative to the United States, it has also developed impressively its capabilities for warfare in Europe. These include tactical air power, a new generation of armored vehicles such as the T-72 tank, and a capacity for the conduct of chemical warfare. Such capabilities extend far beyond what would be prudently deemed necessary simply for the deterrence of war in Europe. Instead, the Soviet Warsaw Pact forces have evolved both a doctrine and capability for the conduct of warfare against NATO. These developments have occurred at the same time that NATO and the Warsaw Pact have been engaged in negotiations for mutual and balanced force reductions (MBFR) in Europe.

As recently as 6 October 1979, President Brezhnev announced that the Soviet Union was prepared to withdraw as many as twenty thousand Soviet troops from East Germany during the next year. According to Brezhnev, the Soviet Union would withdraw up to one thousand tanks, in addition to "a certain amount of other military hardware." Brezhnev's ploy was designed to forestall the deployment by NATO of new generation theater-nuclear systems such as the Pershing II and the ground launched cruise missile. In recent years, the Soviet Union has deployed an increasing number of new generation systems—the SS-20—that provide for Moscow for the first time a counterforce capability against NATO targets in Western Europe. The Soviet Union has also deployed the Backfire Bomber for use in missions against Western Europe. These systems substantially add to Soviet strategic capabilities against China and Japan.

Although Soviet intentions, as usual, remain murky behind the secretive approach taken by the USSR to security issues, U.S. defense officials have expressed concern that the potential marrying of Soviet quantitative missile advantages permissible under the interim agreement with recent MIRV advances could permit the Soviet Union to "develop a clear preponderance of counterforce capabilities."[9]

The picture in the strategic area thus is clouded by uncertainty as to whether the Soviet Union will press ahead with new programs intended either (1) to yield some permanent margin of strategic power in its favor or (2) to improve its bargaining position in further negotiations, or both.

In more specific terms, the key strategic policy issue facing the Kremlin leadership is the extent to which the Soviet Union should attempt to incorporate new MIRVed missiles into its strategic arsenal during the next few years, as against reaching agreement on MIRV limitations and reduction of numbers of Soviet missiles so as to maintain an overall balance of strategic forces. It cannot be predicted with confidence what the Soviet decision will be, but if the first alternative is chosen the prospect of stabilizing the strategic arms competition through SALT will probably diminish and the ABM treaty concluded in May 1972 may even become subject to abrogation. In effect, if the issue is so framed by the United States,[10] the Soviet leaders must decide whether to pay in SALT coin for the economic and technological benefits they would like to extract from détente.

In the case of negotiations on the reduction of theater forces in Europe, the exploratory phase of which ended on 28 June 1973, the negotiations had not gone far enough to indicate what moves the Soviets are prepared to make with regard to cutting back their large military presence in central and eastern Europe.

In the preliminary sparring the Soviets did succeed in persuading the Western participants to drop the formula of mutual and *balanced* force reductions (MBFR) in favor of simply mutual reductions, a change in terminology that accomodates Soviet objections to the principle of "balanced" reductions. Under this principle the Soviet Union would have been expected to take proportionately greater cuts in its deployments to compensate for the fact that withdrawn Soviet forces would be in closer proximity to Europe than American forces withdrawn to the continental United States.

The central consideration for Soviet policymakers with respect to European security issues would appear to be how far to go in the direction of a genuine military détente without endangering Soviet hegemony in the eastern half of Europe. To the extent that the continuation of political détente seems both desirable to the Kremlin leadership and to require some lowering of the level of military confrontation between the opposing NATO and Warsaw blocs, the Soviet Union may be prepared eventually to cut back its force levels in Europe, which would have the additional advantage of freeing some military assets for buttressing the Soviet position in Asia.

But, given the long-standing importance in Soviet eyes of having a formidable Soviet military presence in Europe, it seems warranted to conclude that any mutual reduction agreements the USSR may sign will be such as to permit it to preserve a substantial military advantage in the European arena. In a sense this is simply to say that, whatever fluctuations there may be in the political climate, the Soviet leadership is likely to operate on the traditional assumption that the USSR's interests as a great continental land power call for the continued maintenance of strong ground-air theater forces in both the European and Asian extremities of the Eurasian continent.

But the situation is somewhat reversed in the sphere of naval and maritime states, and in the process the Soviet leadership faces issues for which the traditional pattern of Soviet military policy provides relatively little precedent.

Perhaps the most basic issue is what share of Soviet resources available to the military establishment can "rationally" be allocated to the further expansion of sea power as an instrument for the achievement of Soviet military-political goals. Given a military structure in which the outlook of army marshals has long predominated, it might be surmised that the Soviet admirals have not found it altogether easy to establish a claim to a larger slice of military resources.

They may, for instance, have had to dispose of arguments like that made many years ago by the late Marshal Tukhachevsky, who wrote that the spending of a "significant part" of German military resources on the navy rather than the army prior to World War I represented an ill-timed and irrational use of available capital, since the navy could contribute little to Germany's immediate strategic goals.[11]

In any event the development of Soviet naval and maritime power is proceeding, with most Soviet naval programs lying outside the area of negotiations affecting the U.S.-Soviet military balance. Only the strategic or SLBM component of naval forces has thus far been dealt with in SALT, with the interim agreement of May 1972 allowing the Soviets to complete programs that will give them numerical superiority in SLBMs. The main issue before the Soviet leaders here has already been mentioned—whether to begin incorporating MIRV technology into the Soviet SLBM force as well as the land-based missile arsenal.

Perhaps the single most knotty naval policy issue to be threshed out, at least in terms of the ultimate resource commitments involved, is whether the Soviet Union should attempt to match the United States in large carrier strike forces. Expert opinion in the West is divided on this question, although most students of Soviet naval affairs believe that Soviet carrier construction programs will stop short of such an ambitious goal. On the other hand, it is not improbable that the Soviets may at some point seek to reduce the existing disparity in carrier strength through negotiated restrictions on deployment of U.S. carriers. Indeed, the position already taken by Soviet negotiators in SALT on withdrawal of forward-based systems (the FBS issue) would seem to point in this direction.

Whatever course the Soviets may elect to take on the carrier questions, it does seem likely that programs of surface ship construction to improve the worldwide general-purpose capabilities of the Soviet navy will continue. Among the factors entering into the rationale for such programs, increasing importance may be given to the role of sea power in any future international scramble for access to raw materials, especially oil, and in the control of sea routes for distribution of oil to Europe and Japan.

Finally, one may bring up a question pertinent to the whole sweep of Soviet military policy at the present juncture of history. For more than a decade the Soviet Union has poured immense resources into the buildup of its armed forces. The quantitative buildup of these forces may have reached a peak, at least for those forces for which levels have been set in negotiated agreements, although qualitative improvements are still being made. To what use, then, can the Soviet leaders be expected to put the enormous military power they have now acquired?

Although one can predict precisely how the Soviet Union may try to turn its expanded and still growing military assets to account beyond the deterrence of nuclear war alone, it seems fair to conclude that the general thrust of Soviet military policy will be to help create an international environment favorable to the achievement of Soviet political aims or—to borrow the previously cited formulation of a Soviet writer in the military daily *Red Star*—to insure broader opportunities "for consolidating the successes of the policy of peaceful coexistence."

At this point it is useful to quote Robert Pfaltzgraff's (Chapter 12) summary analysis of Soviet military strategy and force levels that are significant relative to the United States, Europe, and the Third World:

> Soviet conceptions of military strategy and force levels differ substantially from conceptions prevalent in the United States and in the Western world more generally. For the Soviet Union, military power is considered to have military and political utility for the achievement of political objectives. It is not communist ideology, per se, but instead the possession of a *strategy* for the maximization of available capabilities—sometimes against a militarily superior adversary—that has contributed decisively to the growth and influence experienced by the Soviet Union especially since World War II. Soviet strategy is based on the principle enunciated by Clausewitz that "warfare is always an extension of politics—that it is subordinate to the political objectives and the foreign policy interests in a 'grand strategy.'" Strategy in the Soviet conception is, first and foremost, a political concept related to an unfolding reality interpreted in Marxian dialectical terms grounded in the political objectives of the state. Military *power* related to military *strategy* is a crucially important element not only in accelerating the inevitable forces of history, but also in holding in check the military capabilities especially of the United States, which might otherwise be tempted to utilize military force to

thwart the unfolding course of history. The sustained growth of military power is designed to permit the Soviet Union to protect the Soviet homeland from attack and then to provide the basis for hastening the weakening of the West both in the Third World and on the rimlands of the vast Eurasian land mass.

Soviet strategic writers reject the concept of "mutual assured destruction" so popular in the United States and Western Europe in the 1960s and 1970s. Whereas in the West the terms "deterrence" and "defense" have been viewed as somehow separate phenomena, Soviet logic holds that the possession of a war-waging and war-winning capability is the necessary prerequisite to the deterrence of an adversary. In the Soviet conception, therefore, deterrence and defense are for all practical purposes one and the same. Soviet writings reject the idea of mutuality in assessing the destructive potential inherent in nuclear conflict. Soviet forces must be configured in such a way as to insure the survival and, indeed, the ultimate victory of the Soviet Union. Thus, Soviet military strategy postulates the need not for the deterrence of *both* sides, but rather for the deterrence of the United States and, in the event of war, the victory of the Soviet Union.

Western conceptions of strategic military stability are largely alien to the Soviet Union. Strategic military stability is consistent with a status quo conception of world politics. Since the Soviet leadership rejects such a conception it follows that military power represents a temporary "correlation of forces" subject to change. If nuclear war is both "thinkable" and "winnable," as Soviet literature maintains, Soviet strategy must contain concepts and provide for force levels designed to maximize for the Soviet Union the element of surprise. This concept is linked directly to the idea stated explicitly in Soviet literature that nuclear weapons will be employed as required by the dictates of battle. The advent of nuclear weapons has not altered the objective postulated in Soviet nuclear doctrine, i.e., to destroy the enemy's potential for the conduct of warfare. The idea of surprise contained in Soviet doctrine applies at both the strategic-nuclear level and on the battlefield. In one scenario, the Soviet Union preempts a U.S. first-strike. In a second scenario, the Soviet Union launches a first-strike against the United States. Both scenarios contain surprise as a decisive element.

There is a remarkable correspondence between Soviet force levels and strategy. For example, the United States has maintained its fixed, land-based strategic missile arsenal of 1054 since 1967 in the belief that such a force, together with other components of the triad, would be adequate to preserve a *deterrent* relationship with the Soviet Union. In contrast, the Soviet Union has mounted an effort to develop, test, and deploy a series of new strategic systems far beyond the needs of deterrence postulated in U.S. doctrine. In sharp contrast to the assumptions about Soviet behavior inherent in mutual assured destruction, the Soviet Union has placed substantial emphasis upon active and passive defense. This emphasis is evident both in Soviet doctrine and in practice. If the Soviet Union anticipates a potential U.S. retaliatory strike in response to a Soviet attack against the fixed, land-based component of the American strategic force, it follows that Soviet defensive efforts must be directed against such a contingency. Civil defense has been steadily increasing as a component in the Soviet program for war survival. There is a general consensus in the Soviet military affairs community that the Soviet Union attaches greater importance both in doctrine and practice than the United States to active defense. This is evident in the substantial allocations of restrictions to the air defense forces (PVO-Strany).

Nowhere is the Soviet emphasis upon war-waging and war-winning capabilities, including the means for chemical warfare that form part of a "combined arms" concept, integrated into a broader offensive. Such weapons may be used on the battlefield without necessarily escalating to a strategic-nuclear exchange with the United States. The possession by the Soviet Union of superior strategic-nuclear forces, in the Soviet view, can play a decisive role in neutralizing the strategic-nuclear capabilities of the United States. Central to Soviet–Warsaw Pact doctrine in Europe is the capability to use surprise to minimize NATO warning time and to overrun forward NATO positions in the initial phase of a conflict; to cut vital supply lines to the United States and other NATO forces on the central front; and to prevent resupply from the United States, Canada, or Great Britain.

In the 1970s the role of tactical airpower underwent a change in Soviet doctrine from an emphasis principally upon support of Soviet ground forces to which it was traditionally subordinated toward an offensive capability designed to secure control over the skies far behind enemy front lines. This use of airpower accords fully with Soviet–Warsaw Pact doctrine based on the primacy of the offensive.

Only since the late 1960s has the navy become an important component of Soviet military power with the development of the "blue water" fleet capable of operating in any of the world's seas. Thus the emergence of the Soviet Union as a superpower with global interests coincided with the attainment by the Soviet Union of a navy second only to the United States. The missions given the Soviet navy in the late twentieth century include, first and foremost, strategic-nuclear strikes against the United States. The Soviet Union also has configured its naval forces to interdict sea lines of communication to thwart U.S. resupply efforts to NATO in the event of a Soviet–Warsaw Pact attack. The peacetime operation of Soviet warships in the world's major oceans — the Atlantic, Mediterranean, Indian, and Pacific — provides for Moscow a military presence that is deemed useful for political purposes.

In sum, there are major differences between the Soviet Union and the United States with respect to conceptions of deterrence, the role of military power in relation to other capabilities for the achievement of political objectives, the conception of nuclear weapons as deterrence and war-fighting instruments, the threshold or "firebreak" between conventional and nuclear warfare, the meaning and implications of strategic-military superiority, the importance attached to offensive and defensive capabilities, and, perhaps most important, the differences that separate the superpowers in their conceptions of strategy itself.

Conclusions and Prospects

The influence of Soviet foreign policy in world politics has increased steadily since the Bolshevik Revolution, climaxing after the end of World War II. In the postwar era Moscow has succeeded in creating disorientation and disconcertion in most areas of the world. Either directly or indirectly, it has compelled most governments to formulate their policies with a view toward Soviet reactions.

As a result, pro-Western and "neutral" countries formed groupings to protect themselves against possible Soviet pressure. Policy decisions became more or less "collective," meaning that no country could stand alone without at least leaning to either one of the other group of nations. France, the exception, was led back to the nineteenth century by President Charles de Gaulle, who favored old-fashioned nationalism; Georges Pompidou, his successor, basically adhered to this policy. Giscard d'Estaing is less doctrinaire but still retains a Gaullist tinge, therefore France remains part of the West but in fact stays outside the Western "collective." The "nonalignment" of nations of the Third World is unrealistic — to say the least.

This troubled condition has deeply affected international behavior and thought. There is still too little understanding of the Soviet Union's political system. Indeed it has become popular in the West and the Third World to deprecate the body of communist ideology as no longer pertinent. Those who seek to get to the center of the Soviet mind are called "cold warriors." By contrast, Charles E. Bohlen, a former American ambassador to Moscow who has studied Soviet affairs for forty years, has written, "It seems fashionable nowadays to conclude the cold war is over. I do not see how anybody can reach this conclusion if he takes the trouble to read the Soviet press or speeches of Soviet leaders and to examine the daily drumfire of Soviet propaganda that is directed toward the United States."[12]

Public attacks are also directed toward other Western or neutral states whenever the Kremlin's policy decisions need support or when threats or "explanations" are needed.

I am well aware that changes — such as they are — have taken place as a result of the so-called détente. These changes began with the treaties signed by the Federal Republic of Germany with Moscow, Warsaw, and other East European countries — the outcome of former Chancellor Willy Brandt's dangerous *Ostpolitik*.[13] Then came President Nixon's visit to Moscow and Brezhnev's return visit to Washington. A rapprochement between Washington and Peking that had been in the making for some years also came to fruition.

For Soviet purposes détente is required to safeguard the USSR's western borders at a time when Soviet and Chinese armies face each other along the

Sino-Soviet frontiers. A Soviet–West German détente favors Soviet penetration of Western Europe. Soviet détente in the United States will help the
Soviet economy with food imports and technological know-how. Last but
not least, détente could contribute to the creation of a false sense of security
in the West, particularly in America.

In the United States a great many people developed the naive hope, even
the belief, that the troubles with the Soviet Union were over at last.
Members of Congress, ever alert to taxpayers' complaints, have tried to
deplete American contributions to NATO and to weaken the U.S. military
establishment at home and abroad. Meanwhile the USSR has become
militarily stronger in the nuclear area, and, even more, in conventional armaments. While a nuclear parity of sorts has been sought, not very successfully, in the SALT talks, the United States and NATO are far below
the conventional strength needed to match Soviet armies and, if present
trends continue, it will not be long before this will be true of naval power as
well.

To be sure, the continued buildup of the Soviet military does not necessarily indicate that war with the West is contemplated. It rather serves the
purposes of Soviet foreign policy, a kind of "gunboat diplomacy." This
strength cannot help but produce a more recalcitrant stance by the USSR
in East-West negotiations, and more particularly it seems to coincide with a
renewal of Stalinism within the Soviet Union.

It is significant that even as détente with the West is greatly publicized,
there has been a continued crackdown against dissenters who were courageous enough to condemn the Kremlin's methods of domestic suppression.
As in Romania, a greater degree of maneuverability in foreign affairs appears to go hand in hand with totalitarian suppression against those who
dare to differ with the regime. But domestic policy cannot be divorced from
foreign policy; the two are indivisible. The persecution of literary and
scientific men of distinction, without apparent regard for world public
opinion, is a clear sign that Moscow regards maintaining a true Communist regime as more important than improving its image abroad.

Here we must raise the fundamental question of whether a totalitarian
dictatorship can maintain a reasonably stable relationship with countries
whose basic political beliefs are dichotomously opposed to those of the dictators. Prior to the world wars, there existed a relatively uniform code of
behavior for Western nations and recognition of a body of international
law. With the victory of the Bolshevik Revolution, the international order
based on this law of nations was virtually ended. But since the Bolsheviks
eventually realized that they lived in this world and not outside of it, they
found themselves in a dilemma. To a degree they had to abide by what they
called "capitalist" international law, but at the same time they tried to create

a "socialist" international law. This duality has permeated Soviet foreign policy ever since the October Revolution.

In the early days, one level of Soviet foreign policy was official and went through government channels while the other was unofficial, Communist, and directed over the heads of governments to their peoples. The Commissariat for Foreign Affairs was the official channel and the Comintern the unofficial one.

Today, the Foreign Ministry implements Soviet decisions that originate in the Politburo. There is now more consultation among the Soviet leaders than in Stalin's time, but it is the general secretary of the party who has the last word. The party rules and the government organs merely carry out the order of the party leaders. The secret police, the KGB, also helps to implement policy decisions; every Soviet embassy has resident KGB agents on its rolls, posing as foreign service officers.

Gradually the two levels of Soviet policy have merged, which is to say that national and Communist-international elements are now combined to form one whole. This makes it extremely difficult for outsiders to determine which of the policies are national and which are Communist. Basically these two aspects reflect strategy and tactics by adjusting tactics to meet long-range strategic goals. Moscow has learned how to exploit the customs of noncommunist diplomatic establishments or menial employees.[14]

Another important example of Soviet political dualism is the concept of peaceful coexistence, as discussed earlier. I point to it again because the true meaning of the term in Communist eyes cannot be clarified too often to Western countries that might take it for what it is not. Peaceful coexistence means a state of nonwar—the term "peace" is not entirely applicable—during which the Soviet leaders will continue what they call "ideological warfare."

Earlier in the genesis of this concept, Mikhail Suslov, the CPSU ideologue and Politburo member, never ceased to advertise this concept. Significantly, détente did not prevent Brezhnev from highlighting in his important August 1973 speech at Alma Ata that "we are confident of the correctness of our Marxist-Leninist ideology" and that more contacts between East and West would promote "the propagation of the truth about socialism," thereby winning more and more supporters for the ideas of "scientific communism."

Thus a somewhat schizophrenic character of Soviet foreign policy emerges: national aspiration formulated to achieve Communist strategic objectives, peaceful appearance hiding revolutionary objectives, and fundamentalist ideology behind unconventional tactics.

Soviet leaders know well how to use their dialectical methods while non-Communist statesmen are not certain whether or not to take specific gestures by Moscow at face value. One could argue that the less familiar non-Communist leaders are with the background, beliefs, and psychology of Soviet policy, the more vulnerable they are to its intrinsic dangers. It is therefore not surprising that Soviet ruses more often than not have been quite successful.

This volume outlines a condition that many noncommunist states — and statesmen — do not fully acknowledge. Lacking in-depth knowledge of Soviet communism — or socialism, as Moscow calls it — many statesmen, deceived by appearances, fail to distinguish between tactics and goals. The same pertains to many younger writers who, unfamiliar with the history of communism and the basic nature of changes in world politics, do not feel they need to investigate more thoroughly what lurks beneath the Soviet veneer. Yet this is comparatively easy to do when one uses primary material from Soviet publications and statements by Soviet leaders intended for domestic consumption. For example, on 21 December 1972, Brezhnev, in a "Father Frost" (Christmas) message said, "The Communist Party of the Soviet Union has proceeded and still proceeds on the basis of the continuing class struggle between the two systems — the capitalist and the socialist — in the sphere of economics, politics and, of course, ideology. It could not be otherwise since the world outlook and class aims of socialism and capitalism are opposed and *irreconcilable.*"[15]

Despite this often announced enmity, every opportunity must be seized to prevent another conflagration — this time nuclear. Full cooperation to that effect with the Soviet Union (and the People's Republic of China) is to be encouraged. But at the same time, the study of all aspects of Soviet affairs must become part of our educational curriculum, beginning in the high schools. The Soviet Union cannot be understood without knowledge of the events that led to the Bolshevik Revolution, its Marxist-Leninist principles, and subsequent developments.

This book seeks to advance this understanding.

Notes

1. Kurt London, *The Permanent Crisis* (Waltham, Mass.: Xerox College Publishing, 1968), p. 1.

2. Bernard Ramundo, *Peaceful Coexistence* (Baltimore: Johns Hopkins Press, 1967), p. 2.

3. Charles E. Bohlen, *Witness to History* (New York: Norton, 1973).

4. Ibid., p. 208.

5. See the author's "Communism in Eastern Europe," in Kurt London, ed., *Eastern Europe in Transition* (Baltimore: Johns Hopkins Press, 1966), pp. 19ff.

6. Bohlen, *Witness to History,* p. 539

7. *Kommunist,* no. 15 (October 1971), p. 59.

8. I. Sidelnikov, "Peaceful Coexistence and the People's Security," *Krasnaia Zvezda* [Red Star], 14 August 1973.

9. Statement by Defense Secretary James R. Schlesinger at a press conference, 17 August 1973, reported in *Washington Post,* 18 August 1973.

10. That is to say, "linkage" between the strategic arms negotiations and other issues would have to be established. It is not clear, of course, whether U.S. diplomacy is prepared to insist on linking economic-technological cooperation with a satisfactory outcome of the SALT negotiations.

11. Reference to this appraisal by Tukhachevsky appeared in a recent Soviet book on the economics of force planning by Yu. S. Solnyshkov, *Ekonomicheskiye Faktory i Vooruzheniye* [Economic Factors and Armament] (Moscow: Voenizdat, 1973), pp. 13-15. Solnyshkov, incidentally, is a Soviet naval officer. The thrust of his argument, that rational force planning can be facilitated by careful analysis of goals and missions in the light of newly expanded capabilities of one service or another, is consonant with the Soviet navy's bid for a larger place in the sun.

12. Bohlen, *Witness to History,* p. 273.

13. A treaty with Czechoslovakia was signed in December 1973, followed by other East European agreements.

14. For a description of Soviet foreign policy formulation and implementation see Kurt London, *The Making of Foreign Policy — East and West* (Philadelphia: J. B. Lippincott Co., 1965) pp. 183 ff.; and Vladimir Petrov, "Formation of Soviet Foreign Policy," *Orbis,* vol. 17, no. 3 (fall 1973); see also John Barron's *KGB — The Secret Work of Soviet Secret Agents* (New York: Reader's Digest Press, distributed by E. P. Dutton, 1974) on the role of the KGB in foreign affairs.

15. Quoted by Bertram Wolfe in an address on "Some Problems of the Russo-American Détente" at Oklahoma State University on 2 November 1973.

Index